The Psychology of Survey Response

This valuable book examines the complex psychological processes involved in answering different types of survey questions. It proposes a theory about how respondents answer questions in surveys, reviews the relevant psychological and survey literatures, and traces out the implications of the theories and findings for survey practice. Individual chapters cover the comprehension of questions, recall of autobiographical memories, event dating, questions about behavioral frequency, retrieval and judgment for attitude questions, the translation of judgments into responses, special processes relevant to questions about sensitive topics, and modes of data collection.

The Psychology of Survey Response will appeal to (1) social psychologists, political scientists, and others who study public opinion or who use data from public opinion surveys; (2) cognitive psychologists and other researchers who are interested in everyday memory and judgment processes; and (3) survey researchers, methodologists, and statisticians who are involved in designing and carrying out surveys.

Roger Tourangeau is Senior Methodologist at the Gallup Organization and has been a survey researcher for more than 18 years.

Lance J. Rips is Professor of Psychology at Northwestern University. He is the author of *The Psychology of Proof* and coeditor of *Similarity and Symbols in Human Thinking*.

Kenneth Rasinski is Research Scientist at the National Opinion Research Center, University of Chicago, where he conducts research in survey methodology, substance abuse policy, and media and politics.

The Psychology of Survey Response

ROGER TOURANGEAU
The Gallup Organization

LANCE J. RIPS
Northwestern University

KENNETH RASINSKI
National Opinion Research Center

CAMBRIDGE
UNIVERSITY PRESS

PUBLISHED BY THE PRESS SYNDICATE OF THE UNIVERSITY OF CAMBRIDGE
The Pitt Building, Trumpington Street, Cambridge, United Kingdom

CAMBRIDGE UNIVERSITY PRESS
The Edinburgh Building, Cambridge CB2 2RU, UK   http://www.cup.cam.ac.uk
40 West 20th Street, New York, NY 10011–4211, USA   http://www.cup.org
10 Stamford Road, Oakleigh, Melbourne 3166, Australia
Ruiz de Alarcón 13, 28014 Madrid, Spain

© Cambridge University Press 2000

First published 2000

Printed in the United States of America

Typeface Sabon 10/13 pt.   *System* DeskTopPro$_{/UX}$ [BV]

A catalog record for this book is available from the British Library.

Library of Congress Cataloging in Publication Data
Tourangeau, Roger
The psychology of survey response / Roger Tourangeau, Lance J.
Rips, Kenneth Rasinski.
p. cm.
Includes index.
ISBN 0–521–57246–0 (hb.). – ISBN 0–521–57629–6 (pbk.)
1. Social surveys – Psychological aspects. 2. Public opinion
polls – Evaluation. I. Rips, Lance J. II. Rasinski, Kenneth A.
III. Title.
HN29.T68   2000
300'.723 – dc21   99–34664
                                                          CIP

ISBN 0 521 57246 0 hardback
ISBN 0 521 57629 6 paperback

To Karen, Julie, and Linda

Contents

Preface   *page* xi

1 An Introduction and a Point of View   1

  1.1 Earlier Theories of the Response Process   3
  1.2 A Proposed Model of the Response Process   7
  1.3 Other Recent Proposals: High Road/Low Road
      Theories   16
  1.4 Applications of the Model   19
  1.5 Implications of the Model   20

2 Respondents' Understanding of Survey Questions   23

  2.1 What Is a Question?   26
  2.2 Two Views of Comprehension: Immediate
      Understanding versus Interpretation   30
  2.3 Syntactic Difficulties in Question Wording   34
  2.4 Semantic Effects: Presupposition, Unfamiliarity,
      and Vagueness   40
  2.5 Survey Pragmatics and Its Effects on
      Comprehension   50
  2.6 Summary   59

3 The Role of Memory in Survey Responding   62

  3.1 Survey Questions and Memory for Events   63
  3.2 Organization of Autobiographical Memory   67
  3.3 Factors Affecting Recall of Autobiographical
      Events   81
  3.4 Summary   97

4   Answering Questions about Dates and Durations   100

   4.1   A Typology of Temporal Questions   101
   4.2   Cognitive Processing of Temporal Questions   108
   4.3   Indirect Effects of Time on Survey Responses   121
   4.4   Summary   133

5   Factual Judgments and Numerical Estimates   136

   5.1   Cognitive Studies of Frequency   138
   5.2   Studies of Frequency Estimation in Surveys   145
   5.3   Probability Judgments   160
   5.4   Conclusions   163

6   Attitude Questions   165

   6.1   The Traditional View   166
   6.2   Alternative Paths to an Answer   172
   6.3   The Belief-Sampling Model   178
   6.4   Tests of the Belief-Sampling Model   185
   6.5   Conclusions   194

7   Attitude Judgments and Context Effects   197

   7.1   Forms of Context Effects   198
   7.2   Mechanisms Producing Context Effects   200
   7.3   Variables Affecting the Size and Direction of
       Context Effects   214
   7.4   Serial Position Effects   228
   7.5   Conclusions   229

8   Selecting a Response: Mapping Judgments to Survey
   Answers   230

   8.1   Open Items and Rounding   232
   8.2   Rating Scales and Scale Anchors   239
   8.3   Unordered Categories and Satisficing   250
   8.4   Summary   254

9   Editing of Responses: Reporting about Sensitive
   Topics   255

   9.1   What Is a Sensitive Question?   257
   9.2   Sensitivity and Nonresponse   261
   9.3   Measuring Misreporting   264

9.4   Misreporting in Surveys   269
9.5   Processes Responsible for Misreporting   279
9.6   Editing for Other Purposes   286
9.7   Conclusions   287

10   Mode of Data Collection   289

10.1 The Range of Methods for Survey Data
     Collection   290
10.2 The Method of Contact and Administration   293
10.3 Other Characteristics of the Data Collection
     Method   298
10.4 Psychological Effects of the Differences among
     Data Collection Methods   305
10.5 Conclusions   312

11   Impact of Cognitive Models on Survey Measurement   313

11.1 The Anatomy of a Survey Response   315
11.2 Impact on Conceptions of Survey Measurement
     Error   318
11.3 Impact on Survey Practice   323
11.4 Impact on Psychology   335
11.5 Barriers to Further Accomplishments   337

References   343
Author Index   381
Subject Index   392

Preface

This book examines surveys from a psychological perspective. It proposes a theory about how respondents answer questions in surveys, reviews the relevant psychological and survey literatures, and traces out the implications of the theories and findings for survey practice. We hope the book appeals to a variety of audiences, including survey researchers, methodologists, statisticians, and others who are involved in designing and carrying out surveys; political scientists, social psychologists, and others who study public opinion or who use data from public opinion surveys; cognitive psychologists and other researchers who are interested in everyday memory and judgment processes; and demographers, market researchers, sociologists, and anyone else who uses survey data and is curious about how such data come into being.

Although we have written the book to be read from cover to cover, we recognize that not every reader will share our enthusiasm for all the topics the book includes. Readers who are most interested in public opinion may want to focus on Chapters 1, 2, 6, 7, and 8, skipping or skimming the other chapters. Those who care mostly about survey data on factual matters may want to focus instead on Chapters 1–5, 9, and 10. Those who are most interested in traditional issues in survey methodology, such as question order effects and differences across methods of data collection, may want to concentrate on Chapters 4, 7, 9, 10, and 11. And those who are most curious about the cognitive psychology of survey responses may want to focus on Chapters 1–5, 8, and 11.

This book took shape over a period of four years. During that time, many people contributed to the book in many different ways, and we'd like to pause here to acknowledge their contributions and to offer our gratitude.

First of all, we thank the various undaunted souls who braved the early drafts of this book, hacking their way through thickets of tangled prose and negotiating mountains of conceptual confusion along the way. Their suggestions marked out our route through the later drafts of the book and have, we hope, blazed a trail that will be easier for later readers to follow. We start by singling out three good friends and careful readers – Stanley Presser, Jon Krosnick, and Reid Hastie – who made it through the entire manuscript and survived to give us their very useful comments. In addition, Fred Conrad and Norman Bradburn used drafts of the chapters in courses they were teaching; they and their students gave us numerous helpful suggestions for improving the book. Other colleagues and friends read individual chapters or sections and also gave us useful feedback; these include Fred Conrad, Mick Couper, Bob Groves, Beth Proffitt, Michael Schober, Norbert Schwarz, and Michael Shum. We are grateful to all of these clear-sighted, kind, and tactful critics. Without their help, this book could have been a whole lot worse.

There are also several people without whose help this book couldn't have been written at all. One of us (Roger Tourangeau) took shelter for three terms from his regular duties (first at the National Opinion Research Center [NORC] and later at the Gallup Organization) at the Joint Program in Survey Methodology (JPSM) on the campus of the University of Maryland. We thank Bob Groves and Stanley Presser for arranging this happy (and much-needed) haven; our thanks to Nancy Mathiowetz, Martin David, and Mick Couper for their encouragement during Tourangeau's stints at JPSM. In addition, we thank Phil DePoy and Kirk Wolter at NORC and Max Larsen and Susan Nugent at Gallup for their patience and support during Tourangeau's various part-time leaves of absence from his day job. We are especially grateful to the Gallup Organization, which gave Tourangeau a partial subsidy during the final, critical birth pangs. Lance Rips also took a leave from his regular duties – as a professor at Northwestern University – to serve instead as a Fellow of the Bureau of Labor Statistics (BLS) during the 1997–1998 academic year. It greatly speeded the completion of this book. We thank the BLS, the American Statistical Association, and the National Science Foundation for sponsoring this fellowship. We especially thank Fred Conrad for his help during the fellowship period and Douglas Medin for support from Northwestern.

A project of this size and duration inevitably becomes something of a trial to one's family, and we'd like to thank ours for putting up with us during the past four years. We recognize that forgetting curves, context effects, and response strategies are not exactly everyone's cup of tea. We are grateful to our wives for feigning, on many occasions quite convincingly, interest in these and other equally arcane topics that are not the stuff of fascinating dinner table conversation. We are grateful as well to our children, all of whom managed to stay out of jail and other mischief during this period of more than usual paternal preoccupation.

Some of the heretofore unpublished data in Chapter 6 were collected under a grant from the NORC's Director's Fund. We gratefully acknowledge NORC's support and thank Norman Bradburn, NORC's director at the time, who arranged it.

CHAPTER ONE

An Introduction and a Point of View

Survey research rests on the age-old practice of finding things out by asking people questions. In this respect, it has much in common with a diverse set of activities ranging from police interrogations and courtroom proceedings to medical interviews and quiz shows. At the heart of each situation, one person asks another person questions for the purpose of obtaining information (Schuman & Presser, 1981).

In surveys, this pair is the *interviewer* and the *respondent*. Interviewers can put questions to respondents face-to-face, over the telephone, or through a computer. However, the interviewer's questions and the respondent's answers are always the central ingredients. The questions can ask about the personal activities or circumstances of the respondent (often called *behavioral* or *factual questions*) or they can seek the respondent's opinion about an issue (*attitude questions*). The examples in (1) are factual questions, and those in (2) are attitude questions from national surveys:

(1) a. Was anything stolen from you while you were away from home, for instance at work, in a theater or restaurant, or while traveling? [NCS][1]

b. Since the 1st of (month, 3 months ago), have you (or any members of your C[onsumer] U[nit]) received any bills for telephone services? Do not include bills used entirely for business purposes. [CE]

[1] In citing examples from surveys, we follow the typographic conventions of the surveys themselves. We indicate the source of the survey in brackets after the example, using the following abbreviations for the five surveys from which we draw most of our examples: CE for Consumer Expenditure Survey, CPS for Current Population Survey, GSS for General Social Survey, HIS for the U.S. Health Interview Survey, and NCS for National Crime Survey.

(2) a. In general, do you favor or oppose the busing of (Negro/Black) and white school children from one school district to another? [GSS]
   b. Everything considered, would you say, in general, you approve or disapprove of wiretapping? [GSS]

The factual/attitude terminology fits some survey questions more comfortably than others, but these examples give a rough idea of the types of questions that will concern us here.

One might suppose that survey researchers would long ago have developed detailed models of the mental steps people go through in answering survey questions, models that spell out the implications these steps have for survey accuracy. After all, the accuracy of surveys depends almost completely on the accuracy of people's answers. Of course, with attitude questions, it is often difficult to decide what an accurate answer is. Still, answers to such questions are prone to a variety of well-documented *response effects* – differences in survey outcomes that reflect seemingly irrelevant procedural details such as the order in which the answer categories are presented. These response effects may be due to problems in understanding the question, remembering relevant information, producing an appropriate answer, or other mental processes. Despite their importance for understanding and evaluating surveys, the study of the components of the survey response process is in its infancy, having begun in earnest only in the 1980s.

By contrast, rigorous mathematical formulations of *sampling errors* have been available since the early 1950s, when the major texts on survey sampling appeared (Cochran, 1953; Deming, 1950; Hansen, Hurwitz, & Madow, 1953). Sampling error arises because it is usually impossible to interview everyone in the target population; thus, there is some uncertainty about the relation between estimates that come from the interviewed respondents and the answers that might have come from the population as a whole. The study of survey sampling is devoted to reducing errors attributable to such effects, and it is both precise and scientific. But the study of questionnaire design, whose aim is to reduce response effects, remains an art (as Sheatsley, 1983, and Sudman & Bradburn, 1982, have noted).

A major goal of this book is to provide a framework for understanding response effects in surveys. We will propose a model of the survey response process and trace its implications for survey error. Our hope is to unify what is known about response effects by relating existing findings to a cognitive model of the survey response process. Many reviews of the literature on response effects in surveys have noted the fragmentary character of the research on this topic. We believe that a cognitive model of the survey response process can offer an improved map of this varied landscape.

The terms *response effects*, *response process*, and *respondent* misleadingly suggest a behavioristic focus on the way that people respond physically to survey questions. We will continue to use these terms because they are universal in the survey literature, but we have already indicated that we do not share this point of view. Errors on surveys can be due to internal features of language comprehension, memory, and choice, as well as to the way people execute a response, and our theory builds on current research in cognitive psychology and artificial intelligence. We view response effects in surveys as a challenging test case for cognitive science, one that goes beyond the simple tasks that typically find their way into the cognitive laboratory. In studying survey errors, we follow Newell's (1973) advice to consider large-scale domains that draw on many mental abilities and that can therefore shed light on how cognition works as a unified system. We believe (and hope to persuade you) that a cognitive model of how people answer survey questions can offer as many insights to cognitive and social psychologists as to survey methodologists.

1.1   Earlier Theories of the Response Process

Before presenting our own view of how people answer survey questions, we consider two important antecedents: psychometric theories of attitude measurement and early proposals within the survey methodology tradition. Comparing these theories to our own approach highlights what's distinctive to the point of view presented in this book.[2]

---

[2] We concentrate in this section on historical antecedents, but contemporary research in artificial intelligence (AI) and linguistics has also influenced our thinking about the way people answer survey questions, as will be evident in later chapters. For instance, work in AI has examined the process by which computers can be programmed to answer questions framed in everyday language (e.g., Allen, 1995; Graesser, McMahen, & Johnson, 1994; Lehnert, 1978). The AI and linguistics research has concentrated on the difficult problem of identifying the specific information that ordinary questions seek. So far, however, this research has had little direct impact on models of the survey response process. We attempt to correct this oversight in Chapter 2.

1.1.1   Psychometric Theories

Perhaps the first models of the survey response process were the ones developed by psychometricians – Guttman, Guilford, Likert, and their colleagues. This research produced the first systematic attitude measurement techniques, techniques that quantified the strength of a person's conviction in an opinion (e.g., *How strongly do you favor increasing aid to the homeless?*). Of these early pioneers, Louis Thurstone was perhaps the leader in describing the underlying psychological processes that made attitude measurement possible (see, e.g., Thurstone, 1927).[3] Thurstone's goal was to develop mathematical models that described the outcome of comparisons among several stimuli, including several statements about an issue (e.g., *Aid to the homeless should be increased; Society already does enough for the homeless; The homeless are a nuisance*).

Thurstone's formal models rested on a psychological theory of judgment: the idea that people represent stimuli as points or regions on an internal dimension (e.g., the dimension of strength of agreement with a position). Thus, his psychological models distinguished several component processes, including the identification of the dimension of judgment (or, as Thurstone referred to it, the *psychological continuum*), the judge's reaction to the stimulus (the *discriminal process*), the assignment of scale values, and the comparison of pairs of stimuli (the calculation of their *discriminal difference*). In the case of an attitude question, Thurstonian theory predicts that people compare their own position with what they take to be the position implied by each statement in the scale. The result of the comparison determines which statements they endorse.

For a variety of reasons, these psychometric models have not played a prominent role in discussions of survey error. One major problem is that, even though their emphasis is statistical, the psychometricians' mathematical models are not easily translated into the terms that have come to dominate discussions of survey error; the survey error models are extensions of those used to analyze random sampling error, and they focus on factual questions, for which it is possible (at least in principle) to measure the accuracy of the answer (e.g., Hansen et al., 1953; see Chapter 11 and Groves, 1989, on the differences between the survey and psychometric approaches to measurement error). In addition, from our

---

[3] Perhaps another antecedent can be found in Frank Ramsey's (1931) work on measurement of utility, although this approach did not join the mainstream in psychology until the 1950s.

current vantage point, the earlier psychometric models are hamstrung by the absence of a detailed description of the judgment process. Although Thurstone's model presents one view of how people choose among response options, it is silent on questions of how they identify the psychological continuum on the basis of the survey question, how they recruit relevant attitude information from memory, and many other crucial issues.

1.1.2   Cannell's Process Theory

The model proposed by Cannell, Miller, and Oksenberg (1981; see Cannell, Marquis, & Laurent, 1977, for an earlier version) was perhaps the first model of the survey response process to reflect the new cognitive outlook within psychology. Their model distinguished two routes to an answer, one based on relatively careful processing of the question and the other based on superficial features of the interview situation, such as the interviewer's appearance (see Cannell et al., 1981). Careful answers are, according to this model, the product of the five sets of processes in (3):

(3) a. Comprehension of the question;
   b. Cognitive processing (i.e., assessments concerning the information sought, retrieval of relevant memories, and integration and response formulation);
   c. Evaluation of the accuracy of the response;
   d. Evaluation of the response based on goals other than accuracy;
   e. Accurate responding.

We illustrate the arrangement of these steps in Figure 1.1. Cannell, Miller, and Oksenberg (1981) view these five sets of processes as more or less sequential, although their model explicitly allowed for the possibility that respondents might cycle back to an earlier stage if they judged their preliminary answer not to be accurate enough. Prior to the fifth stage, when respondents give an accurate (or at least adequate) answer, respondents could switch to the parallel track and alter their answer based on relatively superficial cues available in the interview situation – cues such as the interviewer's appearance or the implied direction of the question. Responses based on such cues were likely to be biased by *acquiescence* (the tendency to agree) or *social desirability* (the need to present oneself in a favorable light).

The model by Cannell and his colleagues has many attractive features,

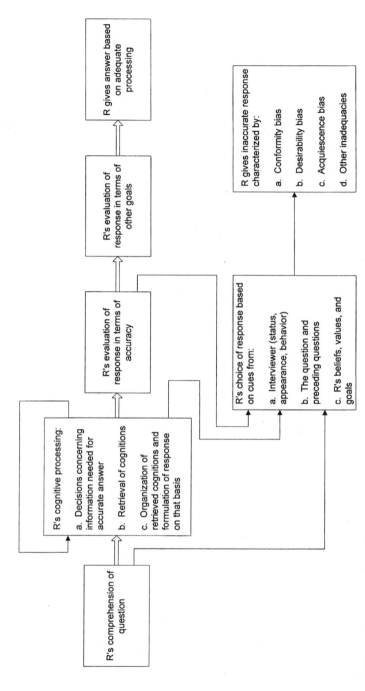

Figure 1.1. Cannell, Miller, and Oksenberg's model of the survey response process. The boxes along the bottom of the figure represent the processes needed for a careful answer; those along the top represent the processes leading to an inadequate answer. Adapted from Cannell et al. (1981). Copyright © 1981. Adapted with permission of Jossey-Bass.

and it has spawned many related approaches (see Section 1.3). The notion that respondents might take different routes to arrive at an answer is an appealing one, and the specific routes in the Cannell model – one based on systematic processing of the question and the other based on more superficial processing – have a number of parallels in the psychological literature. For example, discussions of attitude change have identified central and peripheral routes to persuasion (Chaiken, 1980; Petty & Cacioppo, 1984). Hastie and Park's (1986) distinction between *memory-based judgments* and *on-line* (i.e., situation-based) *judgments* also bears similarities to the two tracks in Figure 1.1. Another attractive feature of the model is its explicit concern with the respondent's motivation, including such motives as the desire to provide accurate information, to appear agreeable, and to avoid embarrassment.

From our viewpoint, the model suffers from two major drawbacks. The first is that, because the model never assumed a central place in Cannell's work, it was never worked out it much detail. The most complete exposition of the model (in Cannell et al., 1981) runs no more than three pages. Most of the research inspired by the model has focused on improving respondent motivation in a general way rather than on testing predictions regarding the model's specific components. The second drawback is related to the first. It is the model's rather sketchy treatment of the cognitive processes involved in responding to a question, which the model's second stage lumps together. By contrast, the model distinguishes several stages in describing what happens *after* the respondent derives a preliminary answer. The respondent evaluates the initial answer in terms of its accuracy, then in terms of its compatibility with other goals, and finally may modify or discard it based on these earlier assessments. The model seems to assume that respondents could answer questions accurately if only they wanted to and concentrates on whether they decide to answer accurately or not. We favor a different emphasis.

1.2 A Proposed Model of the Response Process

We have organized this book around a model that divides the survey response process into four major components – comprehension of the item, retrieval of relevant information, use of that information to make required judgments, and selection and reporting of an answer (Tourangeau, 1984, 1987; Tourangeau & Rasinski, 1988; see also Strack & Martin, 1987). Table 1.1 lists each of these components along with

TABLE 1.1 Components of the Response Process

Component	Specific Processes
Comprehension	Attend to questions and instructions
	Represent logical form of question
	Identify question focus (information sought)
	Link key terms to relevant concepts
Retrieval	Generate retrieval strategy and cues
	Retrieve specific, generic memories
	Fill in missing details
Judgment	Assess completeness and relevance of memories
	Draw inferences based on accessibility
	Integrate material retrieved
	Make estimate based on partial retrieval
Response	Map judgment onto response category
	Edit response

specific mental processes that they might include. In describing these processes, we don't mean to suggest that respondents necessarily perform them all when they answer a survey question. Although some processes may be mandatory, others are clearly optional – a set of cognitive tools that respondents can use in constructing their answer. Exactly which set of processes they carry out will depend on how accurate they want their answer to be, on how quickly they need to produce it, and on many other factors. In this respect, the theory presented in Table 1.1 resembles approaches to decision making that emphasize the array of strategies that people bring to bear on a problem (Payne, Bettman, & Johnson, 1993). These processes are also not exhaustive. We suggest some additions to the list in later chapters when we take up the components in more detail.

Each of these components can give rise to response effects; respondents may, for example, misinterpret the question, forget crucial information, make erroneous inferences based on what they do retrieve, or map their answers onto an inappropriate response category. Both psychological and survey research provide ample evidence of the errors each component produces, and to understand how the response process can go awry, we need to take a closer look at them. In reviewing these components, we also preview the material we will cover in the rest of this book.

1.2.1 Comprehension

Comprehension encompasses such processes as attending to the question and accompanying instructions, assigning a meaning to the surface form of the question, and inferring the question's point – that is, identifying the information sought (Clark, 1985; Graesser, McMahen, & Johnson, 1994; Lehnert, 1978). Current research on the pragmatics of natural language emphasizes the reasoning people must perform in order to grasp the full implication of a sentence (Grice, 1989; Lewis, 1979; Sperber & Wilson, 1986); research on conversation emphasizes the way conversational partners cooperate to shape their mutual understanding (Clark & Schober, 1992).

As survey researchers have known for some time, many reporting problems arise because respondents misunderstand the questions. Respondents' attention may wander during an interview, and they may miss part of the question; in a self-administered questionnaire, they may not notice essential instructions or, having noticed, they may not bother to read them. The question may be double-barreled, inadvertently asking two or more questions at the same time. The question may include terms that are unfamiliar to the respondent or terms that are understood in different ways by different respondents. The question may be too complicated syntactically or it may contain detailed qualifications that are hard to understand. Familiar terms may nonetheless be vague, and even seemingly clear categories (such as *siblings*) may include borderline cases that can be misclassified (stepbrothers). With attitude questions, a key step in the comprehension process is identifying what issue the question is about. Chapter 2 of this book examines the comprehension of survey questions in more detail; it presents a more detailed theory of this component and reviews what is known about comprehension problems in surveys.

1.2.2 Retrieval for Factual Questions

The retrieval component involves recalling relevant information from long-term memory. This component encompasses such processes as adopting a retrieval strategy, generating specific retrieval cues to trigger recall, recollecting individual memories, and filling in partial memories through inference. Several characteristics of the recalled material and of the initiating questions can affect the accuracy and the completeness of this component (Jobe, Tourangeau, & Smith, 1993). These include the distinctiveness of the events, the degree of fit between the terms used in the question and the events' original encoding, the number and quality of the cues that the question provides, the source of the memory (direct experience or secondhand knowledge), and the length of time since the events occurred. Chapter 3 examines these issues.

1.2.3   Judgment for Factual Questions

Retrieval often does not yield an explicit answer to survey questions. The question may concern the total number of visits to the doctor in the last six months, the number of hours worked, or the total amount spent on retail purchases during the reference period. If so, respondents must sum the individual events they recalled during the retrieval phase in order to find the total number. The judgment component comprises the processes that respondents use to combine or supplement what they have retrieved. There are at least five major types of judgment processes that may come into play:

(4) a. Judgments regarding the completeness or accuracy of retrieval;
   b. Inferences based on the process of retrieval;
   c. Inferences that fill in gaps in what is recalled;
   d. Integration of the products of retrieval into a single overall judgment;
   e. Estimates that adjust for omissions in retrieval.

The first three types of judgment depend on the relation between judgment and retrieval. Type (4a) determines whether further retrieval is warranted and whether specific memories fall within the scope of the question. Some judgments of this type can be seen as an extension of the comprehension component as respondents attempt to implement their understanding of the nature of the events covered by the question. The second type of judgment involves drawing conclusions from features of the retrieval process; for example, when retrieval is difficult or sketchy, respondents may conclude that the events in question happened infrequently or long ago or never took place at all (Brown, Rips, & Shevell, 1985; Gentner & Collins, 1981; Tversky & Kahneman, 1973). The judgments of the third type are attempts to reconstruct what happened by inferring missing details, often based on what typically happens during an event of a given type.

Respondents undertake the remaining types of judgment to transform the retrieved information into an appropriate answer. The fourth process is necessary because people often retrieve fragmentary information that they must combine to produce a single response. This combination may involve simple numerical averaging (Anderson, 1981) or more complex types of estimation. The final process involves situations in which what is remembered forms part of a larger estimation strategy. For example, to answer a question about a lengthy time period, respondents may recall the number of events in a recent, easily remembered portion of the period and then extrapolate to cover the entire period.

The processes in (4) usually operate on retrieved information, but sometimes judgment supplants retrieval entirely. As Reder (1987) has argued, people sometimes answer retrospective questions by considering the general plausibility of a response. Respondents who have never heard the term *health maintenance organization* (HMO) can probably infer from that fact alone that they do not belong to one. People can bypass retrieval of specific information in such cases.

Judgments about Dates and Durations

Survey questions often ask about events that occurred within some specific time frame; for example, the National Crime Survey asks question (5):

(5) During the last 6 months, did anyone steal things that belonged to you from inside ANY car or truck, such as packages or clothing? [NCS]

Question (1b) is a similar item. Because people have difficulty remembering exact dates (Friedman, 1993; Thompson, Skowronski, Larsen, & Betz, 1996; Wagenaar, 1986), they may report events that took place before the specified *reference period* (i.e., the time period that the question asks about – the last six months in question (5)). This sort of error is known as *forward telescoping*, and this phenomenon has been the subject of theorizing by both survey methodologists and cognitive psychologists since Neter and Waksberg (1964) first documented it.

Reporting errors due to incorrect dating seem to arise through several distinct mechanisms. People may make incorrect inferences about timing based on the accessibility (or other properties) of the memory, incorrectly guess a date within an uncertain range, and round vague temporal information to prototypical values (such as 30 days). We take up these issues in detail in Chapter 4.

Judgments about Frequencies

Another popular type of survey question asks about the number of times the respondent has engaged in some activity or about the rate of events that happened in some reference period. Question (6) is typical of the sort of item we have in mind:

(6) During the past 12 months (that is since __(date)__ a year ago), about how many times did _____ see or talk to a medical doctor? (Do not count doctors seen while a patient in a hospital.) (Include the _____ visits you already told me about.) [HIS]

Individual visits to the doctor may be difficult to remember, but it is often possible for people to reconstruct what must have taken place (e.g., Means, Nigam, Zarrow, Loftus, & Donaldson, 1989; A. F. Smith, 1991; see also Lessler, Tourangeau, & Salter, 1989, on the reporting of dental visits). For example, people may recall only the regular pattern of events and use this rate to make an estimate for the full reference period (Burton & Blair, 1991). Chapter 5 considers the judgment processes involved in answering such questions.

1.2.4   Retrieval and Judgment for Attitude Questions

When we have to decide our attitude toward an issue, we need to consult our memory for relevant information. But what exactly do respondents retrieve when they answer a question about their attitudes? What does it mean for a respondent to give an inaccurate report about an attitude? Most attitude research seems to take it for granted that having an attitude means having a preexisting judgment about an issue or a person and that people automatically invoke these judgments when answering a relevant question (e.g., Fazio, 1989); responses to attitude questions do not, as a result, seem to present much of a problem or to require an elaborate cognitive theory.

We regard this view as overly simple. Along with Fischhoff (1991), we assume that there is a continuum corresponding to how well articulated a respondent's attitude is. At the more articulated end, the respondent has a preformed opinion just waiting to be offered to the interviewer; at the less articulated end, the respondent has no opinion whatever. Between these extremes, he or she may have a loosely related set of ideas to use in constructing an opinion or even a moderately well-formed viewpoint to draw on.

Respondents probably do not have perfectly well-articulated opinions on all attitude questions that survey researchers pose. First, evidence from large-scale attitude surveys indicates that on any given issue – no matter how familiar – a substantial portion of the population simply does not have stable views. As Converse (1964, 1970) and others have shown, attitude responses over time sometimes show seemingly random shifts at the individual level even when no clear trends show up in the aggregate. Moreover, survey responses can shift dramatically in response to minor changes in question wording or order. Second, even if respondents do have more crystallized views about an issue, these views may not lend themselves to a clear-cut answer to the question at hand. The survey item may ask about an aspect of the issue that the respondent has not thought about. For instance, an item on the GSS asks whether abortions should be permitted in the case of rape; this item may give even ardent pro-life advocates reason to stop and reflect before they answer.

The judgment processes outlined in (4) are also relevant to attitude questions. For example, people may moderate or withhold their judgment if they feel that the information they possess is not sufficient (Yzerbyt, Schadron, Leyens, & Rocher, 1994); they may base their attitudes on what's most easily brought to mind (Ross & Sicoly, 1979); they may use stereotypes and schemas to fill in information they can't recall (e.g., Hastie, 1981); and they may combine piecemeal evaluations into a single assessment (Anderson, 1981). In Chapters 6 and 7, we present a detailed model of the attitude response process; we return there to the issue of when people base their answers on existing evaluations and when they base them on more specific considerations.

1.2.5   Reporting and Response Selection

The model's final set of component processes involves selecting and reporting an answer. We include two groups of processes here – mapping the answer onto the appropriate scale or response option and "editing" the response for consistency, acceptability, or other criteria.

Even when respondents have a clear answer to report, it may not be clear to them how to report it. The response options offered by the question are sometimes vague: In the case of attitude questions, where is the exact boundary between "Strongly agree" and "Agree"? In the domain of factual questions, how often do you have to eat in a restaurant in order for the frequency to qualify as "seldom" or "often"? Beyond the difficulties respondents may have with particular answer categories or response formats, they may differ in their approaches to selecting an answer. More than one response option may present a reasonable answer for a given respondent. Some respondents may work hard to choose the best possible answer; others may be content to pick the first acceptable answer they consider. Respondents may also differ in their willingness to give an answer at all or to opt out of a question by saying they do not know the answer. Survey researchers have examined many questions regarding formats for answer categories, including how many categories should be offered, whether each one should be labeled, how the categories should be ordered, and whether "Don't know" should be included among them. We discuss these issues in more detail in Chapter 8.

Surveys often venture into areas that people do not ordinarily discuss with strangers. For example, a number of national surveys ask about the use of illicit drugs; other surveys ask about abortions, preferred methods of contraception, consumption of alcohol, medical conditions, or other topics that may cause embarrassment or resentment on the part of respondents. In fact, some respondents may regard one of the most basic of survey questions – *Who lives here?* – as an unwarranted intrusion (Tourangeau, Shapiro, Kearney, & Ernst, 1997). It is apparent that respondents do not always answer such questions truthfully. In Chapter 9, we consider the processes that govern the respondents' level of candor in answering sensitive questions – how respondents weigh the risks and benefits of responding truthfully (and of responding at all), what risks concern them, and what characteristics of the survey can raise or alleviate these concerns. Some respondents may decide in a rational way whether to respond truthfully or to give evasive answers; others may decide in an unconscious and automatic way, in accord with rules that originally evolved for dealing with other situations.

1.2.6   Summary

The theory of Table 1.1 sets out 13 cognitive processes that people may use to respond to a survey item. Despite the sheer number of processes, we should emphasize that survey responses are not the product of lengthy deliberations. On the contrary, respondents take less than 5 seconds to answer typical attitude questions (Bassili & Fletcher, 1991; Tourangeau, Rasinski, & D'Andrade, 1991).

In any model of this sort, a question immediately arises about the sequencing of the processes. Are the four main components distinct, nonoverlapping stages or are they simply classes of related processes? There is little evidence to help us decide this issue, and theoretical arguments can be made for either position. On the one hand, it seems likely that for many questions respondents methodically follow the logical sequence of first comprehending the item, then retrieving the relevant facts, then making whatever judgment is called for, and finally reporting that judgment in the appropriate format. After all, how would respondents know what to retrieve before they have understood the question? How could they make a judgment if retrieval has not produced the necessary input? How could respondents report an answer before they have arrived at it?

On the other hand, it is equally clear that there can be many variations in the response process. In the first place, there will often be at least partial overlap among components. For example, retrieval is likely to commence before comprehension is complete; the very act of understanding key words in interpreting a question may trigger the spread of activation that is thought to be a central mechanism in retrieving memories (Anderson, 1983). In some cases, it may even make sense to think of retrieval as preceding comprehension; respondents may already have retrieved the information they need to answer one question in the process of answering earlier questions. Similarly, judgment may parallel rather than follow retrieval. In answering an attitude question, respondents may sequentially update their judgment about an issue as specific considerations come to mind. Or they may make judgments based on accessibility while they continue to retrieve memories. So any adequate model of the survey response process must allow for some overlapping processes.

In the second place, the model must allow respondents to backtrack from a "later" stage of the process to an "earlier" one. When retrieval yields little information, respondents may ask the interviewer for clarification or try to reinterpret the question on their own. At least one class of judgments involves deciding whether additional retrieval is warranted. An adequate model of the survey response process must therefore allow for cycling between the judgment and retrieval components. Similarly, selecting a response may require respondents to alter their judgment so that they can map the judgment onto one of the choices. Whenever the output from one component does not meet the requirement of another component, respondents may have to reexecute the earlier one.

A third complication is that respondents can sometimes skip or truncate a component. This accords with the cognitive toolbox approach that we mentioned in Section 1.2; respondents needn't employ all their response strategies in answering every question. Having understood a question as intrusive, respondents may skip retrieval and judgment altogether and go directly to response selection – offering an evasive response or refusing to answer. In fact, inattentive respondents may even skip the comprehension stage and simply respond by saying they do not know the answer. With attitude items, respondents may omit the judgment component once they have retrieved an overall opinion (or at least a definite impression), provided that the form of the question permits an answer based on an existing judgment. With factual items, retrieval may yield an answer that requires little further cognitive processing; respondents do not need to use much in the way of judgment to answer questions about their age, date of birth, or sex. And, as we have already noted, judgment may replace retrieval when people answer on the basis of plausibility or familiarity rather than specific memories.

Because respondents can carry out components in parallel, because they can backtrack from later components to earlier ones, and because they can completely skip components, it would be misleading to describe the four components as nonoverlapping stages. Although we suspect that comprehension – retrieval – judgment – reporting is the most common order for the components, there is little evidence to support (or refute) this hypothesis, and other common patterns are worth noting.

1.3   Other Recent Proposals: High Road/Low Road Theories

The model in Table 1.1 constitutes an idealized list; the response process for a given item is likely to include only a subset of the processes identified there. Are there sequences other than the comprehension – retrieval – judgment – reporting sequence that are likely to arise in practice? As it happens, several models of the survey response process identify such sequences as alternative paths to responding.

We have already described the model proposed by Cannell and his colleagues in Section 1.1.2. This model features one track that includes most of the same processes that we have identified – comprehension, retrieval, judgment, and mapping – and a second track that modifies the response due to motives other than accuracy. This second track takes into account cues from the interview situation itself (see Figure 1.1).

We have also discussed some reasons for preferring a different model from that of Cannell and his colleagues. Here we consider an additional issue – the question of whether there are two distinct routes to arriving at an answer. It is certainly possible that, for some items, the conscientious and superficial routes represent sharply distinct tracks consisting of clearly distinguishable processes; however, in many cases the distinction between these two modes of processing is likely to blur. For example, even when respondents are trying to be conscientious, prior items can affect their answers; indeed, the effects of retrieving information relevant to one item may have an automatic effect – an impact outside the respondent's awareness or control – on retrieval for related questions later on. Similarly, respondents may use both information retrieved from memory and cues from the situation in formulating their answers. There is no reason, in principle, why both sources could not contribute information to a response. Perhaps it is best to view Cannell's two tracks as two extremes on a continuum of processes that vary in the depth and the quality of thought that respondents give to their answers.

1.3.1   The Satisficing Model

Two other models of the survey response process have appeared in the last few years, and they share with the Cannell model the assumption of dual paths to a survey response – a high road and a low road. The first is the satisficing model that Krosnick and Alwin have presented (Krosnick & Alwin, 1987; see also Krosnick, 1991). Krosnick and Alwin distinguish between respondents who *satisfice* (the low road) and those who *optimize* (the high road) in answering survey questions. In their view, satisficing is not so much a strategy for choosing among response options as an overall approach to answering the questions (cf. Tourangeau, 1984). Satisficing respondents do not seek to understand the question completely, but just well enough to provide a plausible answer; they do not try to recall everything that is relevant, but just enough material on which to base an answer; and so on. Satisficing thus resembles the more superficial branch of Cannell's two-track model. Similarly, optimizing respondents would seem to follow the more careful branch.

Like the Cannell model, Krosnick's satisficing theory makes a sharp distinction among processes that probably vary continuously. Respondents may process questions to differing depths, and they may not carry out each component process with the same level of care. There is no reason to assume that respondents who are inattentive while reading a question will necessarily do a poor job of retrieval. The key point is that respondents may carry out each cognitive operation carefully or sloppily.

1.3.2   Strack and Martin's Two-Track Theory

Strack and Martin (1987) have also proposed a two-track model, one that focuses on the response process for attitude questions. The two routes they identify correspond to the distinction between responses based on an existing judgment and those based on a new judgment that respondents derive at the time they answer the question. The route for new judgments closely parallels the model presented here; the key processes comprising that route are interpreting the question, accessing relevant information, "computing" the judgment, and formatting and editing the response. The other route leaves out the judgment step and replaces retrieval of more specific information with retrieval of a prior judgment. Although we certainly agree that processes resembling both tracks occur in surveys, we believe that both of Strack and Martin's tracks can be seen as special cases of the more general model we presented in Section 1.2.

There are several reasons for the choice of the general model over Strack and Martin's more specific one. First, we believe there is little evidence that respondents retrieve either an existing judgment or more specific beliefs about an issue but never retrieve both. In fact, in Chapter 6, we review evidence that a mix of specific beliefs and existing judgments may be the most common output of the retrieval process for attitude questions (in line with Fischhoff's, 1991, *partial perspectives* philosophy). In any case, it seems unnecessary to exclude this possibility a priori. Second, we question the model's assumption that, when people retrieve an earlier opinion, they circumvent the judgment process entirely. Although it may be possible to recall an attitude (e.g., that *The Last of the Mohicans* is boring) without being able to remember anything else about the topic, it is unclear how often this happens in surveys. Many attitude items require respondents to make new judgments even when they retrieve a prior opinion. For example, agree/disagree items such as those in (2) force respondents not only to retrieve their own views, but also to determine how close those views are to the position expressed by the item. Respondents must still perform some sort of comparison process, however abbreviated.

Like the routes in Figure 1.1, Strack and Martin's two branches represent pure cases. These ideal types are certainly worth noting, but it would be a mistake to see them as exhausting the possibilities.[4]

---

[4] Closer to our own approach is Schwarz's (1990) model for factual questions. Although this theory differentiates reports based on individual memories from those based on summary estimates (a high road/low road difference), it allows some variety in the relations between judgment and retrieval processes.

1.3.3   Summary

We prefer to think that quite a large number of paths to an answer are possible, depending on the effort that respondents are willing to invest and on the interplay between retrieval and judgment. In each case, the path traverses a subset of the processes identified here – which may be carried out well or sloppily, in parallel or in sequence, and with or without backtracking – as circumstances and motivation dictate.

A recent review by Jobe and Herrmann (1996) describes seven models of the response process, including several we have already discussed. Some of the others encompass the same processes listed in Table 1.1, differing from the present model only in how they group these processes into larger components. For example, Forsyth, Lessler, and Hubbard (1992) include separate comprehension and interpretation components; Willis, Royston, and Bercini (1991) include separate judgment and decision processes. These differences seem more a matter of emphasis than of substance. Two of the models attempt to account not only for the mental operations of the respondents but for those of the interviewer as well (Esposito & Jobe, 1991; Sander, Conrad, Mullin, & Herrmann, 1992).

1.4   Applications of the Model

Models like the ones summarized here are useful in part because they offer a new understanding of the sources of response effects in surveys and suggest methods for reducing such effects. For example, survey items such as (6) ask about the frequency of a specific class of events – visits to the doctor, days of illness, incidents of crime victimization, sexual partners, and so on. The outcome of each component of the response process will affect the number of events reported in answer to such questions. Depending on how respondents understand the question – in particular, on how broadly or narrowly they define the class of events to be reported – more or fewer events will qualify. Similarly, the number of events they report will reflect the outcomes of retrieval and judgment: The more relevant events they can remember, the greater the number they will report, and the more events they see as falling within the reference period for the question, the more events will be included in the answers.

Reporting errors are not the only place where cognitive models can shed light on survey problems. Chapters 7 and 10 of the book extend this model to two additional problems encountered in surveys – the impact of the order of the questions and the effects of new computer-assisted methods of data collection.

One of the most puzzling sets of findings in the survey literature concerns the impact of item context. In Chapter 7, we describe our theory of how earlier questions in the interview or questionnaire can affect each component of the response process (Strack & Martin, 1987; Tourangeau & Rasinski, 1988). Prior items can change how respondents interpret later questions, what considerations they retrieve in formulating their answers, which standards or norms they apply in judging the issue, and how they report their answers. In addition, different mechanisms that produce context effects influence responses in different ways. Prior items sometimes influence later responses in the direction of consistency but sometimes have the opposite effect, producing apparent inconsistencies. Complicating matters further, the context of an item can change the overall direction of the answers or it can alter the correlations between answers to different items.

Over the last 25 years, the face of survey research has changed dramatically as computers have supplanted pencils and clipboards as the survey interviewer's most indispensable tools. Allowing the computer to collect the data has had a variety of effects, some of which have been subjected only to cursory investigation so far. The different methods of collecting survey data – self-administered questionnaires, interviews conducted by telephone or face-to-face, computer-assisted telephone and personal interviews, automated self-administered questionnaires – differ along many dimensions. We propose an analysis that singles out three key characteristics of the method of data collection – the degree of impersonality it conveys, the perception of legitimacy it fosters, and the level of cognitive burden it imposes on the respondent (and interviewer). Chapter 10 reviews the evidence regarding the effects of the method of data collection on the answers obtained.

1.5   Implications of the Model

In discussing the relationship between philosophy and psychology, William James once remarked that "metaphysics . . . spoils two good things when she injects herself into a natural science." There are those who might argue that the attempt to apply concepts and methods from the cognitive sciences to issues of survey methodology has had equally unhappy results. Innovations based on this attempt, sometimes dubbed the

CASM movement (for cognitive aspects of survey methodology), have been widely accepted within the federal statistical community, but there is also widespread scepticism about the value of this approach. In our final chapter, we consider the results that CASM has achieved so far.

Any effort to apply findings from one field to the problems of another raises several questions: Are researchers addressing the right problems? Are they applying valid theories? Have they developed the right applications of the theories for the problems at hand? We consider these questions in detail in Chapter 11, attempting to evaluate both our specific model and the more general movement to use cognitive science to improve survey practice.

Although the emphasis in this book is on the application of cognitive models to problems in survey methods, the findings in this growing literature clearly have something to offer the cognitive sciences in return. We single out several areas where survey findings have implications for cognitive theory. First, apart from survey-related studies, there have been few formal investigations of memory for everyday events, the happenings that are the stuff of daily life. Surveys routinely ask about consumer purchases, visits to the doctor, searches for jobs, hours spent at work, illnesses, hospital stays, courses taken in school, and a host of other daily occurrences. To be sure, a few landmark investigations of everyday memory have appeared within cognitive psychology (see Chapter 3), but these are meager compared to the large number of studies conducted with a view to improving survey reports about such issues.

The survey-inspired studies on everyday memory have yielded dividends bearing on several theoretical issues in the cognitive sciences. For example, some of the clearest evidence for the existence of generic memories – idealized memories of a class of recurring events – comes from attempts to understand survey reporting on dietary intake (A. F. Smith, 1991) and visits to the doctor (Means et al., 1989).

Similarly, investigations of how respondents answer questions about the frequency of everyday events have yielded rich insights into estimation processes and their role in filling in information that memory alone cannot provide. Herrmann (1992) describes some 15 strategies that respondents use in answering survey frequency questions, many of them involving estimation. To cite one example, Burton and Blair (1991) explore a strategy in which respondents recall events during a recent period and then make a rate-based projection for the entire period in question. This strategy is far closer to the estimation procedures employed by statisticians or engineers than to the heuristics that have taken center stage in discussions of frequency judgments within the psychological literature. Investigations of rounding in survey reporting (e.g., Huttenlocher, Hedges, & Bradburn, 1990) have shed further light on how respondents compensate for vague or incomplete memories. Since the time of Bartlett's classic work (1932), psychologists have acknowledged that memory involves both retrieval and reconstruction; the survey-based studies on generic memory, estimation, and rounding have added considerable detail to this picture.

Another area where the survey literature has much to offer cognitive psychology involves what might be called *proxy memory* – memories for events experienced by other people. This topic has been almost completely neglected within the mainstream memory literature (see Larsen, 1988, for an exception) but has been a lively area within the movement to apply cognitive theories to issues of survey methods (e.g., Blair, Menon, & Bickart, 1991).

In addition to its implications for the study of memory, the recent efforts to apply cognitive theories to survey issues have much to contribute to the study of attitudes. As we've remarked, investigations of attitudes in social psychology often seem to assume that respondents have a preexisting answer to most attitude questions and need only to read out this answer. The results from the survey literature present quite a different picture: Responses to survey questions can become unreliable over time (Converse, 1964, 1970) and show fluctuations as a consequence of seemingly minor changes in question wording (Schuman & Presser, 1981). In fact, simply changing the order of the questions can produce large swings in the answers (Tourangeau & Rasinski, 1988). If answers to attitude questions are simply readouts of stored judgments, it is not clear why question order should make such a difference. The study of order effects on responses to attitude questions has been a particularly fruitful area for the application of cognitive methods to a long-standing survey problem (Schwarz & Sudman, 1992; Tourangeau & Rasinski, 1988). These models are aimed at explaining survey results, but they have greatly expanded our understanding of assimilation and contrast effects in judgment more generally.

In several areas, then, the effort to apply concepts and methods drawn from psychology to problems in surveys has yielded benefits to both fields. Still, the sailing hasn't always been smooth. In Chapter 11, we consider some of the barriers to further progress.

CHAPTER TWO

Respondents' Understanding of Survey Questions

Survey designers don't need to be reminded that the wording of the questions has an important impact on the results. Respondents can misinterpret even well-formulated questions, and when that happens, the question the respondent answers may not be the one the researcher intended to ask. Because of this obvious danger, the questions on national surveys are often subjected to empirical pretests. For example, the questionnaire designers may conduct cognitive interviews or focus groups in which they probe respondents' understanding of the questions and invite them to describe how they go about answering them (see Willis, DeMaio, & Harris-Kojetin, 1999, for a survey of these methods; we present a briefer discussion of them in Chapter 11). This practice is useful in bringing to light problems the designers may have overlooked.

This chapter looks at those aspects of survey questions that make them difficult for respondents to understand. These aspects are of many different sorts, ranging from features of grammar and word meaning to the broader situation in which the respondent and interviewer find themselves. Grammar can come into play either because the sentence is structurally ambiguous or because it includes complex clauses that respondents cannot parse. As an example of structural ambiguity, Item (1) asks respondents whether they agree or disagree with this statement:

(1) Given the world situation, the government protects too many documents by classifying them as SECRET and TOP SECRET. [GSS]

As Fillmore (1999) points out, this sentence has two readings: According to one reading, the government, motivated by the world situation, protects too many documents; according to the other, the government protects more documents than can be justified by the world situation. The ambiguity relates to syntactic structure (it depends on what part of the sentence the initial clause modifies), and it may affect how a respondent answers the question. A recent study by Stinson (1997) centered on a question that illustrates the sort of grammatical complexity that can lead to trouble:

(2) Living where you do now and meeting the expenses you consider necessary, what would be the smallest income (before any deductions) you and your family would need to make ends meet EACH MONTH?

Although syntax can present hurdles for respondents, most studies of question wording have focused on semantic problems – problems of meaning – especially those involving the meaning of individual words. Many words in natural language are *ambiguous* (have more than one meaning) or are *vague* (have imprecise ranges of application). In addition, survey questions may include obscure or technical terms that are *unfamiliar* to respondents. Opinion surveys, for example, may ask about newly emerging issues that are unfamiliar to many of the respondents.

Vagueness and ambiguity can lead respondents to interpret questions in variable ways. For example, when Belson (1981) probed respondents in a follow-up interview about the meaning of Question (3), he found differences among respondents in the age range they attributed to *children*:

(3) Do you think that children suffer any ill effects from watching programmes with violence in them, other than ordinary Westerns?[1]

The respondents' difficulties might have been due to the ambiguity of the term *children*, which can refer either to sons and daughters of any age (as in *How many children do you have?*) or to youngsters in particular. Vagueness may be a more likely source, however, because the meaning of *youngster* is not crisply bounded (the division between youngster and adult is not well defined). And, of course, the term *ill effects* is deliberately vague. Similarly, Belson found that respondents gave a wide range of interpretations to the adverbial quantifier *usually* in (4):

(4) For how many hours do you *usually* watch television on a weekday?

---

[1] Questions (3) and (4) are not from actual surveys. Belson (1981) composed them for research purposes in order to embody the types of question-wording problems most often found in items "provided by research organizations whose representatives made available questionnaires which they had used over the past two years" (p. 23).

Question (4) also illustrates a further problem that affects comprehension. Many questions *presuppose* that certain characteristics apply to the respondent and then *focus* on an associated aspect. In (4), for example, *usually* presupposes that there is some usual pattern in the respondent's weekday television viewing, and the question focuses on how many hours per day make up that pattern. Presupposition and focus are normal components of a sentence's meaning, but they lead to difficulties in surveys when the presupposition fails to apply. If there is no regular pattern to the respondents' TV watching, then they must either opt out of the question (e.g., by responding *don't know*) or reinterpret the question in ways that apply to them. Difficulty with presuppositions may also occur in (5), another item from the General Social Survey, in which respondents have to rate their agreement or disagreement:

(5) Family life often suffers because men concentrate too much on their work. [GSS]

This item presupposes that men concentrate too much on their work and focuses on its effect on family life. A respondent who agrees with the subordinate clause (men concentrate too much) and disagrees with the main clause (family life suffers) should have no special difficulty answering (5). But a respondent who disagrees with the subordinate clause may feel that the question doesn't properly apply to him or her (Fillmore, 1999).

This item raises another difficulty: What sort of position would someone be advocating by making the statement in (5)? Is the intent to convey the feminist view that men should take on a fairer share of the household chores and child-rearing responsibilities? Or is the intent to convey a more fundamentalist position that family life should take priority over outside activities? Depending on which reading the respondents give to the item, they may embrace or reject its implied sentiment.

These examples illustrate the major classes of interpretive difficulty that survey designers encounter. The question's grammatical structure (its *syntax*) may be ambiguous or too complicated for respondents to take in. Lengthy or complex questions can exceed respondents' capacity to process them, resulting in misinterpretations (e.g., Just & Carpenter, 1992). The question's meaning (or *semantics*) may elude respondents if they misunderstand vague, unfamiliar, or ambiguous terms or if they are misled by inapplicable presuppositions. Finally, the intended use of the question (its *pragmatics*) may create difficulties, as in (5). To begin exploring these comprehension difficulties more systematically, we begin by looking at the nature of questions and the processes involved in understanding them. The remaining sections then examine the contributions of grammar, meaning, and use in respondents' approach to questions.

2.1   What Is a Question?

The comprehension difficulties that respondents face usually involve understanding questions, and we will focus on questions here. Obviously, respondents also have to comprehend sentences of other sorts, especially at the beginning of the survey interview, in explanatory passages, and during transitions between parts of the survey instrument (e.g., *Now I'd like to ask you some questions about your children*). With self-administered questionnaires, comprehension of various kinds of instructions, especially those about the route respondents are supposed to take through the questionnaire, can create problems as well (Jenkins & Dillman, 1997). But many of the aspects of comprehension that we will discuss in connection with questions carry over to other sentences as well.

One immediate difficulty in thinking about questions, however, is that we can view them at different levels of analysis. Questions are associated with certain surface forms, generally give rise to a particular class of meanings, and are usually intended to perform a specific kind of action. But although these levels of form, meaning, and action are correlated with each other, the correlation is far from perfect. We cannot concentrate on one level at the expense of the others.

Like other complex linguistic objects, questions display a characteristic grammatical and phonological structure. For example, questions often have inverted word order (*Where was Catherine working last week?* rather than *Catherine was working where last week?*) and a rising intonation contour.[2] Thus, the term *question* often refers to a class of lin-

---

[2] But not always. *Echo questions* can preserve the order of a preceding statement in conversation (e.g., *I fed your headband to the gerbil. You fed my headband to the gerbil?*). *Subject questions*, such as *Who fed your headband to the gerbil?*, also have normal word order (cf. *I fed your headband to the gerbil;* see Radford, 1997, Section 7.7). Rising intonation likewise appears at the ends of some questions but not all. Bolinger (1957, p. 1) cites the following example from Raymond Chandler, noting that the final question probably doesn't rise:

Mr. Hady is on nights and Mr. Flack on days. It's day now so it would be Mr. Flack would be on.
Where can I find him.

guistic objects – interrogative sentences – that we typically use in asking for information. This meaning looms large in survey designers' talk of *question wording*: Given the sort of information that we want, what's the best way of structuring the question as a linguistic object to get at those facts or opinions?

But once we begin to consider the possibility of alternative wordings, we seem to presume that there is *something* of which they are alternative versions: an abstract question that we can ask in different ways. If we're interested in finding out when someone begins his or her commute, we might ask (6), adapted from the Long Form used in the decennial census:

(6)   What time did Calvin usually leave home to go to work last week?

But we could also use *Could you please tell me when Calvin usually left home to go to work last week?* or *On those days when this person worked last week, when did he or she usually leave home?* These versions have clearly distinct linguistic forms, but, at least in some situations, they get at the same information and should receive the same answer. It is not easy to say exactly what the something is that each of these items expresses in common, but according to recent theories of the semantics of questions (e.g., Groenendijk & Stokhof, 1997; Higginbotham, 1996), this shared aspect of meaning is what we will call a *space of uncertainty*. This space consists of a set of possibilities, each of which constitutes a potential answer to the question. One of these possibilities is the correct answer. For Question (6) and its variants, this uncertainty space might be the set of all propositions of the form *Last week, Calvin usually left home to go to work at time t* for all clock times *t*. A respondent could give any of these propositions as an answer to the question, although only one of them (perhaps *Calvin usually left home to go to work at 9:15 a.m.*) would be the correct answer. We indicate this space in a schematic way in Figure 2.1a, where the different points in the space correspond to different answer possibilities and the starred point indicates the correct possibility. If respondents also have response options for Question (6) (e.g., 7:00–7:59 a.m., 8:00–8:59 a.m., etc.), each option will correspond to a single possibility, collapsing the earlier set of points (see Figure 2.1b). If the response options are vague (e.g., *morning, afternoon*, or *evening*), then the possibilities may share some of their propositions, as in Figure 2.1c. We discuss this last case in Section 2.4.2.

An interrogative sentence is a common way to express an uncertainty space, but it's not the only way. We can ask the same (abstract) question using an imperative sentence (*Please tell me when Calvin usually left home for work last week*) or a declarative sentence (*I'd like to know*

What time did Calvin usually leave home to go to work last week?

Uncertainty Space a:

> • Calvin leaves home at 12:00 a.m.
> • Calvin leaves home at 12:01 a.m.
>
>   .
>   .
>
> * Calvin leaves home at 9:15 a.m.
>
>   .
>   .
>
> • Calvin leaves home at 11:59 p.m.

Uncertainty Space b:

> • { Calvin leaves home at 7:00 a.m.
>   { Calvin leaves home at 7:59 a.m.
>
> • { Calvin leaves home at 8:00 a.m.
>   { Calvin leaves home at 8:59 a.m.
>
> * { Calvin leaves home at 9:00 a.m.
>   { Calvin leaves home at 9:59 a.m.

Uncertainty Space c:

> * morning   { Calvin leaves home at 5:00 a.m.
>   { Calvin leaves home at 11:30 a.m.
>
> • afternoon { Calvin leaves home at 11:00 a.m.
>   { Calvin leaves home at 5:30 p.m.
>
> • evening   { Calvin leaves home at 5:00 p.m.
>   { Calvin leaves home at 9:30 p.m.

Figure 2.1. A schematic view of the uncertainty space for the question *When did Calvin usually leave home to go work last week?* Panel a shows the uncertainty space without response options; panel b, for precise response options (6–7 a.m., 7–8 a.m., etc); panel c, for imprecise options (*morning, afternoon,* and *evening*).

when Calvin usually left home for work last week). And interrogatives do not necessarily express an uncertainty space; they can express a statement (*Did you know that Calvin usually left home for work at 9:15 last week? How could you possibly think that I wiped my feet on your mouse pad?*) or request an action (*Could you please stop wiping your feet on my mouse pad?*), as well as laying out a space of possible answers.

Finally, we can define questions not as a certain type of form or meaning, but as the activity that people perform when they ask for information. Seen this way, questions are one sort of speech act (Searle, 1969). When someone asks when Calvin usually leaves home for work, he or she is usually making a request – that the listener provide information about the time Calvin leaves home for work. If the meaning of a question is an uncertainty space, then the request to the listener is to provide information about which possibility in the space happens to be true. The standard way to make this request is to use an interrogative sentence, and when that way is used we have the typical alignment of sentence form, meaning, and use that appears in Table 2.1 (adapting the view of Higginbotham, 1996). In using the interrogative sentence (6), the questioner is expressing a space of uncertainty (that Calvin usually left home for work last week at time t for all relevant values of t) and requesting that the listener provide information as to which of these possibilities is correct. As Table 2.1 also shows, this correlation between grammatical form, meaning, and use for questions parallels a similar correlation for statements (including answers to questions).

The correlation between form, meaning, and use in Table 2.1 is easy to break because interrogative sentences do not necessarily lay out an array of possibilities, as we've already noted. Likewise, one can use interrogative sentences without requesting information. Graesser, Huber, and Person (1992) distinguish four classes of grammatical questions, only one of which corresponds to a request for information of the sort found in surveys. The others monitor common ground in conversation

TABLE 2.1 Components of Questions and Statements

	Grammatical Structure	Meaning	Use
Questions	Interrogative sentence (e.g., "When did Calivn usually leave home to go to work last week?")	Space of uncertainty (e.g., the set of propositions *that Calvin usually left home to go to work last week at time t*)	Requesting information (e.g., requesting someone to inform you when Calvin usually left home to go to work)
Answers	Declarative sentence	Proposition	Informing (in response to a request)
	(e.g., "Calvin usually leaves home for work at 9:15")	(e.g., the proposition *that Calvin usually leaves home for work at 9:15*)	(e.g., asserting that Calvin usually leaves for work at 9:15)

(*Do you follow me?*), coordinate social action (by issuing instructions or seeking permission), or control conversation and attention (as with rhetorical questions). As Bolinger (1957, pp. 2–3) put it, "No one element suffices to define a [question]. . . . For persons who demand rigorous definitions, the term *question* cannot be defined satisfactorily. . . ."

But despite this play in the connection between them, when interrogatives, uncertainty spaces, and requests for information line up, we have something like a prototypical question. Although questions can deviate from the prototype in many ways, it provides a starting point for our discussion of survey questions in the sections that follow.

2.2   Two Views of Comprehension: Immediate Understanding versus Interpretation

Before tackling other aspects of question comprehension, we need to address one other preliminary issue: What *is* comprehension? What is the product of the question-understanding process? Unfortunately, the term *comprehension* is itself ambiguous. On the one hand, the meaning that we get from a word or a sentence must be relatively stable across people; how else could we understand each other? But this stability implies that the interpretation of sentences has to be at least somewhat immune to differences in the amount of knowledge about the concepts. When a survey includes a question about commuting times, both the transportation planner who formulated the question and the commuter who answers it must share some essential set of meanings, even though the two may differ in both the depth and kind of information they bring to bear on the concept *commuting*. But, on the other hand, it seems quite reasonable to think that a transportation planner attaches a much richer and more abstract meaning to *commuting* than the typical commuter does. So how can their interpretations of a question about commuting really be the same?

This discrepancy in our intuition about the stability of meaning across listeners mirrors a similar discrepancy in our intuitions about when we have successfully understood a sentence. In the normal course of a conversation, we process sentences in a seemingly effortless way, and we feel we have interpreted each sentence adequately as soon as (or perhaps a bit before) we come to the end. Unless we are brought up short by a difficult grammatical construction (as in garden path sentences such as *The horse raced past the barn fell*) or an unfamiliar word or phrase (say, *computational lexicography*), we understand the sentence immediately and are ready to move on to the next one. But it is also clear that comprehending a sentence doesn't always end at the period, with the reader or hearer secure in the right interpretation. If someone says that *Bill gave another great sermon*, and the hearer realizes that Bill is neither a minister nor a priest, then he or she may interpret the sentence nonliterally – inferring that the speaker intends it ironically. But another hearer who doesn't know Bill might interpret the same statement literally. There is obviously plenty of room for misunderstanding and contradictory interpretations in ordinary talk.

2.2.1 Representation-of and Representation-about the Question

How can we accommodate these intuitions – that understanding is generally shared and immediate but that it can reflect idiosyncratic knowledge and change or deepen over time? We assume that the product of comprehension consists of two parts, one obligatory and the other optional. Both parts are mental representations centered on the sentence that a person has just read or heard, but they differ in their content. One representation consists of a specification of the underlying grammatical and logical structure of the sentence, together with the lexical representation of the individual words it contains. The other representation consists largely of inferences that the interpreter draws from the sentence in conjunction with other knowledge that he or she has available on that occasion. We call the first a *representation of the sentence* and the second a *representation about the sentence* (Rips, 1995). The representation *of* the sentence is more or less constant across individuals competent in the language. The representation *about* the sentence varies, however, depending on the interpreter's standpoint, knowledge of the subject matter, knowledge of the speaker or writer, knowledge of the context in which the sentence was uttered or written, and probably many other factors. The representation-about will also vary with the amount of time and effort that the individual devotes to interpreting it: The greater the amount of interpreting that goes on, the richer this representation will be.

Consider, once again, Question (6), *What time did Calvin usually leave home to go to work last week?* According to some current theories in syntax and semantics (e.g., Higginbotham, 1996; Larson & Segal, 1995), the underlying structure of this sentence (its logical form) is similar to that in (6'):

(6') [[Which(t)] [?[Last week, Calvin usually left home to go to work at t]]],

where *Which(t)* specifies the questioned element of the sentence, *?* marks the construction as a question, and *t* is a variable ranging over clock times. We discuss this type of formulation in more detail in the next section, but for now we can assume that (6') gives the skeleton of the representation-of the question, the framework that people compile as the result of hearing it. In addition, the representation-of the Calvin question must also contain some information about the meanings of the words and other lexical items in (6'). For example, the representation has to specify that *Calvin* is an expression that refers to an individual, that *work* refers to an event, *t* to a time, and so on.

2.2.2 Constructing the Representation-of a Question

If we step back from the formatting details, it is apparent that deriving the representation-of a question involves several cognitive operations:

- Representing the question in some format (like 6') that makes its logical structure clear;
- picking out the question's focus (*[Which (t)]*);
- linking the nouns and pronouns to the relevant concepts in memory (e.g., associating the terms *Calvin* and *last week* with their cognitive representations);
- assigning meanings to the predicates in the underlying representation (*usually, leave home, go to work*).

Graesser and his colleagues include essentially these same operations in their model of the question interpretation process (e.g., Graesser, Bommareddy, Swamer, & Golding, 1996; Graesser et al., 1994).

What's controversial about the representation-of is its lexical content, the concepts that represent the meanings of the noun phrases, pronouns, and predicates. This component must suffice to determine the range of potential answers – the uncertainty space of the question – but beyond that point there is disagreement. According to some theories (e.g., Fodor, 1981, 1994; see also Anderson, 1983), the mental representations of the lexical items are fairly similar to words in natural language. According to others (e.g., Jackendoff, 1991; see also Schank, 1975), the mental representations are deeper and more fine-grained, specifying both the primitive conceptual elements that underlie words and the larger conceptual structures that these elements are embedded in.

2.2.3 The Representation-about the Sentence

Respondents do not stop interpreting a question when they have finished determining its representation-of. The question about Calvin's commuting time, for example, seems to imply that Calvin has some set pattern, a regular time when he leaves for work. For this reason, a respondent might infer that if Calvin works irregular hours, then the question doesn't apply to him. If the question is accompanied by a set of response options, the respondents may use the options to refine their interpretation of the question. If the response options are 6:00–7:00 a.m., 7:00–8:00 a.m., 8:00–9:00 a.m., 9:00–10:00 a.m., and "other," then they know that the question doesn't require an answer that's precise to the minute. Likewise, they may take the response options as tacitly specifying the usual range of answers that people give to such questions – the typical times people begin work. Perhaps they even assume that the actual frequency of starting times in the population is about equal for each of the response options.

There is an endless set of possible inferences that respondents can make about the question that could be included in their representation-about it. Graesser and his colleagues distinguish 13 types of inferences that readers can make as they read a story (Graesser, Singer, & Trabasso, 1994). Only two of them (inferences that identify the referents of pronouns and noun phrases and those that assign case roles to the noun phases) are needed for the representation-of; the remainder all help elaborate the representation-about. Which inferences respondents actually make will depend on factors like the amount of time they have to think about the question, their understanding of the purpose of the survey, the amount of information they have about the topic, and so on. Although some of these inferences might be more common than others, it's unlikely that every respondent will draw exactly the same ones. Thus, the representation-about the question is likely to vary across respondents and may even vary for a single respondent across occasions.

2.2.4 Relation between the Two Representations

Although we are treating the two representations as distinct entities, we do not mean to imply that there is no interplay between them.

Certainly, people may use the representation-of the sentence as the basis of inferences that become part of the representation-about it. And it is possible that the representation-about the sentence is involved in constructing its representation-of. As a person listens to a question, he or she may form hypotheses about how it will continue, hypotheses that may guide the construction of a representation-of the question. However, these hypotheses are not themselves part of the representation-of the sentence, and the listener may need to revise or discard them later when more of the sentence comes in. Thus, we needn't assume that people first construct the representation-of and then the representation-about in strict sequence.

Both the representation-of and the representation-about the question have an impact on respondents' answers, but these effects come from different directions. Complex wording or complex logical requirements can prevent respondents from being able to compute the representation-of, and in such a case, respondents are in much the same situation they would be in if they had heard only a fragment of the item. They are missing basic information they need to determine the question's space of uncertainty and, as a result, they cannot be expected to come up with a relevant answer. Difficulties surrounding the representation-about the question, however, usually stem from too much information rather than from too little. Respondents may make unwarranted inferences about the question and use those inferences in constructing an inaccurate answer. Suppose, for example, that respondents infer that the response options provide the typical answers to the question and base their own answers on whether they believe they are above or below average. Then their answers will vary with the particular set of categories the survey designer has chosen, no matter what the correct answer happens to be (Schwarz, 1996). In general, then, respondents' problems with representations-of a question may require clarifying and supplementing the question itself. But problems with representations-about the question may require explicitly canceling inferences that the item seems to invite. In the remaining sections of this chapter, we make use of this representation-about/representation-of distinction in examining effects due to the interrogative form, meaning, and use of survey questions.

2.3   Syntactic Difficulties in Question Wording

Let's return to the interrogative form, the first component of typical questions in Table 2.1, to see what difficulties it can pose for respondents. In processing this component, the respondent's job is to get the question into its underlying propositional format (as in (6')) and to identify the question's focus. Difficulties in accomplishing these tasks partly reflect surface features of the interrogative form. In addition, they may reflect syntactic ambiguity or excessive complexity.

2.3.1   Interrogative Form

As we noted earlier, interrogatives usually involve displacement of words from the positions they occupy in the corresponding declarative sentences. In *yes/no questions* (i.e., questions calling for a yes or no answer), these changes are small, involving a switch in the position of the sentence's subject and an auxiliary verb. For example, the interrogative *Have you had a mortgage on this property since the first of June?* [CE] corresponds to the declarative *You have had a mortgage on this property . . .* , where the auxiliary *have* has changed places with the subject *you.* When the declarative has no auxiliary, a form of the word *do* appears instead at the beginning of the question. *Do you have a home equity loan?* is the interrogative form of *You have a home equity loan.*

Matters are more complicated, however, for questions that begin with *wh-words,* such as *who, where, when, why, what, which,* and *how.* Most of these wh-questions shift the position of the subject and the auxiliary, just as yes/no questions do. For example, *What would you have to spend each month in order to provide the basic necessities for your family?* flips the order of *you* and *would.* But the more dramatic difference is the position of the wh-word *what.* The corresponding declarative seems to be of the form *You would have to spend X each month . . .* ; so the wh-word has switched to the front of the sentence from the position X occupies in the declarative version. In fact, there can be many embedded clauses separating the wh-word in complex questions from its corresponding position in a declarative. According to current generative theories of grammar (see, e.g., Radford, 1997), wh-questions take shape through a process that moves the wh-word to the front of the sentence, leaving behind a silent (i.e., unpronounced) grammatical marker or *trace* in the original position. Thus, the representation of (7a) will contain a trace t^* in the position shown in (7b):

(7) a. What would you have to spend each month in order to provide the basic necessities for your family?

b. What would you have to spend t^* each month in order to provide the basic necessities for your family?

c. I would have to spend *$1,000* each month in order to provide the basic necessities for my family.

The trick in understanding wh-questions is to determine the trace position, since it is the trace position that determines the question's focus – the information that needs to be filled in to answer the question. For example, (7c) can serve as an answer to (7a), where *$1,000* occupies the position of t^* in (7b).

In (7), the trace can occupy only one position, but questions can be ambiguous in this respect. The question in (8a), for instance, has two readings, depending on whether the question is asking about the time of the telling (trace at the position shown in (8b)) or the time the telephone will be repaired (trace at the position shown in (8c)):

(8) a. When did Lydia tell Emily the telephone would be fixed?
 b. When did Lydia tell Emily t^* the telephone would be fixed?
 c. When did Lydia tell Emily the telephone would be fixed t^*?

How do people determine the position of the trace in understanding wh-questions? Research on sentence parsing in artificial intelligence (AI) suggests some approaches to this problem (see Allen, 1995, Chapter 5, for a review). The basic idea is that when people encounter the wh-word at the beginning of a question, they store in memory information predicting that they will encounter a missing part in the remainder of the sentence. Which component will be missing is partly determined by the nature of the wh-component itself. Because the trace shares the grammatical properties of the wh-phrase, the trace and the phrase will belong to related grammatical categories. In (7), for example, the missing piece will have to be a noun phrase because *what* fills the role of a noun phrase. The missing part of (8) will be a prepositional phrase, since *when* fills the role of a prepositional phrase (i.e., *at what time*)? As they process the sentence, people look for the missing component. If they run into a stretch of the sentence that is ungrammatical because it lacks the predicted part, they can plug the trace in to fill the gap. If the sentence is grammatical without the predicted part, they must nevertheless find a spot where the trace can go.

Because monitoring for the trace position requires the listener to use working memory, this process is likely to make comprehension more difficult until he or she finds the correct location. (See Just & Carpenter,

1992, for an account of the role of working memory in sentence comprehension.)[3] Psycholinguistic research suggests that people make guesses about the position of the trace in wh-argument questions as soon as they process the sentence's verb (e.g., Crain & Fodor, 1985). They may even make preliminary decisions about trace positions before they reach any potential trace sites (see Tannenhaus, Boland, Mauner, & Carlson, 1993).

Consider how this trace-location process works in comprehending (7) and (8). In the case of (7a), the wh-word *what* alerts the listener that a noun phrase will be missing later in the question. As he or she processes the rest of the sentence, the listener encounters the word *spend*, a transitive verb that is missing its object (*You spend* is not grammatical). Since the expected noun phrase can fill the role of this missing component, the trace must occur after *spend*, as in (7b). Parsing (8a), however, is a bit more difficult. One would expect a missing prepositional phrase because of *when*, but there are no clues about the location of the phrase in the rest of the question. *Lydia told Emily the telephone would be fixed* is perfectly grammatical by itself, so there is no need for the prepositional phrase to patch up the syntax. Since the phrase could attach to either verb in the sentence (*tell* or *would be fixed*), the trace could appear in either the position it occupies in (8b) or the one in (8c). To decide between these two readings, the listener must rely on plausibility, intonation, or other external factors (e.g., stressing *tell* – *When did Lydia TELL Emily the telephone would be fixed?* – favors (8b) over (8c)).

As these examples illustrate, wh-words differ in whether or not the component they represent is an obligatory or an optional part of the remaining sentence. The words *who(m)*, *which*, and *what* often begin components called *arguments* that are required by verbs or prepositions in the rest of the sentence. The words *where* (in what place?), *when* (at what time?), *why* (for what reason?), and *how* (in what manner?) often begin components called *adjuncts* that are optional parts of the question. Argument questions tend to provide more guidance than adjunct questions about where the trace should go. There is also evidence that ambiguous adjunct questions like (8a) are somewhat easier to understand when

---

[3] According to some parsing theories, grammatical rules determine the position of the trace automatically without needing a separate monitoring process. We can assume, however, that the rules that carry out this process draw on extra memory resources in handling these questions, so the effect on working memory may be the same.

people interpret the trace as occurring in the main clause (i.e., (8b)) than when they interpret it as occurring in the subordinate clause (i.e., (8c)).

In summary, questions with different surface forms impose different demands on the listener. Relative to yes-no questions, wh-questions increase the load on working memory, since they require the listener to reconstruct the position of the queried component. Among wh-questions, those that concern arguments (questions about *who, which,* or *what*) may be somewhat easier to process than those that concern adjuncts (questions about *where, when, why,* or *how*). Finally, among adjunct questions, those that focus on an uncertain aspect of the main clause are easier to understand than those that focus on an uncertain aspect of a subordinate clause.

2.3.2   Ambiguity and Complexity

The examples we have touched on so far have already indicated two further sources of difficulty that can result from the syntax of a question – ambiguity and complexity. In the framework presented here, grammatical ambiguity arises because the missing trace (the focus of the question) can be linked to more than one component of the underlying representation of the sentence. For example, in (8), the queried time may involve when Lydia told Emily about the telephone or when the telephone will be fixed. In general, ambiguities arise in complex questions with multiple embedded clauses, so rewriting the question to eliminate the embedding seems a natural strategy for clarifying the intended meaning. Closed questions can also clarify things, since the answer options will point to the focal component of the question.

Even when the complex form does not introduce syntactic ambiguities, it may overload the processing resources of the respondents. Consider this example from Fowler (1992), modeled on a question in the Health Interview Survey:

(9) During the past 12 months, since January 1, 1987, how many times have you seen or talked to a doctor or assistant about your health? Do not count any time you might have seen a doctor while you were a patient in a hospital, but count all other times you actually saw or talked to a medical doctor of any kind.

Both the syntax and semantics of the question are complicated. The question covers face-to-face and telephone consultations, with doctors "of any kind" as well as with "assistants." In addition, respondents are to exclude such consultations if they took place while the respondents were hospitalized (or if they didn't concern the respondents' health) and to restrict their responses to visits that took place during the time frame specified. Processing this question into its underlying logical form is likely to impose quite a burden on working memory, one that may exceed the capacity of the respondent.

Questions like (9) are the product of the practical constraints that questionnaire designers face. On the one hand, the questions need to specify the exact concepts the questions are trying to tap. In the case of (9), most of the question and the accompanying instructions aim to define a particular set of medical visits – outpatient medical visits that occurred during a one-year period, where *visit* is construed broadly to include telephone consultations. On the other hand, there is the need to save time. The cost of a survey is, in part, a function of the length of the questionnaire. So, rather than ask a series of simpler questions to get at the same information as (9), the survey designers compress all four of the main possibilities (face-to-face visits with a doctor, other face-to-face visits with medical personnel, telephone consultations with a doctor, telephone consultations with other medical personnel) into a single question.

In attitude surveys, there is another pressure that makes for complicated questions. Many survey researchers believe that balanced items like (10a) are better than items that state only one side of an issue (10b):

(10) a. Some people feel the federal government should take action to reduce the inflation rate even if it means that unemployment would go up a lot. Others feel the government should take action to reduce the rate of unemployment even if it means the inflation rate would go up a lot. Where would you place yourself on this [seven-point] scale?

   b. Some people feel the federal government should take action to reduce the inflation rate even if it means that unemployment would go up a lot. What do you think? Do you agree strongly, agree, . . .

Question (10a) is taken from Converse and Presser (1986, p. 38), a widely used text on questionnaire design. The respondents are to indicate their answers on a seven-point scale, whose endpoints are labeled *Reduce Inflation* and *Reduce Unemployment*. A simpler alternative would be to present items like (10b) and the parallel question on reducing unemployment; however, Converse and Presser observe that a substantial number of respondents would agree with both of these items, while (10a) encourages such respondents to take a more definite position.

Aside from the conceptual complexity of the underlying representation of the question, several other variables affect the load a question imposes on working memory (Just & Carpenter, 1992). One is the degree of embeddedness; questions along the lines of *Is that the dog that chased the cat that ate the rat that Karen saw?* impose an especially heavy burden on processing capacity. Another is syntactic ambiguity, which increases the burden on working memory by forcing listeners to entertain two interpretations; garden path sentences (which require reinterpretation at the end) are similarly burdensome. A final variable is the individual respondent's working memory capacity. According to Just and Carpenter (1992), individuals differ sharply in how much they can hold in working memory; questions that overburden one respondent may pose no particular problem for another.

There are two main consequences to overloading working memory: Items may drop out of working memory (i.e., their level of activation may get so low that the item can no longer be used in ongoing processing) or cognitive processing may slow down (Just & Carpenter, 1992). Respondents may take a long time to deal with Fowler's item on doctor visits in the past year, their representation of the question may omit some part of the question's intended meaning, or both things may happen, with respondents taking a lot of time to come up with an incomplete interpretation of the question.

2.4   Semantic Effects: Presupposition, Unfamiliarity, and Vagueness

In the framework we have adopted, a question specifies an uncertainty space – a set of possibilities that correspond to the range of legitimate answers (see Figure 2.1). The survey designer's job is to ask a question in such a way as to convey the intended space, and the respondent's job is to reconstruct the space and say where the correct answer lies within it. This perspective is a handy one because it allows us to discuss some of the common semantic problems that can derail a survey question. The question can express a space whose possibilities are not exhaustive, providing no location that the respondent can identify as a correct answer. In the extreme, when the question uses terms that are unfamiliar to the respondent, the question may not express a space of possibilities at all. The question and its response alternatives can also produce a space that is poorly specified – for example, one in which the regions in the space aren't mutually exclusive. Lack of exhaustiveness results from (faulty) presupposition; lack of exclusiveness results from vagueness.

2.4.1 Presupposition

We found that statements like (5) – *Family life often suffers because men concentrate too much on their work* – can carry not-so-innocent assumptions. The same is true of questions. Question (6) – *What time did Calvin usually leave home to go to work last week?* – presupposes that Calvin had a job and asks what time he usually left to go there. If Calvin has no job, the question is ill-posed, and no direct answer is possible. Instead, the respondent would be forced to object that the question is simply not applicable to Calvin. Presuppositions like these arise because questioners must somehow describe the event or state about which they seek information. To answer the question, the addressee must identify the relevant events (e.g., Calvin's departures for work during the last week), identify the queried property of those events (their usual time of occurrence), and search memory for information relevant to the answer. (See Graesser, Roberts, & Hackett-Renner, 1990, Graesser et al., 1994, and Singer, 1985, for theories of question-answering that run along these lines.) Descriptive information in the question allows the addressee to perform these tasks by specifying what the question is about. The presupposed information consists of things that the questioner and addressee normally assume to hold, since they are among the conditions that make the question meaningful. If the addressee does not agree with the information, however, then he or she must make some adjustment, either to accommodate or to reject it.

We can think of a question's presuppositions as limiting the uncertainty space that the question expresses. The uncertainty space that Question (6) expresses is roughly the set of propositions of the form *Calvin left home to go to work at t* for all clock times t (e.g., 8:15 a.m.), as we saw in Figure 2.1. For the question to be correctly posed, some proposition in this space must be true. If none is true (because Calvin has no job) or if more than one is true (because he has several jobs or works irregular hours), then the question has no good answer. Presuppositions restrict the range of possible propositions in the space: The more stringent the presuppositions, the narrower the range of allowable answers. *At what time of the morning does Calvin usually leave home to go to work?* adds to the presuppositions of (6) that Calvin doesn't work a late shift. The uncertainty space of the question in Figure 2.1 is correspondingly narrowed to just those times that occur during the morning.

Research by Loftus and her colleagues has documented the effects of presupposition on people's memory for events. In these experiments, *leading questions* (i.e., questions containing a false presupposition about an event) can cause addressees to misremember the event as if the presupposition were true. A question like *How fast was the car going when it went through the yield sign?* can cause subjects to report the presence of a yield sign on a follow-up memory test, even if no such sign was part of the original traffic event that the subjects witnessed (Loftus, 1979). The cognitive basis of these false-memory effects remains controversial (for a taste of the controversy, see Belli, 1989, Tversky & Tuchin, 1989, and Zaragoza & McCloskey, 1989), but it is clear that under certain circumstances presuppositions can lead respondents to make incorrect inferences about what happened.

The effect of leading questions may be due in part to a normal reaction that occurs in conversation when a question contains a presupposition about which the addressee has no prior knowledge. Presupposed information is something that the questioner assumes (and believes that the addressee also assumes). When the addressee does indeed know it, then all is well, and he or she can proceed to answer without further ado. In some cases, however, the addressee may not know the presupposed information (e.g., may not know that Calvin has a job in the case of Question (6)). The presupposition is not necessarily rejected unless the addressee believes it to be false. In fact, if the addressee thinks the questioner is in a position to know the truth of the presupposition, the addressee may find it informative and remember it as factual. Although this information is not something the addressee knew before, nevertheless the addressee can *accommodate* to the presupposition, treating it as true (see Lewis, 1979, and Stalnaker, 1974).

In the context of a survey, of course, respondents are unlikely to suppose that the interviewer knows more about their personal circumstances than they themselves do, so they would be unlikely to interpret the interviewer's presuppositions in a question like (6) as news. Some survey questions, however, depend on more specialized information, such as facts about medical procedures and conditions (*Have you or any family members ever suffered a myocardial infarction or heart attack? Do you belong to a health maintenance organization?*) or knowledge of public issues (*Do you favor or oppose the Agricultural Trade Act of 1978?*). If the interviewer is asking their opinion about the Agricultural Trade Act of 1978, then respondents may infer that this is something they could (or should) have an opinion about, rather than an issue that is deliberately obscure or even nonexistent.

How do respondents cope with questions that presuppose information respondents do not have? With opinion questions, some respondents (usually a majority) simply state that they don't know (Schuman & Presser, 1981, Chapter 5). Those respondents who do answer may look to the prior questions to support a guess about the meaning of the obscure issue (see chapter 7 for several examples of such context-based inferences with unfamiliar issues). When the item concerns a factual matter (*Do you or any members of you family have dental sealants?*), respondents seem to employ a variety of strategies (Lessler et al., 1989). They may ask for a definition of the unfamiliar term or state that they do not know. The question's apparent presupposition that the respondent ought to know the term may, however, encourage other strategies. (And, as we shall see, standard survey practice leaves interviewers little room to define unfamiliar terms.) Some respondents seem to assimilate the problematic term to a similar-sounding, more familiar one (*denture cream*). Others conclude that the answer must be no, reasoning that they would probably be more familiar with the term if it applied to them (Gentner and Collins, 1981, describe similar inferences based on lack of knowledge). Surely, we would know if we'd had a *myocardial infarction*. But each of these strategies for generating a substantive answer can lead to problems.

Presuppositions are inescapable in natural language questions because they are a necessary part of expressing the range of uncertainty that questions address. It is usually possible, however, to avoid most troublesome presuppositions through standard survey tactics. Questionnaires often include filter questions that route respondents around items that don't apply to them and issues they never heard of. Similarly, it's common to add "don't know" or "no opinion" options in attitude questions to reduce the pressure on respondents to fabricate opinions about issues they are not familiar with (Converse & Presser, 1986; Sudman & Bradburn, 1982). However, such tactics cannot eliminate all presuppositions. Even if we add a filter question that asks whether Calvin has a job, the main question about his commuting habits still presupposes that Calvin has only one job and that he leaves home for that job at a regular time. No question is presupposition-proof. The best any questionnaire can do is to avoid presuppositions likely to be false in a significant number of cases within the intended population.

2.4.2 Vagueness in Questions and in Response Alternatives

Like presupposition, vagueness is impossible to avoid in natural language. Vagueness occurs when it is unclear whether or not some descriptor applies to an object or event. In the case of Question (3), repeated as (11a) later, it is unclear whether the descriptor *children* applies to teens (or to older offspring); there is no fact of the matter that could decide this issue. We might take a step toward making (11a) precise by stipulating the age boundary, as in (11b). Although this cutoff seems somewhat arbitrary, it at least manages to eliminate borderline cases that could make (11a) problematic for some respondents. However, what about *ill effects, programmes with violence*, and *ordinary Westerns*? To deal with *ill effects*, for example, we could try listing ill effects, as in (11c), but in addition to the fact that some ill effects may themselves be vague, it would be very difficult to spell out all the ill effects that are relevant to the question. Ill effects are inherently open-ended, so making the phrase precise by fiat means missing some clearly relevant symptoms. Perhaps the best we can do is to acknowledge this with an *and-so-on* at the end of the list, as in (11c). Much the same is true of *violence* in this context. We can go some way toward clarifying the concept by giving examples, as in (11d), but this is hardly precise enough to settle all questions about whether specific incidents constitute violence.

(11) a. Do you think that children suffer any ill effects from watching programmes with violence in them, other than ordinary Westerns?

  b. Do you think that people under the age of 14 suffer any ill effects from watching programmes with violence in them, other than ordinary Westerns?

  c. Do you think that people under the age of 14 suffer any ill effects from watching programmes with violence in them, other than ordinary Westerns? By *ill effects* I mean increased aggression in school or at home, increased nightmares, inability to concentrate on routine chores, and so on.

  d. Do you think that people under the age of 14 suffer any ill effects from watching programmes with violence in them, other than ordinary Westerns? By *ill effects* I mean increased aggression in school or at home, increased nightmares, inability to concentrate on routine chores, and so on. By *violence*, I mean graphic depictions of individuals inflicting physical injuries on others or on themselves, depictions of individuals wantonly damaging property or possessions, abusive behavior and language to others, and so on.

Vague Concepts

Like the earlier example about doctor visits (9), (11d) would clearly overwhelm the working memory capacity of most respondents, raising the issue of whether the effort to achieve precision is worthwhile. The danger in vagueness is supposed to be that some respondents will choose one way to make a vague question precise, whereas others will choose a different way, leading to uninterpretable variability in the responses. In commenting on his respondents' understanding of (11a), Belson (1981, p. 182) remarks that "It is . . . well worth noting that there was a high degree of variability in the interpretation of terms like 'children', 'ill effects', 'violence' – such that respondents who offer identical choice of answer may well have been considering rather different aspects of the matter concerned." He reports, in fact, that only 8% of respondents understood the question as intended. But the danger in making efforts to clarify vague concepts is that it produces lengthy, complicated questions that are also hard to interpret.

It is certainly possible that respondents to questions like (11a) sometimes adopt interpretations that differ radically from those of others. For example, according to Belson, some respondents understood *children* as kids eight years old or younger, whereas others understood *children* as those 19–20 years old or younger. Later, we will also see evidence that people interpret vague frequency expressions (e.g., *pretty often*) in different ways. Nevertheless, some degree of vagueness seems built into the meaning of important concepts such as *children* and *violence*. If these are indeed the concepts we're interested in, then we cannot avoid imprecision entirely. In fact, as we argue in Chapter 6, part of what it means to have an attitude is to construe an attitude object in a characteristic way; part of the reason why some people favor *welfare spending* and some oppose it is that they see the issue in different terms. Such differences in how attitudinal concepts are interpreted are partly what we seek to measure by asking attitude questions.

Moreover, some of the evidence of variability in understanding may be due in part to differences in the way respondents specify meanings when they are asked to do so after the fact (e.g., in cognitive interviews or follow-up questionnaires), not to differences in their immediate comprehension. It is quite possible that in computing the representation-of the question, respondents do not make a vague expression precise but deal with the expression in its own terms. It is only when asked to explain what they understood by *violence* or *children* that respondents reach for more specific explications – part of their representation-about the question.[4] At that point, variability is unavoidable because there are many ways to draw arbitrary boundaries.

Since the early 1970s, research on categorization has stressed the gradedness of everyday categories, such as *furniture* or *flower* (e.g., Rips, Shoben, & Smith, 1973; Rosch, 1973). Subjects rate some members of these categories as being more typical than others (e.g., chairs are judged to be more typical as furniture than TV sets are), and these typicality ratings predict many other aspects of their responses to these categories. For example, people take longer to decide that atypical members belong to the category than typical members (e.g., it takes longer to judge that a TV set is furniture than that a chair is furniture), and they are more willing to generalize from typical than from atypical members.

Later research has made it clear that these typicality effects are not always due to vagueness about what counts as members of a category. A category member can be atypical without necessarily being a border-line case (Armstrong, Gleitman, & Gleitman, 1983). A dandelion may be an odd flower, for example, but it is clearly a flower nonetheless. In such cases, gradedness of typicality or exemplariness does not necessarily entail vagueness about category membership. For many categories, how-ever, gradedness in typicality and gradedness in membership go hand in hand. A patch of color intermediate between orange and red is not only an atypical red but also a borderline red. TV sets are not just atypical pieces of furniture but also borderline furniture, since there are no tech-nical facts about either furniture or TVs that would reveal their true category status (Malt & Johnson, 1992). For categories like these, at-tempts to draw the boundaries sharply may be useful for certain pur-poses, but they also falsify to some extent the nature of the categories

---

[4] The situation in interpreting vague predicates would then parallel other instances in which people must introspect about their own mental processes (Nisbett & Wilson, 1977). In asking respondents what they understood by *violence* when they first heard Question (11a), we may be asking them to try to be linguists and to analyze the meaning of the term from a theoretical perspective. Since respondents typically have no training in performing such an analysis, the results may be highly variable. This is likely to be especially true when the follow-up question occurs on the day following the interview, as it did in Belson's (1981) study (see Ericsson & Simon, 1984).

themselves. In crafting questions, we may want to distinguish categories that are inherently vague (e.g., *children, violence, ill effects*) from categories whose fuzziness is due to other factors (e.g., respondents' lack of knowledge). Explanatory comments, such as those in (11c) and (11d), may be more valuable with unfamiliar concepts than with inherently vague ones.

Vague Quantifiers

Vagueness affects nearly all facets of language in surveys – not only the content of the questions, but also the wording of the response alternatives. Bradburn and Sudman (1979, Chapter 10) called attention to the fact that surveys often give their respondents a choice among ordered natural-language categories (e.g., *never, not too often, pretty often, very often*) that may not have exact or constant numerical equivalents. Scales of this sort include adverbial quantifiers for frequency (e.g., *never, not too often*), probability expressions (e.g., *very unlikely, unlikely, likely*), and quantifiers for amounts (e.g., *none, few, some, many*). Most of the expressions on these scales correspond, at best, to a range of numerical values. But both the range and the central tendency sometimes depend on the typical frequency of the quantified event (Pepper, 1981), the other alternatives on the scale (e.g., Newstead, 1988), and group and individual differences among respondents (e.g., Budescu & Wallsten, 1985; Schaeffer, 1991). Moxey and Sanford (1993) provide a comprehensive review of such factors. To take an extreme example, the statement that earthquakes occur *very often* in California implies a very different objective frequency (perhaps once a year) from the statement that someone sneezes *very often* (perhaps once a day). Bradburn and Miles (1979) show that *very often* seems to refer to a somewhat higher frequency as applied to incidents of excitement than of boredom. Thus, it may be difficult to compare numerically a *pretty often* response to one question with the same response to a different question (or from a different respondent).

The data in Figure 2.2 (from Schaeffer, 1991a, Table 2) illustrate the difficulty with vague response categories. The results come from a survey of 1,172 respondents who were asked, "How often do you feel . . . particularly excited or interested in something? Very often, pretty often, not too often, or never?" and "How often do you feel bored?" If the respondents gave an answer other than "never," they were then asked, "About how many times a week or a month did you mean?" (Bradburn & Sudman, 1979). The figure plots the mean numerical frequency that

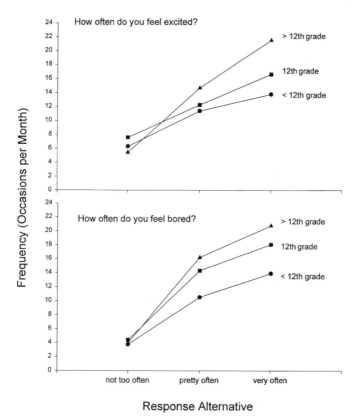

Figure 2.2. Absolute frequency of being excited (top panel) and being bored (bottom panel) for those who said they were excited (bored) "very often," "pretty often," and "not too often." The X-axis shows the highest grade in school completed by the respondents. Data from Schaeffer (1991a, Table 2). Copyright © 1991. Reprinted with permission of the University of Chicago Press.

respondents gave for each of the categorical responses *not too often, pretty often*, and *very often*. For example, the top panel shows that respondents who said that they felt excited "very often" explained that they meant about 17 times per month, those who said "pretty often" meant 13 times, and those who said "not too often" meant 6 times. What's of interest in these data, however, is that the numerical equivalent for "very often" and "pretty often" varied with the respondents' level of education: More educated respondents apparently had in mind larger values for each of these two response categories. Much the same was true for the respondents' age, with younger respondents giving larger numerical values for both "very often" and "pretty often" than did older respondents. Schaeffer (1991a) interprets these results to mean that phrases like "very often" reflect an implicit comparison to a prototypical frequency that varies by group. "Very often" means roughly "more often than typically happens to people like me."

One way to model vagueness in response alternatives is to allow the set of possibilities to overlap in the uncertainty space for the question, as we did in Figure 2.1c. For the response alternatives "never," "not too often," "pretty often," and "very often," the space consists of just four sets, each containing a range of propositions that specify the exact frequency. The set for "not too often" might contain the propositions *I feel bored 1 time a month, . . . , I feel bored 20 times a month*; the set for "pretty often" might contain *I feel bored 5 times a month, . . . , I feel bored 50 times a month*; and so on. Overlap among the sets indicates the fuzziness of the response categories. In line with this model are empirical attempts to map quantifiers like these to regions of a numerical scale by asking subjects whether (or to what degree) *not too often* applies to something that occurs *n* times a week. Results of these studies display extensive overlap between adjacent categories (Moxey & Sanford, 1993). Individual differences or differences due to the content of the question could be handled by reassigning the propositions to the available categories.

Although this uncertainty-space model seems natural, we need to be wary of the idea that the meaning of a quantifier like *pretty often* is equivalent to a distribution of numerical values. In the first place, as Moxey and Sanford (1993) note, the overlap in scale values for even six or seven of these quantifiers is usually so large that they could hardly serve any useful communicative purpose if this were their sole meaning. In the second place, as we discuss in Chapter 5, phrases like *pretty often* are often used to convey the fact that the respondents have only a vague sense of the relevant quantity; it is not as if Bradburn and Miles's respondents knew exactly how often they were bored each month and decided that that exact frequency fell into the range covered by *pretty often*.

It might be more reasonable to think of these quantifiers in their own terms as specifying a relative position within an ordinal series given by the complete set of response options. In part, the meaning of each of these terms reflects the contrast set defined by the alternatives (Fillmore, 1999). Thus, what *pretty often* means in the context of the data of Figure 2.2 is just: more often than *not too often* and less often than *very often*. A respondent's representation-of the alternatives may amount to no more than this, as we suggested in the case of other vague terms. Still, we need a way to capture the plight of the respondent who does recall a specific number of incidents and is then faced with the task of deciding whether this number is *pretty often* or *very often* for the purpose of answering the question. In these terms, overlap among the possibilities in the uncertainty space provides a clear picture of the respondent's dilemma. Perhaps the most important issue, however, from the vantage point of survey designers is that the content of these possibilities changes with question content and with respondent characteristics, as we've noted. This means that translation of the response options back to numerical values is a complex undertaking. If designers want numerical information about frequencies or amounts, then it may be best for them to ask for it directly.

2.5   Survey Pragmatics and Its Effects on Comprehension

The purpose of a question in a survey is to make a request: to get the respondent to provide information as specified by the question's meaning. What the question conveys, however, often goes beyond what it literally says. Respondents can take the question as a starting point for a complicated set of inferences that then influence the answers they produce. Two kinds of factors trigger these inferences, both based on failures of respondents' expectations. The first concerns a question's apparent failure to meet standards of conversational informativeness; the second concerns failure of the interaction between the interviewer and respondent to conform to normal social patterns. We consider these two sources of inferences in turn.

2.5.1   Pragmatic Theory

In a series of lectures entitled "Logic and Conversation," the philosopher Paul Grice (1989) outlined a way to reconcile the strict meaning of sentences (what we have called the representation-of the sentence) with the somewhat different meaning that they sometimes convey (the representation-about the sentence). Grice's main purpose was to square the interpretation that logical words like *or*, *if*, and *some* have in formal logic and the rather different meanings they assume in everyday speech, but his analysis carries over to other differences between what sentences mean and what they convey in conversational settings.

Grice's Conversational Maxims

Grice believed that conversations are governed by what he called a *cooperative principle* – a kind of implicit agreement between participants to make their contributions support the conversation's purpose. Since we often have conversations to accomplish useful things, it's in everyone's interest to make them work smoothly. To flesh out this cooperative principle, Grice divided it into several subprinciples or *maxims* that control the course of conversation. These are supposed to be general rules of reasonable behavior in conversations – a conversational etiquette. For example, Grice discussed a maxim of *Quantity* that asserts that you should (a) make your contribution as informative as is required (for the current purposes of the exchange) and (b) do not make your contribution more informative than is required. This maxim guards against someone's misleading his or her conversational partner by saying too little or derailing the conversation by saying too much. Grice also mentioned a maxim of *Quality* that enjoins: (a) Do not say what you believe to be false and (b) Do not say that for which you lack adequate evidence. There is also a maxim of *Relation* that says to be relevant and a maxim of *Manner* that says to be clear.

Grice's reason for spelling out these maxims was to show that people can convey information indirectly by saying things and expecting the listener to interpret them as cooperative. Suppose you're having a conversation with someone, and he or she utters sentence S. Let's suppose that you have no reason to think that your conversational partner is deliberately being uncooperative. So you should interpret S in a way that makes it seem cooperative and nonmisleading. This sometimes entails adding to what your partner said some additional information I that the partner must believe in order for the sentence to be truly cooperative. Grice calls this extra information a *conversational implicature* of the original utterance. It is an *inference* drawn from the original sentence that preserves its cooperativeness.

Grice gives a number of examples of how this process works. In one of them, the speaker tells Fred that he is out of gas, and Fred says, "There's a gas station around the corner." For Fred to be cooperative in this situation, he must believe that the gas station is not closed, and the inference that Fred believes this is a conversational implicature. More interesting examples are cases in which a speaker deliberately violates (or flouts) one of the maxims. One example is that of a teacher writing a letter of recommendation for a job candidate. If the letter says merely, "Dear Sir, Mr. X's command of English is excellent, and his attendance in class has been regular. Sincerely yours, etc." then the teacher has deliberately violated the first maxim of quantity – make a contribution as informative as is required. Assuming that the teacher is being cooperative (otherwise, why would he write at all?), he probably believes that Mr. X is not a good job prospect because that belief would explain why he is flouting the maxim.

Grice's examples follow the pattern shown in Figure 2.3. If there is

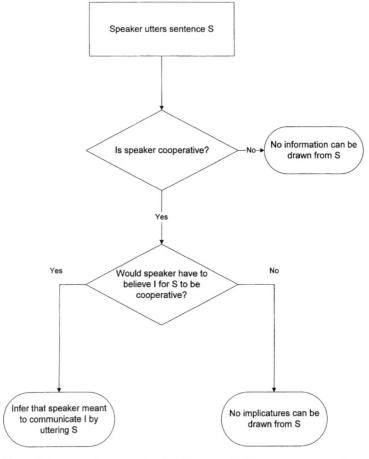

Figure 2.3. Steps in extracting implicatures (I) from a statement (S), according to Grice's cooperative principle.

evidence that a speaker is being uncooperative, then there may be no reason to take what the speaker said seriously. If the speaker *is* being cooperative, however, we can sometimes guess some belief *I* that the speaker must have (or some belief that the speaker must not have) in order for the assumption of cooperativeness to hold. That information is the conversational implicature. If the speaker violates a maxim for some reason (while still remaining cooperative), that often gives us a clue to what the belief might be. The belief that we attribute to the speaker is one that would best explain why he or she violated the maxim. It's not necessary that the speaker violate a maxim, however, to get an implicature across. In the gas station example, no maxim was violated. Still, flouting a maxim can provide clues to what the speaker intended to convey.

Implicatures in Surveys

In the context of surveys, implicatures often arise because the respondents assume (correctly or incorrectly) that the survey designer intends a certain feature of the question to be relevant to their response. That is, respondents assume that the question obeys the maxim of relation (Be relevant!) and thus conveys information *I* that they should take into account in determining their answer. Respondents may even lean on this assumption more heavily in survey interviews than in other forms of discourse; "after all, [the survey designer] prepared and edited the question carefully, and since he knows [respondents] have no way of getting clarification, he must think a question won't need clarification" (Clark & Schober, 1992, p. 27).

For example, respondents may assume that two very similar items convey different questions when they appear in the same part of the questionnaire. The similar items would otherwise be redundant, violating the maxim of relation and the cooperative principle as a whole. To demonstrate this point, Strack, Schwarz, and Wänke (1991) asked respondents to rate both their happiness and their satisfaction with their lives. In one condition, the questions – *How happy are you . . . ?* and *How satisfied are you . . . ?* – appeared next to each other in the same questionnaire. In a second condition, one of these questions appeared as the last item on an initial questionnaire, the second as the first item on a second questionnaire. In line with the prediction, ratings for the questions tended to be more similar when they appeared in *different* questionnaires than in the same one. According to Strack and his colleagues, respondents exaggerate small differences in meaning between happiness and satisfaction when these questions appear in the same questionnaire so that the questions don't fail the cooperative principle. Chapter 7 on context effects in attitude surveys reviews other examples in which the order or grouping of surveys items produces unintended Gricean implicatures.

Clark and Schober (1992) and Schwarz (1996) review findings that suggest that many incidental features of survey questions can produce similar implicatures and so affect responses. The overlap in meaning between survey items, the items' sequencing, the numerical range of the response alternatives, and the range and labeling of ratings scales can all produce implicatures about the survey designer's intent in asking the question, and these in turn shape the way respondents think about the questions. There are, however, many properties associated with each survey item; it is unlikely that respondents attend to all of them. Although some incidental aspects of a question (e.g., the range of numerical values on a rating scale) produce implicatures, respondents must ignore many properties, given normal limits to their ability to process information. They can't overinterpret *everything*. It seems reasonable to suppose that respondents have expectations about the amount of information they can extract from an item in a survey context. They may therefore continue processing the question until this expectation has been achieved or until further effort appears futile (see Sperber & Wilson, 1986). But apart from such general notions based on the respondents' limited capacity and interest, we currently have no method for predicting which elements of a question will produce a pragmatic effect. And without predictability, it is a little too easy to assign survey errors to pragmatic factors. Nearly any effect of wording can appear to be an implicature after the fact. As we'll see, a similar difficulty arises in extending pragmatics beyond implicatures to other aspects of the survey interview.

2.5.2 Pragmatics of Interviews

Grice's theory necessarily views comprehension as a process that's more complicated than passively decoding language: It includes a reasoning component through which listeners and readers infer the ideas behind the sentences. It is possible to go even further, however, and to describe comprehension as an active social endeavor.

Ongoing conversation is a dynamic process in which speakers and listeners collaborate to make sure they understand what's been said, at least well enough for the purposes at hand. Speakers pause to ensure that their listener is still tracking, and listeners provide feedback to the speaker using backchannel phrases like *uh-huh, yeah,* or *okay* to signal that they're following. As Graesser and his colleagues (1992) note, a major use of questions in conversations is to elicit just such feedback. If the listeners have difficulty understanding what's been said, they can ask the speaker to clear up the problem before going on. Clark and Schaefer (1989) call this mutual checking process *grounding* and have shown that it is a feature of casual, spontaneous conversation. The opportunity to do this sort of checking is a benefit that conversation has over the more formalized comprehension that occurs in listening to a lecture or to TV. It also provides an advantage to conversational participants relative to passive overhearers of the same dialogs (Schober & Clark, 1989).

Compared to normal conversations, the survey interview is likely to seem stilted, resembling ordinary conversation in its one-on-one format but, at the same time, limiting drastically the conversational moves participants can make. Suchman and Jordan (1992) argue that these deviations have detrimental effects on survey quality. They argue that the regulations surrounding surveys straitjacket interviewers, keeping them from interpreting answers flexibly and from adapting questions to the respondents' needs.

The standard texts on survey interviewing caution against giving interviewers too much discretion (see, e.g., Fowler & Mangione, 1990). In many surveys, interviewers are not supposed to offer clarifications on their own initiative or to give much help to respondents who ask for aid in interpreting a question. In the interest of standardization, interviewers are often trained to repeat the survey item verbatim when the respondent asks for clarification and to deflect any further queries that respondents make.[5] According to Suchman and Jordan (1992), this lack of responsiveness threatens the validity of survey questions by masking differences

---

[5] At least officially. Some interviewers may simply ignore these restrictions. Others may find their way around them through paralinguistic cues, such as intonation and gestures, or by repeating a question if the respondent gets it wrong. Schober and Conrad (1997) offer the following example of a trained interviewer clarifying the respondent's uncertainty about the meaning of *bedroom* (words in all caps are emphasized):

Interviewer: How many bedrooms are there in THIS house?
Respondent: Uh, there are two bedrooms. And one den is being used as a bedroom.
Interviewer: How many BEDROOMS are there in this house?
Respondent: Two.
Interviewer: (continues)

between the meaning that the survey designer intended and the meaning the respondent extracts. Clark and Schober (1992) similarly contend that when survey interviews suspend normal processes of grounding, they force respondents to make arbitrary, possibly idiosyncratic, assumptions about the questions' meaning.

The Impact of Standardization on Comprehension

Some evidence for this point of view comes from a recent experiment by Schober and Conrad (1997) that deliberately varied interviewers' freedom to interact with the respondents. Experienced interviewers asked respondents 12 questions drawn from national surveys, such as *Has [name] purchased or had expenses for meats and poultry?* Each question included key concepts (e.g., *meat* and *poultry*) with official definitions that the interviewers knew but that were not included in the question itself. (In case you're wondering, *meats* and *poultry* include "beef, lamb, pork, game; organ meats, such as kidney, sweetbreads, chitterlings, heart, tongue; sausages and luncheon meats; poultry, such as chicken, turkey, pheasant, goose, duck. Include canned ham. Do not include other canned meats and canned poultry, or any prepared meats and poultry.")

Half of the interviewers in the experiment used the techniques prescribed by the Department of Commerce's *CPS Interviewing Manual*, asking questions verbatim, rereading questions if necessary, but not providing the definitions. The remaining interviewers also had to read the questions verbatim, but they were free to say anything that could help the respondent understand the question according to the survey designer's intent. The "respondents" in the experiment had been instructed to base their answers on fictitious information that the experimenters had given to them prior to the interview. Half of the time, this information allowed the respondents to answer the question on the basis of typical instances of the key concepts. For example, they answered the question about meat and poultry on the basis of their purchase of beef. The rest of the time, the information was atypical of the key concepts but clearly fell under the official definition or outside the official definition. On such a trial, for example, the respondents might have had to answer the meat-and-poultry question on the basis of their purchase of canned chicken. The experimenters measured the amount of time it took subjects to answer the question and measured their accuracy, as judged by the official definitions. When the stimulus information was typical (e.g., hamburger), both flexible and standardized interviewing yielded highly accurate responses (98% and 97% correct, respectively). When the information was atypical, however, flexible interviewing led to many more accurate responses (87%) than did standard interviewing (28%). There was a drawback to flexibility, though; flexible interviews were more than three times longer than standardized ones.

Limitations on Flexible Interviewing

These results demonstrate that accuracy improves when interviewers know the official definitions of the key terms and can inform the respondents about them. They leave open the question of whether flexible interviewing is also helpful when interviewers are themselves uncertain about the questions' thrust. This latter situation must arise fairly often in interviews, since many words in natural language are inherently vague, as we noted earlier. Not all the key terms in a question will have definitions to make them precise. (We now know the official meanings of *meat* and *poultry*, but what about *had expenses* in the sample question, *Has [name] purchased or had expenses for meat and poultry?*) Even when definitions are available, they probably do not cover all situations that arise, since the categories mentioned in the definition are themselves open-ended. What, for example, are the boundary conditions for *prepared meats or poultry*? It is unclear whether flexible interviewing will produce greater stability or greater variability when both respondent and interviewer are uncertain about the fit between the question and the respondent's situation. Variations across interviewers can be a very large source of error in survey estimates; that's why survey researchers attempted to standardize interviews in the first place (see Tourangeau, 1990).

Moreover, some of the arguments for flexible interviewing depend on some controversial premises. Critics of the standard survey interview (Clark & Schober, 1992; Suchman & Jordan, 1992) assume that words and phrases in questions have no inherent meaning (or that if such inherent meaning exists, it is irrelevant in understanding survey outcomes). They argue that the meaning respondents extract is always a product of the survey situation in which they find themselves. According to Clark and Schober (1992), effects of question wording seem mysterious because of "the common misconception that language use has primarily to do with words and what they mean. It doesn't. It has primarily to do with people and what *they* mean. It is essentially about speakers' intentions. . . ." (p. 15). Similarly, Suchman and Jordan (1992) assert that "the meaning of an utterance does not inhere in the language, but is a product of interaction between speakers and hearers" (p. 256). If the meaning of a survey question must be constructed on the fly through negotiation between the interviewer and the respondent, then standardized interviewing, which deliberately hamstrings this negotiation process, leaves the meaning of the question indeterminate.

No doubt, respondents draw inferences about the intended meaning of the question, but does this imply that meanings are underdetermined in settings where grounding is restricted or impossible? If meanings have to be continually renegotiated by participants, then it would be impossible for us to understand lectures, speeches, TV shows, movies, plays, and other forms of noninteractive speech. We couldn't read a book or understand a newspaper or magazine, since we cannot negotiate meanings with the writers in any significant way. We seem forced to conclude that if comprehension of questions and statements includes what goes on when we listen to speeches and read books, then some large portion of comprehension must be independent of ongoing collaboration. It is possible to maintain that word and sentence meanings depend on cultural processes and facts about language use, but these processes and facts must nevertheless be stable enough to support interpretation in noncollaborative settings.

A related issue for these interaction views is that there are clear limits on the negotiability of the meaning of questions. The collaboration between the interviewer and the respondent might converge on some novel interpretation of a word or phrase during the question-answering process, but not everything goes. Sometimes these ad hoc meanings will be incorrect. Consider a hypothetical survey interview that proceeds along these lines:

Interviewer: Has Martha purchased or had expenses for meats and poultry?
Respondent: What exactly do you mean by *meat*?
Interviewer: Okay, meat and poultry include beef, lamb, pork, game; organ meats, such as kidney, sweetbreads, chitterlings, heart, tongue; sausages and luncheon meats . . . (reads rest of definition)
Respondent: How interesting. So chitterlings are organ meats. I never would have guessed. But what about peanut butter?
Interviewer: Peanut butter? You think peanut butter is an organ meat?
Respondent: No, not an organ meat. But it is the protein equivalent of beef and pork, so it seems fairly similar to the items on your list.
Interviewer: I suppose that's true. Let's see, it doesn't mention peanut butter here. I'm not sure, um, . . .

Respondent: I know that Martha bought a jar of peanut butter a couple of days ago, so I guess she did have expenses for meat and poultry.
Interviewer: Well, allrighty then. (continues with the next question)

Surely this type of agreement is possible, and we could say that for this pair of people meat and poultry includes peanut butter (in the context of this exchange). But most of us have the strong intuition that it's simply mistaken to think that the meaning of meat and poultry extends to peanut butter, no matter what these participants decide (and no matter what's in the official definition or what the question designer intended). This intuition, along with the possibility of noninteractive uses of language, should make us cautious about the idea that what really matters in the survey context is what the participants intend or mutually decide to believe. Pragmatic inferences about questions are still inferences (part of the respondents' representation about the question), and they can be incorrect in the same way as other nondeductive conclusions. It might be best to view these conclusions not as constituting the question's meaning, but as supplementing a more stable framework of meaning that is nonnegotiable.

These considerations do not mean that flexible interviewing is not an improvement over current survey practice, and we certainly do not mean to discourage researchers from studying the pragmatics of survey interviews. We do think, however, that the costs and benefits of flexible interviewing will have to be determined by empirical research; they are not an inevitable outgrowth of the nature of language use. And, as with most attempts to improve survey practice, flexible interviewing is likely to involve trade-offs. In this case, improved comprehension is likely to come at the price of longer interviews with better-trained interviewers who will now need to learn the official definitions for all the key terms.

2.6   Summary

Questions are complex linguistic constructions, and understanding them requires nearly all of our language skills. At the level of English grammar, questions pose special difficulties. Depending on their form, they may require burdensome processing to determine the focus of the question. Attempts to clarify key concepts or to achieve balance in attitude questions can lead to complicated questions that overload the working memory capacity of some of the respondents. At the level of meaning, questions can be too restrictive, carrying presuppositions that may be inappropriate for some listeners. They can also be too unconstrained, including imprecise words and phrases that make a relevant answer difficult. At the level of language use, questions can present incidental features that listeners overinterpret, especially in the context of survey interviews, where respondents receive little guidance from the interviewer.

These difficulties fall into two functional groups that require different remedies. Some difficulties of grammar and meaning make it hard for respondents to build a basic representation of the question. If respondents can't figure out which part of the sentence is being queried (as in ambiguous examples such as (8a)), then they will be unable even to begin answering the question. This sort of problem requires careful pretesting, perhaps using online techniques to discover exactly where in the sentence respondents begin to go astray.

The other sort of difficulty arises from respondents' tendency to use inference to supplement a question. These inferences can occur at all levels of question interpretation, from hypotheses about grammar to hypotheses about the questioner's intentions. In some cases, these inferences may do no harm, even when they are incorrect. For example, it's at least possible that the different interpretations respondents give for complex words like *violence* or *ill effects* in Question (3) may be no worse than the usual problems we all have in defining terms that have no exact synonyms. Such problems do not necessarily mean that we have not grasped the concepts correctly. Nevertheless, there is plenty of evidence to suggest that inferences do sometimes lead respondents to misinterpret questions and to produce discrepant answers. Although we can sometimes use general pragmatic principles to describe after the fact how these inferences arose, we don't currently have an adequate way to predict them. Detecting the inferences may require educating interviewers to detect and cancel the inferences when they arise, but we need to beware of the possibilities of folies à deux. Perhaps the right approach is pretesting with a sample of respondents about whom the relevant background information is independently known, since we then have a direct comparison between the answer to the question we intended to ask and the answer to the question the respondent understood.

Survey texts sometimes offer specific pointers for writing survey questions that avoid the problems discussed here. The guidelines they offer are generally consistent with the evidence and theoretical analyses presented in this chapter (see Bradburn & Sudman, 1979, and Converse &

Presser, 1986, for two particularly good examples). Here's our own attempt to distill the implications of our discussion of the comprehension of survey questions into practical advice for questionnaire designers:

- Keep questions simple;
- Avoid complicated syntax, including adjunct wh-questions and constructions with embedded clauses;
- Decompose questions that cover multiple possibilities into simpler questions that cover a single possibility apiece;
- Define ambiguous or unfamiliar terms;
- Avoid vague concepts, and provide examples when such concepts must be mentioned;
- Replace vague quantifiers with ranges that specify exact probabilities, frequencies, and so on;
- Train interviewers to recognize and repair misunderstandings.

As this chapter has already made clear, there will be exceptions to each of these rules, potential conflicts among them, and trade-offs involved in implementing them. As a result, crafting good survey questions is likely to remain an empirical enterprise, one that requires the testing of draft questions against the data from pretests.

CHAPTER THREE

The Role of Memory in Survey Responding

Surveys aim to discover facts about the respondents – often biographical facts about them. Respondents can sometimes answer factual questions on the basis of external records or documents, such as sales receipts, deposit slips, birth certificates, and the like, but more often they have to rely on memory for the information. Even easy questions like "What is your name?" or "Where do you live?" require respondents to consult their memory. Some survey questions, such as (1), from the 1988 National Health Interview Survey, may require memory feats of considerable difficulty:

(1) In what year did you first have an episode of back pain lasting a week or more? [HIS]

The greater the demands a question places on memory, the less accurate the respondents' answers and, all else being equal, the less accurate the survey estimates derived from them.

Attitude questions, like factual questions, require the respondents to search their memory. When the General Social Survey asks whether "you would approve of an adult male punching a stranger if the stranger was beating up a woman and the man saw it," the respondent must search his or her memory for relevant information before making a response. But attitude questions pose special problems because the respondent may never have considered the issue prior to the survey. For this reason, we postpone considering attitude questions until Chapter 6, and we concentrate here on memory for biographical facts about the respondents. These biographical facts include static information, such as the respondents' name or birthplace, but most of the crucial questions on surveys concern events in which the respondent has participated – episodes of back pain, for example. In Section 3.1, we look more closely at the kinds of information survey questions ask for. Section 3.2 explores theories from cognitive science about the memory structure of autobiographical events, and Section 3.3 examines the implications of these theories for retrieving information to answer questions like (1).

3.1 Survey Questions and Memory for Events

Let's start by considering the kinds of personal facts that surveys try to find out. One way to distinguish among questions seeking such facts involves the temporal restrictions they impose on the answers.

3.1.1 The Time Frame of the Question

Some survey questions ask about enduring properties of the respondent, such as the respondent's race, native language, or Social Security number. These questions are, in effect, timeless, since the answers remain the same regardless of when the question is asked. But most factual questions in surveys are after information that is time bound, and as a result, the questions contain implicit or explicit references to specific time points or time intervals.

Interview Time and Event Time

Some survey questions refer to the time at which the question itself is being posed, which we will call the question's *interview time*. For example, the question "Where do you live?" means "Where do you live now?", not "Where did you live at some time or other?". Similarly, "What is your age?" means "What is your present age?", not "What was your age at some point?". Questions about changing properties, like age or current address, raise issues of how people update their memory (Bjork & Landauer, 1978). These questions demand that respondents determine the current value of some parameter that changes over time.

Survey questions often contain references to times other than that of the interview, and this chapter will mainly be concerned with this kind of question. Such questions generally ask about a class of events or episodes that the respondent is expected to know, either firsthand or through others, as the examples from the HIS in (2) illustrate.

(2) a. Has anyone in the family EVER had a myocardial infarction?
    b. Do you sometimes drink more than you think you should?
    c. When was this structure originally built?

The first two of the questions in (2) refer to some nonspecific time in the past; question (2c) asks more directly for the time – the *event time* – when the event mentioned (the building of the structure) took place.[1] Question (1) about when the respondent first experienced back pain lasting a week or more is also an example of this type. The answers to such questions are largely independent of the interview time (so long as the target event preceded the interview). They require respondents to search their memory for information about individual events of the specified type and to compose their answers on the basis of this information.

Reference Periods

Many survey items, however, depend on both the interview time and the event time. These items include the ubiquitous questions about whether an event happened in the last few weeks, months, or some other time interval, as in (3).

(3) a. During the past 12 months, that is, {since [12-month date] a year ago} ABOUT how many days did illness or injury keep [family member] in bed more than half the day? [HIS]
   b. Have you worked at a job or business at any time during the past 12 months? [CPS]
   c. When was the month and year that you last worked? [CPS]
   d. As of the end of LAST WEEK, how long had you been looking for work? [CPS]

The questions posit a reference period (or a reference date) situated with respect to the time of the interview and ask about events that occurred during that period (or before or after that date). Question (3a), for example, sets up a 12-month reference period ending at the interview time and asks on how many days events of a certain kind (staying in bed more than half the day because of illness or injury) occurred during that period. The answers to these questions will obviously change as a function of both the interview time and the time of the event(s). Figure 3.1

---

[1] Our use of *interview time* and *event time* derives from Reichenbach's (1947) distinction between *point of speech* and *point of the event* in his analysis of verb tenses. We note that survey items typically refer to past event times but not always; for example, the Current Population Survey asks "Does your disability prevent you from accepting any kind of work during the next six months?"

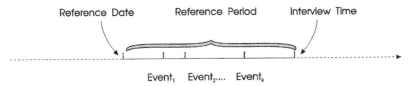

Figure 3.1. The relationship between event time, interview time, and reference period. Events 1 through k fall within the reference period for the question.

depicts the situation schematically. Items like those in (3) implicitly require respondents to search their memory for event information and to locate this information with respect to the bounds of the reference period. In this chapter, we examine the issues involved in memory search; in the next, we consider the problems involved in locating events in time.

3.1.2   First- and Secondhand Events

Another distinction among factual survey items involves *who* the question concerns. The events sought are usually ones in which the respondents themselves took part – for example, episodes in which the respondent was ill, fell victim to a crime, or bought something. Exceptions to this generalization include attitude questions about public events (e.g., "Do you support the bombing of Iraq?") and questions that ask the respondent to report about someone else (i.e., questions in which he or she serves as a *proxy* respondent for another person). Survey designers assume that respondents will be more accurate in reporting incidents they know firsthand than incidents they merely heard about from others. Exceptions are sometimes made in surveys for sample persons thought to be incapable of reporting for themselves (such as the very young or the very old). In addition, some surveys – such as the Current Population Survey – use a single adult to report for everyone in the household; this use of proxies is intended to reduce the number of follow-up visits needed to collect the data.

The idea that people remember firsthand information more accurately than secondhand information is based on the intuition that people store events they experience personally in a more vivid and detailed form than events they merely hear or read about (Larsen, 1988; Sudman, Bickart, Blair, & Menon, 1994). Events we experience firsthand are part of our ongoing autobiographical narrative; memory for such events is aided by the presence of sensory detail and by our knowledge of their antecedents and consequents. Secondhand events often appear to be less integrated into a causal sequence, since our knowledge of their context may be limited.

The comparison of first- and secondhand information is complicated, however, because secondhand facts always reveal themselves in a firsthand context. You learn about your neighbor's recent divorce at a particular time and place – while chatting with a mutual friend, say. Still, the hypothesis that we remember firsthand information better than secondhand information receives support from three types of evidence. First, laboratory studies of memory show that people recognize judgments they made about themselves better than ones they made about others (Keenan & Baillet, 1980). Second, research on strategies used to answer survey questions confirms that proxy reports are more often the result of "wild" or "educated" guesses (Beatty, Herrmann, Puskar, & Kerwin, 1998) or of estimates (Blair et al., 1991) than are self-reports. In some cases, the proxies may simply be unaware of the relevant events that happened to the person they're reporting about (e.g., Brittingham, Tourangeau, & Kay, 1998); in others, they may have trouble recollecting the events. Either way, proxy reporters may be forced to rely on response strategies that do not involve recalling the events in question.

The final line of evidence on the relative accuracy of self- and proxy reports comes from experiments comparing the recall performance of subjects who keep a diary of their activities to the performance of close associates, such as roommates or spouses, who do not keep a diary. In these studies, the diary keepers log events that happen to themselves and sometimes to their partners as well. Then, after completion of the diaries, the diary keepers and the partners are tested on the same events. Table 3.1 shows that this procedure can generate two types of proxy reports: Diary keepers can be tested on events their partner experienced, and partners can be tested on events the diary keeper experienced. It also generates two types of self-reports – diary keepers' reports about their experiences and partners' reports about their own experiences. Although no single study has looked at all four of the possible cells, individual studies have made some of the key comparisons. For example, diary keepers' self-reports about event frequencies are much more accurate than their partners' proxy reports about the same events (cells A and B in Table 3.1; Mingay, Shevell, Bradburn, & Ramirez, 1994). Similarly, the diary keepers' reports about their own experiences are more accurate

TABLE 3.1 Design of Diary Experiments on
Self-versus Proxy Reporting

Individual Being Reported On	Individual Making the Report at Test	
	Dairy Keeper	Partner
Diary keeper	A (self-report)	B (proxy report)
Partner	C (proxy report)	D (self-report)

than their reports about their partners' experiences (cells A and C; Skowronski, Betz, Thompson, & Shannon, 1991). There doesn't seem to be
much difference in the accuracy of self-reports about dates whether they
come from the diary keeper or the partner (cells A and D; Thompson,
1982). Because of the differences among these studies, some caution is
required in interpreting the results. Generalizing from these experiments
to surveys is also tricky, especially since prior survey research on proxy
responding has often turned up inconsistent findings (see Moore, 1988,
for a review). Still, the diary studies hint at an advantage for self-reports
about naturally occurring episodes.

3.2 Organization of Autobiographical Memory

An autobiographical question, such as "Have you ever had a heart
attack?", presupposes that the respondent would have maintained a
direct memory of such an event if it had occurred or would have at least
maintained memories of related circumstances (a hospital stay, perhaps).
In the best case, the respondent can gain access to a mental record of the
event and read from the record some of the event's properties. As we
will see later, there are probably many questions for which a respondent
has to rely on circumstantial evidence rather than memory for the target
event, but there is little doubt that people can remember *some* autobiographical events. Questions about landmark events, such as your first
day at college (Pillemer, Goldsmith, Panter, & White, 1988; Pillemer,
Rhinehart, & White, 1986) or the births of younger siblings (Sheingold
& Tenney, 1982; Usher & Neisser, 1993), are cases in point. It's worthwhile to consider the content and structure of autobiographical memory
in detail, since these may provide clues to methods that can be used to
obtain more accurate answers in surveys.

3.2.1   The Contents of Autobiographical Memory

Knowledge about Events

Most memory researchers appear to agree that what is stored in autobiographical memory is information about events. The notion of an event seems to be a conceptual primitive; attempts to define an event quickly fall prey to circularity. An event might be defined as a change of state, for instance, but we don't seem to have an independent grasp of change apart from that of event.

Psychologists who study event perception usually sidestep this definitional problem, leaving their subjects to decide when an event happens and inferring from the subjects' responses how *they* identify events. In studying the perception of human action, investigators have videotaped actors engaging in common activities and have then asked subjects to indicate places on the tape where the events began and ended (Hanson & Hirst, 1989; Newtson, 1973). These experiments have found statistically significant, but limited, agreement among subjects about event boundaries. Subjects can also vary the size of the event units they select, from coarse activities (e.g., a man sets up a game) to fine ones (a man opens a game box, takes out some dice, etc.). The studies just cited suggest that subjects perceive the fine-grained events as fitting into the coarse-grained ones as parts into a whole, but the evidence for this nesting is fairly weak. One event can be part of another, but events can also clearly overlap.

Although events vary in their extent or granularity, there is some evidence that there is one grain size people prefer for describing events. In an informal study, Rosch (1978) asked students to list events that happened to them that day and on several preceding days. She reported that the students tended to agree in giving approximately the same midlevel descriptions for their daily activities. They mentioned items such as eating breakfast, for example, but not more specific events such as eating a continental breakfast or more abstract ones such as eating a meal (see also Brewer, 1988). Rosch takes these results as evidence for a basic level of events – a normal level of abstractness at which people represent these activities. A basic level for events would parallel earlier findings by Rosch and others for basic object categories: People tend to describe individual objects at an intermediate level of abstractness, labeling a picture of an individual Eames chair as *a chair* in preference to *an Eames chair* or *furniture*. Rosch (1978) believes, in fact, that basic-level events determine the basic level of objects, with basic-level objects being those that serve as props in basic-level events. Later studies appear to confirm the hypothesis of a privileged level of event descriptions (Morris & Murphy, 1990; Rifkin, 1985), although not always the detailed parallels between object and event taxonomies.

Generic Knowledge

Rosch's findings suggest that individual events are grouped into categories that are linked by subordinate–superordinate relations. It's also clear that events can be related by part–whole relations. A continental breakfast, is a kind of breakfast but eating an egg might be part of a particular breakfast. The results on basic-level events concern the kind-of (subordinate–superordinate) relation, but cognitive scientists have also investigated event parts, usually in the context of Schank and Abelson's (1977) theory of *scripts*.

Scripts are mental representations of commonplace action sequences, such as shopping for groceries, visiting a doctor, or going to a movie. The representations consist of a causal sequence of acts – for example, entering the grocery store, finding a cart, finding grocery items, standing in the checkout line, paying, and leaving, in the case of the grocery script – where each act in the sequence is a part of the whole event. Experimental results accord with the notion that people use such script information in understanding and remembering stories about specific events (e.g., a story about Fred's trip to buy soy sauce at the grocery store). The evidence is less compelling, however, for the idea that people store facts about scripts as independent memory units (with one unit for grocery shopping, another for clothes shopping, etc.). It's possible, instead, that general facts about shopping are stored at some still higher level (Bower, Black, & Turner, 1979). There is also no consensus on whether people represent these facts in a strict sequence of episodes (Abbott, Black, & Smith, 1985; Abelson, 1981; Barsalou & Sewell, 1985; Galambos & Rips, 1982; Nottenburg & Shoben, 1980). In more recent versions of Schank's theory, information about routines like grocery shopping is stored not as a whole sequence, but in smaller units (*memory organization packets*, or *MOPs*) that can be strung together on the fly in interpreting discourse (Schank, 1982).

Scripts are one example of a generic knowledge structure that captures common features of many individual events. Although there is disagreement about the exact contents of these structures, there does seem to be widespread agreement among memory researchers that much autobiographical knowledge consists of information about general patterns stored at a relatively abstract level; this generic information is supplemented by additional individuating details that distinguish one event from others of the same type (e.g., Barsalou, 1988; Conway, 1996; Kolodner, 1985; E. Smith, 1999). Information about the overall pattern is often much more easily retrieved than information about the individuating details.

Consider, for example, survey respondents' reports about their diets. Several surveys gather data about respondents' diets in an attempt to link dietary patterns with the development of health problems. In a series of studies, Smith and his colleagues (A. F. Smith, 1991; Smith, Jobe, and Mingay, 1991) compared survey reports about diet with diaries the participants had maintained. A number of findings from these studies indicated that even when the questions asked about foods consumed during a specific reference period, the respondents seemed to be reporting what they usually ate. For example, respondents' reports about what they ate during one week matched diary entries for a different week about as well as they matched the entries for the reference week. In Chapter 5 we review additional evidence that respondents' answers to survey questions seeking biographical facts often reflect their general knowledge about usual patterns rather than their memories for specific episodes.

Extended Events and Lifetime Periods

Multiple events can also form parts of nonstereotypical sequences. Conway (1996) argues that sequences of related individual events, which may last for minutes or hours, can form compound events, which unfold over a period of days or months (see also Barsalou, 1988, and Robinson, 1992). Our knowledge about a trip to Europe may constitute a single sequential event in memory. Such extended autobiographical sequences turn up spontaneously in subjects' recall of past events. For example, Barsalou (1988) found that subjects' descriptions of their summer sometimes included extended events, like "I took a trip to Italy" or "I went on a diet." These events represented 9% of the items subjects listed.

Many personal events seem closely linked to the ongoing circumstances in which they took place. You think of the event as happening when you were in high school or during your first marriage or while you were living in Montreal. These periods may serve as "chapters" in your autobiographical memory and provide a way to locate events that fall under them (Pillemer, Krensky, Kleinman, Goldsmith, & White, 1991). In addition, people often think of a personal event as occupying a posi-

tion in a sequence, with antecedent events leading up to it and conse-
quent events following from it. Many events – including landmarks, such
as your acceptance of a job or your wedding – don't just happen but are
parts of a preceding train of incidents that explain them and a succeeding
train of incidents that they explain, as in stories or narratives. The idea
that memories have a narrative structure is currently fashionable among
revisionist psychoanalysts, developmental psychologists, social psychologists, and linguists, who have stressed the role that personal narratives
play in people's self concept (e.g., Bruner, 1990; Linde, 1993; Schafer,
1992). Usher and Neisser (1993, p. 156) use the same notion to explain
childhood amnesia – the inability of adults to recall personal incidents
that happened to them before they were two or three years old:

Adults think of their lives – past, present, and future – in terms of a series of
well-defined periods and milestones that constitute a rich retrieval structure
and thus facilitate recall. Young children do not have this schema; they do
not think of their experiences as comprising a personal narrative.

Whatever the merit of these more sweeping claims, causal sequences may
provide a possible organizing principle for event memory.[2]

3.2.2   The Structure of Autobiographical Memory

Autobiographical memory contains, then, various kinds of information – details specific to a single event, generic knowledge about categories of events and stereotypical sequences of events, information about
extended autobiographical sequences, and knowledge about the major
epochs of our lives. How this information is organized in memory is
more controversial. In particular, theorists disagree on the relationship
between our knowledge about our own experiences and other types of
knowledge, about the different types of units that store autobiographical
information, and about the nature of the links between the different
units in autobiographical memory.

Tulving's Episodic Memory

Tulving's (1983) early model takes a minimalist approach to autobiographical memory structure. According to Tulving, memories of auto-

---

[2] See Schooler and Herrmann (1992) for a related distinction between periods and sequences in autobiographical memory.

biographical events are the basic units of *episodic memory*, which is a functionally distinct part of the human memory system. A separate memory system, *semantic memory*, contains more general knowledge that we possess, such as our knowledge of the meanings of words and other generic information. Because of the separation between the two memory systems and because events in episodic memory are organized only on a loose temporal basis, episodic memory doesn't allow much in the way of inferences to fill in missing or incomplete information. Visiting an internist about headaches may remind you of a similar event, such as visiting an ophthalmologist about eye strain. If so, information about the earlier event would be stored with information about the later one, allowing you to determine which happened first. But apart from these simple temporal inferences, episodic memory does not include enough general knowledge to allow inferences to be made.

Information that is not tied to specific personal events – for example, knowledge of the lexicon, of science or math, of folk psychology, of (nonautobiographical) history – is all part of semantic memory. The units of semantic memory are concepts, rather than events, and they are organized on a highly interconnected, abstract basis. In particular, scripted information about events (e.g., checking in with the receptionist is part of going to a doctor) is stored in semantic memory, as are the taxonomic relationships among events (a doctor's visit is a kind of health-care visit). Hence, semantic memory can support complex inferences from episodic memory's bare events: If recalling a doctor's visit, you can infer the detail that you probably checked in with the receptionist, even though you don't recall this transaction. Thus, although episodic and semantic memories are distinct, both would be involved in answering questions about individual events.

Tulving's critics have objected that stripping episodic memory of the ability to perform any but the simplest inferences makes it difficult to see its importance as a distinct system of memory (McCauley, 1984). Others have worried about how the episodic/semantic setup can account for generalization from specific encounters in episodic memory to general propositions in semantic memory – for example, from encounters with receptionists in doctors' offices to the generalization that all (or most) doctors' offices have receptionists (Hintzman, 1984). In later work, Tulving himself seems inclined to regard episodic memory as a component of semantic memory rather than as a separate system (see his reply to critics in Tulving, 1984).

Still, Tulving's initial model is a useful starting point. The autobiographical memory he envisioned consists of units of a single type – memories of individual events – that have few links to each other; such links as they do have are based solely on temporal priority. Moreover, Tulving sees this memory system as functionally distinct from the one that holds more general knowledge about classes of similar events.

Kolodner's Model: Memory via Distinctive Properties

As an alternative to Tulving's relatively structure-free autobiographical memory, we consider a model that tries to represent in a single system both the generic properties of similar events and the properties that distinguish one event from similar ones. Visits to a doctor, for example, have similar components, such as checking in with a receptionist, passing time in the waiting room, and finally consulting the doctor. But specific visits differ on dimensions like the purpose of the visit (regular checkup, acute ailment, follow-up), the type of doctor (internist, ophthalmologist, orthopedic surgeon), and so on. It would promote efficiency in retrieving a specific visit – say, to an ophthalmologist for a cataract exam – if that event were originally filed in memory under "doctor's visit," subindexed under "ophthalmologist," and sub-subindexed under "cataracts." If you were later asked "Are there any significant health problems that caused you to consult a doctor during the last six months?" you could mentally follow the path from "doctor's visits" to "cataract exam," retrieve the event in question, and determine whether it occurred in the reference period. This type of memory organization is a *discrimination net* (Simon & Feigenbaum, 1964); it's organized like plant identification manuals that contain keys making successively finer discriminations based on distinctive properties of the plants.

Kolodner (1985) has proposed a computer model of autobiographical memory called CYRUS that contains a discrimination structure for events. CYRUS's memory is composed of descriptions of types of events and descriptions of specific events filed under them. Although CYRUS focuses on the diplomatic events that occurred to former Secretary of State Cyrus Vance, Figure 3.2 adapts the main ideas to our doctor-visit example. CYRUS represents types of events, such as doctor visits, in terms of *event memory organization packets (E-MOPs*, a specialization of MOPs in Schank, 1982). These contain general information about events, including participants (e.g., a receptionist, nurse, and doctor in the case of doctor's visits), locations (doctors' offices), larger events of which this one is a part (e.g., treatment for health-related problems or regular health maintenance), and more general event classes of which

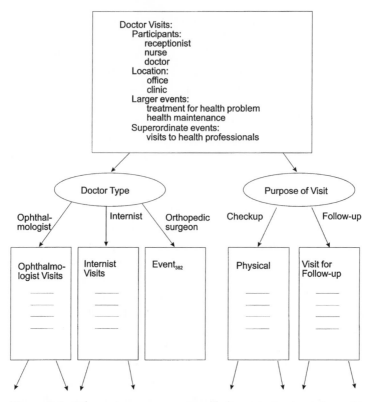

Figure 3.2. Schematic representation of the organization of autobiographical memory for doctor visits. The higher-level E-MOP includes information common to all doctor visits. Indices involving the type of doctor (ophthalmologist) and the purpose of the visit (checkup) lead to lower-level E-MOPs and individual events.

this one is an instance (e.g., visits to a health professional). In addition, an E-MOP contains *indices* to more specific E-MOPs and to particular events. In Figure 3.2, the indices point to subordinate E-MOPs for visits to ophthalmologists and visits to internists, which are specific versions of doctor's visits. If an index discriminates a unique event from others that the E-MOP describes, then the index points to that event. For example, if you've paid only one visit to an orthopedic surgeon, then the orthopedic-surgeon index will point directly to that visit, as shown in Figure 3.2. If an index does not yield a unique event, however, it will point to a subordinate E-MOP. Thus, multiple visits to internists will require a subordinate internist-visit E-MOP, also shown in the figure.

This E-MOP will contain further indices to more specific E-MOPs or events until each internist visit is singled out. (See Wagenaar, 1986, for a related "filing cabinet" model of autobiographical memory.)

A novel feature of CYRUS is that the retrieval process must generate the relevant indices in order for the event to be recalled. In the network of Figure 3.2, for example, the index for type of doctor that branches from the main doctor-visit E-MOP is invisible until the search process guesses it; it's like providing a password to gain access to the rest of the memory. One source that the search can use to determine an index is the question itself: "Have you visited an ophthalmologist in the last six months?" makes salient the type of doctor and allows retrieval of the path to ophthalmologist visits. Some questions, however, don't mention the necessary indices, either because they are too abstract or because they focus on properties different from those used in storing the event. For such questions, CYRUS infers the missing indices from other parts of the question or from related MOPs. "Have you visited a doctor for a work-related injury?" contains no information helpful in traversing the paths below doctor visits in Figure 3.2. Still, the E-MOP for doctor's visits includes the fact that they are parts of treatments for ailments, and the E-MOP for treatments, plus the additional information about work-related injuries, may provide another route to a relevant event.

Conway's Multilayered Model

In contrast to Tulving's model, Kolodner's (1985) allows for two types of units in autobiographical memory – one containing generic information about classes of events and the other containing individuating details about unique events; in addition, Kolodner's model allows for hierarchical linkages among events. It is possible to argue, though, that an organization in terms of general event types and indices is still insufficient, that it neglects the temporal and causal dimensions of events. Conway's (1996) model goes further than Kolodner's in assuming a more elaborate organization that includes three types of memory structures and that allows richer temporal and causal links among these structures.

Conway argues that autobiographical memory consists of information at three levels. The highest level contains information about *lifetime periods*. These are discrete periods, such as one's first job or one's college years, with identifiable temporal boundaries. The memory structures representing these periods include general knowledge about the people, places, activities, and goals associated with each period. Conway argues that lifetime periods have both a temporal and a thematic organization. We store information about the successive phases of our work life, say, separately from the successive chapters of our romantic or residential histories. Any given period in our lives may thus be linked to more than one lifetime period (when I was married to X, living in Y, and working at Z). The themes that organize lifetime periods are linked to important personal goals and may, as a result, vary from one person to the next.

Units at the next lower level capture our knowledge about *general events*, which include extended autobiographical sequences as well as generic events. These general events include memories for key moments in our personal histories, like learning to drive a car or experiencing our first kiss (Robinson, 1992). We may develop narratives, or "mini-histories," for such episodes. The final level in Conway's model contains *event-specific knowledge*, or the details about general events. These details often consist of sensory information, such as visual images. Access to these details is by way of some index or distinctive cue that links the detail to the general event.

Event-specific knowledge differs both in kind and in degree from the information stored at higher levels; it is both more detailed and more perceptual in character. As a result, it is plausible that event-specific knowledge is stored in a separate memory system – similar to Tulving's episodic memory – from the one that holds information about lifetime periods and general events. This latter system may include not only autobiographical knowledge but also other general-purpose knowledge. As evidence for the existence of separate memory systems, Conway (1993) cites studies of patients with severe retrograde amnesia, who often appear to retain some memory for the basic facts of their lives (i.e., for lifetime periods and general events) but can no longer retrieve the details of events.[3]

---

[3] *Retrograde amnesia* refers to the loss of memory for events that took place in the past, prior to the onset of the amnesia; *anterograde amnesia* refers to loss of the ability to form new memories. A somewhat similar proposal regarding the existence of separate memory systems for generic information and novel events has been made by McClelland, McNaughton, and O'Reilly (1995). According to this view, information about novel events is stored for several weeks in a memory system involving the hippocampus and is only gradually consolidated with more generic information in long-term memory over this period.

3.2.3   Implications for the Retrieval Process

These different views of the structure of autobiographical memory have different implications for the process of retrieving information from memory. Before we review the evidence about these implications, it will be useful to consider the fundamentals of retrieval, about which most memory theorists agree.

The Definition of Retrieval

Perhaps the most fundamental fact about human memory is that it contains far more information than is actually being used by any mental process at any given moment. *Retrieval* refers to the process of bringing information held in long-term storage to an active state, in which it can be used. The storage system in which inactive information is held is referred to as *long-term memory (LTM)*; when information reaches a sufficient level of activation to be used in ongoing cognitive processes, it is said to enter *working memory* (Baddeley, 1986).

A basic assumption shared by most memory theorists is that activation spreads from one concept or memory in LTM to related ones (Anderson, 1983; Collins & Quillian, 1969). Thus, an essential component of the retrieval process is the spread of activation along whatever links – temporal, taxonomic, part–whole – connect related memories. The spread of activation is thought to be automatic (i.e., it is involuntary and outside of conscious awareness). Most researchers also believe that there is a controlled component to the retrieval process as well, in which we generate cues that are intended to prompt recall. This controlled process is likely to be cyclic. We start with some partial description of the event we're trying to remember ("Do you remember the time we missed our flight in Orlando?"). The concepts involved in this initial description are activated, and activation spreads from there to related concepts and memories. These new memories may become conscious and serve as additional cues guiding further recall. Or we may intentionally generate other cues to prompt further retrieval ("What exactly were we doing in Orlando?").

The act of retrieving information from long-term memory may or may not be accompanied by conscious awareness of the material that's retrieved or by the experience of remembering a personal event. Studies of *implicit memory* show that we can use information in the course of completing some task without ever becoming consciously aware of it (Schacter, 1987). Similarly, retrieval can be accompanied by the experience of remembering, but this does not always happen (Tulving, 1985). The experience of remembering seems to require the retrieval of a critical mass of perceptual details. Our feeling that a memory is real and that its source is firsthand experience rather than secondhand knowledge seems to be the product of a complicated and error-prone judgment process (Johnson, Hashtroudi, & Lindsay, 1993).

Evidence Regarding CYRUS

Although there is little direct experimental evidence for CYRUS as a model of human memory, some well-documented findings are consistent with its conception of the retrieval process. Many of these findings involve difficulties in retrieving specific events when a large number of events fit the same generic representation, or E-MOP.

According to Kolodner, a person who experiences many events of the same type will have to generate a large number of indices both in storing and in retrieving the events. In trying to recall any one event, the individual may be unable to specify a relevant index and, hence, may recall an E-MOP rather than the specific event. Many visits to an HMO, for example, will make any one visit more difficult to discriminate and cause a person to recall only general information rather than the visit's details (Means et al., 1989). Similarly, Barsalou (1988) found that subjects' recall of events that happened to them during the previous summer was dominated by *summarized events*, such as "I watched a lot of TV," rather than specific events ("We saw a play"). Forcing subjects to recall only specific events disrupted their recall. Linton (1982), in a heroic study of her own memory, also notes that some descriptions of events, which she wrote at the time of their occurrence, later cued only generalized memories. Other memory theories can probably explain the prevalence of summarized events by invoking the idea that similar incidents cause forgetting. However, CYRUS has an advantage in describing this forgetting mechanism precisely.

There have also been attempts to assess CYRUS's assumption that E-MOPs for types of events provide the initial access route to memory. Reiser, Black, and Abelson (1985) measured the speed with which subjects retrieved specific events in response to pairs of cues. The cues consisted of CYRUS's event types (e.g., *went to a doctor*) and general actions (e.g., *sat down and waited*) that are part of many different event types; you can sit down and wait at the theater or in a restaurant, as well as in a doctor's office. The subjects were to recall a specific event involving both cues (an event during which they went to a doctor and sat down and waited), and Reiser and his colleagues varied the order in which they presented the cues. If memory is organized at the top level by event types, as in CYRUS, then presenting the event type first should give subjects a head start in finding an event, allowing them to retrieve the event more quickly. In line with this prediction, these investigators showed that subjects were about two seconds faster when they saw the event type first than when they saw the action first.

The meaning of this finding is not all that clear, however. In a later experiment, Barsalou (1988) compared event-type cues with cues that mentioned participants (e.g., your sister), locations (your home town), or times (noon). On one trial, for example, a subject might have to retrieve a specific event in response to the cue *went to the doctor* followed by *your sister* (event type first); on a second trial, the subject might have to retrieve a specific event to the pair *your best friend* followed by *went to a movie* (participant first). Participants, locations, and times would normally provide indices in CYRUS and should thus be useful only in the context of an event type. CYRUS therefore seems to predict faster retrieval times when the event type appears first. Barsalou, however, found no differences as a function of the order of the cues. Perhaps the easiest way to reconcile these results with the earlier ones is to suppose that the findings of Reiser and his colleagues reflect a handicap for action cues like *sat down and waited* rather than an advantage for event types. Salient participants, locations, and times may be as effective as event types in recalling autobiographical episodes.

The Role of Higher-Level Units

Conway's model of autobiographical memory suggests that retrieval may also utilize high-level cues about extended sequences or periods. As we noted earlier, subjects sometimes spontaneously mention such autobiographical sequences and periods when they recall past events. Brown, Shevell, and Rips (1986) asked subjects to talk aloud as they attempted to determine the dates of public events, such as the first eruption of Mt. St. Helens. To answer these questions, subjects sometimes related the event to personal periods or sequences that occurred at the same time: "I was living in Washington, D.C.; I'd graduated from college already, so [Mt. St. Helens] was definitely post-1979." Use of personal information was more common with nonpolitical events like the eruption than with political items like the signing of the Camp David accord.[4]

A study by Conway and Bekerian (1987, Experiment 3) examined the effectiveness of cues based on periods (e.g., *when I was in college*) as well as cues based on event types (*went to the doctor*); the results indicate that time periods (e.g., *college days* or *while I lived in Memphis*) may be even more effective than event types as retrieval cues. Conway and Bekerian argue that "general personal information, in the form of a category of lifetime periods . . . and related general events . . . , provide[s] faster access to autobiographical memories than do other types of information" (p. 131).

Matching the Question to the Memory

The issues of the content and structure of memory representations have practical relevance for surveys because questions (and other retrieval cues) are more likely to lead to full and accurate recall when the content of the questions matches the content of the information in memory (Tulving & Thompson, 1973). It's clear, for example, that asking respondents for "the last time you did x" will not be an especially helpful probe, since people are unlikely to store an event as "the last x" (unless they happen to know at the time of the event that no more x's can occur). A description like "the last x" doesn't take into account the probable form in which the respondents encoded the event and forces them to generate more useful cues.

Descriptions of events based on autobiographical periods and on event types are less susceptible to this problem, since respondents may originally store a particular event according to the ongoing circumstances or according to the general type of event it falls under. The evidence we have reviewed is far from conclusive about memory structure and about what information provides the best access route to an event memory. It hints, however, that consistent descriptions – ones that

---

[4] Fuhrman and Wyer (1988) presented further evidence that bears on autobiographical periods. They showed that subjects decided more quickly which of a pair of events came first (e.g., *date with Carol* or *starred in My Fair Lady*) when the events were from different periods (high school vs. college) than when they were from the same period (both college events). Moreover, interperiod comparisons did not depend on the ordinal separation of the events within the series of tested items, whereas intraperiod comparisons did. We discuss additional evidence for the effect of periods on recall in Section 3.3.2.

respondents interpret in the same way from one situation to the next – will be more effective than descriptions that change as a function of the situation (e.g., Reiser et al.'s general actions). Of course, successful event recall depends on more than just memory structure. Many empirical variables affect memory storage and retrieval, and these inevitably influence people's ability to answer autobiographical questions. We need to examine some of these additional variables in order to understand how response accuracy varies with memory processing.

3.3   Factors Affecting Recall of Autobiographical Events

It's important to keep in mind that all we ever retrieve from autobiographical memory is a representation of an experience, not the experience itself. The retrieved information may include vivid images, but even images are representations that can differ in accuracy. Retrieval sometimes carries with it a feeling of conviction in the correctness of the memory, but this conviction is not self-authenticating. Studies of *flashbulb memories* – vivid memories of what we were doing when we heard surprising and important news, such as the news of an assassination – show that vivid memories are not necessarily accurate ones (McCloskey, Wible, & Cohen, 1988; Neisser & Harsch, 1992). Everyday memories of the sort that surveys usually probe are even more susceptible to distortion.

Some of what people report about an autobiographical event is undoubtedly the result of inference or reconstruction rather than direct experience (see Bradburn, Rips, & Shevell, 1987, for a review). These inferences can occur at event time, at interview time, or at intervening times when a person thinks about the original incident. If you are the victim of a robbery, for example, you might plausibly infer at the time of the event that the robber has taken $40 on the grounds that you withdrew $40 from the bank earlier that day. Or you may arrive at the $40 figure later when the police recover your wallet. Or you may estimate the figure when you are interviewed about the crime, using your knowledge of the amount of cash that you typically carry. You may be aware that $40 is the product of inference, especially if you estimated it as a conscious strategy at interview time, but it is also possible that you can no longer remember whether you observed or inferred that $40 was taken. We may believe that our memory of an event is due to direct retrieval rather than inference, particularly when little time has passed and the event seems familiar and distinctive (Herrmann, 1994). But it's clear that we often have difficulty distinguishing what we experienced from what we only inferred.

The distinction is important for surveys because surveys often ask for information that respondents may not be able to recall and, as a result, they may use inferential processes to come up with an answer instead. There are several major sources of memory failure:

- Respondents may not have taken in the critical information in the first place;
- they may be unwilling to go through the work of retrieving it;
- even if they do try, they may be unable to retrieve the event itself, but only generic information about events of that type;
- they may retrieve only partial information about the event and, as a result, fail to report it; or
- they may recall erroneous information about the event, including incorrect inferences incorporated into their representation of the event.

When they are unable or unwilling to remember, respondents may resort to reconstructive processes to fill in what's missing. Estimates, inferences, and other reconstructive processes may sometimes lead to more accurate answers than retrieved information does (Loftus, Smith, Klinger, & Fiedler, 1992; Mathiowetz & Duncan, 1988). However, reconstructive processes are subject to error as well. In this section, we outline some of the factors that make it more difficult for respondents to retrieve facts about events and, hence, make it more likely that they will resort to reconstruction and inference to compensate for their lack of knowledge. In Chapter 5, we examine the processes that can lead to error in answers arrived at through these other means.

3.3.1   Recall and the Passage of Time

By far the best-attested fact about autobiographical memory is that the longer the interval between the time of the event and the time of the interview, the less likely that a person will remember it. According to many contemporary theories of forgetting (e.g., Gillund & Shiffrin, 1984; Johnson, 1983), the passage of time doesn't by itself obliterate the event's details. Instead, additional time makes it more likely that the person will experience similar events in the interim, and these later events interfere with the retrieval of the initial one.

Kolodner's theory offers an especially detailed explanation for this interference effect. The longer the time since an event (e.g., $Event_{382}$ in Figure 3.2) the more likely it is that a person will encode another event sharing the same lowest-level index (the person may pay another visit to an "orthopedic surgeon"). This forces the creation of a new E-MOP to record the events' similarities and of new indices to record their differences. The additional indices will mean that a person will have to do more searching in retrieving the event, and this will reduce the chance of correct recall. Even researchers who don't subscribe to Kolodner's view about memory structure acknowledge that similar events may blur together, making it easier to remember the overall pattern but more difficult to remember the details of the individual events. The interference hypothesis implies that the effect of time is mediated by how distinctive the event is in the person's stream of experience. So time may decrease recall by differing increments, depending on the type of event involved.

Differences in the Rates of Forgetting

This variety of rates of forgetting appears in Figure 3.3, which we have adapted from a paper by Bradburn and his colleagues (1987). The data points represent results from studies of very-long-term memory for personal facts: college students' recall of the names of their grade school and high school teachers (Whitten & Leonard, 1981), students' recall of exam grades (Bell, 1992), college alumni's recall of the streets in their college town (Bahrick, 1983), and high school alumni's recall of names of classmates (Bahrick, Bahrick, & Wittlinger, 1975).[5]

What's notable about these data is the extremely slow forgetting rate for names of people (classmates or teachers). Indeed, the figure shows that the recall of classmates' names has not yet leveled off, even after 50 years! The figure includes data from studies in which (a) subjects free-recalled items within a specified category, (b) the retention interval spanned a number of years, (c) there were four or more retention inter-

---

[5] In the recall of street names and classmates, the data are adjusted so that 100% recall is the level of an individual who has just graduated. The data for street names and classmates are also adjusted for the effects of other variables that affect recall – for example, number of visits to the town in the case of street names.

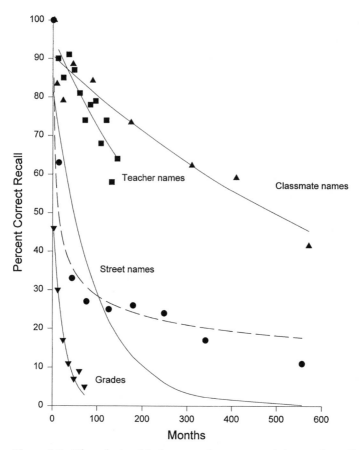

Figure 3.3. The relationship between the passage of time and recall of information in four studies of autobiographical memory. The solid lines indicate the best-fitting exponential functions for the data classmate names (Bahrick, Bahrick, & Wittlinger, 1975), names of teachers (Whitten & Leonard, 1981), and exam grades (Bell, 1992); the dashed line indicates the best-fitting power function for the data from the study by Bahrick (1983).

vals, and (d) some degree of verification was possible. However, similar decreases in autobiographical recall over time appear in studies of cued recall for self-selected everyday events (Wagenaar, 1986), randomly selected everyday events (Brewer, 1988), and tasks that occurred during the subject's previous visit to a psychology lab (Baddeley, Lewis, & Nimmo-Smith, 1978). In some of these cued-recall studies, certain properties of the probed event show forgetting, while others do not; however, the cases of no forgetting are probably due to subjects' ability to infer the properties without having to retrieve them (see Brewer, 1988).[6]

Validation studies in the survey literature also show decreases in accuracy with an increase in the time since the event. Decreasing accuracy with the passage of time is found for reports of hospitalizations (Cannell et al., 1981), visits to an HMO (Loftus et al., 1992; Means et al., 1989), and dietary intake (Smith & Jobe, 1994). There are also cases, however, in which accuracy does not seem to decline over time. Mathiowetz and Duncan (1988) report one such instance for recall of spells of unemployment at a particular company; in their study, accuracy followed a nonmonotonic trend, first decreasing and then increasing. These investigators also found no significant effect of delay after controlling statistically for the effects of other variables (e.g., irregularity of unemployment spells). However, the absence of a delay effect in this study may be due to the fact that an especially large number of layoffs occurred near the middle of the interval in question, providing more opportunities for errors of omission to occur at that point.

Forgetting curves like those in Figure 3.3 can be distorted if respondents do not attempt to recall events but instead base their answers on inferences or estimates. Long retention intervals probably encourage respondents to forgo recall in favor of inference and estimation processes, and when these response strategies are used, they may partially

---

[6] In traditional studies of memory, *free recall* refers to tasks in which subjects study a list of items (e.g., a random list of words) and must later repeat as many of the items as possible (in any order). *Cued recall* refers to tasks in which subjects study a list (e.g., a list of word pairs) and later repeat individual items from the list in response to specific hints or cues (e.g., the second member of a pair in response to the first member). The distinction between free recall and cued recall is often blurred in studies of autobiographical memory. For example, if subjects must recall all of their classmates from high school, are they engaging in free recall or cued recall? In the context of autobiographical memory, it's probably more important to understand the demands of the particular task than to decide on the proper way to extend the traditional free–cued distinction. In what follows, however, we use *free recall* for situations in which subjects are supposed to recall as many instances as possible (in any order) that fit some description or directive, and we use *cued recall* for situations in which subjects are supposed to recall only a single instance. (Thus, the classmates task is free recall in our terminology.) Both of these tasks are relevant to survey research. For example, Question (a) asks for free recall of activities and duties, whereas Question (b) in the same series requires cued recall of a specific event (a deduction from the last paycheck):

(a) What were _____'s most important activities or duties [at work]? [CES, 1991]
(b) Was there any money deducted from_____'s last pay for private pension fund? [CES, 1991]

offset the effects of forgetting (see Chapters 4 and 5; Smith and Jobe, 1994, propose a model based on this assumption). Inferential and estimation processes are less likely to affect the curves in Figure 3.3, since the likelihood of correctly inferring the name of a classmate, teacher, or street is probably small. In such cases, inferences can aid retrieval but not substitute for it.

The Impact of the Length of the Reference Period

It is easier for survey researchers to manipulate the length of the *reference period* – the period about which respondents must report events – than the length of the retention interval for a specific event. For example, survey studies investigating the impact of the length of the reference period may vary whether the respondents report about the last two weeks, last month, or last year (e.g., Neter & Waksberg, 1964). Many of these studies show a net decrease in the number of reported events per unit time as the length of the response period increases, probably due to forgetting (see Sudman & Bradburn, 1973, for a meta-analysis). As Neter and Waksberg point out, however, longer reference periods increase not only the amount of time over which respondents must remember events but also the total number of events they must recall, and both variables are likely to reduce accuracy. Longer reference periods, like longer retention intervals, can also make subjects more likely to estimate an answer, sometimes canceling the effects of forgetting (Blair & Burton, 1987; Burton & Blair, 1991; Chu et al., 1992). Recent validation studies (Mathiowetz & Duncan, 1988; Schaeffer, 1994) suggest that respondents are least accurate when the events they must report are irregular (and thus difficult to estimate) and unimportant (and thus difficult to retrieve).

Theoretical Forgetting Curves

Several survey researchers have attempted to summarize effects of forgetting in terms of a mathematical function relating the probability of recalling an event (or its properties) to the length of the retention interval. (See Rubin & Wetzel, 1996, for a parallel effort by two memory researchers.) For some purposes, a linear forgetting function seems to give an adequate account of survey data (see Sikkel, 1985, for recall of contacts with general practitioners and specialists). It's clear from Figure 3.3, however, that linear forgetting does not always describe the form of retention. Especially when the overall level of recall is low, it is possible to get better fits to empirical results with negatively accelerating curves (in which forgetting is rapid at first but slows down over time).

Sudman and Bradburn (1973) propose that the probability of recall follows a negative exponential function, that is, one of the form ae^{-bt}, where t is time since the event and a and b are constants. Functions of this type decrease to an asymptotic level of 0, are attractively simple, and are in line with some laboratory results. Exponential forgetting most often occurs in the lab, however, for retention intervals of less than a minute; laboratory studies of long-term memory for lists of unrelated items typically support power functions – those of the form at^{-bt} – or more complex functions that include a power component (Wickelgren, 1973, 1974). Power functions also appear in studies of autobiographical memory that employ the *Galton method*. In these experiments, subjects receive a single cue word on each trial and must retrieve a personal event that the cue word reminds them of. Subjects then supply dates for these events, and the dates are used to calculate retention functions. In a review and an extension of such studies, Rubin (1982) showed that power functions provide good fits for the data from college-age subjects (see Rubin, Wetzler, & Nebes, 1986, for data from other age groups). Wagenaar (1986) also found evidence for power-function forgetting in the study of cued recall for events from his own life.

The autobiographical data of Figure 3.3 present mixed evidence for these theoretical forgetting functions (for a more extensive discussion of forgetting curves for autobiographical memory, see Rubin & Wetzel, 1996). Exponential functions do at least as well as power functions for the results on teachers' names, classmates' names, and grades, supporting the Sudman–Bradburn hypothesis; the best-fitting exponential functions appear as solid lines in the figure. However, a power function provides a much better account of the street-name data, which we show as a dashed curve ($R^2 = .96$ for the best-fitting power function and .77 for the best-fitting exponential function). There's no simple explanation for the difference in the shape of this curve, although we suspect that people probably spend less time rehearsing or reviewing the street names of their college town than most of the other types of information that the figure represents. It is also unclear why the remaining experiments in the figure should support exponential functions rather than the power functions more characteristic of other long-term tasks. The power function has received some empirical support from work by Anderson and Schooler (1991), and a meta-analysis by Rubin and Wetzel (1996) suggests that the power function provided the best overall fit to data from studies of autobiographical memory. Unfortunately, we know of no way to predict the form of the forgetting curve for autobiographical information, and we suspect that improvements on this front await attempts to relate the type of information to the structural theories that we discussed in Section 3.2.

3.3.2 Recall as a Function of Other Event Characteristics

Aside from when the event happened (relative to when it is asked about), several other characteristics of the event can affect its subsequent accessibility. Among the key characteristics of an event are its proximity to temporal boundaries (including the reference date), its distinctiveness, and its emotional impact.

Proximity to Temporal Boundaries

We've noted that as the retention interval gets longer, respondents rely more on inference and less on recall in formulating their answers. Part of the reason for this shift in response strategies is that respondents know that events that occurred long ago may not be easily retrieved, and they resort to estimation processes instead (see Brown et al., 1985, and Chapter 5 for discussions of this hypothesis). Another reason for the shift, however, may be that the boundary for the reference period grows less distinct as the reference period grows longer. It is relatively easy to remember your circumstances a week ago and, hence, to distinguish what happened during the last week from what happened before. It's not such a simple matter to recollect what you were doing exactly three months ago. The difficulty here is not uncertainty about the calendar date that marks the beginning of the reference period; including the exact date of the start of the period is unlikely to help. Rather, the problem comes in tying the beginning of the period to one's personal stream of experiences.

Respondents' uncertainty about the start of the reference period implies that they may mistakenly report events that happened before it or mistakenly omit events that happened during it in answering a survey question. The first type of mistake goes by the name of *forward telescoping*, and the second is called *backward telescoping* (e.g., Neter & Waksberg, 1964; Sudman & Bradburn, 1973). Forward and backward telescoping are errors in the temporal placement of events, and we will deal with them in detail in Chapter 4. At this point, we note simply that methods that appear to reduce telescoping call the respondents' attention to personal facts that can serve as a boundary for the reference period. For example, Neter and Waksberg (1964) reduced forward telescoping by enumerating for the respondents all of the critical events that they had reported during earlier interviews, a procedure they dubbed *bounded recall*. Sudman, Finn, and Lannom (1984) similarly found that respondents reported fewer events for the current month if they were first asked about events of the preceding month. Loftus and Marburger (1983) also appear to have decreased forward telescoping by framing the response period in terms of a personally meaningful event (e.g., the first eruption of Mt. St. Helens for respondents living in Washington State).

The results on bounding are consistent with the findings on autobiographical periods, particularly with studies showing that the endpoints marking the boundaries of these periods can be potent cues for retrieval. In independent experiments, Robinson (1986) and Pillemer and his colleagues (1986) found that when college students have to recall events from the last year or two, they tend to recall more events near the points separating school from vacation periods, such as the beginning of the school year in the fall and the beginning of Christmas vacation.

Figure 3.4 shows the results of a similar experiment with students from the University of Chicago (Kurbat, Shevell, & Rips, 1998, Experiment 1). The students in this experiment recalled (in February 1989) 20 unique events that had happened to them during 1988 and then dated these events. The instructions made no mention of the school calendar or of other school-related facts. The figure plots the distribution of these memories over the weeks of 1988, beginning January 1. Vertical lines on the graphs represent the position of term boundaries: In the bottom panel, the divisions show, from left to right, the beginning of the winter quarter, the end of the winter quarter/beginning of the spring quarter, end of spring quarter/beginning of summer, end of summer/beginning of the fall quarter, and end of the fall quarter. The top panel contains data from college freshmen, who had been enrolled for only the fall quarter; hence, the figure shows just the breaks at the beginning of the school year and the beginning of Christmas vacation. The bottom panel consists of data from upperclass students and indicates all quarterly breaks. In accord with earlier results, subjects recalled more events near the relevant endpoints, with freshmen showing an especially large peak at the beginning of the school year (their first term in college).

The calendar effect in Figure 3.4. is apparently due to subjects' spon-

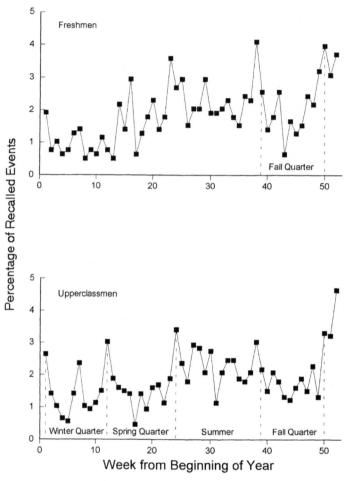

Figure 3.4. The recall of autobiographical events in relation to the school calendar. The top panel shows the data for freshmen; the bottom panel shows the data for upperclassmen. The data are from Kurbat, Shevell, and Rips (1994, Experiment 1).

taneous use of the boundary points to help them recall events. The recall profiles are not the result of (nonschool) holidays or other seasonal factors, since schools with different academic schedules produce peaks that shift with the term breaks (Kurbat et al., 1998, Experiment 1). Nor do the peaks reflect the occurrence of especially important events; subjects do not rate the beginning-of-term or end-of-term items as more important than events that occur at other times (Kurbat et al., 1998; Robinson, 1986). However, the presence of explicit cues does modulate the effect. When students have to write a description of the events on a calendar showing the position of the term boundaries, events near these boundaries increase; but when they use a calendar that shows the position of holidays, such as Valentine's Day and Thanksgiving, events near the school boundaries decrease (Kurbat et al., 1998, Experiment 4).

Robinson and Kurbat and his coworkers speculate that students think of the year as structured by the school calendar and exploit that calendar in retrieval. Students know, for example, that they must have gotten from their home town to their college town at the end of summer and can use that fact to help them retrieve associated events (saying goodbye to their families, shopping for school clothes, reuniting with school friends, moving into a new apartment, and similar activities). A few experiments (e.g., Means & Loftus, 1991) have attempted, with some success, to use personal landmarks or life event calendars (where respondents record personal milestones in their job or residential histories) to improve recall in surveys.

Distinctiveness

We noted that, aside from its impact on our ability to situate the beginning of the reference period with respect to meaningful events in our own lives, the passage of time makes it more likely that we will experience events similar to the one we are trying to retrieve. The presence of multiple similar events can reduce the likelihood of retrieving any one of them (e.g., Anderson, 1983; see also Thompson et al., 1996, who find that infrequent and atypical events are remembered more easily than frequent or typical ones).

There are a number of explanations for this effect. According to Kolodner's model, the presence of similar experiences will require us to generate multiple indices to pick out one of the experiences. Similarly, in Anderson's (1983) theory, retrieval may start with the activation of a single memory structure, such as the structure containing our general knowledge about doctor's visits. When many episodes are linked to that concept, the activation spreading from it to the linked episodes will be dissipated among the multiple pathways; Anderson refers to this as the *fan* effect. Because little activation reaches any of the structures representing the memory for each episode, we are less likely to recall them. Although these and other theories of the retrieval process may differ in the details of their account of the interference produced by multiple experiences of the same type, they share the prediction that repeated experiences are harder to remember than unique ones.

Emotional Impact

Other characteristics of events that affect our ability to recall them are how important they are and how much emotional impact they have. For example, in a monumental study of his own memory, Wagenaar (1986) rated the pleasantness of the events as he recorded them in a diary he maintained for a six-year period. The more intense the rating, the more likely he was to recall the event later on. In addition, he recalled pleasant events better than ones he rated as neutral or unpleasant. Similar findings were reported by Thompson and his colleagues (1996), who had subjects keep diaries recording the events they had experienced. Both pleasant and unpleasant events were better remembered than neutral ones, and among events that aroused feelings in one direction or the other, pleasant events were better remembered than unpleasant ones (see also Holmes, 1970).

Similar results are found in survey studies that examine the accuracy of survey reports by comparing them to records concerning the same events. Important events tend to be reported more accurately than unimportant ones. For example, longer hospital stays are more likely to be reported in a survey than shorter stays (Cannell et al., 1981); costly home repairs are more likely to be reported than inexpensive ones (Neter & Waksberg, 1964); and major purchases are more likely to be reported than minor ones (Sudman & Bradburn, 1973).

The simplest explanation for these findings is that we are less likely to forget important events than unimportant ones; we are more likely to notice them in the first place and to discuss and think about them afterward. Thus, important events have the advantages of both more elaborate initial encoding and greater rehearsal after the fact; both factors probably contribute to their greater retrievability.

3.3.3   Recall as a Function of Characteristics of the Question

The designers of a survey questionnaire can't determine how distinctive or important an event is to the respondents or when the event took place. As a result, if it's necessary to collect information on *all* hospital stays, the best thing that can be done is to shorten the reference period to minimize the number of stays that are forgotten. There are, however, characteristics of the survey questions that can affect the retrieval process, and these can be varied to promote more accurate recall in surveys.

Recall Order

Surveys usually give respondents the option of recalling the target events in any order they choose. Respondents could therefore attempt to retrieve events in the order in which they actually occurred, in reverse chronological order, or in some sequence unrelated to event time. Studies of verbal learning with lists of unrelated items suggest that chronological order produces better recall for auditory material but that the reverse order produces better recall for visual material (Madigan, 1971). It seems likely, however, that chronological order is superior, even for visually presented information, when the items have an intrinsic connection that runs from the beginning to the end of the list. Recalling a sentence in reverse order is obviously a much more difficult task than recalling it in its natural order.

Somewhat surprisingly, however, memory for autobiographical information seems to be superior when subjects recall items in reverse order. Whitten and Leonard (1981) found better performance for reverse order when college subjects attempted to retrieve the names of their grade school and high school teachers. Correct recall of all teachers was more likely (and the time required to name them was less) when subjects worked backward from their 12th-grade teacher than when they worked forward from their 1st-grade teacher or when they recalled the teachers in an (experimenter-determined) random sequence. When subjects were allowed to skip over the names of teachers they could not recall, forward and backward order produced about the same number of correct responses; random order was significantly worse. Loftus and Fathi (1985) also found better memory for the contents of psychology exams when subjects recalled the exams in backward order (from the last exam in the quarter to the first) than in forward order (first exam to last).

It has proved difficult, though, to obtain this advantage for backward recall in surveys. For reports of health-care visits, Loftus et al. (1992) were unable to find a significant difference for backward versus forward versus free recall, and Jobe et al. (1990) found a small advantage for free over forward and backward orders. It seems quite possible that the effectiveness of these recall strategies depends on the type of event in question. For instance, it may be that health-care visits exhibit forward dependencies, especially when an initial treatment necessitates follow-up exams, and these dependencies may work against a backward memory search. So far, however, no work has been done to explore potential interactions between retrieval order and event types.

Time on Task

Any theory of memory ought to predict that the more time subjects have to answer a question, the more accurate their response will be. A slower pace gives respondents more time to comprehend the question and search memory for the appropriate information. Even if the respondents resort to inferences rather than memory search, the slower pace should allow them a better chance to generate inference strategies, to carry these strategies to completion, and to check the conclusions against other facts. There are probably upper limits to improvements in accuracy that come from increasing the response time per question, but for some autobiographical material, people can continue to retrieve pertinent new information over very long intervals. For example, Williams and Hollan (1981) asked subjects to recall the names of high school classmates and found them retrieving new names even after nine sessions, each lasting an hour.

In general, survey research supports the notion that giving respondents more time improves accuracy. Manipulations that slow down the interview – for example, asking longer questions (Bradburn & Sudman, 1979; Cannell et al., 1981), requiring respondents to use lengthier strategies or response methods (Means, Swan, Jobe, & Esposito, 1994a), or giving respondents longer response deadlines (Burton & Blair, 1991) – tend to make their answers more accurate. However, the relation between interview length and response accuracy may need some qualifications. For example, although Cannell et al. (1981) found that including long questions (with redundant wording) increased the number of reported incidents in a survey of health events, this benefit also extended to shorter questions elsewhere in the survey. The longer questions may have increased the time that respondents took to answer each item, leading to more careful responses across the board. Cannell et al., however, did not report the response time per question, so it is unclear exactly how question length changed the pace of the interview.

Burton and Blair (1991) controlled response time more precisely by giving respondents deadlines for their answers. Longer deadlines increased accuracy in one experiment for the number of B grades and the number of courses that the student respondents had taken outside the College of Business. But a somewhat similar manipulation failed to aid respondents' reports of the number of checks they had written and the number of automatic teller transactions they had made. Burton and Blair speculated that longer deadlines can sometimes lead respondents to adopt a more painstaking retrieval strategy, even when a quicker infer-ence approach could have produced better answers.

Decomposition

When respondents have to report counts of events, such as number of purchases or number of health-care visits, they may arrive at better answers if the questions ask separately about smaller subcategories. For example, a question about health-care visits might be broken into sepa-rate questions that get at face-to-face and telephone consultations with a physician or into separate questions about inpatient and outpatient visits. As we note in Chapter 5, respondents report using decomposition spontaneously in answering frequency questions. This method of break-ing an overall question into more manageable pieces (*decomposition*) usually produces better results than holistic estimates in laboratory tasks in which exact enumeration is impossible (Armstrong, Denniston, & Gordon, 1975; MacGregor & Lichtenstein, 1991; MacGregor, Lichten-stein, & Slovic, 1988; Siegel, Goldsmith, & Madson, 1982).

Decomposition has potential for survey use, but so far there is little direct evidence that it improves response accuracy. Means et al. (1994) asked respondents to remember how many cigarettes they had smoked on a given day by breaking up the day into different activities, such as "commuting," "in the office," and "after dinner." Respondents added the separate estimates for these periods to derive their answers. The investigators compared accuracy in this condition to conditions in which respondents tried to recall individual incidents, gave a gut reaction, or used any method they chose. In the first experiment, there were no significant differences between these conditions; in the second, there was a trend toward more accurate responses for decomposition and recall of incidents over the gut reaction and free strategy conditions, although the investigators did not report significance tests. It seems plausible that decomposition is most helpful in situations in which the number of items to be estimated is very large. The total number of cigarettes that respon-dents had actually smoked was approximately 20 per day in Means et al.'s study, and this may have militated against stronger effects.[7]

---

[7] In an earlier study, Means et al. (1989), identified respondents who could recall an undifferentiated group of visits to an HMO but could not recall the individual visits within it. Asking these respondents to imagine the final visit, and then the initial visit, and then subsequent visits to the HMO successfully increased recall for visits within the group. Although Means et al. also referred to this technique as *decomposition*, it seems to have less to do with the recall-and-estimate strategies just discussed than with the amount of time or effort that respondents spent on retrieval.

Retrieval Cues

Discrimination net theories such as Kolodner's predict that people are more apt to retrieve a specific event if they have cues that are distinctive to the event and that match its original encoding. There are clearly limits to the extent to which surveys can provide respondents with cues that will be helpful in these respects, since surveys can't tailor questions to individual respondents' encoding. In some situations, however, surveys can take advantage of the overall effectiveness of certain prompts.

On logical grounds, the most effective type of cue will depend on the goal of the retrieval task. On one hand, if the aim is to retrieve properties of a *specific event*, then the most distinctive cue (consistent with the event's initial encoding) should work best. For example, suppose your task is to remember whether you received a vaccination during your last trip to your HMO. Then the best cues will single out that trip and no others. Studies of autobiographical memory (Brewer, 1988; Wagenaar, 1986) suggest that the most effective cue will often be one that states what went on (e.g., you consulted an internist about an infection); less effective are cues for other people involved in the event (e.g., Dr. Wigton) and where the event took place (e.g., the HMO office on King Drive); least effective are cues to the time of the event (June 25, 1994). The cue for what went on is most distinctive and probably more closely constrains other aspects of the event. Person and place cues are less distinctive (there may be many events that took place with Dr. Wigton or at the HMO location). Time cues are potentially most distinctive. But for reasons that we will take up in the next chapter, events are rarely encoded with precise dates; hence, time cues fail to make contact with the target event.

On the other hand, if the aim of memory search is to find *as many events* as possible that are associated with a given cue, then less distinctive cues (cues that match many incidents) may be superior. If you have to recall as many health-care visits as possible, for example, then you may be better off starting with a cue that will remind you of many visits. Barsalou's (1988) preliminary study suggests that locations (the HMO office) prompt more events than activities (having a checkup) or broad times (weekdays), and these cues in turn prompt more events than participants, although the differences between cue types are not large. We also noted that autobiographical periods can provide fast access to events when the task is to find *any* event that meets the description. In line with this, Means et al. (1989) found that asking respondents to construct a time line containing important personal events helped them recall HMO visits that they had not previously been able to report; however, Chu et al. (1992) reported no facilitation for "key events" in a study of hunting and fishing activities.

Implications for Survey Practice

Table 3.2 summarizes our discussion of the factors that affect retrieval and traces out their implications for survey practice. For example, one implication of the impact of the passage of time (and the distinctiveness of the target events) is that the length of the reference period should be tailored to the frequency of the events. To elicit accurate reports about minor purchases, say, a shorter reference period is needed than if the question concerns major purchases. Aside from manipulating the length of the reference period, questionnaire designers can sharpen the boundaries of the reference period (by providing temporal landmarks or using bounded recall procedures), provide more or better retrieval cues (e.g., by using a life events calendar), or encourage respondents to spend more time on the task. (See Jobe et al., 1993, for a more extended discussion on survey findings on autobiographical memory.)

3.4   Summary

A theme that runs through this chapter and the next two – on placing events in time and making estimates based on autobiographical memories – is that memory for experience is intertwined with general knowledge; similarly, the process of remembering what actually happened is inextricably bound up with the process of inferring what probably happened. Inferences based on general knowledge guide the search of memory for relevant facts by specifying or elaborating partial descriptions of the events we seek, and they fill out the information we retrieve when recall is fragmentary. As time passes, it may be impossible to separate what we experienced from what we inferred. Whatever its exact structure, autobiographical memory must be set up to permit this retrieval–inference interaction; the events it stores are indexed in several ways in terms of basic-level event types, autobiographical sequences, lifetime periods, and key details such as participants and locations.

Respondents will have a better chance of recalling an event when they have cues that distinguish the target event from similar ones and that match the event's original encoding. These goals will be easier to achieve when the event is distinctive or when it's important enough to the re-

TABLE 3.2 Summary of Factors Affecting Recall

Variable	Finding	Implication for Survey Design
Characteristics of Event		
Time of occurrence	Events that happened long ago harder to recall	Shorten the reference period
Proximity to temporal boundaries	Events near significant temporal boundaries easier to recall	Use personal landmarks, life events calendars to promote recall
Distinctiveness	Distinctive events easier to recall	Tailor length of the reference period to properties of the target events; use multiple cues to single out individual events
Importance, emotional impact	Important, emotionally involving events easier to recall	Tailor length of the reference period to the properties of the target events
Question Characteristics		
Recall order	Backwards search may promote fuller recall	Not clear whether backward recall better in surveys
Number and type of cues	Multiple cues typically better than single cue; cues about the type of event (what) better than cues about participants or location (who or where), which are better than cues about time (when)	Provide multiple cues; use decomposition
Time on task	Taking more time improves recall	Use longer introductions to questions; slow pace of the interview

spondent to receive elaborate encoding initially. Survey reseachers obviously have no control over the way respondents encode events. Still, the success of bounding procedures, personal landmarks, and life event calendars indicates that surveys can exploit distinctive events that occur naturally. In addition, surveys can offer retrieval cues in the questions, via decompostion, or from prior interviews to aid recall.

CHAPTER FOUR

Answering Questions about Dates and Durations

A glance at several national surveys reveals a large number of questions that ask respondents about the time of an event. For example, the National Crime Survey asks Question (1) for each crime victimization that the respondent reports:

(1) In what month did (this/the first) incident happen? (Show calendar if necessary. Encourage respondent to give exact month.) [NCS]

We presented similar questions in Chapter 3. Equally common are questions, such as (2), concerning the duration of a state or event:

(2) How much time did you lose because of injuries? [NCS]

These probes for a time point or duration, common as they are, aren't the only questions that require respondents to consider when or how long ago events occurred. Many survey items specify a reference period and ask whether or not an event of a given type occurred within it, or they specify a duration and ask whether an event or state lasted for a longer or shorter time. In answering Questions (3) and (4), for example, a respondent doesn't have to supply a date or duration but must still determine the time of the occurrence or the length of time:

(3) Did the accident happen during the past 2 years or before that time? [HIS]
(4) *IF RETIRED, IN SCHOOL, KEEPING HOUSE, OR OTHER*: Did you ever work for as long as one year? [GSS]

We refer to yes/no questions like (3) and (4) as time *verification* items and to questions like (1) and (2) that demand an explicit time point or interval as *direct* time items.

This chapter examines the cognitive processes involved in answering direct and verification questions about time and their impact on survey accuracy. As a preliminary step, Section 4.1 presents a typology for the time questions that we have found in surveys.[1] Section 4.2 reviews cognitive theories about how people answer such questions, and Section 4.3 applies these theories to two practical difficulties in surveys – telescoping and seam effects in panel studies.

4.1   A Typology of Temporal Questions

So far we've been able to treat events as if they occupied points on a time line. Figure 3.1 in the previous chapter showed individual events, such as doctor's visits, as single moments within the reference period. To understand the full range of time questions, however, we need to elaborate this view to allow for states and events that have their own duration.[2] Having a job, being on layoff, living at a particular address, being ill, having an injury, being in the hospital, and serving in the military are all states whose durations are the targets of questions in national surveys. It is natural to ask how long these states lasted and when they took place. Questions about when a state occurred require respondents either to specify the beginning and ending points of the interval or to specify some standard unit of time that includes the state's full duration. Thus, a respondent could give the time of a spell of unemployment as occurring between March 1 and May 1, 1998, or in the spring of 1998.

States and events thus occupy an envelope in time whose duration can range from a single moment to a protracted interval. When survey questions have to pin down particular instants within the interval, they typically use words like *begin, start, stop, end, finish,* and *complete,* which linguists call *aspectualizers* or *aspect markers* (Binnick, 1991; Dowty, 1979). Events can also occur over discontinuous intervals or in

---

[1] To determine the kinds of time questions in surveys, we canvassed the National Crime Survey, the U.S. Health Interview Survey, the Quarterly Interview of the Consumer Expenditure Survey, the General Social Survey, and the Current Population Survey.

[2] Philosophers and linguists distinguish states from events, partly on grammatical and partly on conceptual grounds. States (e.g., being ill, living in Cincinnati, knowing Reid Hastie) don't have agents and hence don't appear in certain grammatical constructions. It sounds odd to say, for example, *Have chicken pox!* or *What Lily did was have chicken pox.* By contrast, events have agents and can normally appear in these constructions. Visiting a doctor, moving to Cincinnati, and shaking hands with Reid Hastie are all events, and it is possible to say (e.g.), *Visit a doctor!* and *What Lily did was visit a doctor.* See Binnick (1991) and Dowty (1979) for discussion.

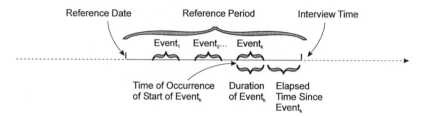

Figure 4.1. A time line for survey questions.

series of like events. For example, writing a book is an event that can take place in interrupted stints over a period of years. Visiting museums is a series of events, each a separate museum visit. Questions about the duration of a discontinuous event or series of events are potentially ambiguous because we can calculate the length of time with or without the gaps. It might take three years from beginning a book to finishing it but only six months of physical writing activity. If so, then either *three years* or *six months* could serve as a correct answer to the question *How long did it take to write that book?*

Figure 4.1 elaborates on Figure 3.1, summarizing our characterization of the temporal dimension of events. As before, we distinguish the interview time and the reference period, but we allow individual events to occupy their own interval (possibly discontinuous). Each event has an inception and a termination point, whose time we can query separately (e.g., *When did you start writing the book? When did you finish writing the book?*). For event series, it is possible to pick out separate events with ordinal adjectives, such as *first* and *last*, and even to combine them with aspect markers (*When did you finish writing your first book?*). This flexibility in naming events is helpful in survey contexts.

4.1.1   Types of Temporal Questions

There are four main types of direct time questions that appear in surveys:

- Time-of-occurrence questions (e.g., *On what date did the event happen?*);
- Duration questions (*How long did the event take? How long did the state last?*);
- Elapsed-time questions (*How long since the event?*);

- Temporal-frequency questions (*In how many* [shorter time units] *per* [longer time unit] *did the event occur?*).

Each of these types has verification counterparts (e.g., *Did the event happen on this date? Did it take longer/less time than this interval? Did it occur longer ago/more recently than this interval? Did the event occur in more/fewer [shorter units] per [longer unit] than this rate?*).

The first three types of temporal questions map directly into segments of the time line in Figure 4.1. Time-of-occurrence items ask about the time of an event (or time point within an event, such as its beginning or end). Duration items query the time between the beginning and end of an event or state. Elapsed-time items query the time between the end of the event and the time of the interview. Example (1) is a time-of-occurrence item, and Example (2) is a duration item. Example (5), from the Health Interview Survey, is an elapsed-time question:

(5) ABOUT how long has it been since _____ LAST went to a dentist? [HIS]

Temporal rate questions are ones like (6) that ask respondents to count or estimate the number of time units in which some event occurred. They differ from other questions about rates or frequencies in that the numerator (as well as the denominator) of the rate is a temporal unit, such as hours:

(6) In the weeks that _____ worked, how many hours did _____ usually work per week? [CE]

Of course, other questions about rates – for example, *How many glasses of wine do you drink per week?* – are clearly related to temporal rates. Research on judgments of frequency, however, is an active endeavor that deserves a chapter of its own (see Chapter 5).

From the four types of direct questions in the preceding list, we can get the corresponding verification questions by specifying some date, interval, or rate and asking about its relation to the target event. For example, Question (3) is a verification question about elapsed time, since it asks whether an event (an accident) happened in the last two years or before (i.e., whether or not it happened less than two years ago). Question (4) is a verification question about duration, which asks whether an activity (working) lasted longer than one year. Verification questions about time of occurrence (e.g., *Did you receive food stamps in August*

1996?) and rates (*Do you usually work more than 35 hours per week?*) also appear in surveys.

4.1.2 Time-of-Occurrence Questions

Time-of-occurrence questions can take a variety of forms; they vary not only in how they describe the target event, but also in the precision with which they specify a possible answer. Direct time-of-occurrence items can ask for the exact time of day, for the date (day, month, and year), for just the month and year, and so on. In addition, these questions can specify a reference period in which the target event takes place. The reference period restricts the time that the question probes, asking when *within this time* the event occurs.

The following schema indicates the diversity of direct time-of-occurrence questions in national surveys. We indicate optional elements in parentheses and alternative choices by a vertical list of items in brackets:

(7)

$$\text{(Within ref period,)} \begin{bmatrix} \text{when} \\ \text{in what dated unit} \end{bmatrix} \text{did} \left(\begin{bmatrix} \text{first} \\ \text{next} \\ \cdot \\ \cdot \\ \cdot \\ \text{last} \end{bmatrix} \right)$$

$$\text{event} \begin{bmatrix} \text{occur} \\ \text{begin} \\ \cdot \\ \cdot \\ \cdot \\ \text{end} \end{bmatrix} ?$$

In this schema, *dated unit* can refer to an exact day, month, and year or to a coarser date (e.g., just month and year or just year). For example, Question (1) from the National Crime Survey – *In what month did (this/ the first) incident happen?* – has this form, with the dated unit specified as *month*. The question allows the interviewer to insert *first* in case the respondent reports more than one incident of the same type. No reference period is specified in Question (1) itself, but an earlier introduction restricts the incidents to those that occurred in the last six months. We note that respondents can answer the *when* version of this question with elapsed time (e.g., three months ago) rather than an exact date (September 1998), depending on the response options that the interviewer gives.

The verification version of time-of-occurrence questions could name the dated unit and ask whether the event occurred then (e.g., *Did the incident happen to you in August 1996?*). However, questions like this are rare in surveys. It is much more common to specify a reference period and ask whether the target event occurred within it.

4.1.3   Questions about Duration and Elapsed Time

Our review of national surveys suggests that questions about duration are the most common direct time items. Although researchers could compute the answers to these items from the answers to time-of-occurrence questions (subtracting the date of the beginning from the date of the end of an event or state), survey designers generally prefer to obtain the duration directly. The critical issues that motivate many of these questions are worker productivity and health status, and for these issues what's important is the length of a spell of unemployment or illness, not necessarily when the spells occurred. In the next section, we consider whether respondents are more likely to keep track of such information in terms of their duration or their onset and offset.

Direct duration questions appear in two slightly different forms that treat time as either continuous or discrete. In the continuous version, the question asks how long the state or event lasted – that is, how *much* time the event consumed – whereas in the discrete version, the question is how *many* temporal units (e.g., hours or days) the event took. Phrases like *how long* or *how much time* typify the continuous questions, as in (2), and phrases like *how many days (months, etc.)* typify the discrete questions. The former seem more appropriate for a state, such as being on layoff, whereas the latter seem best for repeated or discontinuous events, such as purchasing lunch at school.

The schema in (8) shows the common patterns for both continuous and discrete duration questions. The continuous form asks how much time, how long, or what the total time was, whereas the discrete form asks how many temporal units the event took. In our sample of surveys, the temporal units mentioned vary widely, including years, months, weeks, days, and even nights (for hospital stays and vacation trips).

(8)

$$\text{(Within ref period,)} \left(\begin{bmatrix} \text{exactly} \\ \text{about} \end{bmatrix} \right) \begin{bmatrix} \text{how much time} \\ \text{how long} \\ \text{what total time} \\ \text{how many temp units} \end{bmatrix}$$

$$\text{did} \left(\begin{bmatrix} \text{first} \\ \text{next} \\ \cdot \\ \cdot \\ \cdot \\ \text{last} \end{bmatrix} \right) \begin{bmatrix} \text{event take} \\ \text{state last} \end{bmatrix} ?$$

This schema accounts for virtually all the direct duration questions in our sample.[3] Verification questions about duration also appear with respect to the length of time that the respondent worked or was ill. Question (4) provides an example. We can also consider the National Crime Survey's "Did you stay overnight in the hospital?" as a yes/no duration question.

Many duration questions use *about* to inform respondents that they can give an approximate answer. The opposite directive – asking respondents for the exact amount of time – also occurs in survey questions, although much less frequently. For example, the Current Population Survey asks, "Exactly how many weeks had you been on layoff?" Similarly, in Question (1) the interviewer is supposed to "encourage respondent to give exact month." The force of *about* or *exactly* in these questions probably depends on the coarseness of the temporal units and the type of event or state. In general, more fine-grained units (e.g., minutes) demand more precision than coarser ones (hours), and events whose durations are (or ought to be) well known demand more precision than those whose durations are obscure. *How many minutes did you work last week?* seems to require a more exact answer than *How many hours did you work last week?* And *How many hours did you work last week?* requires a more exact answer than *How many hours did you complain to coworkers last week?* (See Sadock, 1977, 1981, for an analysis of the

---

[3] Exceptions are questions about the length of a period covered by a paycheck or bill. For example, the Consumer Expenditure Survey asks, "What period of time is covered by the regular payments [for health insurance]?" and "What period of time was covered by the [telephone] bill?" These questions demand a duration, such as month or year, but are associated with regularly repeated intervals, unlike the questions that Schema (8) represents. They are closely related to questions about temporal rates, which we discuss later in the chapter.

pragmatics of expressions of approximation.) The use of *about* or *exactly* cancels or modifies the implicatures conveyed by the temporal units.

Duration questions are closely related to what we have called elapsed-time questions, since elapsed time is the duration of the interval between an event and the interview. It is also possible to calculate elapsed time from time of occurrence, and perhaps for this reason, direct elapsed-time questions are not common in the surveys we've examined. We show the general form in (9):

(9)

$$\text{(Within ref period,)} \left(\begin{bmatrix} \text{exactly} \\ \text{about} \end{bmatrix} \right)$$

$$\begin{bmatrix} \text{how long since} \\ \text{how long ago since} \\ \text{how many temp units since} \end{bmatrix} \left(\begin{bmatrix} \text{first} \\ \text{next} \\ \cdot \\ \cdot \\ \text{last} \end{bmatrix} \right) \text{event} \begin{bmatrix} \text{occurred} \\ \text{began} \\ \cdot \\ \cdot \\ \text{ended} \end{bmatrix} ?$$

Although all the variations in this schema are possible questions, only a few appear in our sample. Question (5) – "ABOUT how long has it been since _____ LAST went to a dentist?" – is one of a small number of elapsed-time items. These questions may be rare because questions of the form *When did it happen?* can do double duty as time-of-occurrence and elapsed-time questions. Data from Huttenlocher et al. (1990) suggest that respondents prefer giving elapsed time rather than time of occurrence in answering the question *When did the interview take place?* By contrast, verification questions about elapsed time are quite frequent if we count ones of the form *Did the event occur within (during) the last n weeks (months, etc.)?*, as in Question (3).

4.1.4 Questions about Temporal Rates

Survey researchers are sometimes interested in the normal amount of time that the respondent spends on an activity rather than the actual amount of time during the reference period. So, instead of asking a question about duration (e.g., *How many hours did you work last week?*), they ask questions about rates (*How many hours do you work per week?*). Such questions are based on the assumption that respondents are likely to know certain rates directly, especially if the rate is fixed in advance rather than calculated after the fact. Thus, questions about temporal rates appear in our sample most often in connection with hours of work, since respondents often keep track of this rate because of pay schedules. Other rate questions involve number of hours of sleep per night and number of weeks of work per year.

Rate questions nearly always contain *usually* or some other expression that indicates a central tendency or normal value (e.g., *on average*). In fact, rate questions often stress this expression in the same way that duration questions stress *about*. For example, the Current Population Survey asks, "How many hours per week do you USUALLY work at your (main) job?" Asking *How many hours do you USUALLY work per week?* rather than the simpler *How many hours do you work per week?* implies that the rate may vary and that what is sought is the typical rate. Roughly speaking, the former question is supposed to mean *For most weeks (during some reference period), what was your work rate?* (cf. Lewis, 1975). *Usually*, like *about*, may also cue respondents that they can estimate the answer. Both expressions seem to imply a degree of imprecision or approximation: If *about* means *almost exactly* (Sadock, 1981), then *usually* means *almost always* (Lewis, 1975).

The general pattern of these rate questions is presented in (10), where the temporal units in our sample are normally hours per week or weeks per year:

(10)   (Within ref period,) on how many short temp units per long

temp unit did event $\left(\begin{bmatrix} \text{usually} \\ \text{on average} \end{bmatrix}\right)$ occur?

A few related questions ask how often a particular kind of event happens (e.g., a mortgage or insurance payment). But these questions call for answers in terms of events per temporal unit (e.g., payments per month) rather than amount of time per unit, and we consider them along with other frequency questions in the next chapter. Verification questions about temporal rates are possible, although (11) is the only clear example in our sample.

(11) Do you USUALLY work 35 hours or more per week (at your job) (at all jobs combined) (in the family business or farm)? [CPS]

4.2 Cognitive Processing of Temporal Questions

How do respondents answer time questions of the sort we have just catalogued? We strongly suspect that there is no one answer to this question and that even if we limit consideration to one type of temporal question (say, time-of-occurrence questions), we will find that respondents use many strategies to answer it. If we ask a respondent in what month a particular crime incident occurred, as in Question (1), he or she could come up with an answer by (a) recalling the circumstances of the incident, noting that it was very warm then, and using the temperature to infer that it took place in August; (b) recalling that the incident took place just after a child's birthday party and inferring that it therefore took place in July; (c) realizing that the incident caused another – for example, repair or replacement of an item damaged in the incident – and using the date of the repair to estimate the prior date; (d) using a general feeling about the clarity of the incident to estimate that it took place two months ago; or (e) directly remembering the date, perhaps from writing it down on the police report. It seems plausible that respondents sometimes use each of these strategies (and many others) in dealing with time-of-occurrence questions, although not with equal frequency. The same is true of duration questions, if only because people can use strategies for time of occurrence to estimate duration (by recalling the beginning and end of the target event and calculating the difference). This frustrates an attempt to propose a simple theory for time questions that is true to the cognitive goings-on underlying respondents' answers.

Our approach is to admit that people bring to bear different sources of information and integrate them to derive an estimate. Although the specific information they use is idiosyncratic, the types of information and the integration rules have some generality. Specifically, respondents draw on four kinds of information to answer temporal questions:

- *Recall of exact temporal information* (such as a date of occurrence);
- *Recall of relative order information,* such as the fact that an event occurred near some *temporal landmark* or as part of an *extended event* that includes some other incident that can be dated;
- *Recall of other details* from which some temporal information (such as the season of the year) can be inferred;
- *Impressions based on the retrieval attempt,* from which temporal inferences can be drawn (such as the inference that because the memory of an event is sketchy, the event must have happened some time ago).

Information of various types is drawn from memory (and perhaps supplemented with information from written records) to establish initial constraints on the answer to a time question. Respondents add new information as it becomes available to constrain the answer further until they have satisfied the criteria for an acceptable response. We can model this process as a constraint-satisfaction procedure or as a set of interlocking inductive inferences (Collins & Michalski, 1989) in which each bit of information interacts with others to modify the result. The spirit of this proposal is similar to that of work in AI on understanding temporal relations in text and in plans (e.g., Allen & Kautz, 1985).

We intend our hypothesis about answering time questions to coincide with our conclusions about autobiographical memory in Chapter 3: Recalling personal information consists of developing partial descriptions of events that aid the retrieval of additional information in a cyclic fashion (see also Conway, 1996). The information added in each cycle imposes new constraints on our picture of what happened. These partial descriptions include, in particular, temporal information that can help us retrieve further information about when the event took place. Integrating the new facts with the earlier ones often gives us a boost in determining time points and extents.

As an example of the type of process that we have in mind, consider the problem that one of us recently faced (while filing an insurance claim) in answering the question *When did you buy your car radio?* Some of the steps were these: The car is a 1993 model, bought new, and I purchased the radio from a separate dealer just after buying the car. So 1993 is a strong possibility for the year. But, second, car manufacturers release car models for a particular year before the beginning of that calendar year, and this means that 1992 is also a possible year for the purchase. I recall purchasing the car, however, at the end of its model year in order to save some money. In addition, I bought the car for commuting to my new job a couple of months before starting that job in September. Since I've now (July 1996) worked at this job for nearly three years, I must have bought both the car and the radio during the summer of 1993. That's consistent with the considerations about the model year. Furthermore, I can now remember taking my daughter with me to get the radio and playing miniature golf with her while it was being installed. This helps confirm the summer date of the purchase. It might be possible to narrow the date further by pursuing some of these details. My daughter's birthday is in August, and perhaps there was some relation between the miniature golf trip and the birthday. But if so, I can't currently recall it. Given all this information, July or August 1993 seems a reasonable answer.

Figure 4.2 illustrates some of this retrieved information schematically.

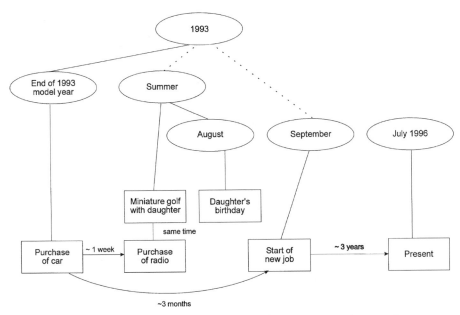

Figure 4.2. An example of retrieved information relevant to answering questions about the time of occurrence of an event (the purchase of a car radio).

Events, such as the purchase of the radio and the start of the new job, appear in rectangles, and dated units (e.g., 1993, summer) in ellipses. Arrows among events (and between events and units) show temporal relationships, which can be metric (e.g., three years before) or merely ordinal (before, during, after). The metric information needn't be exact, but it may take the form of upper and lower bounds (one to three months before) or approximations (about two months). This retrieved information provides the basis for inferences that determine the answer to the time-of-occurrence question. For example, if the car purchase occurred at the end of the 1993 model year and the end of the 1993 model year was in 1993, then the car purchase was in 1993. If the radio purchase occurred just after the car purchase, then the radio must also have been purchased in 1993.

The diagram also illustrates a number of points about locating events in time that we explore later. First, the retrieved information may yield several potential routes to an estimated date (e.g., through the car model or through the start of the new job). In the example, this information is consistent; however, the different routes could lead to inconsistent answers, prompting new inferences to reconcile them. Constraints from these routes are "soft" in that some could turn out to be erroneous. Second, the retrieved dated units are diverse, including independent year and season information. This means that it is possible to be correct about the season in which the event happened but incorrect about the year. This independence of dated units accords with the results of a number of experiments (e.g., Friedman & Wilkins, 1985). Finally, the response depends on information about the event itself (i.e., the radio purchase), relations to other events (e.g., the car purchase, the start of the job), and general knowledge about event types (e.g., that people play miniature golf in the summer) and temporal facts (e.g., if a brief event occurs just after another event, the date of the first must be close to the date of the second). (See Friedman, 1993, and Thompson et al., 1996, for similar *reconstructive* theories.)

There seems to be no limit to the types of facts that can be used to determine the answer to a time question, but they must eventually connect to specifically temporal information if any answer to such questions is forthcoming. For that reason, we concentrate in this section on relevant types of temporal information in memory. We follow the preceding section in organizing our discussion according to information about time of occurrence, duration, and elapsed time. There seems to be no research that specifically targets temporal rates. We discuss related work on the use of rates in frequency estimates in the next chapter.

4.2.1   Memory Information for Time of Occurrence

It is pretty clear that we don't store each event we experience with an explicit date, although the evidence against this possibility is less conclusive than we might like (see Friedman, 1993, for a discussion of this issue). Perhaps the most compelling evidence comes from studies in which participants must produce a date for a personal event and then report the procedure they used to arrive at the date. This methodology is open to the usual objection against retrospective reports of mental processes: Some reports may be after-the-fact theorizing on the subjects' part (Nisbett & Wilson, 1977). Nevertheless, the results suggest that participants usually don't mention deriving the date simply by retrieving it (Burt, 1992a; Friedman, 1987; Thompson et al., 1996). We summarize this evidence in Table 4.1, which lists the percentage of reported strategies that subjects use in dating events they've experienced. In Burt's

TABLE 4.1 Percentage of Response Strategies for Dating Events, by Study

Strategy	Baddeley et. al (1978)	Friedman (1987) Month	Day of Month	Burt (1992a)	Thompson et al. (1996) Recent (1–100 Days Old)	Old (>1 Year Old)
Recall of exact date	—	10	10	21	21	3
Use of landmark event	21	26	30	10	28	12
Use of temporal period	32	53	8	—	37	56
Guessing	—	2	41	49	5	21
Other	47	9	11	20	9	8

(1992a) study, for example, participants reported retrieving dates for about 21% of personal events, where the events spanned an interval of several years. The subjects in this experiment were people who kept personal diaries, and these diaries provided the stimulus items. Since diary keepers may be especially well attuned to dates, these figures may overestimate the normal rate at which people retrieve dates for life events. A hint that this is so comes from Friedman's (1987) study of people's memory for the date of an earthquake they had experienced nine months before. Only 10% of participants reported directly retrieving the month or the day of the month of the event. When people *do* retrieve dates, however, their accuracy is usually good. Participants were correct on 73.5% of trials in Burt's study when they said they had retrieved an explicit date.

Temporal Landmarks

Despite the fact that people don't often retrieve exact dates, they still do fairly well in locating the time of personal events. In Burt's experiment with diary keepers, participants assigned the correct date (year, month, and day of the month) to events on only 5.3% of trials; yet the correlation between the reported date and the correct date was extremely high ($r = .92$). If participants don't remember exact dates, then how do they achieve this level of accuracy?[4] One obvious suggestion is that, although people don't remember the exact date of every event, they remember dates (or can determine them accurately) for certain landmark events and use these landmarks to date less important events nearby. In Figure 4.2, the start of a new job played this landmark role: The event to be dated (purchasing the car radio) connects causally to the new job, since the radio was bought to make commuting to the job more pleasant. Because it's easy to assign a date to the beginning of the job, it is possible to work backward in time to date the radio purchase.

Landmarks could include individual events of special importance (a wedding, the birth of a child, the death of a family member or friend) and calendar-bound events, such as holidays and birthdays (see Shum, 1998, for an extended discussion). Table 4.2 shows the most frequent items that two groups of (mostly freshmen) students produced when asked to list up to six landmark events that had occurred to them in the last year (Shum, 1997). *Landmark events* were defined for the students simply as special times that "stand out from the more ordinary or mundane events that happen to us." The first column of percentages comes from a group of students tested in September 1996; the second comes from a similar group tested in January 1997. Important incidents for freshmen tend to be those associated with the transition between high school and college (Kurbat, Shevell, & Rips, 1998; Pillemer et al., 1986, 1988), and many of the listed events concern high school graduation, acceptance by colleges, moving to college, first day at college, and so on. The remaining nonschool incidents include attending a prom, beginning or ending a romantic relationship, receiving news of the death of a friend or relative, and going on a vacation. The only calendar-based event these students listed was their birthdays. It's possible, though, that the landmarks people use in dating events may differ from those they think of in responding to this more general question.

The frequency with which people report using landmarks to date events varies across studies from 10% (Burt, 1992a) to about 30% (Friedman, 1987; Thompson et al., 1996), as Table 4.1 indicates. Part

---

[4] Caution is necessary here, however, since not all studies of memory for dates reveal this level of accuracy. For example, White (1982) reports correlations in the range .26–.40 between correct date and estimated date for events in a year of his own life. The difference may be due to the choice of events (White sometimes selected commonplace events to record), to the different range of dates (one year vs. up to nine years), or to the frequency of the events.

TABLE 4.2 Percentage of Students Listing Individual Events as
Landmarks

	% of Students Who Mention Landmark	
Event Description	Students Tested in September	Students Tested in January
High school graduation	55	44
Moving from home to college	54	40
Acceptance at college	30	27
Vacation	21	10
Birthday	20	5
High school prom	16	9
Broke up with boy/girl friend	13	6
Death of friend or relative	8	9
Met boy/girl friend	2	8

Note: Sample sizes were 255 in September and 262 in January.
Source: Data from Shum (1997).

of this variability is due to differences in the retention interval across
experiments, since the use of landmarks decreases with the age of the
event to be dated (Burt, 1992a; Thompson et al., 1996). Some of the
variation across studies, however, could also be due to the way in which
the investigators put the question about dating strategies. Participants
choose their response from a fixed list of alternatives (e.g., *Did you date
the event by directly remembering the date, by using a related landmark
event, by using the general period of time during which the event occurred, etc.?*), and the alternatives offered differ from one study to the
next. A conclusion common to these studies, however, is that landmarks
produce better estimates of the correct date than any other strategy
examined, except for direct retrieval of the date ((Baddeley et al., 1978;
Burt, 1992a; Thompson et al., 1996).

Temporal Periods

Chapter 3 noted that several theories assume that temporal periods
or sequences organize memory for autobiographical events (Barsalou,
1988; Conway, 1996). According to these theories, long-term memory
indexes events according to broad time periods or streams of connected
events. It seems possible that these same periods or extended events
could be helpful in determining the time of an individual event that falls
within them. For example, if you can determine through internal cues

that an event occurred while you were on sabbatical in Burma (and if you know the time of the sabbatical), then you can obtain bounds on when the event happened. Temporal periods other than strictly autobiographical ones can also serve this bounding function: The 1993 model year for cars and the summer season in Figure 4.2 both aid in narrowing the time within which the target event (radio purchase) happened. As in the case of landmark events, some of these temporal periods can be calendar-bound (e.g., fall academic semester), whereas others are specific to individuals (e.g., the period when I lived in California).

Studies of the methods people use to date events suggest that temporal periods are a common source of information (see Table 4.1). In one of the studies that Thompson et al. (1996) describe, participants reported using time periods to date 37% of recent events (1 to 100 days old) and 56% of more remote ones (more than 1 year old). Use of time periods, unlike landmarks, thus increases with the age of the event to be dated, perhaps because of the greater fragility of more specific information. Thompson et al.'s experiments also suggest that time periods produce fairly accurate estimates: Participants who report using temporal periods to date events are less accurate than those who directly retrieve a date or a landmark, but they are more accurate than those reporting any of the other strategies recorded, including counting the number of intervening events, using clarity of memory to estimate time, or using information from the event itself (Thompson et al., 1996, Table 7.2).

Using temporal periods to date events, however, leaves a characteristic mark on the data. If a person's only knowledge of the time of an event is that it falls within a specific interval, then there's a tendency for the person to select a date near the center of the interval as the best guess. The result is that events that actually occurred near the beginning of the interval tend to receive too recent a date, and events that occurred near the end of the interval tend to receive too remote a date. This type of bias appears clearly in experiments in which participants know that the stimulus events are drawn from a specified period, such as the last year (Huttenlocher, Hedges, & Prohaska, 1988; Kurbat et al., 1998; Thompson et al., 1996; White, 1982). However, a micro version of the same effect also occurs if participants can localize the event to a shorter interval within the larger period, such as an academic semester or quarter. Events from the beginning of the quarter receive too recent a date, and events from the end of the quarter receive too remote a date (Huttenlocher et al., 1988; Kurbat et al., 1998). There is a similar phenomenon in estimates of duration and of elapsed time, with longer intervals underestimated and shorter ones overestimated. All these related effects should probably be put down to people's general heuristics for selecting numbers from a bounded scale, and it is sometimes called a *response contraction bias* in the psychometric literature (see Chapter 8 and Poulton, 1989).

Of course, landmark events and temporal periods don't exhaust the information people can use to infer the time of an event. For example, they can use elapsed time to estimate the time of occurrence because of the logical interdependence between the two that we noted earlier. This happened in Figure 4.2 in dating the start of the job three years ago. We will return to estimates of elapsed time in Section 4.2.3, but the set of strategies that people can use in reckoning dates is probably open-ended.

4.2.2   Memory Information for Duration

Despite the close logical relationship between time of occurrence and duration, research on these topics has proceeded independently. Laboratory experiments on duration present participants with intervals of varying lengths (usually less than 10 minutes) and ask them to judge length in ordinary temporal units, to compare two lengths, or to reproduce the original length (see Allan, 1979, and Zakay, 1990, for reviews). For example, a participant might hear auditory start and stop signals bounding a first target interval, a brief pause (the *interstimulus interval*), and then a second target interval. The participant must then decide whether the first or the second target interval was longer. The goal is to account for variables that affect the accuracy of participants' judgments. These variables include the lengths of the target intervals, the length of the interstimulus interval, and the characteristics of events that occur within the intervals. Participants in these experiments either learn beforehand that they will make temporal judgments (a *prospective* or *intentional* condition) or learn about the task after the stimulus presentation (a *retrospective* or *incidental* condition). For our purposes, retrospective judgments are the important ones, since survey respondents rarely know prior to an event that they will later have to report its duration. We also concentrate here on studies of intervals that last for more than one minute, since the processing of very brief intervals is less relevant to surveys and may rely on a different set of psychological processes.

Estimates of the length of a temporal interval usually increase linearly with true duration (e.g., Waterworth, 1985). In some experiments, the intercept of the linear function is greater than 0 and the slope is less than

1, so that participants are overestimating short intervals and underestimating long ones. This phenomenon time researchers call *Vierordt's law* (see Woodrow, 1951). It is controversial, however, whether Vierordt's law reflects anything more than participants' bias to respond with estimates near the center of the stimulus range when they are unsure of the correct answer, another form of response contraction.

Most of the relevant research on the relation between real duration and estimated duration has occurred under prospective conditions, since it is difficult to obtain enough retrospective judgments to plot a psychophysical function. It would be useful to know whether retrospective judgments are also linear in real time. We also lack information about how estimated duration varies with length of the retention interval. Investigators seldom vary the retention interval in these laboratory experiments, probably because they tend to view them as studies of time perception rather than time memory (see Schab & Crowder, 1989, for one exception). Loftus, Schooler, Boone, and Kline (1987) report greater overestimates of the length of a videotaped bank robbery when participants gave judgments after a 48-hour delay (Experiments 1 and 2) than immediately after the viewing (Experiment 3). However, Loftus and her colleagues did not vary the retention interval within a single experiment, and their three experiments differ in other potentially relevant ways besides their retention intervals.

Investigators have adopted a number of theoretical positions to explain the results of these duration experiments (e.g., Block, 1985; Ornstein, 1969; Underwood, 1975). However, one thread that runs through these accounts is that the greater the number of subjective segments in an interval, the longer people judge it to be. The best-known finding of this sort is the *filled-duration illusion*: The larger the number of auditory or visual signals that punctuate an interval, the longer it seems (e.g., Ornstein, 1969, Experiment 1; see also Thomas & Brown, 1974, for brief intervals). Similarly, participants estimate the duration of a list of words as longer if highly salient words partition strings of less salient ones (Poynter, 1983; Zakay, Tsal, Moses, & Shahar, 1994) or if participants have to alternate study tasks within the list (Block, 1985). Other factors, such as the number of items that participants can recall from the intervals, the complexity of the items, the variability in item spacing, and the attentional demands of the task, all have less reliable effects on duration estimates.

The effect of segmentation appears to depend, however, on the characteristics of the event. In one experiment (Boltz, 1995, Experiment 2), participants judged the duration of a TV show that included commercial breaks. When the commercials interrupted natural patterns in the ongoing action, the greater the number of commercials the longer and the less accurate participants' estimates of the show's length. However, when the commercials appeared at the seams of the action, the number of commercials did not lead to greater overestimates. A possible explanation for this result is that commercials added further subjective segments only if they did not coincide with the segments imposed by the action.

This segmentation effect may be closely related to (perhaps a special case of) people's tendency to estimate partitioned quantities as greater than equivalent unpartitioned ones. For example, Tversky and Koehler (1994) document a similar *unpacking effect* in probability estimation: People estimate the probability of an exhaustive set of subcategories (e.g., the probability that Calvin died of heart disease, cancer, or other natural causes) as greater than that of the entire category (Calvin died of natural causes). (See Section 5.3.2 for further discussion.) Similarly, Pelham, Sumarta, and Myaskovsky (1994) describe a *numerosity heuristic*: a tendency to estimate overall quantity (e.g., the sum of a set of numbers) from the number of pieces it encompasses (the number of addends). Such a heuristic might be responsible for the segmentation effect in retrospective judgments if participants fail to attend to specifically temporal characteristics of the original events and therefore have to base their estimates on ancillary information, such as the number of segments they remember. Segments may thus be among the stock of information that people can use as a basis for temporal inferences. In addition, there are many (meta-) beliefs about the passage of time that they could also use to adjust estimates based on the number of segments. For example, people tend to think that intervals filled with unpleasant activities, few activities, monotonous activities, or easy activities seem longer than those filled with pleasant, numerous, variable, or difficult ones (Galinat & Borg, 1987).

Some research on autobiographical memory has also examined whether these laboratory effects generalize to everyday experiences. As an analog of the filled-duration illusion, Burt (1992b) asked participants to estimate the duration of two groups of events that he had culled from the participants' personal diaries. One group consisted of "filled events," each a continuous stream of related activities, such as a hospitalization or an official trip; the other group consisted of "unfilled events," each including two related, but temporally separated, incidents (e.g., receiving an invitation and attending a party, applying for a position and hearing the result). The filled-duration illusion would seem to predict greater signed error (i.e., estimated duration − true duration) for filled than for unfilled events, but the results of the study showed no difference in signed error and somewhat smaller absolute error (i.e., | estimated duration − true duration |) for the filled events.[5] The parallels are unclear, however, between the filled–unfilled distinction in this study and in the earlier lab experiments. What fills the laboratory intervals are sequences of sounds or lights, not causally connected incidents. Moreover, the laboratory filler may exert its effect by dividing the overall interval into parts, and there is no guarantee that the autobiographical filler played the same role. In clarifying the relationship, it would be helpful to know the number of perceived subevents within these autobiographical items.

As Burt points out, the relatively small effects of the retention interval may be due to the fact that participants could use the description of the event as the basis of an estimate for its duration, even if they were unable to recall the event itself. When asked the duration of a specific business trip, for example, a participant could use the usual range of business trips to derive a reasonable guess.

4.2.3   Memory for Elapsed Time

These laboratory studies on perceived duration don't distinguish judgments of duration (how long an event lasted) from judgments of elapsed time (how long ago it took place). Participants give their time judgments just after the end of the event, so elapsed time is minimal and approximately constant during the experiment. For naturalistic events, though, there are two studies that focus on elapsed time – one by Ferguson and Martin (1983) and the other by Huttenlocher et al. (1990). Ferguson and Martin's study concerned public events within the past five years; participants judged how long ago each event had occurred (e.g., "How long ago was Pope John Paul II's visit to the United States?"). The study by Huttenlocher and her colleagues was embedded in a follow-up phone call that took place up to 60 days after a General Social Survey interview. During the call, the interviewer asked respondents, "How many days ago did the interview take place?"

Both studies obtained an elapsed-time version of the usual Vierordt pattern: Recent events received estimates that were too far in the past, whereas older events received estimates that were too recent. As we

---

[5] For a description of these and other error measures, see Chapter 8.

noted in Chapter 3, survey researchers refer to such dating errors as telescoping, presumably because, in survey settings, the errors typically involve events reported as happening more recently than they actually happened; from the vantage point of the interview, the events are seen as closer in time than they really are. But errors in the opposite direction (backward telescoping) are made as well. Backward telescoping is more prominent in Ferguson and Martin's data, forward telescoping in the data of Huttenlocher and her colleagues. This could be due either to the difference in the range of dates (two months versus several years) or to the distinction between public and personal events. The time of a recent personal event, such as an interview, may be easier to discern than that of a recent public event. Our knowledge of most public events is probably less vivid initially than our knowledge of personal experiences and may level off more quickly. If so, lack of information about recent public events could allow more room for backward telescoping.[6]

According to Ferguson and Martin, people compute elapsed time from the time of occurrence of the event, which they encode during the initial experience; according to Huttenlocher and her colleagues, people compute elapsed time directly. Both sets of investigators, however, acknowledge at least implicitly that elapsed time estimates probably depend on both sources of information. According to Ferguson and Martin, people use related events to determine an approximate time of occurrence when no direct calendar information is available for the target item. Huttenlocher and her colleagues lean toward event sequences (see Chapter 3) to explain their respondents' preference for elapsed time over calendar dates in answering the question "When did the interview take place?" The model they propose for elapsed time, however, makes no essential use of these sequences; estimates of elapsed time derive from time-of-occurrence information, subject to rounding and to adjustment for the ends of the stimulus range.

4.3   Indirect Effects of Time on Survey Responses

Difficulties people have in determining the time or duration of events show up in survey data as measurement error, often as unexplained

---

[6] Huttenlocher et al. (1990) also show that respondents round estimates to times that are stand-ins for calendar units (seven days, thirty days) or are multiples of five. Hornik (1981) reports a similar tendency to round to multiples of five in duration estimates. The multiples-of-five strategy does not occur, however, when participants must produce time-of-occurrence answers rather than elapsed times (Skowronski et al., 1994). See Chapter 8 for further discussion of rounding.

bunchings of reported incidents: Plotting the data over the time line reveals that events are overreported at certain periods and underreported at others in ways that researchers can't explain. In this section, we consider two such phenomena – the seam effect and telescoping – that survey researchers have clearly documented, and we examine whether temporal inferences, like those we've discussed earlier, can help account for them.

4.3.1   Seam Effects

The placement of an event in time can have dramatic effects on survey reports, even when the respondents don't have to provide an explicit date or time.[7] One example occurs in longitudinal (or *panel*) surveys, such as the Survey of Income and Program Participation (SIPP) and the Panel Study of Income Dynamics (PSID). These surveys interview each respondent at fixed intervals (or *waves*) and ask the respondent for information about the intervening period. SIPP, for example, interviews respondents three times a year; each interview covers their participation in the labor force and income sources in each of the preceding four months. An individual respondent might be interviewed at the beginning of June to report on employment and income for the months of February, March, April, and May; the respondent would be interviewed again in October and would report on June, July, August, and September; and so on, for a total of seven interviews (Jabine, King, & Petroni, 1990). Figure 4.3a shows part of the interview schedule for one group of respondents. (SIPP includes several rotation groups whose schedules are phase-shifted by one month.)

A problematic feature of such surveys is called the *seam effect* – the tendency for month-to-month changes in the data to concentrate suspiciously in adjacent months that were covered in different interviews. For example, a SIPP respondent interviewed in October about June, July, August, and September (as in Figure 4.3a) would show few changes in income and employment status between adjacent pairs of those months but more changes between May (which was covered by an earlier interview) and June; similarly, more changes would be reported between September and October than between other pairs of adjacent months (e.g., June and July).

Seam effects in SIPP, PSID (Hill, 1987), and the Income Development

---

[7] We're grateful to Adriana Silberstein and Monroe Sirken for pointing out previous studies of the seam effect and to Fred Conrad for comments on an earlier draft of this section.

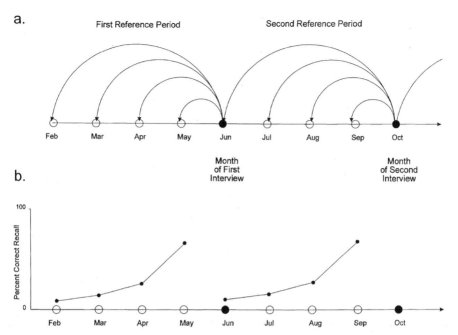

Figure 4.3. (a) Interview schedule for one rotation group in the Survey of Income and Program Participation (SIPP). (b) Hypothetical forgetting curves for information within SIPP reference periods.

Survey Program (Moore & Kasprzyk, 1984) are quite large. Table 4.3 illustrates this in terms of the percentage change from one month to the next on a number of variables collected in SIPP during 1984 (Young, 1989). The first three columns in this table represent changes between adjacent months in the same reference period. The last column is the percentage change between the final month of the old reference period and the first month of the new one – that is, the transition across the interviewing seam. The percentage change on all variables is greater at this point than for any of the within-reference-period transitions. Reports of Social Security income, for example, change by 12% across the seam but by only 1% or 2% within the reference period. The percentages in the table are calculated over all rotation groups, so the differences cannot be due to seasonal trends. (See Martini, 1989, for similar data on employment status.) The seam effect also persists when we look only at data that the same respondent provides about him- or herself in both interviews (Moore & Kasprzyk, 1984), so proxy responding is not the source of the difference.

What factors are responsible for the seam effect? One obvious possi-

TABLE 4.3 Month-to-Month Changes in Income and Other Variables in the SIPP 1984 Full Panel Longitudinal Research Panel

	Percentage Change Between Adjacent Months			
Variable	Month 1 to 2 of Ref. Period	Month 2 to 3 of Ref. Period	Month 3 to 4 of Ref. Period	Month 4 of Old to Month 1 of New Ref. Period
Marital status	0.3	0.3	0.3	0.7
Employment status	4.6	5.0	5.4	10.2
Personal earnings	5.5	6.3	6.4	16.3
Total family income	4.9	5.4	5.7	17.9
Individual Social Security	1.9	1.6	1.8	12.0
Family AFDC* receipt	0.1	0.1	0.1	0.3
Family food stamp receipt	0.2	0.4	0.2	0.9

* AFDC, Aid to Families with Dependent Children.
Source: Young (1989), Table 1.

bility is that memory for the relevant event or quantity decreases across the reference period. Respondents are more likely to remember income they received in the month preceding the interview than income they received four months before the interview. If so, the respondent's data will exhibit a false transition across the seam between adjacent months covered by different interviews. The data in Table 4.3 show a small increasing trend across the first three columns for personal earnings, family income, and employment status, consistent with the idea that respondents remember more changes in the later part of the reference period. (The data in Table 4.3 for changes in marital status, food stamps, and AFDC are too close to zero to be revealing.) The best evidence for forgetting in this context, however, comes from Kalton and Miller's (1991) study of respondents' memory for the amount of their Social Security benefits. An actual increase in benefits during January 1984 was reported by 68.4% of SIPP respondents interviewed in February; however, this percentage decreased to 59.6% for respondents interviewed in March and to 53.0% for respondents interviewed in April. Thus, reports of the change decrease with time, implicating forgetting.

Forgetting might be sufficient to explain the seam effect for some variables, but for others it is unlikely to be the whole story. If forgetting were the only cause of the seam effect, then the change at the seam should approximate the total change within the reference period. We illustrate this effect in Figure 4.3b, which shows hypothetical forgetting curves for the sample rotation group. Respondents report the May data after a one-month interval and the June data after a four-month interval, so forgetting may lead to greater underreporting of income in June and thus to a seam effect. However, respondents also report the February figures after four months. On average, then, the February-to-May change (a four-month difference within an interview) should be about the same as the May-to-June change (a one-month difference across interviews). The data in Table 4.3 don't allow us to calculate precisely the total change within the reference period; however, in the case of Social Security benefits, it's clear that the change within the reference period is too small to explain the change at the seam. Record checks of SIPP data show relatively small effects of forgetting on most variables (Marquis & Moore, 1989).

The forgetting explanation that we've just considered runs into difficulties because it calls for changes within the reference period as well as changes at the seam. This suggests that seam effects may be due in part to respondents' tendency to minimize change *within* the reference period (Kalton & Miller, 1991; Young, 1989). Respondents may simply report their current level of income as the value for previous months in an effort to simplify the task and to avoid memory retrieval. This form of response bias is sometimes called a *constant wave response*. Ross (1988) describes a similar phenomenon – retrospective bias – in autobiographical memory. Lacking detailed memories about earlier periods of our lives, we may extrapolate from our current characteristics (what we eat, how much we drink, what we think about political issues) to our past. If the characteristic is one for which little change is expected (such as political attitudes), we may infer that the past value is identical to the present one. If, on the other hand, the characteristic is one that we expect to change, we may exaggerate the amount of difference between the past and the present in reconstructing the past. For instance, persons who have been through therapy may subsequently exaggerate their pretreatment troubles (see Ross, 1988). A related possibility is that respondents use their current level as a starting point for estimating values from earlier months but fail to adjust sufficiently for intervening changes – an example of the anchoring and adjustment heuristic (Tversky & Kahneman, 1974; see Section 5.1.2 for further discussion).

Constant wave response, retrospective bias, and anchoring-and-adjustment could all produce seam effects since changes will be temporally displaced into the seam. They will also produce correlated errors for data originating from the same interview, with lower correlations for data across the seam (Marquis & Moore, 1989). For example, consider a respondent from the rotation group in Figure 4.3 who begins receiving Social Security income in August, and suppose that during the October interview the respondent reports receiving Social Security for June, July, August, and September. Then the change will appear in the seam between May and June because during the June interview (before receiving the benefit), the respondent reports no Social Security for May. Kalton and Miller's (1991) study of the 1984 Social Security increase provides evidence for displacement of this kind.

Young (1989) showed that the seam effect is different in magnitude for different variables (e.g., food stamp recipiency vs. Social Security income). It seems likely that seam effects are more common when memory retrieval becomes too difficult. The effect varies across questions because retrieval difficulty varies across questions. (Smith & Jobe, 1994, have developed a related model for survey questions about dietary intake.)

4.3.2 Telescoping

We first discussed telescoping – errors in dating events – in Chapter 3, where we considered whether clarifying the boundaries of the reference period could reduce the frequency of such errors. Here we face the issue of why telescoping occurs in the first place.

The most thorough study of telescoping is one of the earliest: Neter and Waksberg's (1964) investigation of respondents' memory for household repairs and modifications. Neter and Waksberg's study was an experimental survey that varied the conditions under which households were interviewed. It compared *unbounded* interviews, which simply asked respondents to provide information about jobs during the reference period, with *bounded* interviews, which provided respondents with a list of jobs from the previous reference period before asking them about the current one. Suppose, for example, that interviews are conducted with a particular respondent in March and again in April. If the April interview is bounded, the interviewer would first inform the respondent of the data that he or she had provided in March and would then inquire about jobs in the current month. If the April interview is unbounded, the interviewer would ask about jobs in the current month with no preliminaries. The reference periods themselves were either one month, three months, or six months long. The premise of the study is that bounding reduces telescoping by discouraging respondents from reporting jobs they'd already reporting in an earlier interview. Thus, the contrast between unbounded and bounded interviews provides a measure of the impact of telescoping in the usual unbounded conditions.

It is worth while to summarize some of Neter and Waksberg's main conclusions. First, the comparison between bounded and unbounded recall for one-month reference periods produced the results in (12):

(12) a. Forward telescoping occurred for both the number of jobs and the total expenditures on them, as indicated by larger reports in the unbounded condition.

b. The amount of forward telescoping was greater for larger jobs.

c. The amount of telescoping was largely unaffected by uncertainties about completion dates of the job, as indicated by similar effects for do-it-yourself jobs and jobs completed by others.

Figure 4.4 shows some of the data supporting these conclusions. The y-axis of this graph indicates the percentage increase in reported number of jobs for the unbounded reference period compared to the bounded period, that is, 100* (jobs reported in unbounded recall − jobs reported in bounded recall)/ jobs reported in bounded recall. This increase is assumed to reflect net forward telescoping. More expensive jobs exhibit a larger increase than smaller jobs, especially for do-it-yourself jobs. If respondents have a more exact notion of when they finished their own jobs than of when contractors finished their work, then precision in knowledge of temporal location does not reduce telescoping. Similar results appeared in the comparison of bounded and unbounded recall for three-month reference periods.

Second, Neter and Waksberg estimated the amount of *internal* telescoping that occurred within the three-month period. Respondents had to assign each job to a specific month within this period, and internal telescoping occurred when they assigned one job to the wrong month. To determine the extent of internal telescoping, the investigators compared the monthly data for the bounded three-month period to the data for bounded one-month periods, making statistical adjustments for possible effects of forgetting. Their conclusions parallel those in (12): Internal (forward) telescoping increased the number of reported jobs and expenditures in the most recent month at the expense of the earliest month within the reference period. Moreover, the extent of telescoping increased with the size but not the type of job (do-it-yourself vs. other).

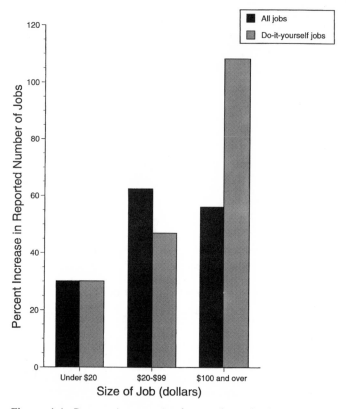

Figure 4.4. Percent increase in the number of jobs reported in 1-month unbounded reference periods compared to bounded 1-month reference periods (after Neter & Waksberg, 1964, Tables 1 and 2). Reprinted with permission from *Journal of the American Statistical Association.* Copyright © 1964 by the American Statistical Association. All rights reserved.

Why do respondents misreport the temporal location of events? Two explanations are possible. The first is that telescoping reflects a subjective distortion of the time line, so that (in forward telescoping) remote events seem closer to the present than they are. The second possibility is that telescoping is due to increasing uncertainty about the time of an event as the elapsed time grows longer.

Temporal Compression

Neter and Waksberg focused their attention on documenting telescoping rather than on explaining it: "This study was concerned mainly with investigating the existence of telescoping and recall losses and measuring their magnitudes, rather than learning about their causes" (Neter & Waksberg, 1964, p. 48). The first important theory of telescoping is due to Sudman and Bradburn, who identified it with time compression: "There are two kinds of memory error that sometimes operate in opposite directions. The first is forgetting an episode entirely. . . . The second kind of error is compression of time (telescoping) where the event is remembered as occurring more recently than it did" (Sudman & Bradburn, 1973, p. 805). Sudman and Bradburn proposed that when respondents try to recall events of (say) the last three months, they in fact consider events from a somewhat longer period. The longer period "feels like" three months to them, enticing them to import earlier events into the reference period. If the true reference period is of length t, then according to Sudman and Bradburn's model, the effective recall period is $t + \log(bt)$, where b is a scaling parameter. This means that if target events occur uniformly on the time line, respondents tend to overreport events by a proportion equal to $\log(bt)/t$. Suppose, for example, that b = 2.5. If respondents must report the number of times they purchased food in the last three months, the effective report period is then 3 + $\log(2.5*3) = 3.88$ months, and the proportion of events the respondent telescopes into the reference period will be $\log(2.5*3)/3 = .29$. The log component in these equations implies that increasing the length of the reference period will *decrease* telescoping. If the reference period in our example is twelve months rather than three, for instance, then the percentage of overreported events is reduced to 12%. This is consistent with Neter and Waksberg's results; their estimates for telescoping were smaller for longer reference periods. Moreover, Sudman and Bradburn's theory also includes a separate forgetting mechanism. Thus, respondents will not necessarily report all the events they have telescoped into the reference period: The number of *reported* events depends on the balance between the increase due to telescoping and the decrease due to forgetting. (See Chapter 3 for a discussion of Sudman and Bradburn's assumptions about forgetting.)

The literature on duration and elapsed time (reviewed in Section 4.2) provides little support for Sudman and Bradburn's psychometric assumption of logarithmic increments in time perception. The usual finding is a linear relation between true and subjective time, with a slope typically less than 1. This implies lengthening of short reference periods and shortening of long ones. Nevertheless, there are several features of the Sudman and Bradburn model that help explain (or at least are consistent with) the conclusions in (12). First, since bounding reduces or eliminates telescoping, the model predicts the observed increase in reports for unbounded versus bounded recall.

Second, respondents' uncertainty about the time of an event need not affect the amount of overreporting due to telescoping, in line with (12c). Events that occur prior to the reference period may be telescoped into it if respondents are uncertain about their time of occurrence. But it is equally true that uncertain events will be telescoped *out of* the response interval, assuming distributions that are roughly symmetric and of equal variance. This is illustrated in Figure 4.5a. Event$_1$ is a hypothetical target event that actually occurred at time$_1$, prior to the beginning of the reference period. Event$_2$ is a second target event that occurred at time$_2$, within the reference period but equally far from its beginning. Suppose that a respondent is unsure of the exact dates but has some sense of approximately when they occurred, represented by distributions of possible dates. When the respondent assigns a date to event$_1$, he or she will sometimes come up with a date that occurs within the reference period. However, when the respondent picks a date for event$_2$, it will equally often be a date *prior* to the start of the reference period. Clearly, this balance between forward and backward telescoping will occur, even if both distributions have much greater or much smaller variance, as long as the variances are equal and the distributions symmetric. Under these conditions, the amount of uncertainty does not affect telescoping.

At first glance, it also seems that Sudman and Bradburn's model should easily predict Neter and Waksberg's finding of greater overreporting for larger jobs (see Figure 4.4). After all, respondents are less likely to forget large, salient jobs than smaller ones, so the data on large jobs should mostly reflect telescoping, whereas the data on small jobs should reflect both telescoping and a countervailing effect of forgetting. Recall, however, that Neter and Waksberg calculated telescoping relative to bounded recall periods. If we hold the length of the reference periods constant, why should there be more forgetting for small jobs in the unbounded period relative to the bounded one? Although Sudman and Bradburn don't address this problem directly, their discussion of Neter and Waksberg suggests that they believe that the bounding procedure (giving respondents their previous reports of home alterations and repairs) may act as a recall cue, enhancing recall for more trivial jobs. Cueing may be less beneficial for large jobs since respondents can recall them readily in any case. If so, we can expect a greater difference in forgetting for small jobs than for large ones in the unbounded relative to the bounded period; this difference in forgetting can offset the effects of

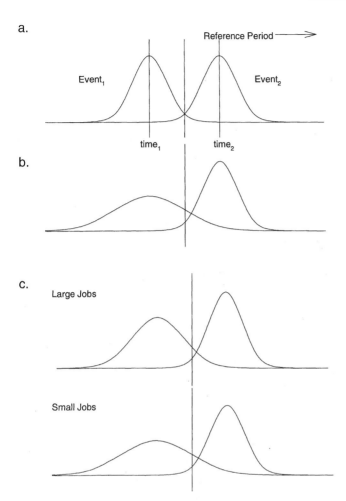

Figure 4.5. Effects of uncertainty about the time of an event on telescoping. The center vertical line represents the beginning of the reference period. Density functions represent a respondent's temporal uncertainty about when an event happened. $Event_1$ occurs at $time_1$, outside the reference period; $Event_2$ at $time_2$, inside the reference period. The area under the $Event_1$ curve to the right of the center line indicates the proportion of forward telescoping, and the area under the $Event_2$ curve to the left of the center line indicates the proportion of backward telescoping. In (a) uncertainty about the two events is equal, and no net telescoping occurs. In (b) the more remote $Event_1$ has greater uncertainty, and net forward telescoping occurs. In (c) a larger increase in uncertainty for small jobs leads to more forward telescoping for small than for large jobs.

telescoping. Thus, Sudman and Bradburn's model gives a reasonable account of (12a) and is consistent with (12c) but needs some additional assumptions to deal with (12b).

Variance Theories

The Sudman–Bradburn theory ascribes telescoping to respondents' misperceiving the length of the reference period, but it is also possible to explain telescoping in terms of uncertainty about when the target events happened. Suppose that a respondent is asked to report how many times he or she purchased food in the last three months. The respondent will typically not be able to remember the exact time of each event but may have an impression of the range of dates on which the event could have happened. To determine whether a specific food-purchasing event occurred during the reference period, the respondent may select a date within this range and compare it to the date of the beginning of the reference period, as we assumed in the discussion of Figure 4.5a. The respondent will count the purchase if the event occurs after the start of reference period and otherwise will not count it. By themselves, however, these response assumptions do not predict net telescoping, as we noted earlier. Although respondents sometimes perceive events that occur prior to the reference period as having occurred within it, they can also make the opposite error (perceiving events in the reference period as occurring prior to it and hence failing to report them). To get telescoping, we need one more assumption: Uncertainty about the time of an event increases with its age. If remote events have larger variance than more recent ones, then it is more probable that a respondent will import a remote item into the response interval rather than export a more recent event.

To see this, consider the time line in Figure 4.5b. Because event$_1$ is older than event$_2$, the respondent may be less clear about when it occurred, as indicated by the difference in variance of the distributions of possible times of occurrence for these purchases. When the respondent picks a date for event$_1$, he or she will fairly often come up with a date that occurs within the reference period (see the proportion of the event$_1$ curve that falls to the right of the reference period boundary). However, when the respondent samples a date for event$_2$, it will be quite rare for the date to be prior to the start of the reference period (the area of the event$_2$ curve that falls to the left of the boundary is small). The result will be net forward telescoping. Huttenlocher, Hedges, and Prohaska (1988) and Rubin and Baddeley (1989) independently proposed models of telescoping based on this assumption. Since these models are quite similar, we refer to them both as the *variance* model.

The variance model certainly predicts telescoping, and it does so under more realistic assumptions about memory for time than does the Sudman–Bradburn model. Rubin and Baddeley, in particular, present independent evidence for the increase in dating error with the age of an event, and many other studies have obtained similar differences (e.g., Baddeley et al., 1978; Burt, 1992a; Linton, 1975; Thompson et al., 1996). Unfortunately, however, the model has difficulties with the telescoping phenomena in (12b) and (12c). Notice, first, that it is natural to suppose that, as time passes, respondents become more uncertain about the timing of small jobs than about the timing of large ones, and this complicates the model's ability to handle (12b). For example, suppose that temporal uncertainty is roughly the same for small as for large jobs that occurred last month, but uncertainty is larger for small than for large jobs that occurred three months ago, as shown schematically in Figure 4.5c. If a respondent is asked to report jobs that occurred within the last two months, he or she should be more likely to telescope the old small job into the reference period than the old large job, contrary to (12b). To predict greater telescoping for large jobs than small ones, the model can invoke forgetting in the same way that Sudman and Bradburn do. But in the context of the variance model, forgetting of small jobs has to completely offset the expected impact of the increase in the small jobs' variance. An analogous problem afflicts the variance model's ability to handle (12c). If respondents become more confused about the time of contract jobs than of do-it-yourself jobs as time passes, this can again lead to the situation of Figure 4.5c and thus to more telescoping for the contract jobs. Neter and Waksberg's data, however, show no such difference.

It seems likely to us that differences in variance play a role in telescoping, but this doesn't seem to be the complete explanation. At best, we can make the variance model consistent with (12) by including a number of ad hoc assumptions, but these seem to have little independent rationale. This is one area of survey methodology that has motivated some research in cognitive psychology, but the connection to the survey phenomena isn't as tight as one might hope.

4.4   Summary

Answering questions about dates generally requires inferences. Events don't appear to us with dates attached; encoding the date of an event takes a special effort – one we don't normally perform since we don't normally need to. In situations where we unexpectedly have to recall the date of an event, our accuracy will depend on how much we remember about the event itself, on how much we remember about its relation to other datable events and periods, on our knowledge of the times of events in its vicinity, and on how much effort we are willing to put into our calculations. Because the information available to us may not fully determine the date or duration, we often have to introduce simplifying assumptions that give rise to characteristic errors. For example, if all we know about an event is that it fell within a particular period, we may give the event a date too near the center of that period. If we have to determine the duration of an extended event and all we can remember is the number of segments it encompassed, the number of segments may inflate our estimate. It is also possible that the information available for dating an event is contradictory, since the information can come from different sources. Fixing a date means satisfying as many constraints as possible, based on our knowledge of the circumstances, and then adding assumptions to fill out the remaining uncertainties.

Shum (1998) has argued that landmark events – special events whose dates are easily remembered – play a central role in organizing autobiographical memory; the data suggest that landmark events improve accuracy in dating neighboring events. Results of methodological experiments in survey settings also confirm that reminding respondents of these landmarks (e.g., the birthday of the respondent or other important personal or public events) improves dating of more mundane events, such as visits to an HMO (Means et al., 1989). Reminding them of temporal periods within which the target event took place may also increase accuracy, but at the expense of response contraction bias. Little is known about ways to improve duration estimates – an unfortunate state of affairs, given the frequency with which questions about duration appear in national surveys.

Cognitive research on dating errors in surveys has focused on telescoping. Recent theories explain telescoping in terms of an increase in uncertainty about the time of older events, and there's little doubt that such an increase occurs. However, the connections between temporal uncertainty and telescoping in surveys are still not clear. Uncertainty predicts more telescoping for minor events than for major ones, but just the opposite occurs. Uncertainty predicts greater telescoping for events whose timing respondents know less about, but there appears to be no such difference. There's an obvious need to resolve these discrepancies before we can feel confident enough about the proposed theories to use them as the basis for recommending remedies in surveys.

By contrast with telescoping, the seam effect is one that cognitive psychologists have ignored, despite hints that response strategies are its source. Although the seam effect leads to errors about when changes occur, it may be due less to respondents' mistakes about temporal location than to their tendency to simplify the task by giving the same response for each temporal interval. When respondents find retrieving the requested information difficult, they may shift to using their current state to estimate earlier states. If so, simplifying retrieval by encouraging respondents to use written records or probing explicitly about changes may help solve this problem.

CHAPTER FIVE

Factual Judgments and Numerical Estimates

Survey questions often require respondents not only to remember auto-biographical events but also to use that information to make judgments. Having remembered the relevant information, the respondent is still not necessarily in a position to answer the question. Instead, the information must be toted up, averaged, combined, or summarized in some way.

This combination process is especially crucial for survey questions that ask about the frequency of some event – for example, how frequently the respondent has visited a doctor, has been the victim of a crime, or has purchased some item. In national surveys, such questions are extremely common – too numerous for us to catalog completely – but here are some examples that give a feel for the range of these items:

(1) During those two weeks, how many times did _____ see or talk to a medical doctor? (Include all types of doctors, such as dermatologists, psychiatrists, and ophthalmologists, as well as general practitioners and osteopaths. Do not count times while an overnight patient in a hospital.) [HIS]

(2) When you were growing up, how often did your father (FATHER SUB-STITUTE) attend religious services?

> NEVER
> LESS THAN ONCE A YEAR
> ABOUT ONCE OR TWICE A YEAR
> SEVERAL TIMES A YEAR
> ABOUT ONCE A MONTH
> 2–3 TIMES A MONTH
> NEARLY EVERY WEEK
> EVERY WEEK
> SEVERAL TIMES A WEEK [GSS]

(3) Since the 1st of (*month 3 months ago*), have you (or any members of your CU) made payments for hospitalization or health insurance policies which you no longer have? *If YES:* How many policies? [CE]

As our examples make clear, there is often a complex interplay between memory and judgment in responding to such frequency items (Bradburn et al., 1987). Sometimes, judgments integrate what people retrieve from memory, summarizing it as an average or a total. For example, some respondents might answer Question (1) about the number of consultations with doctors by recalling specific consultations and summing them. In these cases, the products of retrieval (specific episodes) become the input to the judgment process. In other cases, judgment is a supplement, or even a replacement, for the memory of specific events. The "approximative" terms in the response options in Question (2) – *about, several,* and *nearly* – suggest that the question is seeking an estimate rather than a total of individual incidents. These terms act in exactly the same way as *usually* in the time questions that we studied in Chapter 4. The distinction between answers that are based on specific information retrieved from memory and those that are constructed from more general information runs throughout the judgment literature.

People may also base their frequency judgments on the process of retrieval rather than on its products (cf. Conrad, Brown, & Cashman, 1998, on memory assessments). When retrieval fails to bring to mind any relevant information, people may conclude from that fact that the event in question is rare, a pattern of reasoning Tversky and Kahneman (1973, 1974) labeled the *availability heuristic.*[1]

No other class of judgments relevant to surveys has inspired more research than frequency estimates. Three distinct research traditions have explored how people make such judgments. The first tradition is an outgrowth of the study of recognition memory; it examines the issue of how people retain information about frequency as a consequence of learning lists of items. The second tradition grows out of studies of risky

---

[1] Of course, judgmentlike strategic processes are often involved in memory. The respondent may have to decide whether an event took place within the reference period and whether it meets the other criteria imposed by the question, as in Question (1). Further, having recalled one or more relevant incidents, the respondent must decide whether retrieval is complete (or at least complete enough). If he or she decides that it is not complete, then there is the additional issue of trying to recall the remaining incidents or applying some sort of correction to compensate for the omissions. Similarly, when no events come to mind, the respondent must decide whether this reflects retrieval failure or the absence of any relevant events.

decision making and concerns the accuracy of people's judgments of frequency and probability. In Section 5.1 we look at the implications of these two traditions for survey research. The third tradition springs from survey methodology itself and specifically examines the processes people use in answering survey questions about frequencies. We discuss this approach in Section 5.2. Section 5.3 takes a brief look at questions about the probability that something will happen. Although such questions are closely related to frequency items, they pose some special problems of their own.

5.1   Cognitive Studies of Frequency

Experiments on frequency within cognitive psychology have usually adopted one of two approaches. The first approach – an outgrowth of traditional studies of verbal learning – presents subjects with a list of words to learn, and some of the words are repeated within the list. Subjects must then decide how many times a given word appears or whether one word appears more often than another. The second approach is more direct, quizzing subjects on the frequency of some public, but often little-known, event or object (e.g., the number of deaths per year due to various natural causes or the number of African nations in the United Nations). Whereas the first approach emphasizes the importance of facts about frequency stored in memory, the second emphasizes the judgment heuristics – the rough estimation strategies – that supplement memory.

5.1.1   Memory Studies of Frequency Reporting

Laboratory studies of memory for frequency differ in many obvious ways from the questions about frequency in surveys. The stimuli in the memory studies are typically word lists rather than autobiographical events, and the subject's task is usually to determine the number of repetitions of an individual item (e.g., the number of times the word *potato* appeared). The lag between presentation and recall is typically minutes rather than weeks or months (although see Underwood, Zimmerman, & Freund, 1971, for an exception). And the range of frequencies tends to be quite narrow, often from zero to two or three (e.g., Hintzman & Curran, 1994). In addition, the task itself is sometimes to identify which of two items was presented more often rather than to report the number of times each one was presented.

Perhaps as a result of these differences, researchers have sometimes portrayed remembering frequency as an effortless process. For instance, Hasher and Zacks (1984, p. 1372) argue:

People are surprisingly accurate at answering such questions without being aware of how they acquired the relevant information in the first place. This observation meshes with recent research in human memory to suggest the possibility that the ability to answer such questions stems from . . . the inevitable encoding into memory of certain fundamental aspects of experience.

Among the aspects of experience that people automatically encode, according to Hasher and Zacks, are both frequency of occurrence and the location of experiences in time. Their conclusion about temporal information seems totally at odds with the literature reviewed in chapter 4. Similarly, their hypothesis about frequency diverges widely from those of Tversky and Kahneman (1973, 1974) and Burton and Blair (1991), as we will see momentarily. A more reasonable (but pallid) summary of the memory literature is that effort at encoding and level of accuracy in recall probably vary widely as a function of both the type of information the subject must report and the conditions in force at encoding and test. Even with simple stimuli, such as individual nouns, the average level of underestimation in a memory study reported by Begg, Maxwell, Mitterer, and Harris (1986, Table 1) ranged from 6% to 35%.

A more consistent pattern of results of the memory studies is that subjects tend to underestimate the frequency of stimuli that were actually presented and overestimate the frequency of those that were not presented (Begg et al., 1986; Hintzman & Curran, 1994; Jonides & Naveh-Benjamin, 1987; Underwood et al., 1971). This is a pattern whose analog in the temporal domain we encountered in Chapter 4 (see the discussion of Vierordt's law). In both cases, the result may be due to subjects giving middling values as estimates when they are unsure of the exact quantity. Suppose that you have just seen many different nouns one after another and now have to say how many times (if any) *potato* appeared on the list. If you don't remember *potato* but suspect that your memory for the list items may be imperfect, a safe course is to give a small number as a compromise. If *potato* wasn't on the list, this strategy will produce overestimates; if it was, underestimates.

Researchers in the memory tradition (e.g., Jonides & Naveh-Benjamin, 1987) distinguish two basic accounts of how we make frequency judgments, which we depict in Figure 5.1. According to the first account, frequency information is stored as a separate characteristic of

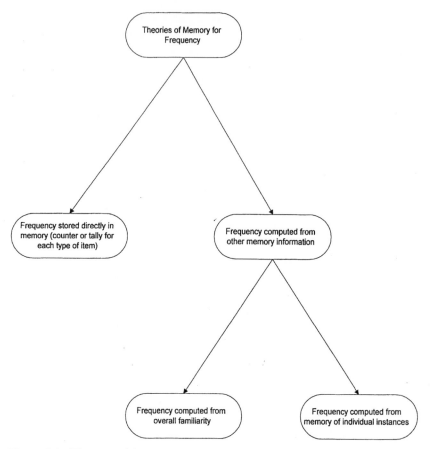

Figure 5.1. Theories of frequency estimation in the memory literature.

an item – a kind of frequency counter – that a person updates each time the item occurs. Just as we update our memory of a nephew's height each time he visits, we might also update a frequency counter tracking the number of visits he has made. This updating might occur automatically (as Hasher and Zacks argue) or it might occur deliberately (Howell, 1973). The second general account sees frequency judgments as a by-product of other information stored in memory. Although people do not store frequency per se, they can compute frequency from other facts that they do remember.

There are two main variants of the second, computed frequency theory, which we show on the right branch of Figure 5.1. The first assumes that people base frequency judgments, as they do recognition decisions, on some underlying dimension of overall familiarity or strength. The other variant assumes that frequency judgments depend on the retrieval of multiple traces that differ in content – individual memories of encounters with the item or event. To derive the frequency from these traces, people might simply add the number of items they recall or they might use the recalled items as the basis of an estimate. Hybrid models are also possible, in which people compute an index of strength at the time of test on the basis of individual traces (Hintzman, 1988).

To draw out the similarity of these hypothesized processes to those recognized in the survey literature, we can categorize the three strategies as (a) recall of an exact tally (whether created deliberately or automatically); (b) estimation based on an impression of an item's familiarity or strength; and (c) retrieval of one or more specific memories, which are then toted up. Notice that the difference between theories (a) and (c) depends on the information available to people when they answer frequency questions. According to the tally view, people have a direct representation of frequency already available; according to the specific memory view, people have memories of particular instances that they must still count up.

For the most part, the evidence from the memory studies suggests that the tally viewpoint does not fully explain frequency judgments. Hasher and Zacks's (1984) case for automatically updated tallies rests largely on two arguments: First, frequency estimates are very accurate; second, their accuracy does not seem to be affected much by the subjects' intention to encode frequency information, the age or cognitive ability of the subjects, or the degree of disruption from other tasks. The first argument is undercut, as we have seen, by the fact that the judgments are not all that accurate; in the aggregate, frequency estimates in the memory studies can be off by 30% or more. The second argument is contradicted by the evidence as well. Encoding instructions can in fact have a large impact on the accuracy of frequency estimates; for instance, subjects who generated synonyms for the test words when they studied them later gave more accurate judgments of their presentation frequency than those who generated rhymes (Jonides & Naveh-Benjamin, 1987). Thus, an account based on automatic tallies runs into considerable difficulty (see Felcher & Calder, 1990, for a thoughtful appraisal of the automatic account). Conscious tallies do not seem to offer a viable alternative either. It seems inconceivable in most of the memory studies that subjects could be consciously keeping a running count of the number of times each item was presented; the sheer number of items (generally, more than 30 in each list) would quickly overwhelm working memory. And when extrapolated to memory for autobiographical frequencies, the tally theory hasn't a chance, since there is an infinite number of possible event types that we can query. As Jonides and Naveh-Benjamin (1987) argue, tallies may be part of the picture but they cannot be the whole story.

Could retrieval of specific items be the key element in explaining frequency judgments? Evidence on this score comes from experiments in which subjects study a long list of nouns drawn from several different categories (e.g., flowers, birds, musical instruments). Subjects then either estimate the frequency of items in each category or recall the items in the same categories. In these experiments, subjects' frequency judgments correlate with the number of category items they can recall even when true frequency is statistically controlled (Bruce, Hockley, & Craik, 1991). This suggests a role for memory of specific items. At the same time, however, the correlation appears too small to explain the accuracy of the judgments (Watkins & LeCompte, 1991). And there are factors, such as the age of the subject, that affect recall but not frequency estimates (Bruce et al., 1991). It thus seems unlikely that memory for specific items is the sole determiner of the frequency responses.

A more probable story is that familiarity and recall of specific items both contribute to the frequency judgments in these studies. Experiments by Hintzman and Curran (1994), for example, suggest that recognition judgments reflect both item familiarity and more specific item information. These experiments timed subjects as they decided whether or not an item had appeared in a previously presented list. When the test item was quite similar to one of the presented items, the rate of false alarms (incorrect "yes" responses) peaked at response times of around 600 milliseconds; thereafter, the false alarm rate declined. According to Hintzman and Curran's theory, the early peak reflects decisions based on the test item's similarity to one of the items that had been presented earlier. The subsequent decline reflects the retrieval of additional information that enabled subjects to distinguish the test items from those presented earlier.

The Hintzman–Curran results suggest that one variable determining which strategy people use to make frequency judgments is the relative accessibility of the necessary information. Impression-based judgments can be made quickly since familiarity information is more accessible than information about the details of the item. Reliance on accessibility or familiarity, however, also leaves a respondent open to error. Although true frequency can increase familiarity, so can factors like ease of perceiving an item, expectation induced by context, and probably many other variables (Jacoby & Whitehouse, 1989; Whittlesea, 1993). Thus, familiarity is an unreliable cue for frequency and can lead people to judge an event as frequent for the wrong reasons. As we're about to see, experiments on judgment and decision making have uncovered exactly the same source of frequency mistakes. To derive a more accurate frequency estimate, people may therefore need to consult less accessible item information.

5.1.2   Studies of Judgment Under Uncertainty

Among the most influential work in cognitive psychology over the last 25 years is the research on judgment by Tversky and Kahneman (1973, 1974). According to Tversky and Kahneman, subjective assessments of frequency and probability are "based on data of limited validity, which are processed according to heuristic rules" (Tversky & Kahneman, 1974). In line with its assumptions about the poor quality of the data and the rough-and-ready character of the heuristics, this work tends to emphasize errors in frequency and probability judgments.

Tversky and Kahneman distinguish three major heuristics. The first – representativeness – applies mainly to probability judgments. Tversky and Kahneman (1974, p. 1125) argue, "In answering such questions, people typically rely on the representativeness heuristic, in which probabilities are evaluated by the degree to which [event] A resembles [causal process] B." For example, we judge the probability that an individual is a member of a class according to the degree of similarity between that person and our stereotype for the class. It is difficult to combine the assessment of representativeness with other information, and, as a consequence, reliance on the representativeness heuristic is thought to produce a host of systematic errors, including insensitivity to base rates, sample sizes, and validity considerations (Kahneman & Tversky, 1973). In addition, the level of confidence in the judgment mainly reflects the degree of representativeness, often leading to gross overconfidence in the validity of predictions.

The second heuristic Tversky and Kahneman described is availability, assessing "the frequency or probability of an event, by the ease with which instances or occurrences come to mind" (Tversky & Kahneman, 1974). Although ease of retrieving instances may generally be a valid cue to the size of a class, other factors can affect the availability of the instances. For example, it is easier to remember famous names than ones we have never heard of, and this may affect our frequency judgments about a list that contains both, causing us to overestimate the number of famous names and to underestimate the number of less famous ones (Tversky & Kahneman, 1973). Similarly, people may judge that there are more words ending with *ing* than ending with _ *n* _, even though the one category includes the other.

Tversky and Kahneman's final heuristic – anchoring-and-adjustment – is a more general strategy in which an initial value is adjusted to arrive at a final estimate. The initial value, or anchor, may be an arbitrary value or it may be the result of a partial computation. Because the adjustments tend to be insufficient, the accuracy of the final estimates depends heavily on the initial anchor. Recent findings suggest that anchor effects occur even when people are forewarned of its potential influence, provided that they pay attention to the anchor and don't already know the answer to the target question (Wilson, Houston, Etling, & Brekke, 1996). The tendencies to underestimate the probability of disjunctive events (e.g., drawing at least one red marble from an urn in seven tries) and to overestimate the probabilities of conjunctive events (e.g., drawing seven red marbles in seven tries) may both result from applying the anchoring-and-adjustment heuristic. In both cases, people may be anchoring on the probability of the simple event (the probability of drawing one red marble) and adjusting inadequately when they try to estimate the compound probability.

It is possible to draw some parallels between the strategies explored in the memory studies and Tversky and Kahneman's heuristics. Consider the representativeness heuristic. It is the same sort of impressionistic, unidimensional assessment as the assessments of similarity that are sometimes thought to determine recognition judgments. For example, Hintzman's (1988) echo intensity on which, he argues, frequency judgments are based mainly reflects the resemblance between the test item and the traces left by the items studied earlier. Similarly, what Tversky and Kahneman label availability may be just another name for familiarity. As we've seen, memory researchers claim that false recognition can result from misattributing a feeling of familiarity to past encounters with an item when it actually arises from another source.[2] Only anchoring-and-adjustment, then, seems to lack an analog in the memory literature.

---

[2] Another possibility is that the availability heuristic is more closely akin to the retrieval of specific instances. Tversky and Kahneman are never very detailed about the actual pro-

If Tversky and Kahneman seem to concentrate on the impressionistic end of the spectrum of possible strategies for estimating frequencies, this emphasis may reflect the tasks they use. Typically, their studies ask subjects to say which of two outcomes is more likely or which of two categories is more frequent. It is easy to see how respondents could make a quick assessment of the availability or representativeness of each option, compare the two, and make their selection. These heuristics seem ideally suited to comparative judgments, especially when there is a premium on speed rather than accuracy. Gigerenzer and Goldstein's (1996) *take-the-best* heuristic is an extreme example of a strategy that produces fast and reasonably accurate comparative judgments. This heuristic involves selecting the option that is favored by the first consideration that comes to mind and that supports one option over the other. Often, that consideration is the fact that one has heard of one of the alternatives but not the other. But although these heuristics might be reasonable for comparisons, they seem less effective for direct estimates of frequency or probability. It is the latter type of judgment that survey items typically require.

5.2   Studies of Frequency Estimation in Surveys

One of the first survey problems to which psychological theories were applied is how respondents answer questions about frequency, such as questions about the number of consumer purchases they have made (Sudman & Bradburn, 1973). As Chapters 3 and 4 made clear, answers to such questions are prey to forgetting and dating errors. The studies done in the last decade or so implicate a third source of errors: flawed estimation strategies.

cesses involved; they are more concerned about the errors produced by the heuristics than by their internal mechanics. But the examples they give suggest that the assessment of availability consists of retrieving a few instances and then assessing how readily they came to mind (e.g., Tversky & Kahneman, 1974, p. 127):

For example, one may assess the risk of heart attack among middle-aged people by recalling such occurrences among one's acquaintances. Similarly, one may evaluate the probability that a given business venture will fail by imagining various difficulties it could encounter.

Bruce and his colleagues (Bruce et al., 1991) and Watkins and LeCompte (1991) have examined this process in the context of memory experiments.

TABLE 5.1 Strategies for Answering Frequency Questions in Surveys

Type of Information Used	Strategy
Information about specific events	*Recall-and-count* (episodic enumeration): Recall each event and count the events to get the total number
	Recall and count by domain (additive decomposition): Recall and count events separately by domain
	Recall-and-extrapolate (rate estimation): Recall a few events to estimate a rate and then project that rate over the reference period
Exact tally	*Tally:* Recall current tally of events
Generic information	*Retrieved rate:* Retrieve existing information about rate
	Recommended rate: Retrieve information about the recommended rate and then adjust upward or downward
General impression	*Guess* (rough approximation; direct estimate)
	Context-influenced estimate: Use the value given by the middle response category as an anchor and adjust it based on the impression

Note: Alternative names for a strategy are given in parentheses.

5.2.1 Response Strategies for Frequency Questions

The early work on frequency questions in surveys, including the classic studies by Neter and Waksberg (1964) and Sudman and Bradburn (1973), presuppose that respondents recall each episode relevant to the question (each household repair or consumer purchase) and then total them up to get the answer. This strategy, variously labeled *episodic enumeration* (e.g., Blair & Burton, 1987) or *recall-and-count* (e.g., Menon, 1993), appears to be used only by a minority of respondents when they are asked to describe their strategies retrospectively (Blair & Burton, 1987; Brown & Sinclair, 1997; Burton & Blair, 1991; Conrad et al., 1998; Means & Loftus, 1991; Menon, 1996; Willis, Brittingham, Lee, Tourangeau, & Ching, 1999) or to verbalize them as they answer (Menon, 1993).

Despite these findings, it is possible that respondents sometimes do, in fact, recall each episode in many surveys. Survey questionnaires often include an initial frequency question only as a preliminary that is followed by additional questions gathering detailed information about each event. In the Neter and Waksberg study, for example, respondents were asked not merely about the number of household repairs they had made, but also about the nature and cost of each one. Since this study used a longitudinal design, it is likely that even if respondents started out by estimating the number of repairs to answer the initial frequency question, they would soon bow to the inevitable and recall each repair in anticipation of the detailed follow-up questions they knew were coming. When survey questionnaires embody this organization – first eliciting the number of events of a given type (doctor's visits, household repairs, consumer purchases) and then the details about each one – respondents probably realize rather quickly that estimation and rough guesses are not very useful response strategies. They may delay some of the cognitive work involved, but they do not reduce it.

The data from respondents' reports about how they arrive at their answers to frequency questions indicate four main routes:

(4) a. Recall of specific information, typically individual episodes;
 b. Estimation based on the recall of generic information, typically summary information about the rate of occurrence;
 c. Recall of an exact tally;
 d. Estimation based on a general impression.

Each of these strategies has a number of variants (see Bickart, Blair, Menon, & Sudman, 1990, for a more detailed taxonomy). We describe these themes and variations in the rest of this section, summarizing the major possibilities in Table 5.1.

Recall of Specific Information

One strategy, of course, is simply to remember the events and then to count them up. Researchers have distinguished two variations on this basic recall-and-count theme, as shown in Table 5.1. One involves recalling and counting separately within each of several subdomains; these counts are then summed to obtain the overall total (see, e.g., Bradburn, et al., 1987, and Lessler et al., 1989, who call this strategy *additive decomposition*). In answering a question about how often they ate in restaurants during the past month, respondents may recall and tote up lunches separately from dinners and fast-food places separately from other restaurants. Another variation on the recall-and-count strategy involves recalling several episodes and using them to estimate a rate of occurrence; this rate is then applied to the entire reference period. We will refer to this as the *recall-and-extrapolate* strategy (cf. Conrad et al., in 1998, on rate estimation). People can also estimate a rate from the spacing between episodes. If one's last two visits to the dentist were 6 months apart, this implies a rate of two dental visits per year (Lessler et al., 1989; see also Blair & Ganesh, 1991).

Estimation Based on Generic Information

One of the main obstacles to the recall of specific information about individual episodes is the tendency for memories of similar events to blend together into a generic representation that captures the overall pattern but not the distinguishing details of the episodes (see Chapter 3, as well as Means & Loftus, 1991; A. F. Smith, 1991; E. R. Smith, 1999). Because it is so difficult to recall the individual episodes, respondents may resort to recalling generic information instead, information such as the typical rate of occurrence for the behavior in question.

Perhaps the most striking demonstration of the use of generic information comes from a series of studies of dietary recall by A. Smith (1991). Smith's respondents attempted to recall the types of food they had eaten during a two- or four-week period; their reports were subsequently matched with their entries in a food diary they had kept during that period. The rates at which the reports matched the diary entries were not very high even when the reports were obtained immediately after the end of the reference period. Further, when the reports were obtained sometime after the reference period had ended, there was some drop in the match rates initially but no further drop after six weeks (at which point about a third of the reports still matched the diary entries). In addition, there were high rates of intrusion errors; more than a third of the food items that respondents reported could not be matched to a diary entry. All these findings led Smith to conclude that respondents "list foods they routinely eat without regard to when they ate them" (A. F. Smith, 1991, p. 11).

In another study, Smith, Jobe, and Mingay (1991) had respondents maintain diaries for two separate reference periods. Respondents' reports matched the diary entries for the second period almost as well as they matched the entries for the first. In a parallel result, Menon (1993) found identical levels of accuracy whether respondents reported behavioral frequencies for the same week in which they had maintained a diary or for the preceding week (Experiment 3; see also Menon, 1996). Of course, these findings could reflect the sheer regularity of the behaviors in question. If respondents eat the same items in any two-week period, then the reports will match one period as well as another even if the respondents are recalling specific information from the period they are reporting about. Two types of evidence argue against this interpretation of Smith's findings. First, the level of accuracy in these studies is not very high, suggesting that the "dietary reports . . . consist, in large part, of individuals' guesses about what they probably ate." (A. F. Smith, 1991, p. 11). These guesses, in turn, reflect generic knowledge of their usual dietary habits. Second, respondents' reports about their strategies for answering these questions often indicate a reliance on rates or other generic information.

Several studies suggest that the generic information on which frequency estimates are based is sometimes information about *recommended* rather than actual rates (see Table 5.1). Respondents may, for example, base their reports about how often they have seen a dentist in the last year on the fact that two visits are recommended. This figure serves as an anchor that respondents then adjust up or down, depending on what specific information they recall (Lessler et al., 1989). Similarly, some parents report that they attempt to recall the number of recommended doses in order to answer questions about how many vaccinations their children had received (Willis et al., 1999).

Recall of an Exact Tally

Another route to an answer is available to respondents who have kept tabs on the frequency sought; they can simply report that frequency. It seems likely that most parents remember the number of children they have without recalling each one. A novelist may keep track of the number of books he or she has written; a slugger may know the number of home runs he has hit in his career. If the figure is important enough, if it is asked about often enough, or if it is small enough, we may simply know the answer. In a study of 190 students who reported having at least eight sexual partners, Brown and Sinclair (1997) found that a substantial proportion claimed that their reports were based on the retrieval of an exact tally.

Estimation Based on a General Impression

Studies in which respondents attempt to verbalize their strategies for answering frequency questions typically include a residual category for those respondents who report no particular process; instead, such respondents indicate that they "just guessed" or something similar. This strategy has been labeled *direct estimation* (Blair & Burton, 1987), *rough approximation* (Brown & Sinclair, 1997), or *general impression* (Conrad et al., 1998), although it is hard to be sure that the different authors (and their informants) are really referring to the same process.

A series of studies by Schwarz, Hippler, and their colleagues (Schwarz & Hippler, 1987; Schwarz, Hippler, Deutsch, & Strack, 1985) suggest that one version of this strategy may involve translating a general impression ("very often" or "a great deal") into a numerical answer, using the information provided in the response categories to anchor this mapping. These studies show that the range of frequencies in the response categories affects the answers the respondents give (see also Bless, Bohner, Hild, & Schwarz, 1992; Gaskell, O'Muircheartaigh, & Wright, 1994; Menon, Raghubir, & Schwarz, 1995; Tourangeau & Smith, 1996). For example, respondents report watching more TV on average when the response options for the question start with "up to two and a half hours" per day than when they start with "up to a half hour" per day. (We review this result in more detail in Chapter 8; see Table 8.2). Schwarz and Hippler argue that respondents interpret the response options as conveying information about the population distribution, taking the middle category to represent the average or typical value. Based on this inference, respondents with only a vague sense that they watch more (or less) TV than the average person can nonetheless place themselves in a response category. The middle response option serves as an anchor, which they adjust upward or downward in light of their impression. The effect of the response categories disappears when the behaviors in question are very regular, presumably because the respondents have a more exact sense of their rate of occurrence (Menon et al., 1995); the effect increases when the question asks for a judgment that is hard to compute (Bless et al., 1992).

When the question does not provide any response categories, respondents may have a harder time translating their impression into a frequency estimate. One indicator of this difficulty is their use of round numbers to report answers based on general impressions (Conrad et al., 1998). Respondents' impressions may consist of very inexact rate information – perhaps simple familiarity or strength – that is crudely mapped onto round values.

Summary

Table 5.1 lists the strategies discussed thus far, grouping them according to the type of information they use. It is also apparent from a number of studies that respondents may use mixed strategies; they may, for example, recall-and-count within one subdomain but calculate a rate-based estimate within another. In addition, an answer that respondents derive through one of these strategies may serve as a starting point that they adjust using information from a second source (Bickart et al., 1990; Blair & Burton, 1987; Lessler et al., 1989). Respondents may first recall-and-count, then compare the result with their overall impression; if the initial total seems too low, they may try to recall further episodes. Or they may adjust an estimate based on the typical rate if they remember specific information about departures from the usual pattern.

There is a reasonably close correspondence between the survey strategies (Table 5.1) and those that come from memory experiments (Figure 5.1). Memory researchers see frequency estimates as arising from retrieval of specific traces, exact tallies, or impressions (of item familiarity or strength); these parallel the first, second, and fourth groups of strategies listed in the table. Watkins and LeCompte (1991) have also suggested that subjects in memory experiments use rates or other generic information to remember the frequency of list items belonging to semantic categories (e.g., the number of flowers or trees on the list). This suggestion corresponds to the third of the survey strategies (see also Watkins & Kerkar, 1985).

The relationship to Tversky and Kahneman's heuristics is a little harder to see. Anchoring-and-adjustment appears to underlie the effects of the range of response categories on frequency reports; respondents apparently anchor their estimates on the middle response category and adjust them to conform to their general impression. In addition, respondents sometimes come up with an initial answer and then adjust it as they remember other information. But there do not appear to be direct analogs to the representativeness and availability heuristics. Both of these involve fast, impressionistic assessments, and they may be responsible for some of the "guesses" and uncodable protocols found in the survey studies of frequency estimation. Still, the absence of direct evidence for the availability heuristic is puzzling; that heuristic seems especially well suited for the quick estimation of frequencies. Conrad, Brown, and Cashman (1998) argue that because the availability heuristic does not involve the actual retrieval of instances (but only an assessment of their retrievability), it leaves no trace in working memory that a respondent can report. The brief descriptions Tversky and Kahneman give of the heuristic (which we quote in footnote 2) suggest, however, that availability involves actually retrieving a few instances. In that case, applications of the availability heuristic may be labeled *recall-and-extrapolate* (or *rate estimation*) in the survey studies.

5.2.3   Determinants of Strategy Selection in Surveys

We noted earlier that most respondents in the survey studies of frequency do not enumerate episodes to arrive at their answers. This conclusion comes from several studies that asked respondents to describe their strategies. Table 5.2 displays the results from five of these studies: Blair and Burton (1987) examined students' reports about their frequency of dining out; Willis and his coauthors (1999) reviewed parents' reports about the number of vaccinations their children had received; Brown and Sinclair (1997) studied students' reports about the number of their sexual partners; and Conrad and his colleagues (1998) considered telephone respondents' reports about 10 routine behaviors (such as using an ATM or shopping in a grocery store). In four of these studies, roughly a fourth of the respondents used recall-and-count; in the Brown and Sinclair study this strategy was somewhat more popular, being reported by 40% of the respondents.

In the studies of vaccination reporting, respondents often mentioned trying to recall other types of episodic information besides memories of the vaccinations themselves. Some said they tried to remember information recorded on the vaccination card (which lists the child's vaccinations to date); others reported that they tried to recall what the child's pediatrician told them about the child's vaccination status. We list these in Table 5.2 as "other" strategies based on recall of specific information. The tally strategy appears only in connection with reports about sexual partners; about a fourth of Brown and Sinclair's respondents (all of whom had reported having at least eight partners) claimed to base their answers on a running count of the total.

In their early paper, Blair and Burton (1987) anticipated most of the strategies found in later survey studies on frequency estimation and also most of the variables now known to affect the selection of response strategies. They argued that the choice of a response strategy depends on:

(5) a. The level of effort needed, specifically for recall-and-count;
    b. Motivation (i.e., willingness to make the necessary effort);
    c. The accessibility of episodic information;

TABLE 5.2 Relative Frequency of Response Strategies, by Study

Strategy	Blair & Burton (1987)	Willis et al. 1999 Study 1	Willis et al. 1999 Study 3	Brown & Sinclair (1997)	Conrad et al. (1998)
Recall of specific information					
Recall-and-count	27%	27%	24%	42%	27%
Other	3%	48%	68%	—	12%
Estimate based on generic information					
Rate	53%	—	—	2%	15%
Other	9%	11%	3%	—	9%
Tally	—	—	—	28%	—
Impression	5%	11%	5%	14%	18%
Other/uncodable	3%	3%	—	14%	18%

d. The availability of alternative processes;

e. Task conditions, including question wording.

Their own and later research has provided considerable support for each of these hypotheses about the selection of response strategies.

Level of Effort and Motivation

The cognitive effort needed for the recall-and-count strategy depends directly on the number of events that must be recalled and totaled. It is both harder to remember the events and harder to count them as their number grows. Blair and Burton (1987; see also Burton & Blair, 1991; Conrad et al., 1998, and Means & Loftus, 1991) showed that the more events respondents have to report, the less likely they are to try to enumerate them. Table 5.3 provides evidence for this decrease from three separate studies. Although it is by far the most popular strategy when there are only one or two events to report, recall-and-count virtually disappears when respondents have to report as many as ten. In a similar vein, Tourangeau and Smith (1996) found that about two-thirds of the respondents who reported having more than eight sexual partners gave a round number for the total, suggesting that their answers were estimates. Among respondents who do report using the recall-and-count strategy, response times grow longer as more events are reported; each episode appears to take nearly a second to recall (Conrad et al., 1998).

The effort needed for the other response strategies depends on varia-

TABLE 5.3 The Number of Events and Percentage of Respondents Using Recall-and-Count

Study	Number of Events	% Using Recall-and-Count
Blair and Burton (1987)	1–3	84%
	4–5	63%
	6–10	15%
	11 or more	0%
Burton and Blair (1991)	1–2	86%
	3–10	40%
	11 or more	7%
Means and Loftus (1991)	1	81%
	2	70%
	3 or more	47%

Note: Blair and Burton (1987) classified respondents by the number of events they reported; the other two studies classified them by the number of events indicated in records.

bles other than the number of events. The difficulty of estimating a rate of occurrence would, for example, depend on the regularity of the events in question. The results of several studies by Menon and her colleagues indicate that respondents find it harder to answer frequency questions when the behaviors in question occur on an irregular schedule than when they occur regularly (Menon, 1993, 1996; Menon et al., 1995).

Although there is little direct evidence for the effect of the level of motivation on the selection of a response strategy, it seems plausible that respondents would be more willing to make the effort needed to recall-and-count if their motivation were high enough. When Burton and Blair's (1991) respondents were told that the questions were important and were instructed to take more time to answer, they were more likely to say they enumerated individual episodes.

Accessibility of Episodic Information

Aside from affecting the level of effort needed to enumerate episodes, the number of events may decrease their accessibility. The more we experience events of a given type, the harder it becomes to retrieve the details of any one of them. In addition, the length of the reference period and the distinctiveness of the episodes will affect their accessibility, as Blair and Burton (1987) and others have pointed out. All these variables make recall-and-count less attractive by decreasing access to individual events. For example, as the reference period gets longer, respondents are less likely to report using the recall-and-count strategy (Blair & Burton, 1987; Burton & Blair, 1991; see also Chu et al., 1992). Blair and Burton (1987) showed that the impact of the length of the recall period is independent of that of the sheer number of events. Several studies have also demonstrated that when the questions concern easily confused events, recall-and-count becomes a less common strategy than when they concern distinctive events (Conrad et al., 1998; Menon, 1993; see also Means & Loftus, 1991, on recurring versus acute medical conditions).

Accessibility of Alternative Information

Some of the strategies in Table 5.1 require the respondents to have previously stored certain information. An answer cannot be based on a tally unless a tally already exists; it cannot be based on an existing rate unless the respondent has previously noticed the rate and stored it in memory. As Conrad and his colleagues put it, "Strategy selection is restricted by the contents of memory, [though] not dictated by them" (Conrad et al., 1998, p. 360). We would expect more generally that when the information needed to carry out a given strategy is highly accessible, respondents will be more likely to use that strategy (Menon et al., 1995). This principle seems to apply to the recall-and-count strategy, which is used less often as individual episodes become harder to retrieve, and it applies to rate-based estimates as well. As the events in question occur on a more regular schedule, respondents are more likely to estimate their number from their rate of occurrence and less likely to use recall-and-count or impression-based strategies (Conrad et al., 1998; Menon, 1993, 1996; Menon et al., 1995). These findings presumably reflect the increased accessibility of rate information (and the decreased accessibility of information about individual episodes) for regular events. Men and women may use different strategies for counting their sexual partners, perhaps because they notice and remember different things about their partners (Brown & Sinclair, 1997).

Task Conditions

The exact nature and conditions of the task can also affect the selection of a response strategy. Giving respondents more time, as we have seen, encourages them to recall-and-count episodes (Burton & Blair, 1991). The wording of the question can also affect the response strategy they use. Asking respondents "how many times" they have done something may encourage them to count each time, whereas asking them "how often" they have done something may encourage them to base their answers on a rate. The data, however, offer only weak support for these hypotheses (Blair & Burton, 1987). Menon (1996) shows that decomposing an overall frequency question into more specific questions encourages respondents to enumerate episodes. Asking respondents to express their answers as a percentage rather than as a raw amount increases their reliance on the information that the response categories convey, suggesting a switch to impression-based strategies (Bless et al., 1992); prior items on the same topic may also increase the impact of the response options (Gaskell et al., 1994).

No Events to Report

A final factor that may affect the choice of a strategy is whether respondents have experienced *any* relevant events. Conrad and his colleagues (1998) show that respondents who report no events of a given type report using strategies to arrive at their answers that are somewhat different from the strategies used by respondents who report one or more events. We might expect that impression-based strategies, reflecting assessments of the apparent familiarity, accessibility, or plausibility (Reder, 1987) of the events in question, would account for many of these zero answers. In memory studies, familiarity and accessibility do seem to play a role in recognition judgments (see, for example, Hintzman & Curran, 1994); when an item seems unfamiliar or inaccessible enough, respondents judge that they never saw it before. In survey settings, respondents might do something similar, concluding that they never experienced events of a type that they never heard of before. For example, the NHIS asks respondents whether they have experienced a series of health conditions (*Bursitis?*; *Eczema or psoriasis?*). Many respondents may conclude that they probably haven't had these conditions since they've never heard of them before.

Many of the respondents who gave zero answers in the study by Conrad and his colleagues (1998) reported that they had attempted to retrieve specific episodes but had failed to come up with any. Gentner and Collins (1981) explored the conditions under which such retrieval failures lead to the inference that no relevant events took place. They argue that when the question concerns the sort of thing we typically would remember (such as recent or unusual events), we are more likely to conclude from our failure to retrieve specific memories that no such events happened.

Summary

Table 5.4 summarizes our discussion of the selection of response strategies. Two principles seem to account for most of the findings. The first is the relative accessibility of the types of information that the different strategies depend on. In most cases, survey respondents probably do not carefully consider all the options before deciding which strategy to carry out. Instead, the frequency question may trigger the retrieval of two or three pieces of information from memory, and the nature of this information then dictates which response strategy they apply. Both retrieving information and applying a response strategy may take place more or less automatically. A question about frequencies may trigger the recall of two or three episodes, which the respondent unthinkingly counts up, or it may trigger the retrieval of a rate, which the respondent uses to estimate a total. Many of the variables in Table 5.4 (including the number of events, the length of the reference period, the regularity and distinctiveness of the episodes, and the wording of the question) affect the accessibility of one or more types of information that respondents use to answer frequency questions. This point of view is similar to

TABLE 5.4 Variables Affecting Strategy Choice for Frequency Questions

Study	Main Strategies Compared	Topic of Reports	Variables Related to Strategy Choice
Blair and Burton (1987)	Recall-and-count vs. rate-based estimation vs. other	Dining out; 5 other routine behaviors	Length of reference period Number of events reported Question form Sex of respondent
Brown and Sinclair (1997)	Recall-and-count vs. "rough approximation"	Sexual partners	
Burton and Blair (1991)	Recall-and-count vs. rate-based estimation	Courses and grades (Study 1) ATM transactions, checks written (Study 2)	Length of reference period Number of events to be reported Time for response Number of events to be reported
Conrad et al. (1998)	Recall-and-count vs. rate-based estimation vs. impression	10 routine behaviors	Response latency Regularity of events Distinctiveness of events
Means and Loftus (1991)	Recall vs. estimation	Visits to an HMO	Number of events to be reported
Menon (1993)	Recall-and-count vs. rate-based estimation	12 routine behaviors	Regularity of events Distinctiveness of events
Menon (1996)	Recall-and-count vs. rate-based estimation	6 routine behaviors	Regularity of events Question form (decomposition question)
Menon et al. (1995)	Rate-based estimation vs. "context-based"	9 routine behaviors (Experiment 1) Washing hair, unplanned visits to friends (Experiments 2 and 3)	Regularity of events Subject of question (self vs. other person) Question format (open vs. closed)
Tourangeau and Smith (1996)	Reporting round vs. raw values	Sexual partners	Number of partners reported

the one we developed in Chapter 4 for answering questions about time of occurrence, and it is consistent with the approach to inductive inference outlined by Collins and Michalski (1989).

The principle of relative accessibility suggests that strategy selection is simply a matter of which type of information reaches working memory first. The second principle acknowledges the role of controlled processes – the conscious consideration of effort and accuracy – in selecting a response strategy. Under certain circumstances, respondents may choose to ignore or deviate from the path suggested by the information that comes to mind first. They may, for example, adjust an answer derived through one strategy because the answer seems too high or too low (presumably because it conflicts with other information that the respondent has retrieved). In addition, if the question seems important enough or if they have been told to take their time, respondents may deliberately choose to adopt a more burdensome strategy (such as recall-and-count) than they would otherwise have chosen (Burton & Blair, 1991). Or when multiple types of information come to mind, respondents may construct a mixed strategy that allows them to use them all. Thus, conscious considerations such as the manifest inadequacy of the answer or a belief in the special importance of the question may lead respondents to pursue a different, more effortful strategy than they ordinarily would have used. Unless such controlled processes intervene, most survey respondents are probably swept along by whatever information comes to mind and by whatever response processes this information sets in motion.

Drawing on a framework proposed by Feldman and Lynch (1988), Menon, Raghubir, and Schwarz (1995) have proposed a similar model for the selection of response strategies for frequency questions. Menon and her coauthors argue that information will be used in answering a frequency question if it is accessible and if it is seen as diagnostic (i.e., sufficient to answer the question). For example, respondents seem to rely more on the information contained in the response categories when the behaviors in question occur frequently but at irregular intervals than when they occur on a regular schedule. With irregular behaviors, rate information may be accessible but it is no longer diagnostic; as a result, respondents base their estimates on the information that the response options convey. The accessibility of the information is presumably a function of automatic processes; the assessment of its diagnosticity is, by contrast, likely to involve controlled processing.

5.2.3   Implications for Accuracy

Several studies have examined the accuracy of the answers to survey frequency questions, typically by comparing the survey reports to records about the same events. Two accuracy measures – the absolute deviation between the survey report and the record (expressed as a percentage of the value given in the record) and the correlation between the reports and the records – have turned out to be useful. In the first of their two studies, Burton and Blair (1991) found that accuracy improved when they gave respondents more time to answer, but time to respond had no effect in their second study. They also reported that, for ATM transactions, recall-and-count produced more accurate answers than those based on estimates; of course, those who used the recall-and-count strategies had fewer episodes to report and thus may have had an easier time reporting them accurately. Menon (1996) found that decomposition improves the accuracy of reports about irregular, but not regular, events (see also Means & Loftus, 1991, on recurring medical conditions). An earlier study showed only marginal effects of the regularity and distinctiveness of the events on the accuracy of reports about them (Menon, 1993).

5.3   Probability Judgments

Far fewer survey questions ask respondents to judge probabilities than ask them to judge frequencies, although the two types of judgments are obviously closely related. Surveys may avoid asking for probability or likelihood estimates because they are seen as imposing even greater cognitive burdens on the respondents than frequency estimates do (Bless et al., 1992), and there is some evidence to back up this hypothesis (Bless et al., 1992; Gigerenzer, 1991; Tversky & Koehler, 1994). Still, a few survey-minded economists have advocated the collection of probability judgments in surveys to assess intentions or expectations (e.g., Dominitz & Manski, 1997; Juster, 1966), raising the issues of the accuracy of such judgments and of the best way to collect them. It is difficult to paraphrase some probability questions into frequency terminology – for example, "What do you believe the likelihood is that you will lose your job next year?" – so probability questions are sometimes indispensable. The literature on judgment under uncertainty, however, raises serious concerns about both the external calibration of probability judgments and their internal consistency.

5.3.1   External Calibration

Some of the problems in probability estimates are illustrated in an early study that examined lay judgments regarding the risks of death from various causes (Lichtenstein, Slovic, Fischhoff, Layman, & Combs, 1978). Lichtenstein and her colleagues found a nonlinear relationship between judged and actual risk. This nonlinearity partly reflected the systematic overestimation of low risks and the systematic underestimation of high risks (Lichtenstein et al., 1978, Figure 10). Besides these tendencies to overestimate the likelihood of rare events and to underestimate the likelihood of common ones, probability judgments can be distorted by a second phenomenon involving the extremes. We seem prone to exaggerate the differences between a sure thing and a very likely outcome at the high end of the distribution and between an impossible event and one that is merely highly unlikely at the low end (e.g., Tversky & Kahneman, 1979). More generally, we seem to make finer discriminations among probabilities that are near 0 and 1 than among less extreme probabilities (see, e.g., Tversky & Kahneman, 1979, Figure 4). Quadrel, Fischhoff, and Davis (1993) have developed a procedure for eliciting probabilities that reflects this differential sensitivity; their method uses a more finely graded scale to capture very low probability estimates.

A review of the literature on the calibration of probability suggests that accuracy varies according to the events being judged, the expertise and training of the judges, and the exact nature of the judgment task (Lichtenstein, Fischhoff, & Phillips, 1982). One recent survey study showed high levels of accuracy in the aggregate for estimates of the risk of job loss and loss of health insurance coverage but low levels of accuracy for the risk of being burglarized (Dominitz & Manski, 1997). On the average, the respondents grossly overstated their chances of being burglarized.

5.3.2   Internal Consistency

We can also assess probability judgments in terms of their consistency with the axioms of probability theory. Several systematic departures are evident. One of these is the conjunction effect, in which a compound event (a heart attack victim is an overweight, middle-aged male) is judged to be likelier than one or both of its constituents (a heart attack victim is a male). According to one account, the effect results from the representativeness heuristic (Tversky & Kahneman, 1982); adding conditions can increase the match between the description and the relevant stereotype even though it necessarily reduces the probability of the event described. A second departure from the dictates of probability theory involves disjunctive events. We judge a disjunctive event to be more likely when the event's description explicitly mentions each of the possibilities it encompasses than when it does not mention them (Tversky & Koehler, 1994). For instance, subjects rated the probability of death from unnatural causes to be some 66% higher on average when the "unnatural causes" were unpacked into accident, homicide, and other unnatural causes (Tversky & Koehler, 1994, Table 1). When the specific possibilities are not expressly mentioned, we overlook some of them and produce lower probability estimates. The more possibilities the disjunction includes, the more mentioning each of them affects the estimates (Tversky & Koehler, 1994, Figure 1). The technique of unpacking a probability judgment is similar to that of decomposing other complex judgments (e.g., Armstrong et al., 1975).

The one constraint that probability judgments do appear to follow is that the probabilities assigned to an event and its complement generally sum to 1 (Tversky & Koehler, 1994; Wallsten, Budescu, & Zwick, 1992). Even here, however, anecdotal evidence suggests that problems may arise. For example, if the questions eliciting the probability judgments of the event and its complement are widely separated in a questionnaire, we suspect that their sum may often depart from 1.

5.3.3   Judgments of Probability in Surveys

As we noted in our discussion of vague quantifiers in Chapter 2, most survey items that elicit probability judgments use qualitative response categories ("very likely," "unlikely," and so on). Some items do, however, elicit numerical answers. A study of expectations by Dominitz and Manski (1997) is one recent attempt; their questions asked respondents in a national telephone survey to rate the "percent chance" that they would lose their jobs or their health insurance coverage over the next year or that they would be burglarized. As we have already noted, the responses seemed better calibrated to the actual risks of job loss and loss of insurance coverage than to the risk of burglary. In addition, the ratings seemed to illustrate the greater differentiation of probabilities near 0 and 1 that Lichtenstein and her colleagues observed (Lichtenstein et al., 1978). As is apparent in Table 5.5, most of the responses to the

TABLE 5.5 Distribution of Responses to Three Probability Items

	Loss of Health Insurance	Burglary	Job Loss
Value			
0, 100	49.1%	14.2%	37.3%
Other multiples of 10	30.0%	47.7%	30.8%
25, 75	3.0%	3.7%	2.7%
1–5, 95–99	15.8%	30.7%	26.5%
Other raw values	2.2%	4.8%	2.8%
Total n	2,060	2,050	1,837

Source: Dominitz and Manski (1997). Copyright © 1997. Reprinted with permission of the University of Chicago Press.

three items are multiples of 10 and 25, suggesting that the responses are based on vague underlying expectations that are hard to map onto the scale; of the answers that are not round values, the vast majority are close to 0 or 100. For each item, about 80% of the answers are concentrated at the value 5 or one of the multiples of 10. Most respondents apparently simplify the task of estimating the probabilities by treating the scale as though it included 12 points – the multiples of 10 plus the value 5.

5.4 Conclusions

The few studies that assessed the accuracy of responses to frequency questions indicate that it is far from perfect. The correlations between the survey reports and records data observed by Burton and Blair (1991) range from a low of .25 to a high of .86. The technique prescribed most often in efforts to improve accuracy decomposes the judgment into simpler components (Armstrong et al., 1975; Henrion, Fischer, & Mullin, 1993; MacGregor et al., 1988; Means & Loftus, 1991; Menon, 1996; Tversky & Koehler, 1994). Decomposition offers at least three possible advantages over a single composite question: It clarifies what is included in the question, provides an organized framework for responding, and reduces the computational burden on the respondent. Still, it is hardly a cureall for response error. Although decomposition typically increases the magnitude of an estimate, it doesn't always improve its accuracy (see Section 3.3.3 for a discussion).

Many of the strategies described here have analogs in the literature on statistical estimation. The strategy of sampling, computing a rate, and then extrapolating to get a total is a less formal version of the method used to estimate population totals in national surveys. Developing separate counts for different domains is analogous to subdividing a population into strata and making separate estimates for each stratum. Anchoring-and-adjustment is a fair description of a number of statistical techniques (such as poststratification or iterative proportional fitting) that begin with an approximate value and then adjust it, sometimes repeatedly. Even the availability heuristic can be seen as a kind of crude sampling procedure. The strategies used by survey respondents, then, are often quite reasonable in principle even if they are flawed in execution.

CHAPTER SIX

Attitude Questions

At first glance, the memory and estimation processes we described in the last three chapters might not seem very relevant to attitude questions. Questions about attitudes and opinions differ in some important respects from factual and behavioral questions, and these differences would seem to demand different cognitive processes. For instance, consider the example with which we began Chapter 5:

(1) During those two weeks, how many times did _____ see or talk to a medical doctor? (Include all types of doctors such as dermatologists, psychiatrists, and ophthalmologists, as well as general practitioners and osteopaths. Do not count times while an overnight patient in a hospital.) [HIS]

There is clearly a determinate set of facts that a respondent ought to consult in answering this question, and, in principle at least, a researcher could check this same set of facts to determine whether the respondent's answer was accurate. Of course, as we saw in Chapter 5, respondents don't necessarily review any specific episodes in answering questions like (1), but such questions clearly refer to a demarcated set of episodes. That's why it makes sense to talk about the accuracy of the answers.

By contrast, attitude items rarely refer to any well-defined set of facts. Here are some attitude questions from the General Social Survey:

(2) a. Do you think the use of marijuana should be made legal, or not?
   b. Would you be for or against sex education in the public schools?
   c. On the average, (Blacks/African-Americans) have worse jobs, income, and housing than white people. Do you think these differences are mainly due to discrimination?

Although there are public facts relevant to deciding whether the respondent's answers to these questions are "accurate" or not, the questions don't refer directly to these facts. For example, whether the respondent personally smokes marijuana or publicly advocates its legalization is clearly relevant in deciding the accuracy of his or her answer to Question (2a), but they are hardly definitive. Public facts are, at best, indirect evidence about the validity of the respondent's answers. If there is a set of facts that determine the accuracy of answers to questions like (2a), they are presumably facts about the respondent's beliefs or attitudes. The subjective character of attitudes makes it difficult, if not impossible, to verify survey reports about them. Moreover, the respondent may have a number of beliefs about marijuana and other illicit drugs – some of them contradictory – that he or she could reasonably consider in framing an answer to (2a). Because of this open-ended character, it doesn't make much sense even to discuss the accuracy of answers to questions like those listed in (2).

As this chapter will make clear, however, there are more similarities than differences between the response process for the two types of questions. The same four types of information from which frequency estimates are derived – tallies, impressions, generic information, and specific memories – have their counterparts with attitude questions. Moreover, the same automatic and controlled processes that govern how frequency judgments are made also determine what sources of information respondents use in answering attitude questions. In the rest of this chapter, we describe the traditional view of attitudes, in which responses to attitude questions are seen as reports of existing judgments. We then lay out the empirical problems with this view and discuss the alternative sources of information that respondents may draw on in answering attitude questions. In the final section, we discuss a model – the belief-sampling model – that tries to capture what's common across the different sources of information that feed into attitude responses.

6.1   The Traditional View

Behavioral frequency questions like (1) seem to presuppose a naive theory about how respondents will go about answering them; although respondents may in fact prefer other strategies, such questions seem to call on the respondents first to remember any relevant incidents and then to tote them up. Attitude questions also seem to presuppose a theory of how the answers will be produced, although this theory involves very different processes from those assumed in the naive theory for frequency questions. Wilson and Hodges (1992, p. 38) call this implicit theory the *file drawer model*:

When people are asked how they feel about something, such as legalized abortion, their Uncle Harry, or anchovies on a pizza, presumably they consult a mental file containing their evaluation. They look for the file marked *abortion, Uncle Harry*, or *anchovies*, and report the evaluation it contains.

For our purposes, the file drawer model makes two main points: First, attitudes are preexisting evaluations of some target; second, they are relatively stable. This model is the moral equivalent for attitude questions of the tally model for frequency judgments. Both assume that the answer to the question is there for the asking and that, unless new information forces the tally or evaluation to be updated, the answer won't change over time.

6.1.1   Automatic Activation of Attitudes

It's clear that Wilson and Hodges intend the file drawer model as a kind of straw man, but it's equally clear that it does capture some of the main features of traditional discussions of attitudes: If an attitude isn't a stable disposition to evaluate something favorably or unfavorably, then it's not clear what it is. Allport's (1935) classic discussion of attitudes argued that attitudes formed in childhood can last a lifetime. In a more recent discussion, Petty and Cacioppo (1981, p. 7) defined an attitude as "an enduring positive or negative feeling about some person, object, or issue."

Most contemporary versions of the traditional viewpoint retain the key assumptions captured (and perhaps parodied) in the file drawer model. The most completely worked-out model of the attitude response process in the traditional vein is that of Fazio and his collaborators (Fazio, 1989; Fazio, Sanbonmatsu, Powell, & Kardes, 1986; Fazio & Williams, 1986). They argue that an attitude consists of an association between some object or person – the target of the attitude – and an evaluation of it (see Judd, Drake, Downing, & Krosnick, 1991, for a similar view). For some respondents at least, confronting the target automatically activates the evaluation. The traditional account of the response process seems to fit these respondents and their highly accessible attitudes quite well. Mention the target of the attitude and the attitude is activated; all that's left is to report it.

Fazio and his colleagues present two types of evidence for the automatic activation of attitudes. First, they show that repeated expression of an attitude leads to faster responses to questions about it (e.g., Fazio, Chen, McDonel, & Sherman, 1982). These differences in response speed are, in turn, related to the impact of attitudes on later behavior (Fazio et al., 1982; Fazio & Williams, 1986). Fazio and his colleagues argue that repeated expression of an attitude strengthens the crucial target-to-evaluation link; as this link gets stronger, the target is more likely to activate it, and it is more likely to affect subsequent behaviors. Second, they demonstrate that presenting attitude targets affects the subject's ability to classify adjectives (e.g., *appealing*) as positive or negative (Fazio et al., 1986). The attitude targets in these studies were mostly referents of commonplace words (such as *landlord* or *spider*); subjects were supposed to remember these words and repeat them after they had classified the adjective. Their findings indicated that when the adjective and the noun evoked opposite reactions (e.g., *spider* and *appealing*), respondents were slower to classify the adjective; when the two evoked similar reactions (e.g., *spider* and *appalling*), respondents were faster. Fazio and his colleagues argue that reading the noun automatically triggers the retrieval of its evaluation (at least among respondents with highly accessible attitudes) and that this evaluation affects reporting the evaluation of the subsequent adjective.

6.1.2   Problems with the Traditional View

Several findings raise questions about the assumptions of the traditional view, including Fazio's contemporary version of it.

Reaction Times and Accessibility

To begin with, a number of researchers have questioned Fazio's interpretation of the reaction time results. Although it is quite plausible that repeated expression of an attitude would lead to faster response times, it is not clear that this reflects a stronger, more accessible link between the attitude target and the evaluation. According to Fazio, the increased speed reflects the automatic activation of the attitude or a faster retrieval process. But it is equally possible that practice increases the speed of other cognitive operations as well as or instead of retrieval. For example, respondents could report their evaluation more quickly (this is, after all, what they've practiced) or simply recognize the issue more quickly.

Similarly, it isn't clear that the priming Fazio and his coworkers

(1986) observed is *attitudinal* in character. It's possible, for example, that presenting pairs with opposite valence like *spinach–appealing* sets off interfering semantic processes as respondents retrieve the very different connotations of these words. A series of follow-up studies supports these doubts about Fazio's interpretation of the findings (Bargh, Chaiken, Govender, & Pratto, 1992; Bargh, Chaiken, Raymond, & Hymes, 1996; Chaiken & Bargh, 1993; but see Fazio, 1993). The most compelling evidence comes from a study by Bargh, Chaiken, Raymond, and Hymes (1996). They replicated the procedures of Fazio and his colleagues but required subjects merely to say the target adjective aloud rather than to evaluate its connotation. The connotation of the prime affected the time it took just to say the adjective. Moreover, this effect wasn't restricted to primes that respondents could evaluate quickly (i.e., those linked to highly accessible attitudes). The study by Bargh and his colleagues suggests that whatever is activated in processing the noun is probably not attitudinal. Reading a noun may automatically trigger the retrieval of its connotation, and the noun's connotative meaning – either positive or negative – may affect the processing of subsequent words. In any event, this priming/interference effect does not depend on *attitude* accessibility.

Variability Over Time

The traditional view is also difficult to reconcile with findings from the survey and social psychology literatures that responses to attitude questions are inconsistent over time and sensitive to variations in question order and context. Converse's classic studies, for example, showed that political attitudes can be quite unstable across interviews (Converse, 1964, 1970). Converse traced this instability to the process by which people generate answers to attitude questions. Responses to attitude questions, according to Converse, often reflect evanescent opinions fabricated through a nearly random process; such "nonattitudes" do not provide a basis for responses that correlate highly over time (for a review, see T. W. Smith, 1984a).

Subsequent researchers have questioned Converse's interpretation of this instability, citing measurement error and true attitude change as alternative explanations for the variability across interviews (see Judd & Krosnick, 1982; Judd & Milburn, 1980; and Krosnick, 1988, for especially careful attempts to partition the different sources of instability). Still, there is considerable evidence that respondents may often not have ready-made attitudes to report.

TABLE 6.1 Responses to Item on Government Spending in Two Interviews

	January 1980			
June 1980	Cut	Middle	Keep Same	Don't Know
Cut	195	46	39	47
Middle	65	29	20	14
Keep same	40	30	122	21
Don't know	62	17	27	56
Total	362	122	208	138

Note: Table entries are the number of respondents giving each combination of answers in the two interviews. The question in both interviews was: "Some people think the government should provide fewer services, even in areas such as health and education, in order to reduce spending. Other people feel it is important to continue the services it now provides even if it means no reduction in spending."
Source: Zaller (1992, Table 2.1). Copyright © 1992. Adapted by permission of Cambridge University Press.

In the first place, many respondents simply don't know very much about the issues that appear in public opinion surveys. Here's a representative finding: In late 1986, some 24% of the American public could not say what office George Bush held (Zaller, 1992). At the time, Bush had been vice president for six years; in two more years, he would be elected president. Despite this low level of engagement in public issues, respondents in surveys seem reluctant to admit that they don't have an opinion. Substantial minorities will respond to questions about very obscure or fictitious issues (Bishop, Oldendick, & Tuchfarber, 1986; Schuman & Presser, 1981). Clearly, *some* answers to attitude questions are cobbled together on the spot.

Another problem is that the level of attitude change would have to be quite high to account for the instability over time that is typical in panel surveys of attitudes. Table 6.1 shows the distribution of responses to the same question administered to respondents in interviews in January and June of the same year; the data are from a study by Zaller (1992). Only 48% of the 830 respondents gave the same answer in both interviews. It just doesn't seem plausible that more than half of the respondents would have changed their minds about government spending in a few months.

The Effects of Thought

Studies that examine the effects of thought on attitudes provide further evidence that people base answers to attitude questions on something other than a static underlying evaluation.

The earliest demonstrations of the effects of thinking about an issue are the studies by Tesser and his colleagues on self-generated attitude change (Tesser, 1978). These studies show that thinking tends to increase the extremity of views about the issue. This polarization appears to be mediated by the cognitive structures that the issue activates (Chaiken & Yates, 1985; Tesser & Leone, 1977): Respondents with well-developed cognitive structures are more likely to show polarization than those with poorly developed ones. The apparent corollary that attitudes based on well-developed structures tend to be extreme is contradicted by findings that such attitudes are sometimes associated with moderate evaluations (Linville, 1982; Linville & Jones, 1980). However, studies by Millar and Tesser (1986) indicate that thinking about an issue can produce either moderation or polarization, with polarization being more likely with complex structures that include a number of correlated dimensions.

Similarly, Wilson and his colleagues have examined what happens when respondents have to give the reasons for their evaluations. Wilson and Dunn (1986) showed that asking respondents to focus on the reasons for their attitudes reduced attitude–behavior correlations, apparently by changing responses to the attitude questions. A later study by Wilson, Kraft, and Dunn (1989) showed that the disruptive effects of asking for reasons is limited to respondents with little knowledge about the issue. Like Tesser's studies of self-generated attitude change, then, the studies of Wilson and his colleagues show attitude change with minimal external prompting.

Context Effects

Finally, a large number of studies indicates that the context in which an attitude question is asked – typically, the questions immediately preceding the target item – can have large effects on the answers. We review these context effects in detail in Chapter 7. For now, we simply note that it is hard to see why changing the order of the questions should have so much impact on the answers if all respondents are doing is reporting an existing evaluation.

6.1.3   Extensions of the Traditional View

Of course, many researchers recognize that there may be more than a single path to a response to an attitude question. Fazio and his colleagues, for example, acknowledge that attitudes are automatically activated only when they are highly accessible (e.g., Fazio, 1989; Fazio & Williams, 1986; see also Krosnick, 1989). Respondents with less accessible attitudes presumably come up with answers to attitude questions through some other process. Fazio's model requires at least two response processes to accommodate both groups of respondents (see also Strack & Martin, 1987).

Many other attitude researchers have recognized the limitations of the traditional view of attitudes capsulized in the file drawer model; in particular, they have acknowledged that it fits some respondents better than others. There is considerable debate about what distinguishes the two types of respondents. Researchers have measured the degree of centrality, importance, extremity, knowledge, strength, and accessibility of attitudes (see Krosnick & Abelson, 1992, and Raden, 1985, for a discussion of these dimensions). The general argument is that a subset of respondents (those with strong attitudes, say) answer attitude questions by retrieving and reporting an existing evaluation and that the rest do something else. The well-documented measurement problems with attitude questions (e.g., question order effects) are attributed to those with weak attitudes, the ones whose answers are generated through some process other than retrieving an existing judgment. Still, that leaves the question of how respondents who lack answers that are central, important, extreme, strong, and so on answer questions about their views.

6.2   Alternative Paths to an Answer

The literature on attitudes suggests three possible alternative sources for answers to attitude questions:

(3) a. Impressions or stereotypes;
   b. General attitudes or values;
   c. Specific beliefs or feelings about the target.

Just as we may have only a hazy sense of how often we've done something, we may have an equally vague impression of a person or issue we're asked to evaluate. In such circumstances, we may nonetheless base our answer on that impression (Sanbonmatsu & Fazio, 1990). Or, lacking any ready-made evaluation (even a very hazy one), we may attempt to construct one either from the top down, deriving a position from more general values or predispositions (Zaller, 1992), or from the bottom up, using specific beliefs about the issue to construct an opinion about it (Tourangeau & Rasinski, 1988). For example, in responding to Question (2a) about the legalization of marijuana, we may draw on our general values (e.g., about drug use or about personal freedom) to construct an answer or we may try to recall or generate specific arguments about this issue to come to some conclusion about where we stand. The latter two strategies resemble the use of generic information and the retrieval-and-enumeration of specific episodes to answer frequency questions.

6.2.1 Impression-Based Responses

When we don't have a very clear sense about an issue, we may fall back on a general impression about the target or the category to which it belongs (Sanbonmatsu & Fazio, 1990). Under these circumstances, our responses to an attitude question may reflect this overall impression.

A study by Sanbonmatsu and Fazio (1990) seems to illustrate this sort of impression-based response. Subjects in their study read about two department stores. One of the stores (Smith's) was described in generally glowing terms, whereas the other store (Brown's) was described in mainly negative terms. The camera department at Brown's store was an exception to the unfavorable overall picture; the information about that department was positive. The camera department at Smith's store was, by contrast, described unfavorably. Subjects were asked to select the store they'd choose to shop for a new camera. The study thus pitted the subjects' overall impression of the stores against the more specific information about the two camera departments. When the subjects were under time pressure or were *not* given any special reason to worry about the quality of their decisions, they seemed to rely on their impressions; they were more likely to choose Smith's Store (with its crummy camera department) than Brown's. It was only when the subjects had both the time and the motivation to make a valid judgment that their choices were consistent with the specific information about the camera departments at the two stores.

Lodge, McGraw, and Stroh (1989) argue that evaluations of political candidates are similarly impression-driven. Over the course of a political campaign, we receive a lot of information about the candidates, including their political affiliation, their stand on the issues, their endorsement by various interest groups, their chances of winning, and so on. It seems quite likely that we process this information as we receive it, updating our evaluation of the candidates throughout the course of a campaign (cf. Hastie & Park, 1986, on online processing). The evidence on which these evaluations were originally based may gradually be forgotten or distorted over time. As a result, we may come to see the candidates we like as agreeing more with us than they actually do, and we may remember their positions as being more consistent with the party label than they really are (Lodge et al., 1989). Our evaluations of political candidates may reflect our impressions, not the specific information on which we originally based them.

6.2.2 Responses Based on General Values and Predispositions

Another source we can draw on to answer attitude questions consists of more general values and ideological predispositions (Rokeach & Ball-Rokeach, 1989). Zaller (1992) argues that the public's reaction to press coverage of political issues is, in large part, determined by such predispositions; these involve basic political values, such as economic individualism, tolerance for nonconformists, attitudes toward racial equality, and belief in religious authority. Studies of attitudes toward specific issues also suggest that these attitudes may reflect deeper underlying principles. Luker (1984), for example, argues that attitudes toward abortion derive from more basic views about religion, the role of women, and sexual freedom.

Some of the clearest examples involve foreign policy issues. For example, Bradburn and Danis (1984) discussed the differences between the results for two items on the Korean War, one used by the Gallup Organization, the other by the National Opinion Research Center (NORC):

(4) a. Do you think the United States made a mistake in deciding to defend Korea or not? [Gallup]
   b. Do you think the United States was right or wrong in sending American troops to stop the Communist invasion of South Korea? [NORC]

The NORC item consistently drew more support for the war. Question wording effects like this one prompted Mueller (1973) to observe that public support for U.S. involvement in the Korean and Vietnam wars seemed to depend on whether or not the question mentioned the threat of a communist takeover. In a series of experiments prompted by Mueller's remark, Schuman and Presser (1981) demonstrated that adding the phrase "to stop a communist takeover" increased support for U.S. military interventions by about 15%. Adding the phrase "to stop the spread of communism" had an even more dramatic effect on responses to an item about aid to the Nicaraguan contras (Zaller, 1992). Several studies have shown similar wording effects on other topics: There is far more support for increased spending on halting the rising crime rate than on law enforcement, for aid to the poor than for welfare, for dealing with drug addiction than with drug rehabilitation, and so on (Rasinski, 1989; T. W. Smith, 1987; for related findings, see Kinder & Sanders, 1990). Finally, Schuman and Presser (1981) showed that most respondents didn't venture an opinion about the very obscure Monetary Control Bill, but those who did based their answers on their views about inflation (see also Table 7.1).

The simplest explanation for all of these findings is that respondents don't have fixed views about the relatively narrow issues mentioned in the questions but do have general values from which they can derive an answer should the need arise (see also Fischoff, 1991, on partial perspectives). Part of the reason why answers to attitude questions can shift so dramatically in response to seemingly minor changes in question wording or context is that these changes can alter how respondents apply their general values in answering the question.

6.2.3   Answers Based on Specific Beliefs

There is evidence, then, that respondents may construct answers to attitude questions from the top down, deducing their positions on the issue at hand from ideological predispositions or broad values they hold. It's also clear that respondents may retrieve more specific beliefs related to the issue and combine these to arrive at their answers. If the top-down approach bears some resemblance to the use of generic information to produce a frequency estimate, the bottom-up approach has similarities to the recall-and-count strategy.

Two types of evidence suggest that respondents recall and integrate specific considerations relevant to an issue in answering attitude items. The first comes from studies that examine the open-ended answers respondents give in discussing their views about issues. The second comes from the results from "priming" studies that attempt to alter the relative accessibility of material related to a later item.

Open-Ended Material

A study by Zaller and Feldman (1992) illustrates the use of open-ended material to explore the considerations on which responses to attitude questions rest. They asked respondents to report "what ideas came to mind" as they were answering conventional attitude items in a pretest for the National Election Study. One of these items concerned the federal government's role in ensuring that everyone has a good standard of living. Respondents cited a number of considerations in discussing their answers on this item, including the impact on taxes, government red tape, and society's duty to the poor. Similarly, a study by Mason, Carlson, and Tourangeau (1995) found that views about the local economy reflected considerations like the local unemployment rate and prospects for job growth.

Parallel findings have been reported in studies examining the determinants of overall life satisfaction. Respondents in these studies are asked about their satisfaction with a number of domains – such as their marriages, jobs, and housing – and then are asked about their overall happiness. The results indicate that the overall rating is strongly affected by the ratings of the specific domains (e.g., McClendon & O'Brien, 1988). These findings are not just correlational. As we shall see in the next chapter, when the order of the questions raises the salience of some particular domain, it tends to affect the rating of overall happiness. Moreover, if respondents are instructed to think about recent incidents when they were happy or sad, this, too, can change the overall rating (e.g., Strack, Schwarz, & Gschneidinger, 1985). These results suggest that respondents base their overall satisfaction ratings on the specific domains or incidents they consider as they answer the question.

Priming Studies

Reaction time studies provide further evidence that respondents base answers to attitude questions on the retrieval and integration of specific considerations. Tourangeau, Rasinski, and D'Andrade (1991) showed that prior questions about an issue affected how quickly respondents answered a subsequent attitude question on the same issue (see also Judd et al., 1991). Tourangeau and his colleagues systematically varied the relation between pairs of adjacent items – an initial item (or prime) and a subsequent item (or target). All the attitude questions asked whether respondents agreed or disagreed with a statement about an issue. Sometimes the prime and target concerned completely unrelated issues (e.g., abortion and U.S. policy toward Central America); sometimes they concerned related issues (abortion and women's rights); sometimes they concerned different aspects of the same issue (society's role in regulating abortion and whether a fetus should be considered a human life); and sometimes they concerned the same aspect of a single issue (whether abortion is murder and whether life begins at conception).

The main result of the study was a significant priming effect as a function of topical distance between the target and prime. The prior items affected the speed of answers to the target questions, and the size of this effect depended on how closely related the two items were. (Judd et al., 1991, report similar findings.) If respondents were answering all the questions about an issue using the same overall evaluation, then it's not clear why there should have been an additional increase in response speed when the target and prime were about the same *aspect* of the issue. The results are easier to understand if respondents retrieved specific considerations to answer the attitude questions: The closer the two questions, the more that retrieving considerations for the first question would reduce the time needed to retrieve considerations for the next.[1]

6.2.4 Determinants of Strategy Choice

Answers to attitude questions seem to be based on several types of information. They may reflect earlier evaluations, vague impressions, general values, specific considerations, or some combination of these. The chief determinant of which source of information respondents draw on is probably relative accessibility. The results of the reaction time studies indicate that respondents answer attitude questions more quickly when the previous question makes relevant material (of whatever sort) more accessible. In addition, the results of numerous studies (reviewed in the next chapter) suggest that changes in accessibility of relevant considerations can affect not only the speed but also the direction of the answers.

Still, respondents do sometimes seem to take into account the *quality* of the considerations they retrieve, at least when they've been given enough time and motivation to do so. They may reject accessible considerations if they feel they are invalid (Schwarz & Clore, 1983) or biased (Wilson, Hodges, & LaFleur, 1995); they may shift from relatively effortless impression-based answers to more effortful answers based on specific information (Sanbonmatsu & Fazio, 1990).

It may seem likely that if respondents have an existing judgment

---

[1] Tourangeau and his colleagues also included a control task in which respondents classified each item as stating a liberal or conservative position. No priming effects were observed in the classification task. If the reaction time results for the agreement items were based on changes in the accessibility of material used in, say, understanding the questions, then similar priming effects should have been apparent in the agreement and classification data. Instead, the facilitation effects seem to be based on changes in the accessibility of attitudinal material (i.e., considerations related to the target item).

about an issue, they will use it to answer questions as often as they can. (This is one implication of Sanbonmatsu and Fazio's study; unless prodded to be more careful, the subjects in their study based their answers on global impressions.) But although respondents often sidestep extra cognitive work, there may be times when they retrieve an existing attitude but still render a new judgment in answering the question at hand. The question may, for example, focus on some aspect of the issue that the respondent has not yet fully thought through. For example, respondents with generally favorable attitudes toward the environment may not have worked out their positions on, say, greenhouse gases or some new piece of environmental legislation. A question on these issues may force the respondent to generate a new judgment even if the question does trigger the retrieval of existing attitudes

A related situation involves items dealing with difficult or borderline cases. Many pro-life partisans acknowledge that there are situations – such as when the pregnancy endangers the life of the mother – in which abortions should be permitted. Because of such difficult cases, answers to specific questions about an issue often show gross inconsistencies with answers to general questions. For example, people strongly support capital punishment in the abstract but reject it in many specific instances (Ellsworth & Gross, 1994; see also Schuman, 1972). Clearly, in such cases, the answers to the specific questions reflect something other than a previously formed general evaluation.

Besides forming new judgments when the question concerns new aspects of an issue or presents vexing particulars, respondents will sometimes retrieve other considerations along with (or instead of) their existing evaluations. Open-ended responses to attitude questions suggest that respondents sometimes retrieve both specific considerations and an existing overall evaluation. Models that distinguish two separate routes to answering an attitude question – one based on retrieving an existing evaluation and one based on retrieving more specific considerations – would seem to overlook the possibility that respondents might retrieve both (cf. Strack & Martin, 1987).

6.3   The Belief-Sampling Model

The evidence suggests that there are multiple paths to an answer to an attitude question, just as there are multiple routes to placing an event in time or making frequency judgments. Which path is taken in any given instance depends on the accessibility of the necessary information and on strategic considerations, such as the amount of time the respondent takes and his or her motivation to render a defensible judgment. Despite the differences among these routes to an answer, it is possible to make some general predictions about the stability of responses to attitude questions over time and across changes in question context. We propose a model – the belief-sampling model – that traces response instability to variations in the retrieval and judgment processes for attitude questions.

6.3.1   Assumptions of the Model

Retrieval

The key assumption of the belief-sampling model is that retrieval yields a haphazard assortment of beliefs, feelings, impressions, general values, and prior judgments about an issue; we will refer to this material simply as *considerations* about the issue (cf. Zaller, 1992). We will refer to the memory structures that encompass these considerations (whether retrieved or not) as *attitudes* According to this conception, an attitude is a kind of database consisting of feelings, beliefs, and knowledge about an issue. Which considerations a person retrieves will depend on their momentary accessibility. In fact, we assume that the probability of retrieving a specific consideration is proportional to that consideration's accessibility. Accessibility, in turn, will be affected by a large number of determinants, some chronic and some temporary. These include the wording of the question, the nature of the judgment to be made (Hastie & Park, 1986; Wyer & Hartwick, 1984), the instructions given to the respondent (Ottati, Riggle, Wyer, Schwarz, & Kuklinski, 1989; Wilson et al., 1989), long-term accessibility or strength (Fazio, 1989; Fazio et al., 1986), and the content of earlier questions (Tourangeau & Rasinski, 1988; Tourangeau, Rasinski, Bradburn, & D'Andrade, 1989b).

A person does not necessarily use everything that comes to mind in constructing an answer to an attitude question. Some considerations may be plainly irrelevant to the topic; respondents presumably discard such considerations in formulating an answer. Other considerations may consist of arguments that the respondent rejects or assertions that he or she disbelieves. Respondents may also disregard considerations they ordinarily would take into account if the considerations seem biased or redundant in the context of the current question. For example, Wilson and his colleagues show that when respondents are conscious that the considerations they have retrieved are biased toward one side of an issue, they may attempt to compensate for that bias (Wilson et al., 1995). Respondents may also disregard accessible material that they have already used in making a prior judgment if they decide that the new question requires a judgment based on new considerations (Martin, 1986; Mason et al., 1995; Schwarz, Strack, & Mai, 1991; Tourangeau, Rasinski, & Bradburn, 1991). Accessible considerations may be disregarded, then, if they are seen are irrelevant, invalid, or redundant.

The process of rejecting accessible considerations is likely to require conscious thought and deliberate effort. It will, as a result, occur only when respondents have the motivation and ability to carry it out. When the answer must be made quickly – limiting the respondent's ability to weigh the relevance and validity of what comes to mind – accessible considerations may affect judgments regardless of their relevance or validity (e.g., Martin, Seta, & Crelia, 1990; see also Petty & Wegener, 1993; Wegener & Petty, 1995). Similarly, the question context or nature of the task must make the shortcomings of the material quite obvious before respondents disregard it (Stapel, Martin, & Schwarz, 1998).

Judgment

Under many circumstances, multiple considerations about an issue will come to mind, and the respondent will have to combine them to produce an overall judgment. This combination process may involve constraint satisfaction to resolve discrepancies among considerations, as in the process we sketched in Chapter 4 for judgments of time of occurrence. For simplicity and tractability, however, we can assume that the output from the judgment component is a simple average of the considerations that are the input to it. The relevant considerations include those retrieved from long-term memory and new ones the respondent generates at the time he or she answers the question. The old considerations may include any existing evaluation of the issue; the new ones are likely to include new arguments, newly made judgments, and transient considerations such as social desirability.

We don't assume that respondents actually compute an average. Instead, averaging is the algebraic equivalent of an underlying process of successive adjustments: The respondent retrieves (or generates) a consideration and derives its implications for the question at hand; this serves as the initial judgment, which is adjusted in light of the next consideration that comes to mind; and so on (Lopes, 1982). The formation of an attitude judgment is similar to the accretion of details and inferences that produces a frequency or temporal estimate. The final judgment can be represented by the average:

$$J = \frac{\Sigma s_i}{n} \qquad\qquad (6.1)$$

In the equation, J denotes the output of the judgment component, s_i is the scale value assigned to a consideration retrieved from long-term memory (or generated when the question is asked), and n denotes the number of considerations the respondent takes into account. The scale values represent the implications of the consideration – the answer it points to, pro or con – for the particular question. Equation 6.1 applies equally well when an existing evaluation is the only consideration taken into account, when an existing evaluation is adjusted in the light of other more specific considerations about the issue, or when a new judgment is derived from specific considerations at the time a question is asked.[2]

Equation 6.1 recalls Norman Anderson's (1981) averaging model for a range of judgments; ours is a simplified version that assumes the assignment of equal weights to each consideration. As Anderson has pointed out, integration actually involves three major components – valuation (the assignment of weights and scale values to the considerations that affect the judgment), integration (the combination of these considerations via averaging or some other algebraic rule), and response generation (the translation of a subjective judgment into an overt answer). We postpone our discussion of the response generation until Chapter 8; here we assume that the process yields an output that is a monotonic function of J.

6.3.2   Implications for Response Stability

According to the belief-sampling model, responses to attitude questions are inherently unstable because they are based on a sample of the relevant material, a sample that overrepresents whatever considerations happen to be accessible when the question is asked. There is no guarantee that respondents will see an issue in terms of the same set of considerations every time their attitudes are measured. In fact, there are many opportunities for divergence across occasions. The number of considerations on which respondents base a particular answer is likely to be quite small, on the order of one or two (e.g., Tourangeau, Rasinski,

---

[2] A more complicated version of the model would allow respondents to assign weights to each consideration. In this augmented model, considerations that respondents disregard would receive a weight of 0.

Bradburn, & D'Andrade, 1989a); by contrast, the relevant attitude structures may encompass large numbers of considerations about the issue (e.g., Tourangeau, Rasinski, & D'Andrade, 1991). This disparity between the small (and nonrandomly selected) sample of considerations on which answers are based and the large, sometimes diverse, set of considerations that attitudes may encompass constitutes a major source of unreliability in the answers.

A second source of unreliability is in the values (the s_i's in Equation 6.1) that respondents assign to the considerations. This valuation process is not necessarily easy, and it won't necessarily yield the same results every time, even if the judgment is based solely on an existing evaluation. The exact scale value assigned to a consideration is likely to depend on whatever points of comparison are salient to the respondent. In addition, it may be difficult to assign a scale value to a consideration because its implications for the specific issue mentioned in the question may have to be worked out.

With a few additional assumptions, we can use Equation 6.1 to make quantitative predictions about the correlation between responses to the same question over time. The key assumption is that the response actually given to an attitude is a simple linear transformation of the judgment (J) described by Equation 6.1. Although the function that maps judgments onto response options is often more complicated than this (see Chapter 8), it is generally monotonic, and, as a result, the assumption of a linear mapping between judgment and response probably provides a reasonable approximation across a wide range of situations.

According to the model, three key parameters determine the level of the correlation between responses to the same item on two occasions. The first is the reliability of the scaling process, measured by the correlation between the scale values assigned to the *same* consideration on two occasions. Even if a respondent retrieves the same set of considerations each time a question is asked, the responses derived from them will be correlated only to the extent that the scaling process assigns similar values to them every time. We will denote the expected correlation between the scale values assigned to the same consideration on different occasions by ρ_1.

The second parameter that affects the correlation between answers over time is the degree to which any two considerations retrieved by the same respondent are correlated. The considerations in memory (and those generated in response to a question) are likely to show some degree of internal consistency. Thus, even if answers on different occasions are based on completely nonoverlapping considerations, the answers will still be correlated if the different sets of considerations imply similar answers. We will use ρ_2 to denote the degree of internal consistency among considerations; ρ_2 represents the expected value of the correlation between the scale values assigned to any pair of different considerations retrieved or generated by a respondent on a single occasion.

The final parameter that affects the correlation between responses over time is the degree of overlap in the sets of considerations taken into account on different occasions. We will use q to denote the proportion of considerations reflected in the second response that the respondent also took into account in the first. Other things being equal, the greater the overlap in the considerations, the higher the correlation between the responses.

Equation 6.2 shows the expected level of the correlation between responses on two occasions as a function of these three parameters:

$$\hat{r}_{12} = \frac{n_1 n_2 \rho_1 \rho_2 + n_2 q \rho_1 (1 - \rho_2)}{([n_1^2 \rho_2 + n_1 (1 - \rho_2)][n_2^2 \rho_2 + n_2 (1 - \rho_2)])^{1/2}} \tag{6.2}$$

in which n_1 represents the total number of considerations taken into account on the first occasion and n_2 represents the total number of considerations total into account on the second. We give the derivation of Equation 6.2 in the appendix to this chapter.[3] This equation underscores the role of several variables in explaining response consistency over time and across contexts. It asserts that a key characteristic of an attitude is the homogeneity of the considerations on which it rests (ρ_2). On a qualitative level, the model predicts that the correlation between responses will generally increase with ρ_1 (the reliability of the scaling

---

[3] To simplify the derivation, we have assumed that the individual scale values (the s's in Equation 6.1) have a variance of 1; this is a purely technical assumption that does not effect the generality of the results. A second assumption is potentially more limiting; Equation 6.2 assumes that the expected correlation between considerations taken into account on two occasions is described by $\rho_1 \rho_2$ – i.e., it is the same as the consistency within an occasion except for the effects of unreliability in assigning scale values. Of course, as more time passes and there are larger amounts of attitude change, this assumption will become less tenable. In such situations, a third parameter ρ_3 – representing the expected correlation between distinct considerations retrieved on different occasions – would be needed in place of $\rho_1 \rho_2$ in the numerator of Equation 6.2 (cf. Kenny, 1991). Because the discussion concerns situations in which attitudes are measured twice over relatively short periods of time (such as a few weeks), we focus on the simpler model in Equation 6.2.

process), ρ_2, and q (the degree of overlap in the samples of considerations taken into account on the different occasions). The model also clearly calls for some interactions between these variables. The most obvious of these involves the interaction between the overlap and homogeneity parameters: As ρ_2 approaches 1.0, the impact of q nears 0: As the underlying considerations point more uniformly in the same direction, it matters less whether the respondent retrieves the same ones on different occasions. The exact effects of n_1 and n_2 – the number of things considered on each occasion – also depend on the values of the other parameters of the model.

Equation 6.2 has a special case worth mentioning. When both n_1 and n_2 are equal to 1 and that one consideration is the same on both occasions (i.e., q is equal to 1), then the expected level of the correlation between target responses is ρ_1: The only factor affecting response consistency is the reliability of scaling. This special case describes the situation in which target answers in both interviews come from the same previously formed evaluation on the issue.

6.3.3   The Effects of Thought

The belief-sampling model might seem to imply that responses to attitude questions mainly reflect variability in the retrieval or generation of relevant considerations: Respondents who think about the issue more deeply before answering should exhibit greater consistency over time; the larger the sample of considerations, the less variability in the average. There are, however, a number of findings indicating that thinking more deeply about an issue may *decrease* the stability of responses.

According to the model, additional thought on a topic primarily means retrieving additional considerations about it. The effect of continued retrieval depends on several variables. One of them is the size of the underlying pool of relevant considerations. If the respondent knows only a few things about the issue, then additional thought is unlikely to yield much; even with limited retrieval, the pool will quickly be exhausted and further retrieval will add few new considerations. Thus, with poorly developed attitudes, additional thought should not produce change in either direction, and that's what was reported by Tesser and Leone (1977) and Chaiken and Yates (1985). Among respondents who do have more extensive attitude structures, a key variable is whether the considerations they encompass mostly favor the same side. If the retrieval process adds considerations that are consistent with those already re-trieved, the result will be a more extreme judgment; similarly, adding inconsistent considerations will produce a less extreme judgment. Thus, according to the model, whether polarization or moderation occurs de-pends on the level of attitude conflict. This may explain Millar and Tesser's (1986) finding that attitude structures that yield polarization consist of correlated (i.e., evaluatively consistent) dimensions.

A series of studies by Wilson and his colleagues has examined what happens when respondents are asked to give the reasons for their evalu-ations. Asking respondents for the reasons for their answers might lead to deeper thought about the issue (i.e., a larger sample of considerations) or it might shift attention from the feelings that are the usual basis for their judgments to more cognitive considerations (cf. Millar & Tesser, 1986; see also Breckler & Wiggins, 1989, on the relative independence of the cognitive and affective components of attitudes). Wilson and Dunn (1986) showed that asking respondents to focus on the reasons for their attitudes can reduce the correlation between answers to attitude questions and subsequent behaviors. A later study (Wilson et al., 1989) showed that the effect of asking for reasons was limited to respondents with little knowledge about the issue (see also Zaller & Feldman, 1992). Such respondents have only a small pool of relevant considerations that they can draw from; asking them to give reasons for their attitudes may force them to cast a broader net than usual – to retrieve or generate reasons that aren't necessarily consistent with their existing evaluation. By forcing respondents to take into account considerations that wouldn't otherwise have occurred to them, asking for reasons may change the answers to attitude questions and reduce their ability to predict subse-quent behaviors toward the attitude target.

Thinking more deeply about an issue won't increase response stability if it decreases the consistency of the considerations respondents take into account. This drop in consistency can occur if respondents retrieve or generate considerations they would not ordinarily think of or if they shift from affective to cognitive considerations in answering the ques-tions.

6.4   Tests of the Belief-Sampling Model

Three studies have examined the stability of responses over time in order to test hypotheses from the belief-sampling and similar models (e.g., Zaller, 1992). These studies have focused on two main questions – the impact of mixed views about an issue on response stability and the effects on stability of overlap in the sample of considerations respondents take into account on each occasion. All three studies used retrospective probes that asked respondents, in effect, to recount the considerations on which they'd based their answers to conventional attitude questions.

The first study, by Zaller and Feldman (1992), used data from a pilot study for the National Election Study (NES). Three hundred sixty respondents were interviewed in May and again in June 1987. All had taken part in the 1986 NES. In both pilot interviews, respondents received identical items about job guarantees, government services, and aid to blacks:

(4) a. Some people think the government in Washington should see to it that every person has a job and a good standard of living. Others think that government should just let each person get ahead on their own.

  b. Some people think the government should provide fewer services, even in areas such as health and education, in order to reduce spending. Other people feel it is important for the government to provide many more services even if it means an increase in spending.

  c. Some people think the government in Washington should make every effort to improve the social and economic position of blacks. Others feel that government should not make any special effort to help blacks because they should help themselves.

The respondents reported their views about these issues on seven-point scales. They also reported what things came to mind as they thought about these issues, either just before or just after they answered the questions. Interviewers recorded these thoughts verbatim, and the open-ended material was subsequently coded.

Two other studies used similar methods to investigate the stability of answers to attitude questions. Tourangeau and Rasinski carried out a telephone survey of attitudes on welfare and abortion with a random sample of households in Chicago; 499 respondents were interviewed twice, three weeks apart. In both interviews, respondents answered open-ended probes like the one Zaller and Feldman used and also responded to five agree-disagree items each about abortion and welfare. Like Zaller and Feldman, Tourangeau and Rasinski varied whether the open-ended probes immediately preceded or followed the agreement items. One of the agreement questions about each issue was repeated verbatim in both interviews.

A potential drawback shared by this study and the one by Zaller and Feldman is that the attitudes concerned issues on which at least some of the respondents had existing, even long-standing, views; as a result, key characteristics of the underlying attitudes (such as the degree to which they encompass a mix of considerations) may be confounded with other characteristics (such as their extremity). To address this problem, Tourangeau and Rasinski carried out a second study in which they examined newly formed attitudes (i.e., attitudes about a fictitious issue). A sample of 192 adults read a set of arguments about a proposed highway project and completed a questionnaire assessing their views about the project. Two weeks later, the participants were reinterviewed by telephone. The number and composition of the arguments in the initial session were systematically varied across experimental conditions. Half of the participants read eight arguments about the highway project; the other half read only four. Some participants got mainly pro arguments, some mainly con arguments, and the rest received equal numbers on both sides. The initial session and the follow-up interview included both conventional attitude items on the highway project and open-ended probes designed to elicit the considerations on which participants based their answers.

The Impact of Mixed Views

One of the clearest implications of the belief-sampling model is that the instability of answers across interviews is due to sampling variability; the impact of sampling variability, in turn, depends on whether respondents have a mix of considerations they can bring to bear on the question. Respondents with relatively homogeneous or one-sided views will still produce consistent answers even if they don't retrieve the same considerations, since whichever considerations they do take into account will still point in the same direction. Those with mixed underlying views, by contrast, are likely to give different responses when their answers are based on different considerations.

There are many ways to assess the degree of consistency in the underlying pool of considerations (see Priester & Petty, 1996, for a thorough exploration). Equation 6.2 uses the expected correlation between any two considerations a respondent holds (ρ_2). Zaller and Feldman (1992) developed a measure based on the open-ended answers in the two interviews. They took the absolute difference between the number of statements on one side of the issue and the number on the other, divided by the total number of statements:

$$\frac{|\text{Number pro} - \text{Number con}|}{\text{Total number}}$$

This measure is the size of the majority of considerations favoring one side, expressed as a proportion of the total number of considerations mentioned (cf. the ambivalence measure introduced in Kaplan, 1972; see also Bargh et al., 1992). Tourangeau and Rasinski used a similar measure; they classified respondents by the size of the majority of considerations on one side of the issue (i.e., they used the numerator of Zaller and Feldman's measure).[4] Tourangeau and Rasinski also included a self-report measure of mixed views in their first study:

(5) Would you say that you are strongly on one side or the other on the [abortion/welfare] issue or would you say your feelings are mixed?

Table 6.2 shows the correlation of answers to the attitude questions repeated across interviews in the three studies. For all six issues in these studies, the correlations between answers to the same question in different interviews were significantly higher when the considerations respondents cited in explaining their answers were more consistent. In addition, the correlations across interviews were significantly higher for respondents who said their views were strongly on one side of the issue than for those who said they had mixed views.

The Impact of Overlapping Considerations

The belief-sampling model also indicates that as respondents take into account more of the same considerations each time they answer a ques-

---

[4] In applying their method, Zaller and Feldman (1992) pooled the considerations mentioned in both interviews. Tourangeau and Rasinski classified respondents based solely on their open-ended answer in the *first* interview. A potential problem with Zaller and Feldman's procedure is that it could confound mixed underlying views about an issue with changes in those views across the interviews. If respondents mentioned considerations in the second interview that were on the opposite side from those they cited in the first interview, then the problem might be attitude change rather than ambivalence.

TABLE 6.2 Correlation of Answers Across Interviews, by Consistency
of Considerations

| | Zaller and Feldman (1992) | | |
	Job Guarantees	Government Services	Aid to Blacks
Size of Majority			
Equally pro and con	.50 (7)	.59 (11)	.57 (7)
Up to half of total	.80 (20)	.70 (25)	.71 (19)
More than half of total	.77 (15)	.78 (16)	.80 (15)
All considerations on one side	.91 (63)	.87 (54)	.96 (71)
	$p < .01$	$p < .02$	$p < .01$

| | Tourangeau and Rasinski | | |
	Abortion	Welfare	Highway Project
Size of majority			
Equally pro and con	.61 (40)	.58 (51)	.65 (26)
Majority on one consideration	.76 (416)	.62 (416)	.80 (35)
Majority of two or more	.81 (34)	.82 (22)	.89 (53)
	$p < .05$	$p < .05$	$p < .01$
Self-Report			
Mixed views	.58 (175)	.54 (306)	—
Views all on one side	.81 (314)	.72 (184)	—
	$p < .001$	$p < .001$	

Note: The parenthetical entries are sample sizes. See text for a detailed description of the size of majority and self-report measures of consistency of considerations. The Zaller and Feldman results reflect only the open-ended material gathered from the retrospective probes.

tion about an issue, their answers will be more consistent. (In Equation 6.2, this effect is captured by n_2q, which represents the number of considerations taken into account both times.) The coders in the Tourangeau and Rasinski studies noted whether each consideration cited in the open-ended answer in the second interview was substantially the same as one cited in the first interview.[5]

As Table 6.3 shows, the results for overlapping considerations support the belief-sampling model. For all three issues Tourangeau and Rasinski examined, respondents with at least one overlapping statement in their open-ended answers showed significantly higher correlations across interviews than those with no overlapping statements. For example, the correlations between responses to the abortion target item were .35 among respondents whose open-ended answers showed no overlap across interviews, .79 among those whose open-ended answers included one shared consideration, and .84 among those whose open-ended answers shared two considerations across interviews.

Quantitative Models of Response Stability

Once values for the two parameters – ρ_1 and ρ_2 – are estimated, Equation 6.2 can also be used to make quantitative predictions about the correlations between target responses across interviews. The coding of the open-ended data in the Tourangeau and Rasinski studies yielded values for each respondent for the other key variables in the model:

- n_1, the number of considerations taken into account in the first interview,
- n_2, the number taken into account in the second interview, and
- q, the proportion of the considerations mentioned in the second interview that were also mentioned in the first.

---

[5] A potential problem with the method employed in these studies is that the open-ended responses may not reflect the considerations on which respondents actually based target responses. When the open-ended questions followed the target, the respondents may have generated post facto rationalizations for their target answers. When the open-ended questions came first, respondents may have changed the basis for target answers (as in the studies by Wilson and his colleagues). Because the design of two of these studies varied whether the open-ended questions preceded or followed the target questions, they yield some data relevant to these possibilities. The relative position of the open-ended and target questions had no discernible effect on the direction, extremity, or reliability of the target answers or on the content of the open-ended responses in the Tourangeau and Rasinski study. More important, question order had little impact on the relation between the open-ended responses and the target answers. The Zaller and Feldman study did find some differences, depending on when the probes were administered. They attributed these differences, however, to the greater length of the answers to the prospective probes and the increased unreliability of coding these answers compared to those of the retrospective probes.

TABLE 6.3 Correlation of Target Answers Across Interviews, by
Number of Overlapping Considerations Mentioned

	Abortion	Welfare	Highway
Overlap in open-ended responses			
No shared statements	.35 (68)	.04 (95)	.77 (71)
One shared statement	.79 (386)	.72 (374)	.91 (71)
Two or more shared statements	.84 (27)	.63 (12)	.96 (28)

Note: Parenthetical entries are sample sizes.

Tourangeau and Rasinski used nonlinear regression to estimate values
for ρ_1 and ρ_2 for each issue. Figure 6.1a–c displays the predicted and
observed correlations as a function of the number of considerations
respondents took into account on the two occasions and the overlap
between these considerations. The values on the horizontal axis indicate
the number of considerations mentioned in the initial interview (n_1, the
first digit of the group label), the number mentioned in the second
interview (n_2, the second digit in the label), and the number of overlapping considerations (n_2q, the final digit of the label). For example, in
the group labeled 222, the same two considerations were cited in the
open-ended answers in both interviews.[6]

The fit is quite good for all three issues. The model accounts for 81%
of the variance in the abortion correlations, 74% of the variance in the
welfare correlations, and 57% of the variance in the highway correlations. (The poorer fit in the highway study may partly reflect the smaller

---

[6] One of the observed welfare correlations was actually nonsignificantly negative; prior to
fitting the model, we replaced the actual value with .00. We also dropped cells involving
fewer than 10 respondents.

In the highway study the number of respondents was small, and to increase the number
of observations on which each correlation was based, we combined the data for respondents who cited similar numbers of considerations. Respondents gave especially detailed
answers to the open-ended questions in the first session (when they wrote out their
answers). For the initial session, we combined those who listed one consideration with
those who listed two; those who listed three considerations with those who listed four;
and those who listed five considerations with those who listed more than five. These
groups were treated as though they had cited one, two, or three considerations, respectively. In the follow-up interview, we combined all those respondents who listed three or
more considerations, treating them as though they had cited three. Finally, we grouped
all respondents with one or more overlapping considerations, treating them as if they had
cited a single overlapping consideration in both open-ended answers.

a) Welfare

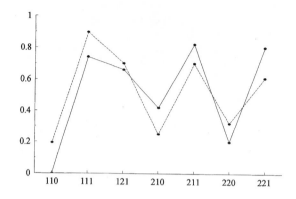

b) Abortion

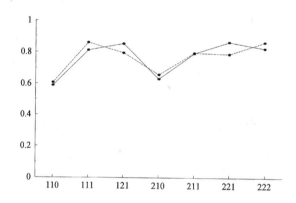

c) Highway

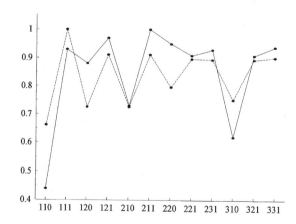

sample sizes – about 12 per cell – on which the correlations from that study were based.) The estimated value of ρ_1 (the reliability of the scaling process) was similar for the three issues – .86 for abortion, .90 for welfare, and 1.00 for the highway project. By contrast, the estimates of the homogeneity parameter ρ_2 differ quite sharply across the issues – .71 for abortion and .66 for the highway project but only .22 for welfare. Apparently, the considerations underlying responses to the welfare item are more diverse than those underlying responses to the other two issues. This result is consistent with the finding that far more respondents described their views on welfare as mixed (62% of the sample) than described their abortion views that way (36%).

Other Findings

One of the less obvious implications of the model summarized in Equation 6.2 is that the impact of the number of considerations sampled depends on their homogeneity. When the considerations clearly favor one side of an issue, sampling more of them will increase response consistency; when the considerations are mixed, however, increasing the sample size may *decrease* consistency. The highway study provides an opportunity to test this hypothesis; that study experimentally varied the size and composition of the considerations initially presented to the respondents.

Table 6.4 shows the correlations between overall evaluations across occasions (final column) and between two items administered in the initial session (the middle column). The logic of Equation 6.2 applies equally well whether one item is administered on two occasions or two items are administered on one occasion.

For the correlation across occasions, there is a significant interaction between the number of arguments initially presented and their overall direction (biased toward one side vs. mixed). The pattern is somewhat similar (although not significant) for the two items in the initial session. The impact of the number of arguments on response consistency depends

Figure 6.1 (opposite). Predicted (dashed line) and observed correlations (solid line) between target responses in the two interviews. The labels on the horizontal axis indicate the number of considerations cited in the first interview (the first digit), the number cited in the second (second digit), and the number judged to be the same in both interviews (the final digit). Panel (a) presents the results for welfare, panel (b) presents the results for abortion, and panel (c) the results for the highway project.

TABLE 6.4 Correlation of Target Answers Across Interviews, by Number of Mix of Considerations in Initial Session

Experimental Group	Overall – Economy (Time 1)	Overall (Time 1–Time 2)
1 pro/3 con arguments	.485 (32)	.785 (30)
2 pro/6 con arguments	.382 (32)	.880 (30)
2 pro/2 con arguments	.536 (31)	.912 (29)
4 pro/4 con arguments	.431 (31)	.814 (30)
3 pro/1 con arguments	.405 (31)	.743 (30)
6 pro/2 con arguments	.598 (31)	.917 (28)

Note: Parenthetical entries are sample sizes. "Overall" refers to an item asking for an overall evaluation of the proposed highway project; "Economy" refers to an item about its effects on the local economy.

on whether they point in the same direction. When the arguments clearly favored one side, the correlation between responses to the same question over time was greater when the respondent read eight arguments rather than four. When the initial arguments were mixed, however, the correlations were lower when respondents had initially read more of them.

6.5   Conclusions

In a thoughtful paper, Wilson and Hodges (1992) distinguish the file drawer and the construal models of attitudes. According to the file drawer model, attitudes are existing evaluations that people look up when they need to; it is only when no evaluation is found that they take the trouble to form a new judgment. According to the construal view, the file drawers contain contents other than evaluations, and these are the basis for answers to attitude questions.

In this chapter, we argue for an intermediate view. We see attitudes as a kind of memory structure that contains existing evaluations, vague impressions, general values, and relevant feelings and beliefs. On any given occasion when we think about an issue, some subset of these contents will come to mind. Depending on which considerations we retrieve and the exact requirements of the task at hand, we may simply reiterate an existing evaluation, update it, or extend it to cover a new aspect of an issue; or we may make an entirely new judgment about the issue.

As with the strategies we use to answer temporal and frequency questions, the type of information we tap in answering attitude questions depends both on its relative accessibility and on more strategic considerations, such as our level of motivation to reach a defensible position. Regardless of the type of information we use to make our judgment, the stability of our answers over time will depend on the internal consistency of our views about the issue, the extent to which we consider the same information on both occasions, and the extent to which we construe that information in the same way.

APPENDIX. DERIVATION OF EQUATION 6.2

Equation 6.1 asserts that the answers to a question on two occasions reflect judgments (J_1 and J_2) that are simple averages (i.e., $J_1 = \Sigma s_{1i} / n_1$) – that is, sums divided by a constant. The covariance of two sums is the sum of the covariances of the terms in each sum. The covariance of one term with a second term times a constant is just the covariance of the two terms times that constant. Thus, the covariance of J_1 and J_2 is

$$\mathrm{Cov}(J_1, J_2) = \Sigma \mathrm{Cov}(s_{1i}, s_{2i}) / n_1 n_2,$$

where the summation is across the $n_1 n_2$ pairs of scale values assigned to the considerations taken into account on the two occasions. This sum includes both overlapping and nonoverlapping pairs. There are $n_2 q$ overlapping pairs; the covariance of between the members of these pairs is $\rho_1 \mathrm{Var}(s_{1i}) \mathrm{Var}(s_{2i})$ – that is, their correlation times the product of their variances. Because we have assumed that scale values have a variance of 1, the covariance of the scale values of an overlapping pair reduces to ρ_1, the correlation between the scale values assigned to the same consideration on different occasions. There are $n_1 n_2 - n_2 q$ pairs of considerations that do not overlap; these have a covariance of $\rho_1 \rho_2$, the correlation between the values assigned to different considerations on different occasions. Thus, $\mathrm{Cov}(J_1, J_2)$ can be expressed as

$$\Sigma \mathrm{Cov}(s_{1i}, s_{2i}) / n_1 n_2 = (n_1 n_2 \rho_1 \rho_2 + n_2 q \rho_1 (1 - \rho_2)) / n_1 n_2$$

The variance of J_1 is the covariance of J_1 with itself:

$$\mathrm{Var}(J_1) = \Sigma \mathrm{Cov}(s_{1i}, s_{1j}) / n_1^2$$

The summation is across n_1^2 pairs. Of these pairs, n_1 consists of the same consideration and has a covariance of 1. The remaining $n_1^2 - n_1$ pairs have an expected correlation of ρ_2 (this is just the definition of ρ_2). Thus, the variance of J_1 is

$$\begin{aligned} Var(J_1) &= \Sigma Cov(s_{1i}, s_{1j}) / n_1^2 \\ &= (n_1^2\rho_2 + n_1(1 - \rho_2)) / n_1^2 \end{aligned}$$

The same reasoning holds for the variance of J_2 and implies that

$$Var(J_2) = (n_2^2\rho_2 + n_2(1 - \rho_2)) / n_2^2$$

Finally, the correlation between J_1 and J_2 (and the overt responses that are linear transforms of J_1 and J_2) is

$$\begin{aligned} \hat{r}_{12} &= Cov(J_1, J_2) / [Var(J_1)Var(J_2)]^{1/2} \\ &= \frac{n_1 n_2 \rho_1 \rho_2 + n_2 q \rho_1 (1 - \rho_2)}{([n_1^2\rho_2 + n_1(1 - \rho_2)][n_2^2\rho_2 + n_2(1 - \rho_2)])^{1/2}} \end{aligned}$$

which is the same as Equation 6.2.

CHAPTER SEVEN

Attitude Judgments and Context Effects

The view of attitudes presented in the preceding chapter implies that attitude judgments are temporary constructions (Wilson & Hodges, 1992). They may rest on long-standing evaluations and beliefs about a topic, but the judgments themselves must often be created in response to a question, sometimes quite quickly. Moreover, the judgments called for by attitude questions are rarely absolute but are typically made in relation to some standard, generally an implicit one. It is hardly surprising, then, that attitude judgments turn out to be quite context-dependent. As survey researchers have demonstrated repeatedly, the same question often produces quite different answers, depending on the context (see Bradburn, 1982, and Schuman & Presser, 1981, for numerous survey examples). To cite just one particularly well-documented example, the level of support expressed for legal abortions when the "woman is married and does not want any more children" depends on whether that question comes before or after a similar question on abortion when "there is a strong chance of a serious defect in the baby" (Schuman, 1992; Schuman & Presser, 1981). Asking the birth defect question first can greatly reduce support for abortion for married women who simply don't want any more children.

According to the belief-sampling model, the stability of attitude responses across different occasions or contexts largely reflects three factors – the homogeneity of the underlying pool of considerations related to the topic, the overlap in the samples of considerations that are the basis for responses to the different questions (or the same question in different contexts), and the reliability of the process of evaluating these considerations. As we shall see, question context can affect all three of these variables, altering the pool of considerations that are seen as relevant, the specific considerations tapped in making the judgment, and the use of these considerations in forming a judgment.

7.1   Forms of Context Effects

Two different patterns of evidence have been cited as demonstrating the effects of question context. In the typical context effects study, context is varied by changing the order of two or more questions. The target question comes either before or after some related question (or set of related questions). When the target question follows the context items, one of two things can happen. The first is a shift in the overall mean (or marginal proportions) of responses to the target. For example, in the case of the two questions on legalized abortion, administering the chance-of-birth-defect question first changes the marginal distribution of responses to the woman-is-married question, lowering the overall level of support for abortions under this circumstance. We will refer to such changes in the overall direction of answers to a question as *directional* context effects. The second thing that can happen is a change in the correlations between the target and context questions. For example, it is possible that the correlation between the answers to the two abortion questions could depend on the order in which they were administered. We will refer to context effects that alter the relation between two (or more) questions as *correlational* context effects.

Most of the mechanisms cited in explanations of survey context effects seem to call for correlational effects. For instance, the preceding questions in the questionnaire or interview may suggest considerations that are relevant to a later question. Because responses to both the prior and subsequent questions are based on these overlapping considerations, one would expect the correlation between the two to be higher than under ordinary circumstances – when the questions are, say, administered in separate interviews or in widely separated sections of the same interview. According to Equation 6.2, the increased overlap should lead to an increased correlation. In practice, however, what is generally reported in the literature are directional effects: Answers to a target question shift one way or the other as a function of the context in which they are embedded.

One reason for the preponderance of directional effects is that context questions are often chosen because they tend to elicit more or less uniform responses. Almost everyone – more than 80% of the general population – favors giving women the right to choose an abortion when there is a strong chance of a serious birth defect. As a result, respondents may vary little in their evaluations of the context questions. When there is little or no variation in answers to the context questions, it's hard to see a heightened correlation between answers to these questions and responses to the target question. Instead, everyone will be moved in the same direction by the context questions, producing a directional effect on target responses.

The distinction between correlational and directional effects is closely related to a second distinction in the survey literature on question context effects – the distinction between conditional and unconditional context effects (T. W. Smith, 1986, 1992a). *Unconditional* effects refer to cases in which the context items have the same impact on answers to a subsequent question regardless of how respondents answer the context questions themselves. For example, an experiment by Tourangeau and his colleagues compared the answers of three groups of respondents to a question on defense spending (Tourangeau et al., 1989a). One group received a series of questions about the military threat posed by the Soviet Union just before the question on defense spending; a second group received a series of questions about the need for arms control before the defense spending question; and the final group received a set of unrelated questions before the defense spending question. Regardless of how they answered the Soviet threat items, the respondents who answered these questions first showed higher levels of support for increased defense spending than respondents in the other two groups. Evidently, even among those who did not see the Soviets as posing much of a threat, the questions still engendered favorable reactions to an increase in the defense budget. In other cases, the direction or size of the effect of the earlier questions does depend on how respondents answer those questions (see, e.g., the cases cited by T. W. Smith, 1992a).

When the effects of context are unconditional, everyone is, by definition, moved in the same direction by the context questions and a directional effect is the necessary result. When the impact of the context questions is conditional (i.e., dependent on how the respondents answered them) – so that some respondents are moved in one direction and some are moved in the opposite direction – the overall result is generally an altered correlation between the context questions and the target question. There is an intermediate possibility considered by T. W. Smith (1992a), in which the magnitude but not the direction of the context effect is conditional on responses to the context items. For instance, it is possible that respondents who disagree with the Soviet threat questions are less affected by those questions than are respondents who endorse them.

Thus far, we have treated question context as being virtually synonymous with question order – as if the context of one question consisted solely of the questions that precede it in the questionnaire. In principle, of course, question context could have a much broader meaning, reflecting the purposes of the survey (as these were presented to the respondent), the climate of opinion at the time of the survey, the presence of other people during the interview, the characteristics of the interviewer, or even the weather at the time of the interview (Schwarz & Clore, 1983). As a practical matter, though, most research on question context has focused on the effects of earlier questions on answers to later ones.

An exception to this rule involves questions in self-administered questionnaires (SAQs). Several studies have attempted to determine whether question order effects are reduced or eliminated when the questions are self-administered (e.g., Ayidiya & McClendon, 1990; Bishop, Hippler, Schwarz, & Strack, 1988; Schwarz & Hippler, 1995). In an SAQ, the respondent has the freedom to look ahead or to go back to earlier questions. As a result, the order in which the questions are presented is less likely to affect the answers they elicit. For the most part, the expected interaction between mode of administration and question order has not been found in these studies, although the trend is generally in the right direction. Even when respondents have the option of ignoring the order of the questions in the questionnaire and completing them in whatever order they please, it's not clear how often they take advantage of this freedom. The important point made by these studies is that the key variable that determines the context of a question is the order in which the questions are *processed*, which may or may not be the same as the order in which they are presented in the questionnaire.

7.2   Mechanisms Producing Context Effects

Researchers have cited a wide range of principles in explaining context effects. Schuman and Presser (1981) distinguished several types of context effects based on the relative generality of the context and target questions and on the overall direction of the impact of context. Both of these distinctions have proved useful and have been retained in most later explorations of the effects of question context.

The *level of generality* variable refers to whether the context question(s) concerns a broader issue than the target question, an issue at the same level of generality, or an issue that is more specific than the one raised by the target question. A question on free speech is broader than one on free speech for extremist groups, which is broader in turn than a question on free speech for members of the Ku Klux Klan (Ottati et al., 1989). In some cases, the level of generality variable reduces to a matter of class inclusion (see Schwarz & Bless, 1992a, for an example). The issue of free speech includes free speech for extremist groups (among others) as a special case; similarly, the class of extremist groups includes the Klan (along with other groups). In some cases, though, establishing the relative generality of two questions is not so straightforward. Schuman and Presser (1981) argued that the woman-is-married abortion question is more general than the birth-defect question; it is quite possible, though, that respondents see these two questions as offering reasons that differ in content rather than in generality.

The other distinction proposed by Schuman and Presser concerns the direction of the effect of context on the answers to the later question. They distinguished between *consistency* and *contrast* effects. In a consistency effect, responses to the target question move in the direction of answers to the context question(s); in a contrast effect, responses to the target question move away from the direction of answers to the context questions. Both terms imply correlational (and conditional) effects, but most of the examples investigated by Schuman and Presser involved unconditional, directional shifts in answers to the target question. Again, the observed directional effects may reflect the lack of variation in responses to the context questions. Most subsequent researchers have retained a similar distinction, adopting the terms *assimilation* and *contrast* to describe the two types of effect.

The context effects observed in surveys have parallels in the psychological literature on social and psychophysical judgments, and several investigators have attempted to show that the theoretical mechanisms discussed in the psychological literature account for the survey findings as well (Strack & Martin, 1987; Sudman, Bradburn, & Schwarz, 1996, Chapters 4 and 5; Tourangeau & Rasinski, 1988). These models tend to explain context effects according to the component of the response process during which they arise.

7.2.1   Context and Question Comprehension

Assimilation effects

Although survey researchers place a premium on writing clear questions, as we saw in Chapter 2, the interpretation of survey questions, like the interpretation of most everyday language, is heavily dependent on context. An essential component of the comprehension process is identifying the higher-level structures into which the current sentence (or question) fits. These higher-level structures include any larger ongoing representations – such as narratives – that the sentence is supposed to advance (Mandler & Johnson, 1977), the category or schema it is related to (Abelson, 1981; Bransford & Johnson, 1972), or the speech act it's intended to carry out (Clark, 1985). These higher-level structures are the basis for a host of inferences that enable readers or listeners to fill in missing or implicit information, to disentangle references to earlier information, and to identify indirect speech acts. Context is often the key to determining which higher-level structures should guide the interpretation of a survey question.

With survey questions, the clues provided by context are likely to be particularly important when the question deals with an obscure, ambiguous, or unfamiliar issue. Studies by Tourangeau and Rasinski (1986) and Strack, Schwarz, and Wänke (1991) illustrate the potential effects of context on responses to questions about such issues. The study by Tourangeau and Rasinski examined responses to a question on the Monetary Control Bill, an obscure piece of proposed legislation that figured in earlier experiments by Schuman and Presser (1981). Levels of reported support for the bill increased when the question on the Monetary Control Bill followed a block of items about inflation (see Table 7.1). Under this context condition, many respondents apparently inferred that the question on the Monetary Control Bill was one more item in the series about inflation and that the bill must be an anti-inflation measure. When the inflation questions were scattered among questions on unrelated issues, they no longer affected responses to the question on the Monetary Control Bill. With the blocked inflation questions, respondents seemed to apply Grice's maxim of relevance (see Section 2.5) and inferred that

TABLE 7.1 Context and the Interpretation of Unfamiliar Issues

Context	Responses to "Do you favor or oppose passage of the Monetary Control Bill?"		
	Favor	Oppose	Don't Know
Block of inflation questions	27.5%	17.5%	55.0%
Scattered inflation questions	8.8%	20.0%	71.2%
Neutral questions	12.5%	25.0%	62.5%

Source: Data from Tourangeau and Rasinski (1988).

the topic of the Monetary Control Bill must be inflation; when the questions shifted from one topic to the next (as in the scattered condition), they realized that Grice's maxims didn't apply and they stopped trying to infer the purpose of the bill.

The study by Strack, Schwarz, and Wänke (1991) asked students at German universities (which are tuition-free) about a vague "educational contribution"; that item followed an item either about college tuition in the United States or about government financial support for students in Sweden. Support for the educational contribution was higher in the latter condition. Respondents who got the U.S. item first apparently inferred that the educational contribution was to be taken *from* them, and those who get the item on Sweden first thought that it would be given *to* them.

These findings have numerous counterparts in the literature on social judgments. For example, Herr, Sherman, and Fazio (1983) report that, as with the Monetary Control Bill, subjects in their studies assimilated unfamiliar stimuli to the more familiar ones they had judged earlier, presumably because they saw them as members of the same category. Martin (1986) and Trope (1986) have also shown that the encoding of ambiguous stimuli may depend on prior stimuli or situational cues.

Contrast Effects

Question context can also affect respondents' inferences about the relation between adjacent questions, and these inferences can produce contrast effects. In particular, several studies have shown that when a specific question concerning a topic precedes a more general question on the same topic, it can alter answers to the general question. In most of these studies, the general question concerns the respondents' overall happiness and the specific question their happiness with their marriages or romantic relationships (Schuman & Presser, 1981; Schwarz, Strack, & Mai, 1991; T. W. Smith, 1986; Tourangeau, Rasinski, & Bradburn, 1991). A few studies have examined other topics, such as drivers in general and young drivers (Kalton, Collins, & Brook, 1978) or the state economy and the economy of the respondents' local community (Mason et al., 1995). In most cases, the preceding specific question produces contrast effects on responses to the general question, although there are exceptions (T. W. Smith, 1986; Turner & Martin, 1984).

What all of these studies have in common is that one question asks for an evaluation of some domain or category and the other question asks for an evaluation of a highly salient member of that domain. Marital happiness is, for example, probably the most important single determinant of overall happiness (McClendon & O'Brien, 1988). Moreover, the phrasing of the general happiness question as a summary (*Taken altogether, how would you say things are these days? Would you say that you are very happy, pretty happy, or not too happy?*) must seem a little odd to respondents; it is as if they were being asked to sum up having covered only a single point. Together, the two happiness questions seem to violate Grice's (1975) maxim of quantity (that one's contribution to a conversation should be informative and avoid redundancy). Several investigators have argued that, as a result of this apparent overlap between the two questions, respondents interpret the general question as excluding the specific mentioned in the prior question, taking the general item to mean something like "Aside from your marriage, how would you say things are these days?"

Two similar studies have tested this account (Schwarz, Strack & Mai, 1991; Tourangeau, Rasinski, & Bradburn, 1991). Both included versions of the general happiness question that explicitly instructed respondents about what they should take into account or leave out. In the study by Tourangeau and his colleagues, the inclusion version read "Taking things all together, including your marriage and other important aspects of your life, how would you say things are these days?" and the exclusion version read "Aside from your marriage, how would you say things are these days?" The study by Schwarz and his coworkers used similar wording, but the specific question concerned the respondents' current romantic relationships, allowing unmarried persons to take part. Table 7.2 shows the correlations between responses to the general and specific questions. As expected, these correlations are high when the general question came first (indicating that respondents spontaneously consider their marriages/relationships in evaluating their overall happiness) and when the general question explicitly instructs respondents to include them; they are low when the general question comes second (indicating that respondents exclude their marriages/relationships under this order) and when the question explicitly calls for their exclusion. These findings are displayed in the first two columns of correlations given in the table.

Respondents will not always infer that consecutive general and specific questions are redundant. The general question might seem less redundant (and more natural) if it followed *several* specific questions; it's hardly uninformative to sum up after discussing many specific aspects of an issue. In addition, questionnaires are not necessarily structured like conversations; they frequently change subjects without warning, and when they do, respondents seem to have little trouble understanding that

TABLE 7.2 Correlations between Responses to General and Specific Questions, by Study and Condition

| | | Schwarz et al. (1991) | |
Condition	Tourangeau et al. (1991)	One Specific Question	Three Specific Questions
General–specific	.54 (60)	—	.32 (50)
Specific–general – no introduction	—	.67 (50)	.46 (50)
Specific–general – joint lead-in	.28 (53)	.18 (56)	.48 (56)
Specific–general – exclusion wording	.27 (54)	.20 (50)	.11 (50)
Specific–general – inclusion wording	.52 (59)	.61 (50)	.53 (50)

Note: Parenthetical entries are sample sizes.
Source: Data from Tourangeau, Rasinski, and Bradburn (1991) and from Schwartz, Strack, and Mai (1991) copyright © 1991. Reprinted with permission of the University of Chicago Press.

the rules governing conversations do not apply. Respondents are unlikely to reinterpret the general question to reduce its overlap with the preceding specific question unless they think that the two are supposed to be taken as a unit; the apparent overlap between the questions will not affect interpretations if their juxtaposition is seen as merely coincidental.

Schwarz and his colleagues included conditions that tested these further hypotheses (Schwarz, Strack, & Mai, 1991). Their study varied the number of specific domains that respondents were asked about and whether the happiness questions were administered without any introduction at all or with a lead-in that emphasized the connection between them (*We would like to ask you to report on two aspects of your life, which may be relevant to people's overall well-being*). As it happens, Tourangeau and his colleagues had included a similar, although less explicit, introduction to the happiness questions (*Now for a couple of questions on an unrelated topic*). The final column in Table 7.2 shows the results when the questionnaire includes three specific questions: Unless the general question explicitly asks respondents to leave out their relationships, the correlation between evaluations of romantic relationships and ratings of overall happiness is similarly high, regardless of question order. The results also indicate that when the questions are asked without any introduction at all, the correlation between the two happiness questions is high. For subtraction to occur, then, the respondents must infer that the Gricean maxims apply (i.e., they must see the questions as forming a connected sequence), and they must interpret the general question as calling for information not already supplied by their answers to the specific question.

7.2.2   Context and Retrieval Processes

One of the key assumptions of the belief-sampling model for answers to attitude questions is that respondents tap only a portion of the potentially relevant considerations in formulating their answers. They take a small sample consisting of what comes readily to mind; considerations that are highly accessible are therefore likely to dominate the responses. Prior questions on related topics can affect the accessibility of considerations relevant to a later question. For example, a study by Tourangeau and his colleagues (Tourangeau, Rasinski, & D'Andrade, 1991) showed that answering one question about an issue made respondents able to answer a second question more quickly; the impact was largest when the two questions were on related aspects of the issue (for a summary, see Chapter 6; see also Judd et al., 1991). The changes in accessibility produced by answering prior questions can also produce changes in the answers to later questions if the considerations made accessible by the earlier questions have different implications from those that would otherwise have been taken into account.

Retrieval-Based Assimilation Effects

Tourangeau and his colleagues conducted two studies that illustrate this sort of retrieval-based assimilation effect (Tourangeau et al., 1989a, 1989b). The prior questions in these studies were designed to increase the accessibility of considerations supporting one side of a target issue. For example, some respondents received a series of questions about the government's responsibility to the poor before they answered a question on welfare; other respondents received questions about economic individualism before the welfare item. Similarly, some respondents answered questions about women's rights before a question about abortion; others answered questions about traditional family values. In seven of ten comparisons from the two studies, respondents who had answered different context questions differed significantly in their answers to the subsequent target item. For example, in both studies the respondents who had answered the questions on government's responsibility to the poor were significantly more likely to support increased welfare spending than those who had answered questions on economic individualism. In all ten of the comparisons, the differences between context groups were in the direction of assimilation.

Two other findings from these studies are consistent with an account based on changes in the short-term accessibility of considerations related to the issue. First, the assimilation effects were larger when the context questions were presented in a block placed immediately before the target question than when they were scattered among unrelated questions. Changes in accessibility produced by prior questions wear off over time (e.g., Anderson, 1983). Assimilation effects based on accessibility changes should therefore be reduced when the presentation of the target question is delayed by intervening material. Second, the assimilation effects were larger when the context and target issues were more closely related. Tourangeau and his colleagues used the correlation between target and context responses as a crude measure of the connection between the two issues. When data from the two studies were combined, the correlation between the size of the target–context correlation and the size of the assimilation effect was .55. The degree to which retrieving one question from memory affects the accessibility of another question depends on the strength of the connection between the two; the more closely related two attitude issues are, the more that retrieving considerations about the one ought to affect the retrieval of considerations about the other.[1]

Many other studies have demonstrated the impact of accessible material on responses to survey questions (Bishop, 1987; Rasinski & Tourangeau, 1991; Schwarz & Bless, 1992a, 1992b), judgments of life satisfaction (Schwarz & Clore, 1983; Strack, Martin, & Schwarz, 1988; Strack et al., 1985), and other social judgments (Higgins, Rholes, & Jones, 1977; Srull & Wyer, 1979).

Disregarding Accessible Material

The mere fact that information is highly accessible does not guarantee that it will be used or, if it is used, that it will be included in the sample of considerations on which the judgment is based. As we noted in Chapter 6, material that is irrelevant, invalid, or redundant may be disregarded (see also Wilson & Brekke, 1994).

In a study by Schwarz and Bless (1992a), for example, German college students evaluated the two major German political parties – the Christian Democratic Union (CDU) and the Social Democratic Party (SDP). Evaluations of the CDU were affected by an earlier question

---

[1] A potential problem with this analysis is that the target–context correlations may themselves be affected by the context variable. However, the conclusion was unaffected when the correlations were based on the data from respondents who received the context questions *after* the target question (Tourangeau et al., 1989a).

about Richard von Weizsäcker, who was at the time the president of the Federal Republic of Germany. Von Weizsäcker was a highly respected politician and a long-term member of the CDU; views about him were, therefore, potentially quite relevant to evaluations of the CDU. At the same time, the office of the presidency was widely viewed as above the fray of partisan politics, so it was also quite reasonable for respondents to disregard their views about von Weizsäcker as irrelevant to the CDU. Respondents who answered a prior question on von Weizsäcker's membership in the CDU (*Do you happen to know which party Richard von Weizsäcker has been a member of for more than twenty years?*) gave higher evaluations of the CDU than respondents who answered a question about von Weizsäcker's office (*Do you happen to know which office Richard von Weizsäcker holds, setting him aside from party politics?*). Respondents who did not answer either question about von Weizsäcker gave evaluations that fell between those of the other two groups (see Table 7.3). When the context brought von Weizsäcker's relevance into question, respondents appeared to disregard their views about him in evaluating the CDU (to the detriment of the CDU). Of course, von Weizsäcker was never seen as relevant to evaluations of the SDP, since he had no connection with that party. The fact that the mean evaluation of the CDU in the group that received neither question about von Weizsäcker fell between those of the other two groups suggests that some respondents spontaneously considered von Weizsäcker in evaluating the CDU but that others did not.

Respondents may also discount information that they regard as invalid or unrepresentative in some way. In a study by Wilson et al. (1995), for example, respondents who had recalled an unrepresentative set of characteristics of a target person took this bias into account in rating the person, although only when the intervening task made the bias in recall salient. Similarly, respondents in a study by Schwarz, Bless, Strack, Klumpp, Rittenauer-Schatka, and Simons (1991) who were asked to recall 12 instances of assertive behavior rated themselves as *less* assertive than respondents asked to recall 6 instances; Schwarz and his colleagues argue that the sheer difficulty of recalling the additional examples suggested to the respondents how unrepresentative these examples must be. In another example, studies by Schwarz and Clore (1983) show that mood is an accessible cue used in evaluating life satisfaction; however, mood appears not to affect life satisfaction judgments when respondents are first asked about the weather. The question about the weather ap-

TABLE 7.3 Mean Ratings of German Political Parties by Prior
Questions on Richard von Weizsäcker

	Prior Question on von Weizsäcker		
Party Evaluated	About His Party	No Prior Question	About His Office
Christian Democrats (CDU)	6.5	5.2	3.4
Social Democrats (SDP)	6.3	6.3	6.2

Note: The evaluations are on a scale ranging from 1 to 11, with higher numbers indicating
more favorable evaluations.
Source: Data from Schwarz and Bless (1992a).

parently highlights the invalidity of mood as an indicator of the quality
of one's life.

Respondents may, finally, disregard accessible information simply because they feel that the task or question calls for something new and
different (e.g., Martin, 1986). We have already seen how Grice's maxim
of quantity can lead to the inference that a general question is meant to
exclude material used in answering an earlier, more specific question
(Schwarz, Strack, & Mai, 1991; Tourangeau, Rabinski, & Bradburn,
1991); in such cases, respondents may discount the accessible material
because they see it as repetitious. A study by Mason and his colleagues
provides another example (Mason et al., 1995); they asked respondents
to evaluate prospects for both the state economy and the economy of
their local community. When the local question came first, it affected
both answers to the question on the state economy and the *reasons*
respondents gave in explaining their answers. Job growth and employment were the reasons given most often in explaining views about the
state economy, but respondents were less likely to cite these reasons
when the state question followed the local question than when it came
first. Apparently, having already cited these factors in explaining their
views on the local economy, they felt their answers to the second question should be based on something new.

If respondents do decide to disregard accessible material, it will produce a contrast effect when they end up discounting considerations that
would otherwise have affected their judgments. For instance, in the study
by Mason and his colleagues, respondents who received the question on
the state economy after the question on the local economy ended up
discounting the very considerations mentioned most often by respondents who received the state question first (Mason et al., 1995).

7.2.3   Context and Judgment

It's not always obvious how to use a specific consideration in constructing an answer to an attitude question. Moreover, when multiple considerations come to mind, it may not be clear how to combine them into a final judgment. Following Norman Anderson's (1981) information integration theory, we have argued that this process is something like taking an average. This view implies that respondents must first assign scale values to each consideration – that is, they must figure out its implications for the question at hand. In some cases, they may give different weights to the different considerations that come to mind. In addition, they may, depending on the nature of the question, apply different rules or procedures to combine what they've retrieved into an overall judgment. All of the processes – the assignment of weights and scale values and the application of some rule for combining considerations – can be affected by question context.

The impact of context on attitude judgments may be so marked because so many of these judgments are relative. When we evaluate a political figure, say, that evaluation almost inevitably involves comparisons – to rival candidates, to other salient political figures, to our image of the typical politician, or to other political figures made salient by the question context. The standard of comparison for the judgment is likely to have an impact on which characteristics of the political figure come to mind and, more important, on how those characteristics are evaluated. With other judgments, the standard applied in rendering the judgment may be absolute; for example, a normative standard may be applied. Even here, however, context may play a role in determining which norm is applied.

Assimilation Effects on Judgment

One of the clearest cases of context affecting the norm invoked in making a judgment involves two questions originally used by Hyman and Sheatsley (1950) and investigated in detail by Schuman and Presser (1981) and Schuman and Ludwig (1983). One question asked whether "the United States should let Communist reporters come in here and send back to their papers the news as they see it?" The other asked whether "a Communist country like Russia should let American newspaper reporters come in and send back to their papers the news as they see it?" Support for free access for the Communist reporters varied sharply according to whether that question precedes or follows the question on American reporters (see Table 7.4). In fact, the original

TABLE 7.4 Proportion Endorsing Free Access for Communist
Reporters, by Question Order

	Study	
Question Order	Hyman & Sheatsley (1950)	Schuman & Presser (1981)
Communist question first	36%	55%
Communist question second	73%	75%

Note: The full wording of the question is: "Do you think the United States should let
Communist reporters from other countries come in here and send back to their papers the
news as they see it?"

result may be the largest context effect in the survey literature, with a
shift of 37% in responses to the question on Communist reporters
across the two question orders. Follow-up studies by Schuman and
Ludwig (1983) yielded similar results when the questions involved im-
ports to the United States from Japan and exports from the United
States to Japan.

Most researchers accept the interpretation of these results offered by
Schuman and his collaborators. When the Communist question comes
first, many responses to that question reflect attitudes toward communism or Russia. When it comes after the question on American reporters,
responses are based on the norm of evenhandedness, which requires that
both parties receive similar treatment. (The 19% change from 1950 to
1981 in answers to the Communist question when it came in the initial
position presumably reflects the thawing of the Cold War during that
period.)

Sometimes the considerations retrieved in answering a question can
affect mood, and the mood created can influence that judgment or later
ones. Mood appears to affect the willingness and ability to evaluate
persuasive arguments (Schwarz, Bless, & Bohner, 1991); it may also
affect the evaluations (or scale values) given to the considerations on
which attitude judgments are based. In a study by Johnson and Tversky
(1983), for example, reading about disasters affected respondents'
moods and their subsequent perceptions of risk. A series of studies by
Strack and his colleagues (Strack et al., 1985) revealed similar effects in
judgments of life satisfaction. When asked to recall happy or sad events
from their past lives, respondents showed contrast effects in assessing
their current life satisfaction; however, when they described these events
in vivid detail, it affected mood and produced an assimilation effect on
their assessments of their current lives (see also McMullen, 1997). The

change in mood probably affected both what came to mind and how it was evaluated.

Judgmental Contrast

If many attitude judgments are comparative, then surely the standard of comparison will have a major effect on the judgments that are rendered. Our assessment of our current situation may be quite positive when we recall the worst times of the past but quite negative when we recall the best (Strack et al., 1985, Experiment 1). Similarly, a Democrat may evaluate Bill Clinton quite favorably when the standard of comparison is Bob Dole but less favorably when the standard is Franklin Delano Roosevelt. Such contrast effects may partly reflect how respondents use the response scale, but they also reflect how respondents assign values to the specific considerations retrieved in evaluating their lives or their president. Our lives may actually *seem* better or worse, depending on the context and the standard of comparison it makes salient, just as a hue can seem lighter or darker, depending on its surroundings (see Figure 7.1).

What standards of comparison are respondents likely to adopt in judging a given stimulus? The standard may involve the average or typical value for the stimulus category, or it may involve a prominent or extreme member of the category. Assimilation is the usual result when the standard is seen as representing the typical value, contrast when it is seen as representing an extreme value on the dimension of judgment or a closely related one. In both surveys and laboratory investigations of judgment, contrast effects often seem to result when respondents are asked to judge several things of the same type on a single dimension – when they judge their satisfaction with both their past and current lives (Strack et al., 1985), their favorability toward several politicians (Schwarz & Bless, 1992b), the height of multiple college students (Manis, Biernat, & Nelson, 1991), and the physical attractiveness of many faces depicted in photographs (Wedell, Parducci, & Geiselman, 1987).

With judgments of causality, a special standard of comparison may be relevant; respondents select the causal explanation that specifies what made the difference between what actually happened and what might have happened instead (Chang & Novick, 1990; Hilton, 1990; Wells & Gavanski, 1989). In judging what caused an outcome, respondents implicitly compare the actual outcome against some set of contrasting, counterfactual cases. With extreme or emotional outcomes, such comparisons may be automatic (Roese, 1997). When the wording of the question alters the background cases against which the outcome is contrasted, the explanation changes as well (McGill, 1989). It is one thing

Figure 7.1. A perceptual contrast effect. The square in the center of the box on the right seems darker than the square in the center of the box on the left.

to explain why *Bill* chose this major, quite another to explain why he chose *this major*. In the one case, Bill is compared with other students; in the other, the major he chose is compared with other majors.

Just as respondents may exclude considerations from the judgment process if they seem tainted, they may also try to compensate for what they see as the biasing effects of a salient standard of comparison (Petty & Wegener, 1993; Wegener & Petty, 1995). Once again, the rejection of accessible material – in this case, a standard – is likely to occur only if the bias is relatively blatant and respondents are motivated to root it out (Stapel et al., 1998).

7.2.4   Context and Reporting

Context can alter how respondents map their attitude judgments onto the response scale and also how they edit their answers before reporting them. Once again, both assimilation and contrast effects can result.

Context, Consistency, and Response Editing

Since 1960, it has been known that when questions are placed next to each other in a questionnaire, responses to them may become more consistent (McGuire, 1960). According to McGuire, the juxtaposition of the questions highlights their logical relationship and increases the consistency of the answers; McGuire argued that the reduction of inconsistencies between beliefs takes place over time, but subsequent research has shown that at least some of the reduction in inconsistency takes place immediately (Wyer & Rosen, 1972). The original formulation of the *Socratic effect* also assumed that the questions involved had to have a logical relationship to one another. However, work by T. W. Smith

(1983) suggests that whenever related questions are placed together in a questionnaire their correlation is increased, even when the relationship is not strictly logical but only topical. Respondents are reluctant to give inconsistent answers, and placing related questions near each other encourages greater consistency.

Contrast and the Mapping of Responses

In the next chapter, we examine the mapping of judgments to the response scale in detail. Here we mention the role that scale anchors can play in this process. According to Parducci's range-frequency model (Parducci, 1965, 1974), the mapping of judgments onto response categories partly reflects the range of stimuli being judged. The range of stimuli has an impact because the most extreme stimuli are mapped onto the endpoints of the response scale, thus serving as anchors that define the entire scale. (For a similar model, see Ostrom & Upshaw, 1968.) Extreme exemplars can, of course, also serve as standards of comparison, affecting the judgment itself and not merely how it is reported. In either case, contrast effects result.

In theory, it is possible to distinguish judgmental contrast effects from anchoring effects in reporting. With judgmental contrast, it is the underlying judgment that is affected; with anchoring effects, it is only how the judgment is reported that is affected. In Figure 7.1, the central square *looks* different with the two backgrounds. In practice, though, it can be difficult to determine whether a prior question is serving as an extreme standard of comparison or a scale anchor or both.

7.3   Variables Affecting the Size and Direction of Context Effects

A range of processes creates context effects. The juxtaposition of questions may carry the implication that a question about an unfamiliar issue concerns the same topic as the previous questions or that a general question excludes an important subdomain. Earlier items can increase the accessibility of relevant considerations, making them more likely to be incorporated in later judgments or more likely to be disregarded when they are seen as problematic in some way. Placing two questions next to each other can highlight the need to apply the same treatment in responding to both, or one question can serve as a standard against which the other question is compared. The juxtaposition of related questions can make their logical relationship more salient, promoting consistency, or a preceding question can serve to anchor the response scale, producing contrast effects. The array of processes involved raises questions about when context effects are likely to occur and when they will take the form of assimilation or contrast.

7.3.1   Variables Affecting the Size or Likelihood of Context Effects

Are there general conditions or characteristics of attitudes that either promote or inhibit the emergence of context effects? Several plausible hypotheses have been proposed. Many of these focus on attributes of the attitude, such as its "crystallization," the presence and accessibility of an existing judgment about the issue, the familiarity of the issue, or the respondent's level of expertise about it. But before we turn to the issue of what makes context effects more or less likely to occur, it is worthwhile to consider their "natural" rate of occurrence in surveys.

Overall Frequency of Context Effects

Two studies have investigated the frequency of context effects in general-purpose attitude surveys. Many of the classic results reported by Schuman and Presser (1981) were based on split-ballot experiments in the Detroit Area Surveys (DAS), an "omnibus" survey covering a broad range of topics. Schuman and Presser looked for the presence of context effects among some 113 attitude questions that followed their experimental variations in the 1971 DAS. They had no a priori reason for believing that responses to these later questions would be affected by the experiments, but, having systematically varied the earlier questions, they could compare responses to the later questions when they followed different versions of the questions involved in the experiments. Only 8 of 113 questions showed significant differences by version, only 2 more than would be expected by chance. The General Social Survey (GSS) provides another natural experiment, allowing an estimate of the baseline frequency of context effects. The GSS employs a design in which batteries of questions are rotated across three different versions of the questionnaire; a given set of questions generally appears in only two of the three versions. T. W. Smith (1988) examined 358 questions that varied in their context across different versions of the questionnaire; only about 4% – slightly less than chance – produced significantly different answers under the different contexts.

Relations Among the Questions

These findings suggest that context effects are quite rare under the conditions of actual surveys, a conclusion that seems inconsistent with the sheer volume of studies demonstrating context effects in surveys and in social judgment. One reason why the Smith (1988) and Schuman and Presser (1981) results regarding the baseline frequency of context effects may be a little misleading is that the mechanisms thought to produce context effects presuppose *some* relationship between the context and target questions.

Consider, for example, the mechanisms responsible for the effects of context on the comprehension of a question. When questions shift from one topic to the next without warning, respondents are no longer likely to see earlier questions as carrying implications about the meaning of later questions. (This is apparent from the absence of context effects for the scattered questions in Table 7.1.) Indeed, it may take an introduction that emphasizes the relation between the general and specific questions to produce context effects based on a reinterpretation of the general question (see Table 7.2). Similarly, reaction time studies indicate that when prior questions have little relation to each other, the earlier question no longer speeds up the retrieval process for the later question. Things demand evenhanded treatment only when they are similar; a question and the standard to which it is compared are typically members of the same class (Schwarz & Bless, 1992a). Answers need be consistent with each other only when one answer is logically (or at least topically) related to another and the context makes this relationship salient (Wyer & Rosen, 1972). In a psychophysical judgment task, Brown (1953) showed that respondents used prior weights to anchor their ratings of subsequent stimuli but were unaffected by the weight of a tray they had lifted; to be used as the anchor for the rating scale, the weight had to be seen as part of the same sequence of stimuli.

If these are the mechanisms that account for context effects in surveys, then a precondition for the emergence of context effects is the placement of related questions relatively close to each other in a questionnaire (although see Bishop, 1987, for a context effect involving widely separated, although conceptually related, questions). The relationship between the context and target questions may involve logical implication, class inclusion, membership in the same category, or association in long-term memory, but some meaningful relationship is needed. As T. W. Smith's (1988) and Schuman and Presser's (1981) results show, variations in context that consist of differences in questions on an unrelated subject that are separated by many questions from a target question are unlikely to produce noticeable shifts in target responses.

Characteristics of the Attitude or Attitude Issue

So one key variable is the nature of the relation between the question and its context. It also seems quite plausible that strongly held, well-formed attitudes would be relatively invulnerable to the effects of question context. For example, if the question automatically triggers the retrieval of a highly accessible attitude, there's no reason why the answer should vary across contexts; accessible attitudes should, as a result, be relatively immune to the effects of item context. Similarly, central attitudes have been shown to be more stable over time than noncentral attitudes (Judd & Krosnick, 1982); it seems logical that they would be more stable across variations in question context as well.

Despite scattered support for these hypotheses (Bassili, 1996a; Lavine, Huff, Wagner, & Sweeney, 1998), the results have not, on the whole, been encouraging. In a review of a number of studies, Krosnick and Schuman (1988) found little relation between measures of attitude intensity and importance, on the one hand, and susceptibility to question wording and context effects, on the other. Bassili and Lavine and his colleagues argue that the measures of attitude strength used in the earlier studies have been flawed; these typically have consisted of a single item. Still, the sheer number of context effects involving judgments of life satisfaction suggests that context effects can occur with very familiar topics about which the respondents presumably have strong opinions. If there is one topic that people are sure to have strong views about, it must be the quality of their lives.

Several researchers have even argued the opposite position: that well-formed attitudes may be a prerequisite for certain types of context effect. For questions about one issue to affect the material retrieved in answering questions about another issue, the two issues must be linked in the respondent's memory; this linkage implies a certain level of structural development in the attitudes (cf. Tourangeau, 1992). In a similar vein, Bickart (1992) has argued that experts may sometimes be more affected by context than novices are; some level of expertise may be required to recognize the implications of the material made salient by context.

Variables Affecting Specific Components of the Response Process.

Because different processes are responsible for the impact of context on the different components of the response process, different variables govern whether context effects will occur during each one. Table 7.5 summarizes some of the main findings regarding variables that make

TABLE 7.5 Variables Affecting the Size or Likelihood of Context Effects, by Response Component and Direction

Response Component	Assimilation	Contrast
Comprehension		
Basic mechanism for effect Variables increasing size/ likelihood	Context provides interpretive framework for target • Target item on unfamiliar issue • Presentation (e.g., blocking of items) suggests context and target on same topic	Target seen as redundant with context • Target on general issue, context on subdomain(s) • Presentation suggests context and target on same topic • Context consists of one or two specific items • Wording of target item leaves its scope undefined
Retrieval		

Basic mechanism for effect Variables increasing size/ likelihood	Context primes retrieval of relevant material
	• Context items on related issue
	• Context items processed just before target
	• Respondents have mixed beliefs about target issue
		Context triggers rejection of relevant material
		• Respondents aware of priming items
		• Primed material seen as
		  Unrepresentative
		  Biased
		  Redundant

Judgment		
Basic mechanism for effect	Context triggers application of norm	Context item serves as extreme standard of comparison
Variables increasing size/likelihood	• Same judgment to be applied to liked/disliked objects	• Context item drawn from same category as target • Context item extreme on dimension of judgment • Context item judged on same/related dimension
Reporting		
Basic mechanism for effect	Context heightens consistency pressure	Context item serves as anchor for scale
Variables increasing size/likelihood	• Relation among items made salient (e.g., by presentation in a block)	• Anchoring item extreme stimulus in set • Anchor judged on same dimension as target

context effects more or less likely to emerge. The table indicates, for example, that assimilation effects on the comprehension of a question are more likely when the question concerns an unfamiliar issue than when it concerns a familiar one, and when the question is seen as continuing the same topic as the prior questions than when it is seen as beginning a new topic. Features of the context questions – such as their presentation in a block just before the target – can also increase the likelihood that such context effects will occur. As the table makes clear, the variables tend to be process-specific, affecting the emergence of assimilation or contrast effects during a single component of the response process.

7.3.2   Variables Affecting the Direction of Context Effects

The variables in Table 7.5 determine whether a context effect occurs at all. Numerous studies have also attempted to pinpoint the variables that determine whether the context effect will push responses in the direction of assimilation or contrast, given that a context effect occurs. For example, a study by Wedell and his colleagues (1987) indicates that simultaneous presentation of the stimuli – photographs of faces – produced assimilation effects on ratings of attractiveness, whereas successive presentation produced contrast effects. Table 7.6 lists 14 variables that have been shown to determine the direction of the effect of context in a range of judgment tasks. The studies in the table were all conducted during the last 15 years.

Two general principles seem to underlie the variables listed in Table 7.6. One principle is that deeper processing is required for contrast effects than for assimilation. For example, in the study by Martin and his colleagues, respondents who were distracted (and thus unable to process the stimuli deeply) showed assimilation effects, whereas those who were not distracted showed contrast (Martin et al., 1990). Similarly, contrast effects emerged when respondent motivation was heightened (Martin et al., 1990, Experiments 2 and 3) or when an explicit cue called attention to the context (Strack, 1992), but assimilation effects emerged when respondent motivation was low or when no cue reminded respondents of the potential effect of the context. Taken together, these findings suggest that when respondents are willing and able to process the context and target questions deeply (or when an explicit cue reduces the need for deep processing), contrast effects are more common than assimilation. If we assume that most survey respondents process the questions superficially, then assimilation effects should predominate in surveys.

The results on depth of processing are consistent with our analysis of the mechanisms underlying context effects. Assimilation effects on retrieval are brought about by the increased accessibility of concepts related to the context questions; these accessibility changes are the product of automatic memory processes. If we assume that the default is for respondents to accept the output of the retrieval or judgment processes uncritically, then respondents will need to carry out extra processing to detect the biases in the output from these components and to attempt to correct for them (Petty & Wegener, 1993; Stapel et al., 1998; Wegener & Petty, 1995).

A second general principle linking several of the findings involves conditions that promote or discourage comparisons between the target and context stimuli. Vaguely defined scales for reporting the judgments (Manis et al., 1991), tasks that force the respondents to focus on both the target and the context (McMullen, 1997), and contextual stimuli with extreme values on the dimension of judgment (Herr et al., 1983) promote comparisons and tend to produce contrast effects. Absolute scales for reporting the judgments, tasks in which the focus is mainly on the contextual stimuli (thereby affecting the respondent's mood), and contextual stimuli with typical rather than extreme values discourage comparisons and tend to produce assimilation. Comparisons (at least literal ones) typically involve two familiar members of the same category; thus, when the target is very unfamiliar or completely novel, it will prevent comparisons and promote assimilation effects (Herr et al., 1983).

The Inclusion/Exclusion Model of Schwarz and Bless

The most successful attempt to tie findings like those in Table 7.6 into a single model predicting when assimilation and contrast effects will emerge is the inclusion/exclusion model proposed by Schwarz and Bless (1992a). Their model assumes that, in judging a target stimulus, respondents form a representation of the target and of a standard of comparison against which the target is judged. Both representations rely on information that is accessible when the judgment is formed. By affecting what information is accessible, context can alter the representation of the target, the standard, or both. According to Schwarz and Bless, any one of three things can happen to information made temporarily acces-

TABLE 7.6 Variables Affecting the Direction of Context Effects

Study	Task	Variable	Result
Herr, Sherman, and Fazio (1983)	Rate ferocity, size of animals	Extremity of context questions	Assimilation with moderate context questions, contrast with extreme ones
		Real vs. unreal targets	Assimilation with made-up target animals, contrast with real targets
Manis, Beirnat, and Nelson (1991)	Judge height of models	Scale for judgment	Assimilation when judgment is in feet and inches, contrast when judgment is on 7-point scale
Martin (1986)	Form impression based on verbal description	Interruption during context task	Assimilation when prior task interrupted, contrast when task completed
Martin, Seta, and Crelia (1990)	Form impression based on verbal description	Distraction during target	Assimilation when distracted, contrast when not distracted
		Motivation	Assimilation with low motivation, contrast with high motivation
McMullen (1997)	Imagine alternative outcome for negative event	Focus on actual or counterfactual outcome	Assimilation with counterfactual focus, contrast with focus on actual
Ottati, Riggle, Wyer, Schwarz, and Kuklinski (1989)	Rate agreement with statements	Separation between target and context questions	Assimilation when context separated from target, contrast when adjacent

Schwarz, Strack, and Mai (1991)	Rate life satisfaction	Introduction to target and context questions	Assimilation with no lead-in, contrast with joint lead-in
		Number of context questions	Assimilation with three context questions, contrast with one
Strack (1992)	Rate likability of target	Awareness of context	Assimilation with no reminder of prior context, contrast with reminder
Strack, Schwarz, and Gscheidinger (1985)	Rate life satisfaction	Recall past vs. present events	Assimilation with present events, contrast with past events
		Vividness of recall	Assimilation with vivid recall, contrast with pallid recall
Wedell, Parducci, and Geiselman (1987)	Rate attractiveness of faces	Stimultaneous/successive presentation	Assimilation when context and target presented at same time, contrast when presented successively

sible by context. First, it may be incorporated into the representation of the target, producing an assimilation effect. Second, it may be excluded from the representation of the target, producing a subtraction-based context effect. Finally, it may be incorporated into the representation of the standard, producing a comparison-based contrast effect.

The impact of including or excluding contextually accessible material will, according to the model, depend on what would have been included in the representations of the target and the standard in the absence of the context questions – that is, on relevant information that is chronically accessible to retrieval. Larger assimilation effects will result when the representation of the target incorporates more temporarily accessible information or information with more extreme implications for the judgment; smaller effects will result when the representation draws more heavily on chronically accessible information. When the information in memory is more internally consistent, the impact of contextually accessible information will decrease; it won't matter which considerations are accessible if they all point to the same answer. In addition, when context increases the accessibility of several considerations that can be incorporated into the representation of the target, it will reduce the impact of any one of these considerations on the judgment. Similar arguments apply to the impact of exclusions on the representation of the target. As more information or information with more extreme implications is left out of the representation of the target, the resulting subtraction-based contrast effects will grow larger. In the terms of the belief-sampling model, the key issue is how the inclusion or exclusion of temporarily accessible material affects the average of the sample of considerations on which the judgment of the target is based (see Equation 6.1 in Chapter 6).

One of the most appealing features of the inclusion/exclusion model is its delineation of the conditions that foster exclusion of accessible material from the representation of a target. According to Schwarz and Bless (1992a; see also Sudman et al., 1996, Figure 5.1), material will be excluded from the representation of the target when it fails to meet any of four tests:

- Does the material bear on the question?
- Did it come to mind because of relevant influences?
- Does it "belong" to the target?
- Is the respondent supposed to use it?

These tests imply that irrelevant, biased, false or inapplicable, and redundant information will be left out of the respondent's representation of the target. Information that is dropped from the representation of the target but that nonetheless bears on the dimension of judgment will be used to construct a standard of comparison (or an anchor for the response scale).

The Belief-Sampling Model

As Sudman, Bradburn, and Schwarz (1996) have noted, the assumptions of the inclusion/exclusion model overlap with those of the belief-sampling model of Chapter 6. The inclusion/exclusion model's account of the direction of context effects does not differ much from the one presented here. The mechanisms that produce inclusion-based assimilation effects, according to Schwarz and Bless, are pretty much the same ones that we cite in explaining assimilation effects during comprehension and retrieval. Similarly, the mechanisms responsible for subtraction-based contrast effects appear to be identical to those described here as explaining contrast effects in comprehension and retrieval. Finally, Schwarz and Bless's comparison-based contrast effects cover pretty much the same territory as what we described as contrast effects in judgment and reporting.

While there are similarities between the two models, there are also some differences in emphasis. The inclusion/exclusion model is more explicit about the factors that determine whether a given consideration makes it into the sample on which the judgment of the target is based. The belief-sampling model, by contrast, is much more explicit about how considerations are used once they enter the sample. The belief-sampling model asserts that the consistency of responses to the same question presented on two different occasions – or in two different contexts – depends on three parameters:

- the degree of consistency in the evaluation of the same consideration on the two different occasions (ρ_1 in Equation 6.2);
- the level of consistency of the pool of potentially relevant considerations (ρ_2); and
- the degree of overlap in the considerations on which the two responses are based (q).

Applied to context effects, the model asserts that context will affect responses when it changes the considerations on which responses are based or the scale values assigned to those considerations. Like the inclusion/exclusion model, then, the belief-sampling model explains the effects of context mainly in terms of the impact of context on what enters into the sample of considerations that are the basis for the judgment and on the evaluation of those considerations. The belief-sampling model attempts, however, to model these effects quantitatively.

Level of Generality

We also favor a slightly different account of when respondents are likely to use contextual stimuli as a standard of comparison for the target (or anchor for the response scale). Our account, summarized in Figure 7.2, gives greater emphasis than the inclusion-exclusion model to the importance of differences in the level of generality of the context and target questions.

When the context question concerns an issue that encompasses the one raised by the target question, respondents may make inferences about the target based on what they know about that larger issue. Just as we make inferences about a species of bird based on our knowledge of birds in general, we may make inferences about a specific issue based on our views about the more general issue of which it is an aspect. As we argued in Chapter 6, broader principles are one of the main sources of information respondents draw on in making attitude judgments. We are, of course, unlikely to fill in gaps in our knowledge with category-based defaults when the target issue is a familiar one; there is no need for such inferences when we already know about the specific issue. Instead, inferences from the general to the specific are likely to involve novel or unfamiliar issues (like the Monetary Control Bill). We also make inductive inferences about a category or larger whole based on the instances or parts that we encounter; that is, we develop expectations about the properties of a category from the properties of its members. Such inferences are more likely if the set of members to which we have been exposed are numerous, prototypical, or diverse but consistent with respect to the property of interest (Osherson, Smith, & Shafir, 1986). Respondents are willing, for example, to generalize about their overall happiness based on the recent happy or unhappy events they recall (Strack et al., 1985) or about a political party from a prominent exemplar (Schwarz & Bless, 1992a; see Table 7.3).

So we make inferences both from the members to the category (or from the parts to the whole) and from the category to its members. By affecting which members are accessible, context can affect our judgment

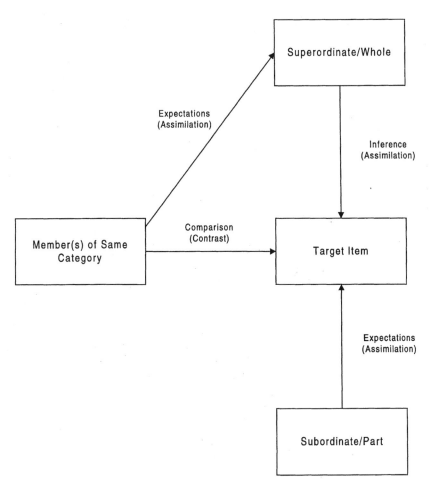

Figure 7.2. Relations between context and target items. The middle box on the right represents the target item; the remaining boxes represent context items at higher, the same, or lower levels of generality than the target. The paths involving assimilation assume that information is not consciously excluded.

regarding the category; by affecting what information about the category is accessible, context can affect our judgment of the members. In either case, assimilation effects will result – unless, of course, the accessible information is consciously discounted by respondents.

Members of the same category can also affect judgments about each other. We may compare one member of a category with another member, and when the member serving as the standard of comparison is extreme or simply quite different from the target on the relevant dimension, contrast is the likely outcome. But there's another way that information about one member of a category can affect judgments about another member. By virtue of the expectations they create about the class as a whole, contextual stimuli – that is, other category members – can indirectly affect judgments about a target (cf., Manis et al., 1991). When the other category members are extreme (and therefore clearly unrepresentative of the category), they will serve as standards of comparison and contrast effects will predominate; when they are numerous or prototypical, assimilation effects will predominate.

According to our analysis, then, information will make it into the sample of considerations on which the judgment of the target is based if it characterizes a superordinate category that includes the target or a subordinate category that the target encompasses. Such information may still be disregarded if it is seen as biased or redundant. It will be incorporated into the representation of the standard – affecting the evaluation of the considerations that are directly taken into account – when its source is another category member, one that is seen as extreme or prominent on the relevant dimension.

7.4   Serial Position Effects

We have argued that context effects depend on some conceptual relation between the context and target questions. There is, however, a class of effects thought to depend only on the position of the target question within the interview, not on the content of the prior questions. T. W. Smith (1992a), for example, discusses fatigue and the development of rapport with the interviewer as examples of such serial position effects. The evidence for serial position effects in surveys is largely anecdotal. It is certainly plausible that respondents report less fully as they become more fatigued (for a related hypothesis on reporting burden, see Neter and Waksberg, 1964) or that they shift from an optimizing to a satisficing criterion in formulating their answers, but there is little direct evidence for these hypotheses (Rasinski, Mingay, & Bradburn, 1994).

The one exception involves a series of carefully designed experiments by Knowles (1988). These demonstrate that the reliability of personality test questions (as measured by the correlation between the individual questions and the overall test score) increases with the serial position of the question within the test. Knowles argues that, as respondents answer more questions related to the same underlying construct, the meaning of the construct becomes clearer to them; they are therefore able to give faster, more knowledgeable answers to later questions than to earlier ones. Knowles's findings are also consistent with an interpretation based on retrieval processes. As respondents answer more questions on the same topic, they retrieve more relevant incidents and behaviors; as a result, their answers to later questions are based on a larger, more representative pool of information than their answers to earlier ones. These two accounts are not contradictory; multiple questions on a single topic are likely to affect both comprehension and retrieval and perhaps other components of the response process as well.

7.5 Conclusions

As we saw in Chapter 6, attitude reports, even those about very familiar topics, may be cobbled together on the spot when respondents answer questions in a survey. Respondents use whatever existing evaluations, vague impressions, general values, or specific beliefs come to mind when they construct their answers. The question's context can affect what respondents consider as they answer the question; in addition, context can, by suggesting a standard of comparison, alter how respondents evaluate what comes to mind. The effects of context may or may not depend on the respondent's answers to the context items, and they can change either the overall direction of responses to the target question or the relation between target responses and responses to the context items.

Respondents generally don't linger over survey questions, but experimental results indicate that if they are given enough time and encouragement, they may detect the whiff of bias and attempt to compensate for the effects of accessible material they see as tainted. Unfortunately, they may overcompensate for the perceived biases, throwing out considerations that would ordinarily have affected their answers.

In everyday life, there are probably advantages to being able to see both sides of most issues, but for attitude surveys this ability can be a nuisance. Broad topics (such as one's overall happiness) are especially prone to context effects. This probably reflects the fact the respondents could consider many things in evaluating such issues but sample only a few of them. This flexibility in what we include and leave out in making attitude judgments explains why context effects crop up so often in surveys.

CHAPTER EIGHT

Selecting a Response: Mapping Judgments to Survey Answers

Survey items use a variety of response formats. Some items allow respondents to generate their own answers in whatever format they choose; others restrict them to selecting a single answer from a preestablished list of response options. Even among items that include a list of response options (*closed-ended* items in the terminology of survey research), there is still considerable variation in formats: The categories may be numbered, given verbal labels, or both; verbal or numerical labels may be provided for all of the response categories or only some of them; the number of categories may range from 2 to 11 or more; the response options may be explicitly ordered (as with categories formed by grouping ranges of numerical values), implicitly ordered (as with many rating scales), or completely unordered. For example, Question (1) orders its response options by intervals based on elapsed time and Question (2) by a labeled rating scale.[1] Question (3) is an unordered list.

(1) When did the accident happen?
   ☐ Last week
   ☐ Week before
   ☐ 2 weeks–3 months
   ☐ Over 3–12 months
   ☐ 1–2 years [HIS]

(2) A working mother can establish just as warm and secure a relationship with her child as a mother who does not work [GSS].

---

[1] Question (2) is an example of a *Likert scale*: one in which respondents must register agreement or disagreement with a statement by providing a number from a labeled list.

Strongly agree	Agree	Disagree	Strongly disagree	Don't know
1	2	3	4	8

(3) What type of insurance plan is it?
   1 – Blue Cross and/or Blue Shield
   2 – Commercial health insurance company
   3 – Health maintenance plan
   4 – Commercial Medicare supplement
   5 – Dental insurance, ONLY
   6 – Other health insurance [CE]

The different formats serve many different purposes. In general, survey researchers favor closed-ended items – they are simpler to code and help clarify the meaning of the question (and the desired form of the answer) – but many surveys include *open-ended* answers (in which respondents formulate their answers rather than selecting them from a list of answer categories). Question (4) is a typical item of this sort:

(4) How many days during the past 12 months has this condition kept him in bed all or most of the day? [HIS]

This chapter examines the processes involved in translating a judgment into an answer. Not surprisingly, these processes differ, depending on the format of the item. We focus on three major response formats:

(5) a. Open-ended items, in which respondents generate a numerical response, such as (4);
   b. Closed-ended items, in which the response categories form a rating scale or some other ordered set, such as (1) or (2);
   c. Closed-ended items, in which the categories are an unordered list of options, such as (3).

Most survey items use one of these three formats.[2] Each format raises different issues for respondents and calls for a different response selec-

---

[2] We treat yes/no questions, which are pervasive in surveys, as a special case of unordered, closed-ended questions. The major category of questions that we do not discuss here are open-ended questions that seek nonnumeric answers, such as "For what condition did_____ see or talk to a doctor during the past 2 weeks?" [HIS] or "What is the name of the company which provides telephone services for (property description)?" [CE]. On national surveys, such questions usually probe for names of entities, where a closed-ended list of possibilities would be impractically long. The difficulty associated with such items probably has more to do with memory than with response selection, although we don't rule out the possibility that people sometimes have trouble formulating their answer.

tion or mapping strategy. With open-ended items, respondents often use round values, suggesting that their answers may not reflect exact underlying values. With rating scales, the answers are subject to the effects of anchors and other contextual influences that can complicate the relation between the underlying judgments and the overt responses. With unordered categories, the order in which the options are listed can nonetheless affect the relative popularity of the answers. All of these potential measurement problems result from the processes used in translating a judgment into an answer.

8.1   Open Items and Rounding

Survey designers often use open-ended items to elicit answers when the required form of the answer is quite obvious. For example, the question "What is your age?" hardly needs the sort of added specification that a set of closed-ended response options might provide. For items seeking numerical answers, open-ended items offer several practical advantages over closed items, especially when the range of possible answers is potentially infinite. First, they are thought to yield more exact information than is possible in a closed format. Even with finely graded categories, there is inevitably some loss of information when the answer is categorical. Moreover, the answer categories must often be truncated at the high or low end of the range. For example, in a special supplement on sexual behaviors, the General Social Survey includes an item on the number of sexual partners respondents have had since they turned 18; the highest response category offered to respondents – 101 or more – is bounded only at the lower end. The closed format loses information about a small, but important, group of highly sexually active persons. Aside from the loss of information from grouping and truncation, closed questions may have another effect on numerical answers. Based on the response categories provided, respondents may draw inferences about the distribution of the behavior in question. They may see the middle category, for example, as representing the population average; similarly, they may interpret the end categories as being very rare. Because of such inferences, respondents may select the middle option too often and the extreme options too rarely (Schwarz & Hippler, 1987).

8.1.1   Evidence of Rounding

Unfortunately, open-ended answers have their own problems. One of the most apparent ones is that respondents often provide round answers

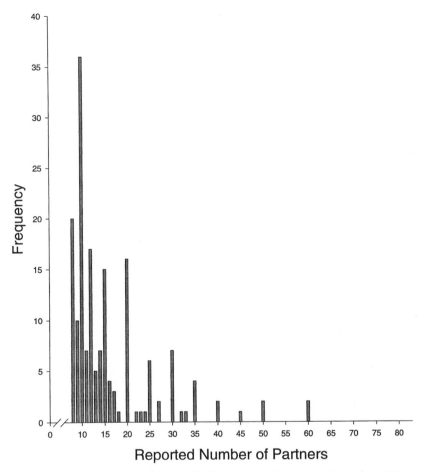

Figure 8.1. Distribution of reported lifetime sexual partners. Data from Tourangeau, Rasinski, Jobe, Smith, and Pratt (1997).

to numerical questions – in effect, creating their own grouped answer categories. For example, data from demographic surveys and population censuses often show evidence of "age heaping" at multiples of 5 (Shyrock, Siegel, & Stockwell, 1976).

Figure 8.1 displays an example of rounding from a survey on sexual behavior. It shows a portion of the distribution of lifetime sexual partners – from 8 to 80 partners – that respondents reported in a survey of adult residents of Chicago (Jobe, Pratt, Tourangeau, Baldwin, & Rasinski, 1997). As is apparent from the figure, the distribution has numerous peaks, nearly all of them at values that are exact multiples of 5. In fact, most respondents (62.4%) who reported having 10 or more sexual partners gave an answer that was an exact multiple of 5. Other data from that study indicate that the proportion of respondents using round values to report their answers is a function of the sheer number of partners reported: The more partners they have to report, the more likely respondents are to use a round value to report them (Tourangeau et al., 1997). The data even suggest a switch to more widely spaced round values as the number of partners increases. Most respondents who reported having more than 25 partners reported a value that is an exact multiple of 10 or 25.

It is tempting to conclude that results like those in Figure 8.1 are a by-product of the sensitive nature of the questions. Respondents with many sexual partners may be embarrassed by the number and may therefore be unwilling to report an exact answer; a round value may serve as a kind of hedge for such respondents, softening the answer by signaling that it should not be taken too literally (Lakoff, 1972; Sadock, 1977).

The use of round values is, however, quite common even with questions that do not raise any obvious sensitivity concerns. For example, a study by Huttenlocher and her colleagues asked respondents how many days ago they had completed an earlier interview (Huttenlocher et al., 1990). Once again, many respondents used either round values or what Huttenlocher and her colleagues refer to as *calendar prototypes* – exact multiples of 7 or 30. The main determinant of whether respondents gave round, prototypical, or exact values was how long ago the prior interview actually took place. In fact, Huttenlocher and her colleagues argue that the relation between elapsed time and the proportion of calendar prototypes is linear. These results closely parallel those for the sex partner question: The larger the number to be reported, the more likely the respondents will report it as a round value. It is plausible that, in both cases, the level of difficulty in producing an exact answer and the tendency to give a round answer instead are proportional to the magnitude of the quantity being estimated. Huttenlocher and her coworkers argue that the quantity being reported – the number of days since the prior interview – is at best inexactly represented in memory; the use of round values signals this imprecision. In Chapter 5, we described a similar use of estimation strategies as an alternative to the retrieval of specific events. Rate-based and other estimation strategies often yield round (or at least inexact) values as their output.

Kennickell (1996) has made a similar point about the use of ranges in surveys that collect information about household finances. He examined data from the Survey of Consumer Finances, a study that collects detailed information from the respondents about their income and assets. A large number of respondents are unwilling or unable to provide exact answers to these questions, reporting instead a range of values (e.g., "$10,000 to $20,000") for the specific asset or source of income. Kennickell argues that in many cases, exact answers to the questions simply do not exist. For example, it is difficult to assign a precise dollar value to one's home or one's car without actually selling them. Reporting the value as a range of round values may be a valid way of expressing this indeterminacy.

8.1.2   Processes Responsible for Rounding

The results reviewed so far suggest that respondents use round values whenever it is difficult (or impossible) for them to come up with an exact answer. The difficulty may arise from imprecise encoding of the information in memory (as in the study by Huttenlocher et al., 1990), from indeterminacy in the underlying quantities (as in the Survey of Consumer Finances), or from the burden of retrieving numerous specific pieces of information (as in the study by Jobe and his colleagues on sexual partners). In each of these cases, the use of round values may reflect problems in the representation of the quantity in question; because of these problems, it may be hard to map the representation onto a single number. By using round values, the respondents may be indicating that their answers in fact represent a range. A respondent who reports having 25 sexual partners may be indicating that the actual value lies somewhere between, say, 23 and 28.

This account suggests that rounding results from fuzziness in the underlying representation of a quantity rather than from difficulty in the process of mapping the quantity onto a response. It is, however, likely that uncertainties in the mapping process also contribute to respondents' tendency to report their answers in round numbers. A study by Schaeffer and Bradburn (1989) illustrates the way imprecise mapping can compound an imprecise initial representation. Schaeffer and Bradburn examined responses to a series of magnitude estimation items intended to assess the stress engendered by various activities involved in caring for a disabled family member.[3] The task was quite difficult, in part because

---

[3] In standard magnitude estimation, participants see an initial stimulus with a number assigned to it. They must then assign numbers to succeeding stimuli "in such a way that they reflect your subjective impressions. There is no limit to the range of numbers that you may use. You may use whole numbers, decimals, or fractions" (Stevens, 1975, p. 30).

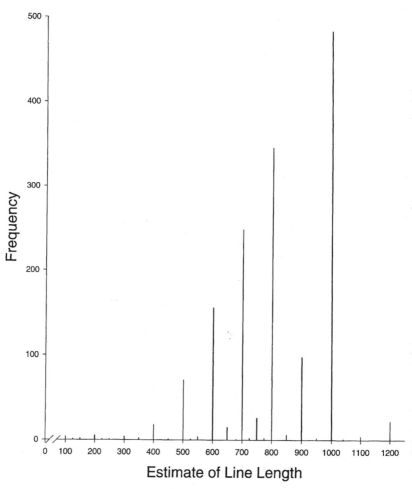

Figure 8.2. Distribution of magnitude estimates. Data from Schaeffer and Bradburn (1989). Reprinted with permission from *Journal of the American Statistical Association.* Copyright © 1989 by the American Statistical Association. All rights reserved.

stress levels are probably not very exactly quantified in the minds of the respondents. But even during the practice task, in which respondents judged the relative length of a line that was exactly eight times longer than a standard line, round values predominate. Figure 8.2 shows the distribution of responses from 100 to 1,200; the standard was assigned the value of 100, so the correctly calibrated answer was 800. The most popular answer was 1,000; that value corresponds to a judgment that

TABLE 8.1 Evaluations of Clinton and Bush in the
1992 ANES

	Number of Responses	% of Total
Clinton		
Multiples of 10	1,907	78.9
15, 85	310	12.8
All other values	199	8.2
Bush		
Multiples of 10	1,948	79.3
15, 85	412	16.8
All other values	98	4.0

the practice line was 10 times longer than the standard. Overall, about 95% of the answers were multiples of 100.

It seems quite likely that in this instance the round values partly reflect respondents' attempts to simplify the task of mapping the judged length of the line onto a numerical response. As Schaeffer and Bradburn argue, ". . . respondents select answers as though the number system were discrete rather than continuous . . . and show a preference for certain round numbers" (Schaeffer & Bradburn, 1989, p. 404). By treating the number system as discrete, respondents reduce the task of generating a numerical estimate to that of selecting a plausible value from a small number of reasonable answers. Similar strategies may simplify the mapping step for other response formats.

Data from the 1992 American National Election Studies (ANES) provide an example in which round values almost certainly reflect difficulty in mapping. Respondents in that survey assessed their attitudes toward various political candidates, including the presidential candidates, on a "feelings thermometer," with values ranging from 0 to 100. Approximately 80% of the evaluations of both Bush and Clinton were multiples of 10, as Table 8.1 reveals. Two other values – 15 and 85 – also drew a high percentage of the responses. The data suggest that at least for these two candidates, the vast majority of respondents treat the feelings thermometer as a 13-point scale. It is difficult to imagine a more familiar political figure than Bush, who was the incumbent president at the time and who had been the vice president for eight years before that.[4] It seems

---

[4] Still, as we noted in Chapter 5, a quarter of the respondents in a national sample were unable to say what position Bush held just six years earlier.

doubtful that the respondents' use of round values was entirely the by-product of the uncertainty in their feelings about Bush (or, for that matter, about Clinton).

The use of round values, then, can reflect uncertainty in the representation of the estimated quantity, uncertainty in mapping that quantity onto a numerical response, or both. In some cases, it may signal sheer unwillingness to come up with a more exact answer. Moreover, by reporting their answers as round values, respondents may be consciously attempting to communicate the fact that their answers are at best approximations. Round values may also serve as a kind of hedge, allowing respondents to soften otherwise embarrassing admissions.

8.1.3   Impact of Rounding

At first glance, it might seem that the use of round values would not, by itself, introduce any consistent bias into survey reports. If respondents round fairly, why should rounding affect the answers in any particular direction? There are, however, two reasons why the use of round values might produce reporting biases. The first derives from the fact that round values are not evenly spaced; as we have already noted, the distances between successive round values increase as the numbers get larger. The change in the spacing between round values means that more reports will be rounded down than rounded up. Suppose, for example, that respondents round their answers to one of the following values – 10, 15, 20, 25, 50, or 100. The net effect of rounding will be to bias answers down, even if respondents unfailingly report the nearest round value as their answer. For example, those who report an answer of 25 will have a raw value that falls somewhere in the interval between 23 and 37; the round value that is ultimately reported is not in the middle of this interval. Similarly, those who report an answer of 50 will have raw values between 38 and 75; again, 50 is not the midpoint of this range.

A second reason that rounding can introduce systematic error is that respondents may *not* round fairly but instead follow a biased rounding rule. According to Huttenlocher and her colleagues, respondents do not necessarily round to the nearest round, or "prototypical," value, but instead may characteristically round up or down. Their model assumes that the "rounding process involves [reporting] a particular prototype r_i whenever the [raw value] is between $r_{i-1} + c(r_i - r_{i-1})$ and $r_i + c(r_{i+1} - r_i)$" (Huttenlocher et al., 1990, p. 205), where r_{i-1}, r_i, and r_{i+1} are successive prototypical values (e.g., 7, 14, and 21 days) and c is a cut point parameter that determines the location of the ends of the interval associated with each prototype. When c is set to 0.5, it implies that respondents always round to the nearest prototypical value; when it is set to 1.0, it implies that respondents always round down; and when it is set to 0.0, it implies that respondents always round up. For example, if the value of c is .5, then respondents report 14 when the underlying value is between 10.5 (= 7 + [.5 × 7]) and 17.5 (14 + [.5 × 7]) days ago; that is, they round fairly. By contrast, if the value of c is 1.0, they report 14 if the underlying raw value is between 14 (7 + [1 × 7]) and 21 (14 + [.5 × 7]) days ago; that is, they always round down. The data suggest that the respondents in the study by Huttenlocher and her colleagues used a value of .7 for their cut point – which is to say that they tended to round down. It is, however, also possible that underlying raw values – the elapsed time since a prior interview – were themselves biased. In any case, it cannot be taken for granted that respondents will adopt a fair rounding rule.

8.2   Rating Scales and Scale Anchors

A wide range of findings suggests that when respondents have the opportunity to report an exact numerical answer or judgment, they may simplify the reporting task by selecting a value from a limited number of ranges; the range selected is reported as a round value. In effect, respondents may implicitly convert open-ended items, which permit any numerical answer, into closed-ended items with an ordered set of response categories. The question naturally arises, then, as to how respondents choose their answers when they are explicitly presented with an ordered set of categories, such as a rating scale.

8.2.1   The Range-Frequency Model

One comprehensive answer to this question is provided by Allen Parducci's range-frequency model (Parducci, 1965, 1974). According to Parducci, the mapping of judgments onto response categories reflects two basic principles. The *range principle* refers to "the matching of successive categories to successive subranges of the stimuli" (Parducci, 1974, p. 129). The most extreme stimuli are mapped to the scale endpoints and serve as anchors that define the remaining scale points; intermediate stimuli are then mapped to intermediate categories. In the simplest version of the model, a stimulus judged as falling midway between the extreme stimuli would be mapped to the midpoint of the scale. The *frequency principle* refers to the tendency for respondents to assign a fixed proportion of the stimuli to each response category; typically, it is assumed that the respondents prefer to use the response categories with equal frequency. If the stimuli are not in fact equally spaced, the frequency principle implies that the reports will make finer discriminations in regions along the dimension of judgment where there are many stimuli than in regions where stimuli are sparse. The range principle ensures that the reported judgments preserve the perceived rank order of the stimuli; the frequency principle ensures that ratings are spread across the entire scale.

The range-frequency model was originally developed to account for context effects on psychophysical judgments, but it applies equally well to the judgments and rating scales used in survey settings. For example, Daamen and Bie (1992) report a study that applies the range-frequency model to probability judgments (made on an 11-point scale). In line with the model, their results demonstrate effects for both the range and distribution of the stimuli; when the stimuli were skewed toward one end of the scale, the ratings were displaced away from that end – a result consistent with the frequency principle.

Although the range-frequency model applies most directly to judgments about multiple objects, it extends to situations in which respondents judge single objects, including political figures. When respondents evaluate a candidate for the presidency, for example, they may make this judgment relative to the category of presidents (or some other relevant category). A respondent's most and least favorite president, then, would serve as the anchors mapped to the extreme response categories, and the respondent's rating of the candidate would be based on the candidate's perceived location relative to these anchors.

8.2.2 Positivity Bias

The range-frequency model suggests that the judgments of a respondent over multiple objects or persons will form a rectangular distribution on the response scale, illustrated as gray bars in Figure 8.3. There are, however, several processes that may introduce distortions into this type of mapping. The first of these is *positivity* or *leniency bias* (Landy & Farr, 1980; Lau, Sears, & Centers, 1979; Sears, 1983). The evidence suggests that respondents are reluctant to give negative evaluations to other persons; as a result, ratings of other people tend to pile up at the positive end of the scale. The tendency to overuse the positive end of rating scales is apparent in performance appraisals of employees (Landy & Farr, 1980), evaluations of political figures (e.g., Lau et al., 1979), and ratings of college courses and professors (Sears, 1983). For example, Sears (1983) reports that the average course rating at UCLA over a five-year period was 7.04 on a scale ranging from 1 to 9; that is, the average course received a rating a full two points higher than the theoretical neutral point of the scale.

The source of the positivity bias is not clear. Zajonc (1968) argues that we are generally inclined to prefer interpersonal configurations in which most of the relations are positive and to assume positive relations between persons in the absence of contradictory information. This preference could account for the positivity bias. Sears (1983) claims that the bias reflects a more specific tendency for us to like what we see as similar to ourselves and to perceive at least some degree of similarity between ourselves and any other person. A third explanation involves self-presentation concerns; respondents may be reluctant to come across as overly negative or critical in their evaluations. Whatever its basis, positivity bias will change the ratings over stimuli from a rectangular distribution, represented by the gray bars in Figure 8.3, to a skewed distribution, represented by the black bars.

8.2.3   The Range of Numeric Labels

A study by Schwarz and his collaborators (Schwarz, Knauper, Hippler, Noelle-Neumann, & Clark, 1991) suggests a second reason why the distribution of observed ratings may depart from the rectangular distribution implied by simple versions of the range-frequency model. They present results from studies comparing rating scales that used two different sets of numeric endpoints. One set ranged from -5 to $+5$; the other, from 0 to 10. The endpoints had the same verbal labels in both cases. With negative numeric scale values, the ratings piled up on the positive end of the scale. Figure 8.4 displays the data from an item asking respondents how successful they had been in life, with the black bars indicating ratings on the -5 to $+5$ scale and the gray bars indicating ratings on the 0 to 10 scale. Regardless of the labels, the ratings tend to fall on the positive half of the scale (in line with the positivity bias), but the pile-up is even more marked when the scale labels run from -5 to

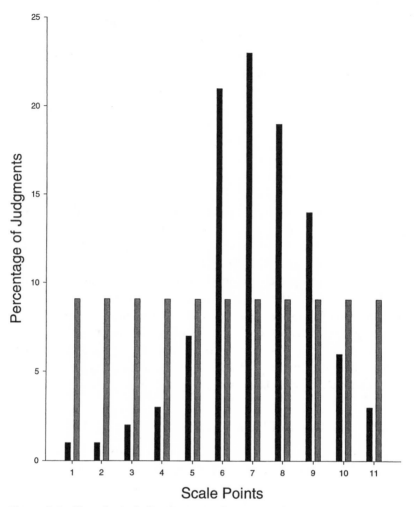

Figure 8.3. Hypothetical distributions of rating scale values. The gray bars illustrate the application of the frequency principle; the black bars show the impact of positivity bias.

+5. It is as if the scale had been compressed; the median answer shifts from the sixth scale point when the scale ranges from 0 to 10 to the eighth scale point when it ranges from −5 to +5.

Negative numbers, according to Schwarz and his collaborators, convey a different meaning from labels that range from 0 up; negative numbers imply that the low end of the scale is the polar opposite rather than the logical complement of the high end. With a unipolar dimension (such as success in life), this implication may be misleading. A value of

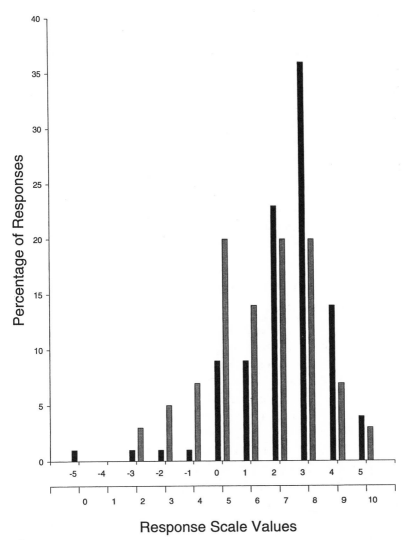

Figure 8.4. Distribution of rating scale values by labels. The black bars represent the distribution of responses on a −5 to +5 scale; the gray bars represent responses on a 0 to 10 scale. Data from Schwarz et al. (1991). Copyright © 1991. Reprinted with permission of the University of Chicago Press.

0 implies a mere lack of success, whereas −5 implies abject failure. What happens when the dimension of judgment is clearly bipolar? Does the use of negative numeric labels alter the meaning of the scale points in the same way? Two studies reported by Schaeffer and Barker (1995) address this issue. The studies examined responses to five items; in each

case, the verbal label given to the category at the low end of the scale was clearly opposite in meaning to the label given to the high endpoint (e.g., "completely satisfied" vs. "completely dissatisfied"). The findings support the main conclusions presented thus far: Even when the scale ranged from 1 to 7, there was still evidence of a positivity bias (i.e., a pile-up of ratings on the positive end of the scale); moreover, when the scale values ranged from -3 to 3, respondents displaced the distribution further toward the positive end. These studies also examined a second variable – whether or not the midpoint of the scale had a verbal label (e.g., "neither oppose nor favor"). The inclusion of a label for the midpoint seemed to reduce positivity bias, mostly by drawing responses from the positive end of the scale to the midpoint. The verbal label may have made the meaning of the numeric midpoint clearer or it may have merely made that response option more salient.

8.2.4   Response Contraction and Cognitive Reference Points

Response Contraction

Although respondents tend to distribute their responses among the response categories, they also show some reluctance to use the extreme categories or scale endpoints. This latter tendency provides another qualification to the basic range-frequency model, and its effect is to moderate response values. Respondents tend to underestimate objects that fall at the high end of the range of items, and they tend to overestimate objects that fall at the low end. In psychophysics, this trend is called *response contraction bias* (Poulton, 1989). It occurs in situations in which respondents know where the scale's midpoint falls, producing response distributions that bunch too close to the midpoint. Responses on a 0-to-10 rating scale, for example, often cluster about the midpoint at 5, with few extreme 0 or 10 responses.

As we mentioned in Section 4.2.1, the same bias occurs quite commonly in experiments in which participants provide dates for specified events (e.g., Kurbat et al., 1998; Thompson et al., 1996). Events that objectively occurred early in the response period receive subjective dates that are too recent, whereas events that actually occurred late in the response period receive dates that are too early. This means forward telescoping for the earliest dates and backward telescoping for the most recent ones.

This tendency to avoid extreme response categories and overuse middle ones has a close cousin: People also overuse categories that contain a standard or prototypical item. That is, just as responses cluster around a central response option, they also cluster around a central stimulus item – either a standard provided by the question itself or one that the respondent knows from past experience. The standard for this *stimulus contraction bias* (Poulton, 1989) can arise in several ways, and we discuss two of them under the headings of cognitive reference points and anchors.

Cognitive Reference Points

As our discussion of rounding has already implied, all numbers are not created equal. Certain numbers seem somehow to stand out, to be prototypical. Rosch (1975) has presented evidence that specific numbers (0, 1, 10, 100, and so on) serve as "cognitive reference points" within the numbering system. In the same way, lines at vertical and horizontal orientations and pure primary colors serve as reference points within the visual system. The prototypical orientations and focal colors are special cases, easily identified and well remembered. In addition, people rate other values as more similar to these prototypes than they rate the prototypes as similar to the other values. Because of this special status, it seems more natural to say that "996 is virtually 1,000" than to say that "1,000 is virtually 996."

Scale values that are numerical reference points may draw a disproportionate share of the responses or, because they are seen as special, they may sometimes be shunned by respondents. A study reported by Kubovy and Psotka (1976) demonstrates the avoidance of prototypical numbers. Respondents in that study were asked to report "the first digit that comes to mind"; the values 0 and 1 were underrepresented in the respondents' answers, presumably because these numbers do not seem random. Further, the special position of 0 within the numbering system may give it a special meaning – the complete absence of the characteristic in question. In a survey context, this meaning may or may not be consistent with the meaning implied by its position within the rating scale.

Anchors

Aside from the range and frequency principles, then, rating scale responses may reflect positivity biases, response contraction, the connotations associated with specific numbers, and the overuse or avoidance of specific values that function as reference points within the numbering system. Other processes may further complicate the picture. One of these is the tendency for respondents to make finer discriminations among stimuli that lie closer to an anchor. Holyoak and Mah (1982), for example, had students at the University of Michigan rate the distance of American cities from the Atlantic and Pacific coasts. Those judging distances from the Atlantic Coast showed less discrimination in their ratings among cities west of the Mississippi than those judging distances from the Pacific Coast; similarly, raters judging distances from the Pacific Coast discriminated less among the cities east of the Mississippi than their counterparts who were judging distances from the Atlantic Coast. The result with either anchor was a distorted cognitive map of the United States. In everyday distance judgments, one's own home (or home town) may serve as an anchor point, so that distances to nearby destinations are exaggerated and distances to faraway places are understated. More generally, respondents may lump together objects that are distant from the anchor and exaggerate the differences among those that are close to it. As Holyoak and Mah (1982) put it, "[Our] results suggest that residents of America's heartland may not be immune to the type of distance distortion of which New Yorkers are commonly accused" (p. 335).

8.2.5 Conversational and Positional Cues

One of the "sincerity conditions" for asking a question is that, if the question lists (or implies) a set of possible answers – an *uncertainty space*, in the terminology of Chapter 2 – then the answer should be among those options (Searle, 1969). A yes-no question implies that the questioner believes that the likely answers are "yes" and "no"; a question that lists one or more specific alternatives implies that the questioner believes that one of these alternatives is the correct answer. One of the clearest findings in the survey literature is that respondents generally act as if the survey questions meet this sincerity condition – they assume, that is, the answer is to be found among the options presented. Accordingly, they overwhelmingly select their answers from among those answer categories rather than volunteering answers from outside the set provided (see our discussion of question presuppositions in Section 2.4.1). For example, even with very obscure attitude issues, many respondents are reluctant to volunteer a "no opinion" response. If, however, the question includes an explicit "no opinion" answer, they are much more likely to indicate they have no opinion (e.g., Bishop et al., 1986; Schuman & Presser, 1981). In one study (Bishop et al., 1986), the proportion of the sample expressing a view on the fictitious "Public Affairs Act" dropped from 42% to 4% when the question included the phrase "or haven't you thought much about this issue," indicating that not having an opinion was among the expected responses.

Besides expecting to find the answer among the explicit response options, respondents may draw additional inferences from the structure or order of the response options. Schwarz and his colleagues argue that respondents answering frequency questions (such as "How many hours of television do you watch in the average day?") may infer that the middle option in an ordered series represents the typical value, the response selected by the average person (Schwarz & Hippler, 1987; Schwarz et al., 1985) . Based on this inference, respondents may tend to assimilate their reports to this perceived average.

Several processes are likely to contribute to this assimilation effect. The first is impression-based processing (Sanbonmatsu & Fazio, 1990) – that is, basing one's answers on a vague impression rather than on specific memories (e.g., about particular television shows one watches regularly). The respondent's impression in this case is likely to involve some sense of his or her standing relative to the population average. The second process is anchoring-and-adjustment, in which the middle response option serves as the starting point for an estimate that the respondent fails to adjust sufficiently (see Sections 5.1 and 5.2). The third process involves reinterpreting the meaning of the object being judged based on the response options. Respondents asked how often they have been annoyed in the past month may interpret "annoyance" as referring to less serious incidents when the response options list high frequencies (e.g., "several times a day") than when they list low frequencies ("once a week"). This reinterpretation process is probably not relevant to relatively well-defined behaviors such as accumulating sexual partners (see Tourangeau & Smith, 1996). The example of sexual partners raises a fourth possibility, however – the desire to avoid embarrassment by selecting a safe, typical answer.

All of these processes will contribute to a pile-up of responses around the middle option; moreover, the exact options offered will influence the overall distribution of the answers. Table 8.2, for example, shows the distributions of responses to two items on television viewing that differ in their response categories (from Schwarz et al., 1985). Both items asked the number of hours per day that the respondent watched TV. When the answer options emphasized the high end of the range, approximately 38% of the respondents reported watching more than 2½ hours

TABLE 8.2 Reported Daily Television Viewed, by Response Options

Low Options		High Options	
Response Options	% Reporting	Response Options	% Reporting
Up to ½ hour	7.4	Up to 2½ hour	62.5
½ to 1 hour	17.7	2½ to 3 hour	23.4
1 to 1½ hours	26.5	3 to 3½ hours	7.8
1½ to 2 hours	14.7	3½ to 4 hours	4.7
2 to 2½ hours	17.7	4 to 4½ hours	1.6
More than 2½ hours	16.2	More than 4½ hours	0.0

Source: Data from Schwarz, Hippler, Deutsch, and Strack (1985). Copyright © 1985. Reprinted with permission from the University of Chicago Press.

of television per day; by contrast, when the options emphasized the low end of the range, only 16% of the respondents reported watching that much television. Two further findings support the contention that these effects reflect inferences about the population rather than simple response contraction: The effect of the scale options is more marked when the question concerns the "typical" person rather than the respondent himself or herself (Schwarz & Bienas, 1990); in addition, the respondents exposed to different options differ in their estimates of the population average (Schwarz & Hippler, 1987).

8.2.6 Summary of Departures from the Range and Frequency Principles

The range-frequency model may serve as a useful starting point for understanding the mapping process for items using rating scales or other ordered categories, but several other processes may interfere with the straightforward application of the range and frequency principles:

- *Positivity or leniency bias* (in which respondents shun the negative end of a rating scale);
- *Scale labels effects* (in which negative numbers are interpreted as implying more extreme judgments than low positive numbers);
- *Response contraction bias* (in which respondents avoid extreme response categories);
- *Reference point effects* (in which specific numbers convey specific meanings that may encourage or discourage respondents from selecting a given response option);

- *Scale range effects* (in which the range changes beliefs about the object being rated or about the population distribution).

The application of the frequency principle may be based on the perceived spacing of salient stimuli even when some of these salient stimuli are not among those to be rated.

One theme that emerges from the findings on both numerical categories and rating scales is that respondents have some difficulty with both formats and use a number of strategies to simplify the task of mapping their judgments onto an acceptable answer. If respondents find it difficult to map their judgments onto rating scales, then it may be possible to develop item formats that make the task easier, allowing them to answer more quickly, more reliably, or both.

A series of studies by Krosnick and Berent (1993) indicates that at least two features of the rating scale formats do, in fact, affect both speed and reliability. They compared the answers given to two types of rating scale items – those that labeled only the end categories and those that provided verbal labels for all the response categories. In addition, they compared typical rating scale items, which present all the response options in a single step, to branching items, which present a preliminary choice (*Are you a Republican, Democrat, or Independent?*) followed by questions offering more refined categories (*Are you strongly or weakly Democratic?*). Both labeling and the two-step branching format increased the reliability of the answers. Moreover, the fully labeled, branching versions of the questions were faster to administer than the partly labeled, nonbranching versions (Krosnick & Berent, 1993, Study 2). Krosnick and Berent argue that the labels help clarify the meaning of the scale points and that the branching structure makes the reporting task easier by decomposing it into two simpler judgments (see Section 5.4).

Aside from labeling and branching, the sheer number of the response categories can affect the difficulty of the item. With too few categories, the rating scales may fail to discriminate between respondents with different underlying judgments; with too many, respondents may fail to distinguish reliably between adjacent categories. Based on a review of the literature, Krosnick and Fabrigar (1997) argue that seven scale points seem to represent the best compromise (see also Alwin & Krosnick, 1991).

8.3   Unordered Categories and Satisficing

A third common format for survey items is a list of categorical response options that do not form an ordered series or rating scale. The respondent's task in this situation is to pick the category that best represents his or her judgment; it should be obvious, however, that respondents may take whatever shortcuts are available to them to reduce the work of selecting an answer. As Tourangeau (1984, p. 90) observed, "Respondents . . . probably do not always wait patiently until all the options have been laid out; they may leap at the first option that seems satisfactory, ignoring the rest." The idea that response selection might reflect a satisficing criterion (Simon, 1957) – choosing an answer that is adequate rather than the one that is optimal – has undergone considerable elaboration since the time of Tourangeau's initial conjecture. Much of this elaboration has focused on the impact that the order of the response alternatives has on the distribution of the answers.

8.3.1   Krosnick and Alwin's Initial Model

Krosnick and Alwin presented a detailed model of response order effects and of respondent and item characteristics that may promote satisficing. In the initial statement of the model, Krosnick and Alwin (1987, p. 203) argued:

When responding to survey questions, there is essentially no cost to the respondent if he or she chooses an acceptable answer instead of an optimal one. And for survey items involving a large number of response options, the cognitive costs entailed by making the optimal choice may be substantial. Therefore . . . we would expect respondents to choose the first acceptable alternative(s) among the offered choices.

According to Krosnick and Alwin, when the response options appear visually (e.g., in a self-administered questionnaire or in a "show card" that lists the response options), three processes may contribute to a tendency for respondents to choose options presented early in the list. First, a satisficing criterion implies that the earlier in the list an acceptable answer appears, the more popular it will be. If respondents choose an early option, they can avoid thinking about the others. Second, respondents are likely to process earlier options more deeply than later ones. As they consider later options, respondents will still be processing earlier ones; as a result, their minds will be "cluttered with thoughts about previous alternatives that inhibit consideration of later ones" (Krosnick & Alwin, 1987, p. 203). Because respondents often fall prey to confirmatory strategies in evaluating each option (i.e., they look for reasons to endorse an option rather than for reasons to reject it), the greater attention given to early options is likely to be positive. Finally, the options presented at the beginning of the list may establish an interpretive framework or standard of comparison for subsequent options.

When the response options are presented visually, it seems reasonable to assume that respondents typically start at the top of the list and work their way through the remaining options in order. Primacy effects would, therefore, seem to be the rule: Respondents will tend to prefer options at the beginning of the list over those at the end. As Krosnick and Alwin observe, the picture becomes somewhat murkier when the interviewer reads the response options to the respondent. Survey interviewers tend to read questions quickly so that respondents will not generally have time to evaluate the first option before they must turn to the next. It is quite likely that respondents will begin by considering the final option, since that option is the one that will remain in working memory when the interviewer stops reading the question. Consequently, we should expect recency effects – the tendency to choose options at the end of the list – when the question is presented aloud to the respondent.

Krosnick and Alwin evaluated these predictions using data from an item on the GSS. The item asks respondents to select the most and least desirable of 13 qualities that a child might have (e.g., "is neat and clean," "obeys his parents well," "has good sense and sound judgment"); in addition, respondents selected the three most and least desirable qualities. All 13 qualities were displayed visually. Respondents received the items either in the order GSS typically uses or in the reverse order. The results showed the expected primacy effects: Respondents more often rated qualities as among the three most desirable when they appeared at the beginning than at the end of the list. A second line of evidence supports the view that respondents may adopt a satisficing rather than an optimizing criterion in selecting their answers. When they must indicate all options that apply to them, respondents endorse fewer options than when the item format forces them to evaluate each option individually (Rasinski, Mingay, & Bradburn, 1994). Apparently, unless they are forced to consider every item, respondents process only enough of them to satisfy the question's perceived requirements.

The impact of response order depends, according to Krosnick and

Alwin, on the mode of presentation of the question. With visual presentation, primacy effects will predominate; with auditory presentation, recency effects. The variable underlying this difference by mode of presentation is the order in which the respondents consider the options. Because respondents process only the first few options deeply, because they adopt a low threshold for evaluating each option, and because they use biased evaluation strategies, they tend to select one of the first options they consider. The mode of presentation determines whether they begin by considering the first or last option.

In addition to mode of presentation, Krosnick and Alwin claim that response order effects are moderated by a second variable – the respondents' cognitive sophistication. The less sophisticated the respondent, the more likely he or she is to satisfice. Krosnick and Alwin partitioned the GSS respondents by education and by their scores on a vocabulary test; response order effects were more marked among respondents in the low education/low vocabulary group than among those high in education and scoring well on vocabulary. Subsequent research has found similar interactions between response order and educational attainment (Narayan & Krosnick, 1996) and between response order and grade point average (Krosnick, 1991).

A reanalysis of the same data reviewed by Narayan and Krosnick suggests that the key variable affecting susceptibility to response order effects is working memory capacity (Knäuper, 1998a; see also Knäuper, 1998b). Knäuper shows that controlling for age eliminates the effects of educational attainment reported by Narayan and Krosnick. (In surveys of the adult population, older adults tend to be less educated than younger ones.) Age, according to Knäuper, is a proxy for diminished working memory capacity. Because respondents who are 55 or older have less working memory capacity, they are more likely than younger respondents to focus on and select a single response option.

8.3.2   Elaborations on the Initial Model

In their initial presentation of the model, Krosnick and Alwin argued that response order effects were more likely with long lists of response options or lists that included multiple options of similar attractiveness. Schwarz, Hippler, and Noelle-Neumann (1991) have offered a variant of the Krosnick and Alwin model in which they claim that each response option acts as a kind of "short persuasive argument" (p. 189) influencing the respondent. Following Petty and Cacioppo's (1986) theory of persuasion, Schwarz and his colleagues claim that the impact of the argument embodied by a response option will depend both on the plausibility of the option and on the depth of processing it receives. Deeper processing will increase the popularity (or persuasiveness) of plausible options but decrease the popularity of implausible ones. Unfortunately, this implication of the model is difficult to test, since the options presented in survey items are typically chosen to sound plausible. However, a second implication of the model of Schwarz and his colleagues – that long lists of response options are not necessary for response order effects – receives some support from experiments conducted at the Allensbach Institute: These experiments demonstrate response order effects even with items presenting as few as two response options. In addition, these experiments demonstrate both primacy and recency effects, depending on the item's mode of presentation (Schwarz et al., 1991).

These effects, however, may have a simpler explanation. Suppose that respondents are more sensitive to the plausibility of the options they evaluate first. As they grow fatigued or lose interest in the question, respondents may make a dichotomous judgment regarding the acceptability of each option they consider, terminating this process when they come to an option they consider good enough. It is not necessary to assume that respondents use test strategies that are biased in the direction of confirmation or that they treat the response options as persuasive messages to account for response order effects. Rather, it is sufficient to assume that some respondents have a low threshold for accepting the options, a threshold that leads them to accept the first plausible option that they consider. For such respondents, the options considered first will have an advantage over those evaluated later.

In subsequent work, Krosnick (1991; see also Narayan & Krosnick, 1996) has distinguished between two forms of satisficing – weak satisficing, in which respondents may take shortcuts but do not abandon any of the major components of the response process, and strong satisficing, in which they jettison whole components (such as retrieval). Weak satisficing takes such forms as selecting the first response option that constitutes a reasonable answer or agreeing with items that make an assertion. Strong satisficing takes such forms as selecting "don't know" as the answer, choosing the most neutral response option, selecting the same response for every item, or even answering randomly. Clearly, these response strategies represent radical attempts by the respondents to minimize effort that go beyond their efforts to reduce the difficulty of mapping a judgment onto a response category. Also, strong satisficing may be a rather rare response strategy. Still, Krosnick's arguments about strong satisficing are consistent with the spirit of the evidence presented in this chapter.

8.4   Summary

Regardless of the response format of the items, respondents are likely to attempt to make the task of reporting their answer as easy as they can. They will use ranges or round values to report numeric quantities, make ratings that follow a few simple principles, satisfice in selecting an answer from a set of options, or adopt answer strategies that entirely bypass serious consideration of the question. To the extent that they are tired, uninterested, or generally unable to cope with the demands of the items, respondents will be more prone to use strategies that reduce the burden that the questions impose. There's no reason why respondents should work hard to answer the difficult questions posed in many surveys. The evidence indicates that many respondents may choose to take it easy instead.

CHAPTER NINE

Editing of Responses: Reporting about Sensitive Topics

National surveys generally steer clear of questions that might offend respondents, keeping to relatively impersonal factual questions or items about abstract attitude issues. But almost every survey includes some items that are likely to seem intrusive or too personal to *some* respondents. For instance, it is quite common for surveys to ask the respondents about their income. Here's a representative income question, taken from the CPS:

(1) (Including overtime pay, tips and commissions,) what are (name's/your) usual monthly earnings on (this job/(your/his/her) MAIN job), before taxes or other deductions? [CPS]

Many surveys try to soften the blow a bit by letting respondents choose from broad income groupings, but the CPS item asks for an exact dollar amount. The census Long Form – sent to one-sixth of the U.S. population – also includes detailed income questions about multiple sources of income (salaries, royalties, Social Security payments, and so on) that seek exact dollar amounts for every adult member of the household.

Even when a survey doesn't ask about the respondent's income, it almost certainly includes other standard demographic questions, and it isn't hard to imagine circumstances in which questions about age, say, or marital status might provoke embarrassment. In addition, surveys often begin by asking respondents for a roster of household members. Here, for example, is the roster question from the CPS:

(2) What are the names of all persons living or staying here?

Household surveys include questions like (2) partly because a roster of individuals is often needed to complete the sample selection process. Once the roster of household members has been obtained, the interviewer selects a random member to be the respondent. But even this most basic of survey questions may seem intrusive and produce misleading answers. Hainer and his colleagues argue that respondents in poor households may deliberately omit males from the household roster for fear of losing welfare or housing benefits (Hainer, Hines, Martin, & Shapiro, 1988). These omissions are an important source of undercoverage both in surveys and in the census.

For these reasons, survey designers find it difficult to avoid asking potentially embarrassing questions even when the main topic of the survey is relatively bland. In recent years, however, surveys have begun to delve into ever more sensitive areas. Since 1971, the federal government has sponsored a series of surveys on illicit drug use. The centerpiece of this effort is the National Household Survey on Drug Abuse (NHSDA), now in its 18th round. (See Turner, Lessler, & Gfroerer, 1992, for a discussion of the survey and the methodological issues it raises.) The NHSDA asks a large, nationally representative sample questions about smoking, consumption of alcohol, and use of illicit drugs. Here are some items from the 1990 questionnaire:

(3) a. During the past 30 days, on how many days did you use cocaine?
  b. When was the most recent time you smoked a cigarette?
  c. How many times in the past 12 months have you gotten very high or drunk on alcohol?

During roughly the same period, the AIDS epidemic has greatly increased the need for data about sexual behavior. As a result, the General Social Survey has sometimes included a self-administered supplement on sexual behavior, and a number of organizations and investigators have carried out free-standing surveys on sexual behavior (e.g., Laumann, Gagnon, Michael, & Michaels, 1994; Sonenstein, Pleck, & Ku, 1989; Tanfer & Cubbins, 1992).

This chapter concerns how respondents react to sensitive or intrusive questions. The model of the response process that we presented in Chapter 1 allows for editing or censoring of responses – respondents' attempts to distort answers to avoid embarrassment, inconsistency, or other consequences. Censoring probably occurs most often in response to sensitive questions, and we spend the bulk of the chapter on such questions. In the final section, we consider other situations that may produce editing or censoring of the answers.

9.1   What Is a Sensitive Question?

No standard definition of *sensitive* (or *threatening*) questions exists, but the concept seems to encompass several distinguishable aspects. We discuss three of them here – social (un)desirability of the answers, invasion of privacy, and risk of disclosure of answers to third parties.

9.1.1   Social Desirability

One dimension of a question's sensitivity is the differential social desirability of the possible answers. Most of us believe that the public opposes the use of illicit drugs, supports voting in elections, and favors regular exercise. Sensitive questions ask, in effect, whether we have violated such norms. In the framework that we developed in Chapter 2, sensitive questions have uncertainty spaces that encompass possibilities that a respondent may not want to contemplate. Question (3a), for example, has as its uncertainty space the following set of propositions: I have used cocaine 0 days during the last 30, I have used cocaine 1 day during the last 30, . . . , I have used cocaine 30 days during the last 30. Only the first of these is socially acceptable.

This notion of sensitive questions presupposes that respondents believe there are norms defining desirable attitudes and behaviors, and that they are concerned enough about these norms to distort their answers to avoid presenting themselves in an unfavorable light. Sudman and Bradburn (1974, pp. 9–10) describe the situation this way:

Some questions call for the respondent to provide information on topics that have highly desirable answers. . . . If the respondent has a socially undesirable attitude or if he has engaged in socially undesirable behavior, he may face a conflict between a desire to . . . tell the truth and a desire to appear to the interviewer to be in the socially desirable category. It is frequently assumed that most respondents resolve this conflict in favor of biasing their answer in the direction of social desirability.

Implicit in this view is the assumption that the respondent is concerned, at least in part, about the interviewer's approval or disapproval. Thus, the distortion, or editing, that sensitive questions provoke is situational: It depends on the presence of an interviewer, the topic of the question, and the facts about the respondent's conduct or attitudes. Change any one of these, and the motivation to misreport will be reduced.

But this situational view of question sensitivity is at odds with much of the psychological literature on social desirability. According to traditional views in social and personality psychology, respondents' concern over social desirability reflects a personality characteristic: Respondents distort their answers because of underlying needs, such as the need for social approval or the need to conform to social standards (see the discussion in DeMaio, 1984). Working in this tradition, Crowne and Marlowe (1964) developed a test that attempts to measure the need for approval, conceived as a personality trait. Of course, as a number of researchers have pointed out, these two views aren't necessarily contradictory. Individuals may differ in their need for social approval; at the same time, the presence or absence of an interviewer and the nature of the topic under discussion may increase or decrease the impact of this need on the answers.

9.1.2   Intrusive Questions

Beyond social desirability is a second dimension of question sensitivity – the notion that certain questions are inherently offensive because they invade privacy. In everyday conversation, many topics are out of bounds, including religion, personal finances, sex, and certain bodily functions. (It is curious that both sex and money fall into the category of taboo topics.) The CPS question about monthly income in (1) is clearly not the sort of thing one could ask a neighbor or a casual acquaintance over lunch. It is not necessarily the answers to such questions that are sensitive but the questions themselves (Schaeffer, in press; Willis, 1997a). This dimension of sensitivity or question threat mostly reflects the topic of the question rather than circumstances in which it is asked or the personality of the respondent. Still, it is easy to imagine that there are individual differences in willingness to make personal disclosures that might affect reactions to intrusive questions.

9.1.3   Disclosure to Third Parties

There is one more dimension to the concept of sensitivity – risk of disclosure. A question is sensitive in this sense if respondents fear disclosing their answers to agencies or individuals not directly involved with the survey. Survey organizations take elaborate precaution to protect the confidentiality of survey data. Employees of survey firms must often sign pledges not to disclose data that might allow others to identify the respondents; interviewers sometimes have formal exemptions from legal requirements to report illicit activities that respondents disclose; official publications of the findings must often suppress results concerning small subgroups of respondents to preserve confidentiality; and the survey organizations themselves keep paper questionnaires under lock and key (and keep their electronic counterparts in password-protected files), strip names, addresses, and other identifying information from analytical data sets, and "sanitize" the data to reduce the risk of inadvertent disclosure.

Despite these precautions, respondents may be wary of disclosure to third parties, such as other government agencies, neighbors, and employers. Individuals appear to vary in the strength of their worries about confidentiality, and the degree of concern has some effect on their willingness to take part in surveys (Couper, Singer, & Kulka, 1998; Singer, Mathiowetz, & Couper, 1993).

9.1.4 Assessing Sensitivity

Sensitivity is, then, a complex concept that is easier to recognize than to define. It depends on respondents' concerns about disclosing *any* information about certain topics, about disclosing information to an interviewer, and about disclosing to third parties. The first two are sometimes lumped together under the heading of *privacy* concerns, reflecting the "desire to keep information about oneself out of the hands of others altogether" (Singer et al., 1993, p. 466). The final worry is often labeled as a concern about *confidentiality* – the "desire to keep information already given to one agent out of the hands of others" (Singer et al., 1993, p. 466).

Methodological studies of sensitive questions have generally relied on the investigators' intuitions about which topics and questions are sensitive. For example, in their classic studies on responses to sensitive questions, Bradburn, Sudman, and their colleagues (1979) examined reports about voting, having a library card, bankruptcy, drunken driving, sex, gambling, and drinking. These topics had not passed any particular operational test but just seemed sensitive to the researchers.

Bradburn and his colleagues did introduce rating scales to assess the topics' level of sensitivity after the fact. They asked respondents to identify any questions they had found "too personal." In addition, they had respondents rate topics on a four-point scale according to how uneasy they would make "most people." Table 9.1 shows the proportion of

TABLE 9.1 Proportion of Respondents
Reporting That Most People Would Be
"Very Uneasy" about the Topic

Topic	Percent "Very Uneasy"
Masturbation	56.4
Use of marijuana	42.0
Sexual intercourse	41.5
Stimulants and depressants	31.3
Intoxication	29.0
Petting and kissing	19.7
Income	12.5
Gambling with friends	10.5
Drinking	10.3
General leisure	2.4

Source: Data from Bradburn, Sudman, and Associates
(1979).

respondents reporting that most people would be very uneasy answering
survey questions about various topics. Judging from the ratings, some
topics (e.g., masturbation) are clearly more sensitive than others (gambling).

Researchers sometimes use two other tests to assess the sensitivity of
a question. Sensitive questions probably yield more missing data than
other questions, since some respondents refuse to answer them. So if the
relation between sensitivity and item nonresponse were strong enough,
then we could use the rate of missing data to measure the sensitivity of
a question. Unfortunately, as we shall see in the next section of this
chapter, the relation between sensitivity and the rate of missing data is
not so striking as to make the one a reasonable measure of the other. A
second potential index of sensitivity stems from the fact that the method
of data collection affects responses to sensitive questions more than
responses to nonsensitive ones (see Chapter 10). Respondents are much
more likely to disclose potentially embarrassing information when the
questions are self-administered than when they are administered by an
interviewer; with nonsensitive questions, the impact of self-
administration is generally negligible. The data on this point are strongly
supportive (see, e.g., Table 10.2).

9.2   Sensitivity and Nonresponse

One method of coping with sensitive questions is simply not to answer them: Those selected for a survey can refuse to take part at all or they can refuse to answer specific questions. The survey literature refers to complete refusal to participate as *unit nonresponse*; refusal to answer specific questions is *item nonresponse*.

9.2.1   Sensitivity and Unit Nonresponse

The topic of a survey has a clear impact on people's willingness to take part in it. But which characteristics of the topic are responsible for this effect? In a meta-analysis of studies on response rates to mail surveys, the topic of the survey emerges as a major determinant of participation (Heberlein & Baumgartner, 1978), but it appears to be respondents' *interest* in the topic (*topic saliency*) rather than the topic's sensitivity that makes a sample member willing to respond. Most people, for example, have more interest in health than in consumer expenditures, and a likely consequence is that surveys on health achieve higher response rates than surveys on consumer expenditures (Groves & Couper, 1998). More recent meta-analyses of the response rates in mail surveys (Yammarino, Skinner, & Childers, 1991) have confirmed Heberlein and Baumgartner's original findings on the impact of the survey topic but have not tried to distinguish this effect from the effect of topic sensitivity.

Still, most survey researchers regard sensitive topics as serious impediments to high response rates (e.g., Catania, Gibson, Coates, Chitwood, & Coates, 1990), and surveys on sensitive topics often resort to extreme measures to achieve respectable levels of participation. The effect of topic sensitivity may be limited to certain segments of the population. If you haven't used illicit drugs lately, you'll find nothing especially threatening about the questions in the NHSDA (although you may, of course, regard them as intrusive).

Confidentiality Assurances and Unit Nonresponse

Survey organizations routinely attempt to allay concerns about confidentiality by offering strong assurances that they will protect the confidentiality of the data. Here, for example, is the assurance to respondents in the National Education Longitudinal Study of 1988, Second Follow-up:

(4) As a matter of policy, the National Center for Education Statistics is required to protect the privacy of individuals who participate in voluntary surveys. We want to let you know that:

1. Section 406 of the General Education Provisions Act (20-USC 1221e-1) allows us to ask you the questions in the questionnaire.
2. You may skip any questions you do not wish to answer.
3. We are asking you these questions in order to gather information about what happens to students as they leave high school and make decisions about postsecondary education and work.
4. Your responses will be merged with those of others, and the answers you give will never be identified as yours.

Other federal agencies offer similar guarantees to respondents in their surveys.

It's not clear, however, whether people pay much attention to these assurances. An experiment by the Panel on Privacy and Confidentiality as Factors in Survey Response varied the wording of the confidentiality assurances given to members of the sample and found little effect on response rates, even though one version stated that data may be given to other agencies and the public. A meta-analysis by Singer, Von Thurn, and Miller (1995) found small, although significant, effects for including confidentiality assurances when the topic of the survey was sensitive (see also Singer et al., 1993). When the topic is not sensitive, elaborate confidentiality assurances can backfire, raising more concerns than they allay (Singer, Hippler, & Schwarz, 1992).

Confidentiality and Participation in the Decennial Census

Despite the weak effects of assurances on response rates, worries about confidentiality may still be an important determinant of survey participation. The assurances may simply not be very effective. It's likely that many respondents don't read or listen to them carefully, and even if they do, they may not fully understand or believe them. Another approach to the question of the impact of such concerns has been to measure the concerns directly and to relate them to willingness to participate in surveys. Singer and her colleagues have used this approach to examine participation in the 1990 census (Singer et al., 1993; see also Couper et al., 1998, and Fay, Carter, & Dowd, 1991).

Participation in the census is mandatory, and estimates indicate that about 98% of all households eventually ended up completing a census form in 1990. At the beginning of the field period, census forms were mailed to all addresses; if a completed form wasn't mailed back by a certain date, the Census Bureau sent an "enumerator" out to collect the information on the form. In this line of research, then, the "participants" are those who complete and mail back their census form without requiring a visit from an enumerator. Mail response rates in the census seem to be declining (Singer et al., 1993), and one reason for the decline may be an increase in concerns about confidentiality and privacy.

Singer and her colleagues analyzed data from the Survey on Census Participation (SCP), a survey carried out after the census. It included eight items designed to tap privacy concerns (e.g., *The census is an invasion of privacy*) and another six that measured confidentiality concerns (e.g., *People's answers to the census cannot be used against them*). They found significant effects for both privacy and confidentiality concerns on census mail response rates, although the impact of both variables was clearer for whites than for blacks. A reanalysis of the same data incorporated a more comprehensive set of predictors of mail response; it still found a significant effect for confidentiality but none for privacy concerns (Couper et al., 1998). In both analyses, the impact of these variables was relatively small compared to that of other determinants of mail response to the census, such as the age or race of the respondent.

9.2.2 Sensitivity and Item Nonresponse

Once they've agreed to participate, respondents still have the option of declining to answer specific questions. Confidentiality assurances may even remind them of that option as an inducement to take part, as in the second clause of the assurance from the National Education Longitudinal Survey that we quoted in (4) (Section 9.2.1). Is the sensitivity of the question related to the rate of item nonresponse? Table 9.2 shows item-level response rates for selected questions in a survey on sexual behavior (Tourangeau, Rasinski, Jobe, Smith, & Pratt, 1997). On average, respondents answered 97.3% of the questions put to them, and this rate varied only slightly by topic. For five demographic questions, the rate was 98.7%; for six items on sexually transmitted diseases, it was 97.4%. So, while the trend is in the right direction, the impact of question sensitivity hardly seems dramatic.

Are there other sensitive topics that have a bigger impact than sex in discouraging responses? One area is questions about income, since these stand out among survey items as producing high rates of missing data. We gave the CPS item in (1) that asks for the respondent's monthly

TABLE 9.2 Mean Proportion of Items Answered in
a Survey on Sexual Behavior

Topic	Percent
43 questions on a range of topics	97.3
5 demographic questions	98.7
9 questions on illicit drug use	98.6
8 questions on sexual behavior	97.9
6 questions on sexually transmitted diseases	97.4

Source: Unpublished data from Tourangeau, Rasinski, Jobe, Smith, & Pratt (1997).

income. More than a quarter of the wage and salary data in the CPS is missing or incomplete and has to be imputed (Moore, Stinson, & Welniak, 1999). This is roughly ten times the rate of missing data for the items in Table 9.2. The CPS includes an annual supplement in March of each year containing particularly detailed questions about income. These questions ask whether the respondent receives certain types of income (such as Social Security or Unemployment Insurance payments) and the amounts received from each source. From 20% to 49% of the data on the amounts received are missing (Moore et al., 1999).

This high level of item nonresponse to questions about income doesn't necessarily reflect unwillingness to report the information. In many cases, respondents may not have the exact figures readily available and allowing them to report income in ranges decreases the level of missing data (e.g., Kennickell, 1996). Still, studies of unit and item nonresponse to the CPS income supplement indicate that both forms of nonresponse depend on the respondent's level of income, suggesting that sensitivity contributes to the large amount of missing data on these questions.

9.3 Measuring Misreporting

It is tempting, but simplistic, to assume that misreporting about sensitive topics is always deliberate. The same cognitive processes responsible for errors in responses to nonthreatening questions can produce errors with threatening ones as well. As we shall see, it can be hard to distinguish between deliberate misreporting and other sources of error (such as biased rounding and other response difficulties that we reviewed in Chapter 8).

Still, there are good reasons to think that deliberate misreporting is a serious problem with sensitive questions. First of all, the accuracy of responses to sensitive questions can be *very* low. For example, Jones and Forrest (1992) compared two sets of estimates of the number of abortions performed each year. One set came from the National Survey of Family Growth (NSFG); the other set came from abortion clinics. The comparison indicated that respondents reported only about half of all abortions in the NSFG. Investigators have explored other sources of error in the NSFG data but have found little support for the hypotheses that forgetting or comprehension problems explain the low level of accuracy (see, e.g., Jobe et al., 1997). The main culprit for the underreporting of abortions seems to be deliberate misreporting.[1]

A second reason to suspect deliberate misreporting is that features of the interview associated with privacy or veracity can have a dramatic effect on the answers to sensitive questions. In one study, for example, women reported having 16–88% more sexual partners when answering self-administered questions than when answering questions from interviewers; the exact size of the increase depended on the time period covered by the question and the specific method of self-administration (see Table 10.3 in the next chapter; for similar findings, see Turner et al., 1998). The impact of self-administration is generally negligible when the questions aren't sensitive. Similarly, the results of several "bogus pipeline" studies indicate that the accuracy of adolescents' reports about smoking improves dramatically when the respondents think that false answers can be detected (Murray, O'Connell, Schmid, & Perry, 1987). *Bogus pipeline* refers to any procedure that respondents believe can detect inaccurate answers, regardless of whether it actually can. Many of the studies on teen smoking have taken saliva or breath samples, which can, in fact, be used to determine whether someone has smoked recently. In these studies, it is possible to compare the accuracy of reports by those who, according to the biochemical tests, have smoked recently and those who have not.

9.3.1   Quantifying Accuracy

Before we describe the findings about accuracy for sensitive topics, we distinguish the different forms that inaccuracy can take and describe the methods used to determine how accurate survey results are.

---

[1] As Jones and Forrest (1992, p. 114) note, although the surveys they examined used sampling designs to minimize bias from women who did not respond, "it is still possible that women with higher than average numbers of abortions could be underrepresented in the final results. Any effect of such underrepresentation would appear as underreporting in this analysis."

Measures of Inaccuracy

The survey literature draws a basic distinction between random and systematic error. According to the standard framework, respondent i's answer on occasion j (Y_{ij}) consists of three components. The first is the true score (X_i), which reflects the facts of the respondent's situation. The second is bias (b), which represents any overall tendency across respondents to overreport or underreport. The final component is random error (e_{ij}), which fluctuates across respondents and, within a single respondent, from one occasion to the next:

$$Y_{ij} = X_i + b + e_{ij}$$

In this conception, one component of the error in survey reports is random and therefore essentially directionless. When there is an external standard (such as a record) to which we can compare the survey response, we can quantify this component using such direction-free measures as the absolute or squared difference between the survey report and the external criterion. Aggregating across respondents, we can compute such overall measures of accuracy as the *mean squared error, the mean absolute difference,* or the *correlation* between the responses and the criterion. Table 9.3 presents the mathematical definitions of these measures. When the report and the criterion are both dichotomous, the mean squared error reduces to the *gross discrepancy rate* – the proportions of cases in which the report disagrees with the standard (see, e.g., O'Muircheartaigh, 1991).

The other component of the error is directional. Respondents answering questions about sensitive behaviors systematically overreport the desirable ones and underreport the undesirable ones. The raw or *signed difference* between the survey report and the external criterion is often used to measure the bias in the reports. For example, if a respondent claims to have a monthly income of $6,000 but the records reveal that the income is only $5,000, then the signed difference (i.e., reported value – true value) is $1,000. Such signed differences may be converted into *relative errors* by dividing the signed difference by the true value. To continue our income example, we can calculate the relative error at 20% ($1,000 / $5,000). At the aggregate level, researchers have looked at the *mean difference* between the survey reports and the criterial values; the mean difference is an estimate of the bias due to reporting error. Again, it is sometimes useful to examine the mean relative error. Finally, when the data are dichotomous, it is possible to look at *the net discrep-*

TABLE 9.3 Some Common Measures of Survey Accuracy

Individual Level	Aggregate Level
Absolute difference: $|Y_i - X_i|$	Mean absolute difference: $\Sigma|Y_i - X_i|/n$
Squared difference: $(Y_i - X_i)^2$	Mean squared difference: $\Sigma(Y_i - X_i)^2/n$
Signed difference: $Y_i - X_i$	Mean difference (estimated bias): $\bar{Y} - \bar{X}$
Relative difference: $(Y_i - X_i)/X_i$	Mean relative difference: $(\bar{Y} - \bar{X})/\bar{X}$
	Gross discrepancy rate: $Pr\ (Y_i \neq X_i)$
	Net discrepancy rate: $Pr\ (Y_i = 1) - Pr\ (X_i = 1)$
	Miss rate: $Pr\ (Y_i = 0 \mid X_i = 1)$
	False positive rate: $Pr\ (Y_i = 1 \mid X_i = 0)$

Notes: Y_i refers to the survey report from respondent i.

X_i refers to the true score for respondent i.

$Pr\ (Y_i = 1)$ refers to the proportion of respondents who reported that they had some characteristic (e.g., the proportion who say that they voted).

$Pr\ (X_i = 1)$ refers to the proportion of respondents who have some characteristic according to the external source.

The last four aggregate measures apply to dichotomous data.

ancy rate (the difference between the marginal proportion having the characteristic according to the survey reports and the marginal proportion according to the external criteria), the *miss rate* (the proportion of those with some characteristic who don't report it), and the *false alarm rate* (the proportion of those without some characteristic who do report it). Table 9.3 provides a summary of some of the more common measures of accuracy. All these are also common measures of error in cognitive tasks.

9.3.2 Designs for Assessing the Accuracy of Survey Reports

A challenge to research on sensitive topics is that many of these involve private acts known only to the respondent and perhaps a few others. Still, the act may sometimes be captured in an official record. It is possible, for example, to obtain arrest reports, voting records, medical records, and other sources of nonsurvey data about potentially sensitive topics. Records are no panacea – they may have inaccuracies of their own – but they provide an important tool for investigating the accuracy of surveys.

Four basic methods have been used to assess the accuracy of survey reports:

(5) a. comparison of survey estimates to estimates based on alternative data sources, such as records;

    b. comparison of individual survey responses with external validation data;

    c. comparisons between estimates based on two different survey sources;

    d. comparisons between individual survey responses from two or more respondents who are expected to agree with each other.

The first method compares population estimates from survey reports to aggregated data from some other source, typically records of some sort. A good example of this approach is Jones and Forrest's (1992) study of abortion, mentioned at the beginning of this section. Similarly, Moore, Stinson, and Welniak (1999) compared income estimates based on reports from the CPS to aggregate figures from the IRS. A variation on this strategy compares estimates derived from two survey procedures, one of which is thought to yield more accurate information. For example, reports about smoking obtained using conventional interview procedures can be compared to the presumably more accurate reports from bogus pipeline conditions (Murray et al., 1987). The estimate from the bogus pipeline group provides the same sort of aggregate benchmark as an estimate derived from external records.

In some cases, validation data are available for individual respondents; thus, a second method for assessing the accuracy of survey data is to compare individual responses to the validation data. Locander, Sudman, and Bradburn (1976), for example, were able to obtain information about library card ownership and driving arrests from official records. They used the records data to assess the effectiveness of different methods of data collection on respondents' propensity to give accurate reports. This way of determining survey response accuracy is predicated on the accuracy of the validation information and of the process that matches the survey reports to the external records. The apparent level of accuracy in survey reports can vary sharply, depending on the stringency of the criteria that determine whether records and reports match (Miller & Groves, 1985).

A third method is to compare estimates based on two sets of survey reports that, in principle, ought to agree. For example, T. W. Smith (1992b) analyzed a number of national samples in which men and women were asked about the number of their opposite-sex sexual partners during some fixed time period. To the extent that the men and women in these samples represent closed populations, the estimates of the total number of sexual partners should converge.[2] Instead, Smith found that men consistently reported having more sexual partners than women did.

A final method carries out the same sort of comparison between reporters at the level of pairs of individual reports. For example, investigators may ask husbands and wives how often they have sexual intercourse with each other and then compare the two answers (Card, 1978; Clark & Wallin, 1964). Or an informant may provide data on the smoking behavior of other members of the household, and these answers may be compared with self-reports about smoking (Brittingham et al., 1998; Gilpin et al., 1994). Disagreement indicates that one or both partners have given an inaccurate answer.

9.4   Misreporting in Surveys

Systematic misreporting on sensitive topics generally takes two forms in surveys: Respondents consistently underreport some behaviors (typically, socially undesirable ones) and consistently overreport others (the desirables ones). Reports about sexual behavior are a particularly interesting case from a methodological standpoint because men seem to be prone to one form of error and women to the other.

9.4.1   Underreporting

The underreporting of sensitive behaviors appears to be common in surveys. Respondents deny having extreme or unpopular attitudes, especially racist attitudes (Devine, 1989; Dovidio & Fazio, 1992; Jones & Sigall, 1971), and they underreport a number of sensitive behaviors, including the use of illicit drugs (Fendrich & Vaughn, 1994; Johnson & O'Malley, 1997), the consumption of alcohol (Duffy & Waterton, 1984; Lemmens, Tan, & Knibbe, 1992; Locander et al., 1976), smoking (Murray et al., 1987; Patrick et al., 1994), abortion (Jones & Forrest, 1992), energy consumption (Warriner, McDougall, & Claxon, 1984), receipt of certain types of income (Moore et al., 1999), crime victimiza-

---

[2] The populations are said to be *closed* if the men draw their sexual partners exclusively from the population of women and the women draw theirs exclusively from the population of men. The assumption is violated to the extent that respondents have sexual partners who fall outside the geographical or age limits of those included in the survey.

tion (Myers, 1980), and criminal behavior (Wyner, 1980). To give a flavor of the findings in this area, we review studies about several of these topics.

Illicit Drug Use

Many studies have examined the validity of self-reports about illicit drug use, mainly among people who have been arrested or are undergoing treatment (see Anglin, Hser, & Chou, 1993; Fendrich & Xu, 1994; Magura & Kang, 1997; and Mieczkowski, Barzelay, Gropper, & Wish, 1991, for some recent examples). These studies typically compare self-reports with results from urine samples and, more recently, hair samples (e.g., Mieczkowski & Newel, 1997). The findings indicate that, even within treatment populations, in which the respondents have openly acknowledged their past drug use, underreporting is still widespread. For example, in the study by Anglin and his colleagues, 39% of those who tested positive for opiates failed to report recent use of opiates in their initial interview (Anglin et al., 1993). Not surprisingly, even higher levels of underreporting are found among individuals who are in jail (e.g., Fendrich & Xu, 1994). The National Institute of Justice sponsors the Drug Use Forecasting (DUF) study, which interviews samples of people in jail and also collects urine specimens from them. Harrison (1995) reviewed evidence from the 1989 DUF comparing reports of drug use in the past three days with urinalysis results. Of those who tested positive for opiate use, 44% denied using opiates in the past three days; similarly, nearly half (49%) of those who tested positive for marijuana denied having used the drug. The rates of underreporting among those who tested positive for cocaine and amphetamines were even higher at 52% and 59% respectively (Harrison, 1995, Figure 1).

Harrison argues that respondents are more likely to underreport recent drug use than drug use in the distant past (see also Turner, Lessler, & Devore, 1992, and Table 10.2 in the next chapter). Other results indicate that even drug use in the distant past may be somewhat underreported: In later waves of a longitudinal survey, respondents sometimes deny ever having used a drug they had reported using in earlier waves (Fendrich & Vaughn, 1994; Johnson & O'Malley, 1997).

Self-administered questionnaires sharply increase the proportion of respondents reporting illicit drug use (Aquilino, 1994; Aquilino & Lo-Sciuto, 1990; Schober, Caces, Pergamit, & Branden, 1992; Turner, Lessler, & Devore, 1992). It is not clear how much underreporting remains when the questionnaires are self-administered.

Smoking

Relative to using illicit drugs, smoking may not seem to be a particularly sensitive topic. Still, for some survey respondents, such as teenagers or those enrolled in smoking cessation programs, smoking may be sensitive enough to produce systematic underreporting. A meta-analysis by Patrick and colleagues (1994) indicated that reports about recent smoking generally agree with biochemical assessments but that the level of agreement is lower within samples of students.

Several bogus pipeline studies also cast doubt on the validity of teenagers' survey reports about smoking. At least five studies reveal significant increases in the percentage of adolescents reporting that they smoke when a bogus pipeline procedure is in place (Murray et al., 1987; see also Aguinis, Pierce, & Quigley, 1993). Some of these studies have used methods that can in fact determine whether the respondent has smoked recently. For example, Bauman and Dent (1982) took breath samples that they subsequently tested for the presence of carbon monoxide; in this case, the bogus pipeline manipulation simply meant warning respondents ahead of time that their answers would be checked against their breath samples. The bogus pipeline procedure affected the reports only of those who subsequently tested positive for smoking (Bauman & Dent, 1982). Self-administration of the questions also appears to increase the percentage of teenagers who admit that they smoke, but does not affect reporting by adults, for whom smoking is presumably less sensitive (Brittingham et al., 1998).

Abortion

Two record check studies have documented the extent of underreporting of abortions, both at the aggregate (Jones & Forrest, 1992) and individual levels (Jobe et al., 1997). In the study by Jobe and his colleagues (1997), only about half of a sample of women (52%) who had an abortion during the previous year reported that abortion in a subsequent survey. More than a quarter denied that they had ever had an abortion.

Several studies have examined methods to improve the reporting of abortion in surveys. Three of them found increased reporting of abortions when the questions were self-administered rather than administered by an interviewer (Lessler & O'Reilly, 1997; London & Williams, 1990; Mott, 1985; see also Mosher & Duffer, 1994), although a fourth (Jobe et al., 1997) did not. In addition, several studies have examined the randomized response technique as a method for improving the accuracy of reports about abortion. In this technique, respondents use a random device (e.g., they spin a dial) to determine which of two questions they will answer. One of the two concerns the sensitive topic (e.g., *Have you had an abortion in the past year?*); the other concerns an irrelevant topic that has a known response distribution (*Were you born in January?*). Only the respondents know which of the two questions they answered; as a result, neither the interviewer nor the investigators can tie individual respondents to specific answers. As Warner (1965) has shown, it is still possible to estimate the proportion of respondents who reported the sensitive behavior. Studies confirm that the randomized response technique increases the proportion of women reporting abortions (Abernathy, Greenberg, & Horvitz, 1970; Shimizu & Bonham, 1978).

Income

The review by Moore and his colleagues (Moore et al., 1999; see also Coder & Scoon-Rogers, 1995) indicates substantial underreporting in the March CPS income supplement. Table 9.4 shows the ratio between the CPS estimates for 1984 and 1990 and those from the National Income Program Accounts for the same years. The level of underreporting by source appears to reflect two factors: People underreport both relatively minor income sources (e.g., investment interest) and relatively embarrassing ones (welfare). Moore and his colleagues argue that the problem is not only that respondents understate the *amounts* that they receive from a given source but also that they deny receiving any income at all from the source. For relatively minor sources of income this com-

TABLE 9.4 March CPS Estimate of Income as a Percentage of NIPA Estimate, by Source

Source	1984	1990
Wage and salaries	97.3	97.0
Interest	56.7	61.1
Social Security	91.9	93.0
Welfare (Aid to Families with Dependent Children)	78.4	71.6
Unemployment compensation	74.8	80.2
Private pensions	57.2	110.8
Military retirement	98.1	89.2

Source: Data from Moore et al. (1999).

plete omission may reflect forgetting, but for more sensitive sources of income it probably reflects deliberate misreporting. The problems of source and amount underreporting are compounded by unit nonresponse to the March CPS and item nonresponse to the income questions.

9.4.2   Overreporting

Respondents may also be reluctant to admit that they have *not* done something that they feel they should have done. As a result, the response editing process may also produce overreporting. Overreporting has been found in reports of voting (e.g., Abelson, Loftus, & Greenwald, 1992; Silver, Abramson, & Anderson, 1986), energy conservation (Fujii, Hennesey, & Mak, 1985), seat belt use (Stulginskas, Verreault, & Pless, 1985), reading, especially among white-collar workers (Stefanowska, 1977), church attendance (Presser & Stinson, 1998), and exercise behavior (Tourangeau, Smith, & Rasinski, 1997). We review the findings on voting and church attendance to give a sense of these results.

Voting

According to Presser (1990), overreporting of voting has been "found in every major validation study." A fair number of such studies have been done, dating back at least to the 1940s. In many jurisdictions, whether an individual voted is a matter of public record, so it is relatively easy to do validation studies that compare reported voting with voting records. Most survey researchers are aware of the potential for bias in responses to questions about voting and use wording that attempts to minimize it. For example, the question used in the National Election Surveys (NES) includes this forgiving introduction:

(6) In talking to people about elections, we often find that a lot of people were not able to vote because they weren't registered, they were sick, or they just didn't have time. How about you – did you vote in the elections this November?

Despite this effort to preempt any embarrassment among nonvoters, 22.5% of the validated nonvoters reported in the 1978 NES that they voted, and the figure rose to 27.5% in the 1980 NES (Silver et al., 1986).

Various tactics have been tried to reduce the overreporting of voting, usually with no success. Abelson, Loftus, and Greenwald (1992) attempted to soften the NES voting question even further by asking respondents whether they "miss[ed] out on voting in the elections." The rate of overreporting was unaffected by this wording change. Presser (1990) varied the context of the voting item in hopes of encouraging more accurate reports. In one study, respondents first had the chance to report voting in prior elections (*Since you were first eligible to vote, would you say that you have voted most of the time, some of the time, or rarely?*). Presser reasoned that letting respondents say they had voted in past elections would reduce their embarrassment about not voting in the most recent one; unfortunately, the change in context had no effect on responses to the main voting item. Similarly, Abelson and his colleagues (1992) asked a prior question about the four previous elections (including the most recent one) but found no effect on overreporting in the most recent election.[3]

Three variables that do affect the rate of overreporting are the race of the respondent, the intention to vote, and belief in the norm of political participation. Black nonvoters are more likely than their white counterparts to overreport voting (Abramson & Claggett, 1984; Traugott & Katosh, 1979), especially when a black interviewer collects the data (Anderson, Silver, & Abramson, 1988a). Those who intended to vote prior to the election and those who strongly endorse the norm of voting are also more likely to report that they voted when they did not (Silver et al., 1986). These findings are consistent with the idea that people who are most embarrassed about not voting are also the most likely to report falsely that they voted.

Religious Attendance

Recently, Hadaway, Marler, and Chaves (1993) questioned the accuracy of survey data on attendance at religious services. They compared

---

[3] A couple of studies have attempted to improve *memory* for voting. Belli and his colleagues (Belli, Traugott, Young, & McGonagle, 1999) provided respondents with a lengthy preamble to the voting question, asking them to think about how they got to the polls, what the weather was like that day, what time of day they went to vote, and whether they went with another person. The point of these preliminaries was to help respondents distinguish between intending to vote and actually voting, although it is possible to see the introduction simply as providing extra cues to improve memory for the event. Similarly, a concern that respondents are sometimes confused about *which* elections they voted in partly motivated the studies by Abelson and his colleagues. In one of two localities, the experimental wording developed by Belli and his colleagues reduced overreporting. The variations reported by Abelson et al. had no effects on reporting; moreover, they found that the rate of overreporting was unaffected by the passage of time, a result that suggests that memory problems are not a major source of overreporting errors.

survey results with attendance counts at Catholic and Protestant churches for a single county in Ohio; the survey data indicated rates of attendance that were twice as high as those implied by the church counts. Although it is possible that errors in the church data and coverage problems in the survey explain some of the difference between the two data sources (Woodberry, 1997), other results suggest that the main source of the discrepancy is reporting error.

Most surveys on attendance at religious services ask an explicit question on the topic. For example, the Gallup Poll has used this item:

(7) Did you, yourself, happen to attend church or synagogue in the last seven days, or not?

The results from questions like (7) consistently indicate that about 40% of the population report that they attended religious services each week (Presser & Stinson, 1998). By comparison, Presser and Stinson also analyzed the results of a time-use survey that didn't mention religion at all:

(8) I would like to ask you about the things you did yesterday – from midnight Saturday to midnight last night. Let's start with midnight Saturday. What were you doing? What time did you finish? Where were you? What did you do next?

The proportion reporting that they attended religious services dropped to about 29%. Additional evidence reviewed by Presser and Stinson suggests that self-administration also reduces the extent of overreporting of attendance at religious services. The effectiveness of both the indirect questioning strategy and self-administration suggests that the over-reporting of church attendance is the product of deliberate misreporting.

9.4.3   Reports about Sexual Behavior

Sexual behavior may be one of the most sensitive subjects in surveys. Sexual behavior is an intimate topic, perhaps *the* most intimate topic. Even in confidential or anonymous settings, questions about sex are likely to be seen as an invasion of privacy. In addition, sexual behavior is deeply intertwined with one's self-concept and self-esteem. Thus, the presence of an interviewer and the potential threat of the interviewer's disapproval are likely to inhibit candid reporting. On top of that, some sexual behaviors, such as marital infidelity and homosexuality, are widely condemned, and others are illegal. A breach of confidentiality in a survey on sexual behavior could have very serious consequences indeed. Questions about sex thus tap all three dimensions of the concept of sensitivity.

Given these barriers to accurate reporting, it is hardly surprising that methodological studies reveal serious problems in survey data on sexual behavior. The most obvious one is the disparity between the reports of men and women about the number of their opposite-sex sexual partners that we discussed earlier. For example, Tourangeau and Smith (1996) found that men in their sample reported an average of 2.9 female sexual partners in the past year whereas the women reported an average of only 1.6 male partners over the same period (see also T. W. Smith, 1992b, 1996; Wadsworth, Johnson, Wellings, & Field, 1996). Most sex researchers believe that the men are overstating the number of their partners, while the women are overlooking theirs (Herold & Way, 1988; Klassen, Williams, & Levitt, 1989; May, Anderson, & Blower, 1989). This difference, in turn, reflects the persistence of the sexual double standard. Both men and women tend to disapprove more of high levels of sexual activity by women than by men.

Aside from this problem in reports about sexual partners, studies also indicate that the reports of members of couples about various sexual behaviors, such as frequency of sexual intercourse and use of condoms, show only moderate agreement (Bachrach, Evans, Ellison, & Stolley, 1992; Padian, 1990; Udry, 1980; Upchurch et al., 1991; Whisman & Allan, 1996). The disagreements seem to be greater among unmarried partners; the disparity in reporting sex parners is also greatest among the unmarried (T. W. Smith, 1992b).

Further evidence suggests that at least some of the error in reports is due to conscious editing of the answers. Reports about sexual behaviors are affected by how well the respondents know the interviewer (Kahn, Lasbeek, & Hofferth, 1988), the context of the questions (Tourangeau & Smith, 1996), the wording of the introductions (Catania et al., 1996), and the mode of data collection (Tourangeau & Smith, 1996; Turner et al., 1998). For example, "forgiving" introductions increased the proportion of men who reported homosexual activity and also increased the proportion who reported no sexual partners at all (Catania et al., 1996). Similarly, a form of computerized self-administration (audio computer-assisted self-interviewing), in which the program simultaneously displays the question on a screen and plays a digitized recording of it to the respondent, dramatically increased the percentage of men reporting several homosexual behaviors (Turner et al., 1998). The study by Touran-

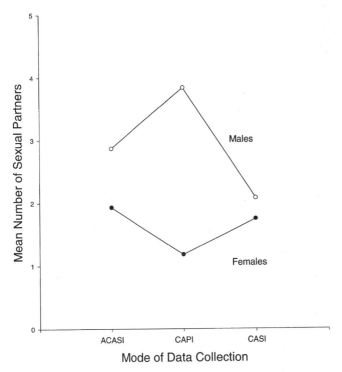

Figure 9.1 The mean number of opposite-sex sexual partners reported by men and women for the past year, by mode of data collection. The upper line shows the average number of sexual partners reported by men; the lower line shows the average number reported by women. ACASI refers to computer-assisted self-interviewing with audio; CASI, to computer-assisted self-interviewing without audio; and CAPI, to computer-assisted personal interviewing (in which an interviewer administers the questions). Data from Tourangeau and Smith (1996).

geau and Smith (1996) found that computer-assisted self-administration (either with or without audio) sharply reduced the gap between the number of sexual partners reported by men and women. We illustrate these data in Figure 9.1. Finally, bogus pipeline studies show that responses to questions about sexual behavior can change dramatically when respondents believe that inaccurate answers can be detected (Clark & Tifft, 1966; Tourangeau, Smith & Rasinski, 1997).

Respondents' strategies for estimating number of sexual partners may play a mediating role in the discrepancy between men's and women's reports. As we saw in Chapter 8, respondents who report large numbers of sexual partners tend to report their answers as round values (see Figure 8.1), suggesting that the answers are estimates. Most of the disparity in the number of sexual partners reported by men and women reflects differences in the tail of the distribution – that is, among men and women who report more than ten partners (Morris, 1993). It is, therefore, possible that highly sexually active men and women use different estimation strategies to answer these questions and that this cognitive difference explains the discrepancy between their answers (Brown & Sinclair, 1997). It isn't clear, however, why men and women should use different strategies unless it is an attempt to raise or lower their totals. For example, women may simply not try as hard as men to recall each of their partners, or men may round their answers up while women round theirs down. We can't rule out the possibility that the response difference is the result of the choice of a response strategy, but the choice itself may be due to self-presentation concerns.

9.4.4   Summary

Respondents systematically underreport or overreport in answering questions about sensitive topics; with some topics (such as sexual partners), some respondents exhibit the one form of misreporting and others exhibit the other. The findings on misreporting support several general conclusions:

- Misreporting gets worse as the topic becomes more sensitive (e.g., underreporting of drug use increases as respondents report on more recent time periods);
- Misreporting is worse among those with something to hide (e.g., teenage smokers as opposed to nonsmokers, nonvoters as opposed to voters);
- Reporting seems to improve when studies use self-administered questions and when they use the randomized response technique.

The findings on the impact of self-administration and the randomized response technique suggest that much of the misreporting on these topics is deliberate. There's no reason why comprehension of the questions or memory for the relevant information should suddenly improve just because the questions are self-administered or because the question has been selected by spinning a dial. Instead, it seems likely that respondents are simply more willing to tell the truth under these conditions. The findings from bogus pipeline studies also indicate that much of the misreporting of sensitive information reflects respondents' willingness rather than their ability to report accurately.

9.5 Processes Responsible for Misreporting

Misreporting about sensitive topics is widespread in surveys, and at least some of it appears deliberate. Although relatively little theoretical work has explored the processes behind this censoring, it is possible to distinguish three general approaches to this question. The first relates misreporting to concerns about privacy and confidentiality; this is the approach typically adopted in discussions of sensitive questions in the survey literature. The second approach views the decisions to take part in a survey and to report truthfully in answering specific questions as the product of rational deliberation; these decisions are based on the respondent's assessment of the potential gains and losses associated with participation and accurate reporting. The final approach views misreporting as an effort to avoid embarrassment; question threat, according to this view, reduces to the threat of embarrassment, and misreporting is just another application of a tactic people use every day to avoid awkward social interactions – lying.

9.5.1 Privacy, Confidentiality, and Third Parties

Earlier in this chapter, we noted that surveys involve several levels of disclosure. The respondent is necessarily asked to disclose information to the researchers and may, in addition, be asked to disclose this information directly to an interviewer. The respondent's answers may also be disclosed to outside parties, such as other family members or other agencies. Respondents may have misgivings about each type of disclosure.

Disclosure to Researchers and Interviewers

Respondents may resent providing information even to the researchers. Studies by Singer and her colleagues (1993) indicate that such privacy attitudes may have played a role in the low rate of mail returns in the 1990 census. Only methods in which the respondents clearly remain anonymous can overcome objections to *any* form of disclosure. Still, there is relatively little evidence that these stringent privacy concerns are behind misreporting about sensitive topics.

Even if respondents are willing to disclose information to researchers, they may be reluctant to disclose it to an interviewer. Sudman and Bradburn's (1974) discussion of sensitive questions (quoted earlier) implicitly traces social desirability effects in surveys to the threat of interviewer disapproval. Many of the most effective survey procedures for improving reporting on sensitive topics, such as self-administration, seem to work mainly by eliminating this threat. These findings (reviewed in more detail in Chapter 10) suggest that concerns about the reaction of the interviewer are a major source of misreporting on sensitive topics.

Disclosures to Third Parties

Respondents may not mind revealing things to researchers or interviewers but may still have concerns about disclosures to third parties. It is useful to distinguish between two types of third parties – other members of the respondent's household and other agencies to which the data might be disclosed. Survey organizations take pains to prevent disclosures to third parties, but most of their efforts are directed at outside agencies and researchers. It is generally up to the interviewers to see that the interview is done in a private setting, where other household members cannot overhear. Interviewers are often unable to do this. For example, roughly half of the interviews for the NES between 1966 and 1982 were conducted in the presence of at least one household member other than the respondent (Silver et al., 1986); Silver and his colleagues report, however, that the presence of a third party had little effect on overreporting of voting. Later studies have also noted that whether other household members were present during the interview has little or no discernible impact on the answers (e.g., Laumann et al., 1994; Schober et al., 1992; Turner, Lessler, & Devore, 1992). A review by T. W. Smith (1997) concludes that the effects of the presence of a third person are minimal.

Several problems may make it hard to demonstrate the effects of the presence of other household members. Most of the studies on this point have been observational rather than experimental, and selection biases may obscure the impact of the presence of others. Survey organizations train their interviewers to conduct interviews in private (see, e.g., T. W. Smith, 1997). Thus, those interviews that end up being conducted in the presence of others may involve respondents who are manifestly unconcerned about the risk of disclosure to other household members. Or the other person present during the interview may be the respondent's spouse or someone else who already knows the information the respondent is being asked to disclose. (See Aquilino, 1993, for a careful analysis of the circumstances under which a spouse is likely to be present during an interview.) The presence of others is also confounded with such respondent characteristics as family size and marital status.

Two recent studies attempted to overcome these problems by varying experimentally whether the interview took place in the respondent's home or at a site outside the home. One study found no effect for the interview site (Jobe et al., 1997). The other study reported an effect for the site on reports about abortion, but that effect may well have reflected the incentive offered to respondents interviewed outside their homes (Mosher & Duffer, 1994; see also Lessler & O'Reilly, 1997). In that study, a random subsample of the respondents interviewed at home was also given an incentive, and the reports of these in-home respondents did not differ from those of the respondents interviewed outside the home.

The evidence indicates that disclosures to local third parties don't have much effect on survey responses. What about concerns about disclosures to more remote third parties? Fear of disclosures to other agencies looms large in discussions of survey undercoverage (e.g., Hainer et al., 1988). Household respondents may deliberately omit some household members in providing a roster in order to avoid a number of tangible consequences, including eviction, deportation, arrest, or the loss of welfare benefits. Two findings suggest that these factors play a role in respondents' thinking. First, undercoverage is worse within households at some potential risk, such as those receiving welfare benefits or those containing immigrants (Fein & West, 1988). In addition, coverage seems to improve when respondents are not required to provide full names for household members, presumably because the data cannot be readily used against the household (Tourangeau, Shapiro, Kearney, & Ernst, 1997).

9.5.2   Subjective Expected Utility (SEU) Theory

The survey literature suggests that question sensitivity is a function of several concerns, raising the issue of how these concerns are weighed and combined in making the decision to take part in a survey and to report accurately or misreport. Utility theory has been applied in an attempt to understand these decisions (Nathan, Sirken, Willis, & Esposito, 1990; Willis, Sirken, & Nathan, 1994); it provides a general framework for understanding how individuals consider losses and gains in making risky decisions (e.g., Pratt, Raiffa, & Schlaifer, 1964; Von Neuman & Morgenstern, 1947). In surveys, respondents deciding whether to give a truthful answer might consider such losses as embarrassment during the interview or negative consequences from the disclosure of answers beyond the interview setting; similarly, they might take into account such gains as approval from the interviewer or the promotion of knowledge about some topic (Rasinski, Baldwin, Willis, & Jobe, 1994).

A pilot study by Willis, Sirken, and Nathan (1994) found that judgments of risks and losses concerning response disclosure were significantly related to the decision to answer a sensitive question truthfully. This initial work was extended in a series of studies that examined the effect of the social context and method of data collection on the willingness to respond accurately in surveys (Rasinski, Baldwin, Willis, & Jobe, 1994; Willis, Rasinski, & Baldwin, 1998). Table 9.5 summarizes the design of these vignette studies.

In the first of these studies, subjects read about a hypothetical interview situation. For example, in one scenario, the respondent was a 28-year-old married woman with two children who'd had an abortion before she met her husband and had been arrested for drunk driving when she was a teenager. The description indicated that her husband knew nothing about either of these incidents. The scenarios varied such features of the interview situation as the age of the interviewer, whether the questions were self-administered or administered by the interviewer, and whether the respondent's family was present or absent during the interview. The second study used a similar methodology, only this time the vignettes were videotaped and all the subjects were female. Again, the scenarios varied the interviewer's age, the mode of administration, and the presence of the respondent's family. In both of these studies, the subjects rated the likelihood that the respondent in the scenario would tell the truth and also judged the likelihood and consequences of several possible outcomes (such as the interviewer's expressing disapproval of the respondent or the respondent's spouse finding out the information revealed in the interview).

The subjects in both studies tended to see the presence of other family members as affecting the probability that the respondent in the scenario would tell the truth. In the first study, the presence of the family had a significant main effect on these probability judgments for one survey topic and interacted with the interviewer's age for both topics that were examined (Rasinski et al., 1994); the presence of the respondent's family seemed to matter more when the interviewer was depicted as being in her mid-50s. In the second study, the presence of the family affected the

TABLE 9.5 Design of Vignette Studies

Study	Sample	Design Features	Key Results
Study 1 (Rasinski, Baldwin, Willis, and Jobe, 1994)	96 males; 96 females	Paper scenarios that vary • Interviewer in 20s vs. 50s • Self vs. interviewer administration • Family present *vs.* absent Topics in hypothetical interviews • Abortion and drunk driving (female subjects) • Sex partners and drunk driving (male subjects)	Respondent judged less likely to tell truth if interviewer is older and family is present Respondent less likely to tell truth if interviewer administers questions and family is present (females only) Disclosure to spouse most important predictor with sexual topics
Study 2 (Willis, Rasinski, and Baldwin, 1998)	192 females	Videotapes that vary • Interviewer in 20s vs. 50s • Self vs. interviewer administration • Family present *vs.* absent Order of ratings also varied Topics in hypothetical interview • Abortion • Number of pregnancies • Drunk driving	Respondents rated less likely to be truthful when family present and interviewer administers questions (abortion and number of pregnancies) Respondents rated more likely to be truthful when subjects judge risks and losses before rating the respondent's likelihood of telling the truth

rated probability that the respondent would answer truthfully only when interviewers administered the questions (Willis et al., 1998). The video study also varied the order in which subjects made the various judgments. The subjects judged that the respondent would be more likely to tell the truth when they answered the questions about risks and losses before the truthfulness questions. This finding is intriguing because it suggests that explicitly considering risks and losses may lead to reduced concerns about them.

The third experiment in the series examined sensitive reporting during an actual survey (Willis et al., 1998). The respondents were 191 women recruited from a women's health clinic; two-thirds of them had undergone an abortion during the prior year. The experiment compared self and interviewer administration of the questions and also varied whether the respondent read a brochure about the societal benefits of health-related surveys. Finally, in one condition, respondents completed a pre-survey questionnaire eliciting their concerns about disclosing sensitive information. The results of this study were somewhat disappointing. None of the experimental variables affected the reporting of abortions or the assessment of the potential risks of disclosure.

In summary, the SEU approach remains a promising approach as a theory of survey reporting. The results of the vignette studies indicate that subjects are sensitive to certain disclosure risks, such as disclosure of information to one's spouse or embarrassment over the interviewer's reaction (Rasinski et al., 1994). Still, the subjects in the vignette studies seemed to worry about variables, such as the privacy of the interview, that don't appear to have much effect in real surveys and downplay variables, such as the mode of administration, that have a large impact. Moreover, none of the studies to date have provided much evidence that respondents carefully weigh the costs and gains associated with truthful reporting or that they combine these assessments in the fashion prescribed by the theory.

9.5.3   Lying to Avoid Embarrassment

Another line of explanation for misreporting about sensitive topics is that respondents are lying to avoid embarrassing themselves (cf. Schaeffer, in press). If the SEU approach emphasizes the rational side of misreporting, this final approach emphasizes its impulsive and emotional character.

Like shame and guilt, embarrassment is a negative emotion that involves self-consciousness and heightened concern about evaluations of the self by others (Tangney & Fischer, 1995; Tangney, Miller, Flicker, & Barlow, 1996). All three emotions tend to be experienced in the presence of others. For example, Tangney and her colleagues (1996) had college students recall instances of each of these emotions. About 90% of the guilt experiences and 82% of the shame experiences that the subjects recalled took place in the presence of other people. Embarrassment was even more public than the other two emotions: Almost 98% of the embarrassment experiences occurred with other people present. According to the ratings of the subjects, embarrassment involved the greatest sense of exposure and the strongest concerns about the judgments of others. The findings also indicated that embarrassment experiences tended to involve exposure to strangers or acquaintances rather than to friends or family members. This parallels the results in the survey literature that show that the involvement of an interviewer has more impact on the answers to sensitive questions than does the presence of other household members.

One way that we avoid embarrassment in everyday life is to lie. DePaulo and her colleagues had samples of college students and community residents keep diaries of their social interactions for a week and to note whether they had lied during each interaction (DePaulo, Kashy, Kirkendol, Wyer, & Epstein, 1996; see also DePaulo & Bell, 1996). Lying is, in these samples at least, a daily occurrence. On the average, the college students reported that they lied about twice a day, or in about 30% of their interactions; the community sample lied somewhat less often – about once a day, or in about 20% of their interactions (DePaulo et al., 1996). Most of the lies reported in the study by DePaulo and her colleagues were white lies intended to spare the teller's or the listener's feelings. Among the common motives for lying was to protect oneself or others from embarrassment. In surveys, two levels of misreporting are generally possible. Respondents can deny an embarrassing fact completely (say, denying that they receive welfare benefits at all) or they can attempt to minimize it (underreporting the amount they receive); both types of underreporting are apparent in income surveys. DePaulo and her colleagues observed a similar distinction between outright lies, on the one hand, and exaggerations and other shadings of the truth, on the other. Regardless of the tactic adopted, the subjects reported that they put little effort into planning their lies and didn't worry much about getting caught. Everyday lies are a spur-of-the-moment decision.

9.6   Editing for Other Purposes

Although most evidence on deliberate misreporting concerns misreporting to sensitive questions, there are also suggestions that respondents edit their answers in at least a couple of other situations.

9.6.1   Politeness to Interviewers

A series of studies has shown, for example, that respondents may tailor their answers to suit the race, class, or sex of the interviewer. Respondents, we have argued, don't want to incur the interviewer's disapproval; they don't want to insult the interviewer either.

Most of these studies concern the effects of the race of the interviewer, but there are similar findings for interviewer class (Katz, 1942) and sex (Kane & Macaulay, 1993). White respondents express more pro–civil rights views to Black interviewers than to White ones (Hatchett & Schuman, 1975–1976; Schaeffer, 1980; Schuman & Converse, 1971). Similarly, Black respondents express more favorable attitudes toward Whites when they are interviewed by White interviewers than by Black ones (Anderson, Silver, & Abramson, 1988b; see also Hyman, Cobb, Feldman, Hart, & Stember, 1954). Some of the earlier studies on race-of-interviewer effects don't fully take into account the clustering of the sample within interviewers; but the results are nonetheless consistent across studies, and the findings hold up when the analysis does make proper allowance for the clustering by interviewers (Kane & Macaulay, 1993).

The most commonly accepted explanation for these effects of the interviewer's visible demographic characteristics is the respondent's reluctance to offend the "polite stranger" conducting the interview, an account first proposed by Schuman and Converse (1971).[4] DePaulo and Bell (1996) demonstrate that people often tone down criticism to spare someone's feelings; they are more likely to shade the truth when they think the recipient cares about the topic. These findings are consistent

---

[4] Schuman and Converse (1971) also found an effect of interviewers' race on a question about the respondent's favorite entertainer. Respondents were more likely to name a Black entertainer when a Black interviewer asked this question. This difference could be due to the respondent's desire to please the interviewer, but it is also possible that the race of the interviewer made entertainers of the same race more available in the respondent's memory – a type of priming effect.

with the survey evidence that the impact of the race and sex of the interviewer is restricted to issues related to race or gender (although see Anderson et al., 1988a, who found that the race of the interviewer affected reports by Blacks about voting). This reluctance to give offense may reflect the norm of politeness (Brown & Levinson, 1987) or a general unwillingness to convey unpleasant news (Tesser & Rosen, 1975).

9.6.2   Consistency

In Chapter 7, we reviewed evidence that respondents may edit their answers to make them more consistent with each other. The survey findings indicate that placing related questions together in a block tends to increase the correlations between the answers (T. W. Smith, 1983). The changes in the answers that produce this effect may simply be an expedient to avoid obvious inconsistencies or they may be the outcome of genuine attitude changes as respondents become aware of the logical inconsistencies among their beliefs (McGuire, 1960).

9.7   Conclusion

Survey respondents' decision to edit their answers can have a big impact on the estimates from surveys, changing the proportion of respondents reporting behaviors like illicit drug use or voting, often by as much as a factor of two. Concerns about disclosure may lead some individuals to withhold information entirely, affecting response rates to surveys and mail return rates in the decennial census. In addition, respondents seem more likely to refuse to answer certain sensitive questions, especially those about income, than nonthreatening survey questions. But beyond this preemptive editing, there is ample evidence of systematic misreporting on sensitive topics in surveys.

Respondents consistently underreport certain behaviors and overreport others. This misreporting may reflect survey-relevant attitudes, such as attitudes about privacy and confidentiality, or more fleeting situational calculations or emotional needs. The same processes that lead to smooth interactions in everyday life, including telling white lies to avoid embarrassment or to spare someone's feelings, can lead to misreporting in surveys (DePaulo & Bell, 1996; DePaulo et al., 1996; Kane & Macaulay, 1993).

Surveys employ a battery of methods designed to improve reporting on sensitive topics. They routinely adopt a number of practices designed to reduce the risk of disclosure to outside agencies, and they offer explicit assurances to respondents on that score. Although elaborate confidentiality assurances can backfire (Singer et al., 1992), on the whole, offering such assurances to respondents seems to improve response rates to surveys (Singer et al., 1995). Surveys also use several tactics to improve reporting among those who do agree to take part. They use forgiving wording, place sensitive questions in contexts designed to promote accurate answers, and let respondents place their questionnaires in sealed ballot boxes. The most effective means of reducing misreporting seem to be self-administration and the randomized response technique. With self-administration, the interviewer is not aware of the respondent's answer; with the randomized response procedure, the interviewer is unaware of the question. Either way, the threat of the interviewer's disapproval is eliminated, and that appears to be a key consideration that motivates respondents to report erroneous information deliberately.

CHAPTER TEN

Mode of Data Collection

Over the last 25 years, the application of computer technology to the collection of survey data has revolutionized the survey industry. From its modest beginnings in 1971, when Chilton Research Services conducted the first computer-assisted telephone interviewing (CATI) survey for AT&T, CATI has become the most commonly used method for collecting data by telephone in the United States and Europe. In a CATI survey, the questionnaire takes the form of a computer program that displays the items to the interviewer on the computer screen; the interviewer then reads the questions to the respondent and enters the answers by pressing the appropriate keys. And, just as CATI has become the standard method for collecting data in telephone surveys, computer-assisted personal interviewing (CAPI) has become the standard method for face-to-face interviews. In the United States, one major federal survey after another – among them the National Medical Expenditure Survey, the National Longitudinal Survey of Youth, the Current Population Survey, the Medicare Current Beneficiary Survey, the National Survey of Family Growth, and the Survey of Consumer Finances – has converted from paper-and-pencil interviews to CAPI as its primary mode of data collection. CAPI uses essentially the same technology as CATI, except that the programs are loaded onto portable laptop computers that can be used in face-to-face interviews. Couper and Nicholls (1998) provide an excellent summary of the history of these developments.

This chapter examines the impact of the new modes of data collection on the respondent and the interviewer and presents a model of the effects of the data collection method on the data that are ultimately obtained.

10.1   The Range of Methods for Survey Data Collection

The new computerized methods have not only supplanted the traditional paper-and-pencil methods for telephone and in-person interviewing, they have also added to the array of methods that can be used to conduct surveys. In a recent review of computer-assisted methods, Weeks (1992) listed five techniques for computer-assisted survey information collection. Besides CATI and CAPI, Weeks discusses prepared data entry (PDE), touchtone data entry (TDE), and voice recognition entry (VRE).

With PDE, respondents are sent an electronic questionnaire, which they complete on their own computers. As in CATI or CAPI, the questionnaire program controls the order in which the questions are administered and carries out edit checks as the answers are entered. In one variant that resembles a mail survey (referred to as *disk-by-mail*, or *DBM*), the electronic questionnaire is mailed to the respondent on a diskette; in another, the questionnaire is transmitted to the respondent by modem or e-mail (Couper & Nicholls, 1998; see also Kiesler & Sproull, 1986, and Saris & Pijper, 1986, for examples of PDE surveys). In TDE (also referred to as *interactive voice response*, or *IVR*), respondents dial in to a computer, which plays a recording of the questions; the respondents indicate their answers by pressing keys on the handset of a telephone. This technology has been adopted by the Bureau of Labor Statistics in its Current Employment Survey (Phipps & Tupek, 1990) and is widely used by market research firms. Voice recognition entry differs from TDE only in the method of conveying the answers: Instead of entering their answers via the telephone handset, respondents simply say them aloud. The VRE technology has also been used in the Current Employment Survey (Harrell & Clayton, 1991).

Since the time of Weeks's review, two additional data collection techniques have emerged and won quick acceptance. The first is audio computer-assisted self-administered interviewing (ACASI), in which the computer displays the question on screen and simultaneously plays a digitized recording of it to the respondent, typically via earphones. Several experimental comparisons between ACASI and other forms of self-administration suggest that ACASI maintains or enhances the advantages of other forms of self-administration (Tourangeau & Smith, 1996, 1998; Turner et al., 1998). The latest addition to the battery of data collection techniques is the Internet survey, in which respondents connect with a Web site, where a program administers the questions. This method of data collection is proliferating rapidly. Examples of recent

Web surveys range from a variety of self-selected polls designed more for entertainment than for scientific value, to large-scale efforts that purport to collect representative information from the broader population, to several government efforts to use the Web to supplement data collection, primarily from establishments (see, e.g., Harrell, Rosen, & Manning, 1998; Lanier, Burrelli, & Fecso, 1998).

These developments have been spurred not only by the widespread availability of computers but also by the need for self-report data on sensitive topics, such as sexual behavior or illicit drug use. In addition to ACASI, researchers have explored a noncomputerized version of audio self-administration for collecting sensitive information; in this method (audio self-administered questionnaires, or ASAQ), a portable cassette player plays a recording of the questions and respondents mark their answers on a paper answer sheet. Researchers have also tried computer-assisted self-interviewing (CASI) without the sound (Couper & Rowe, 1996; Jobe, Pratt, Tourangeau, Baldwin, & Rasinski, 1997).

And, of course, paper-and-pencil methods of data collection are still widely used; paper-and-pencil personal interviewing (PAPI), telephone interviewing, and self-administered questionnaires (SAQ) have not yet disappeared from the scene. The new developments have given survey researchers quite a menu of techniques to choose from. Table 10.1 displays thirteen methods now available for survey data collection.

These modes of data collection differ in several important ways. As the table indicates, they differ in the method of contacting the respondents and delivering questionnaires to them. In one group of methods, the questionnaires are administered over the telephone; in another, the questionnaires are sent by mail (or, in the case of PDE, by e-mail); in the final group, the questionnaires are delivered in person by an interviewer. In addition, an electronic questionnaire may reside on a Web site. At first glance, the method of contact may not seem to matter much, but in practice it can make quite a difference. For example, it may be more difficult to convince the respondent of the legitimacy and importance of the survey over the telephone than through the mail or in person; as a result, respondents may put less effort into responding.

A second way in which the modes differ involves who administers the questions; either interviewers or the respondents themselves read the questions and record the answers. As we noted in the previous chapter, self-administration increases respondents' willingness to disclose information about a number of sensitive topics. Aside from its effect on respondent candor, the active involvement of an interviewer may affect

TABLE 10.1 Current Methods of Data Collection

Method of Contact	Paper-and-Pencil	Computer-Assisted
Telephone	Conventional telephone	Computer-assisted telephone interviewing (CATI) Touchtone data entry (TDE) Voice recognition entry (VRE)
Mail	Self-administered questionnaire (SAQ)	Disk by mail (DBM)
E-mail/Internet	—	Prepared data entry (PDE)/Web surveys
In person	Paper-and-pencil interviewing (PAPI) Self-administered questionnaire (SAQ) Audio self-administerred questionnaire (ASAQ)	Computer-assisted personal interviewing (CAPI) Computer-assisted self-administered interviewing (CASI) Audio computer-assisted self-administered interviewing (ACASI)

the response process in subtler ways. For example, the presence of an interviewer may be distracting, deflecting attention from the task of answering the questions; it is also possible that interviewers help to maintain respondents' motivation, especially with long questionnaires. When interviewers administer the questionnaires, there are inevitably variations in how they ask the questions and probe the answers. Moreover, the race, sex, or other characteristics of the interviewers may affect the responses (see the discussion in Chapter 9). In addition to its other effects, then, self-administration may reduce the impact of the interviewers on the data that are collected.

Another difference among the methods involves whether the questions are presented to the respondent aurally or visually. Methods of data collection such as CAPI or ACASI, in which the questions are read aloud, make it unnecessary for the respondents to be able to read. This characteristic of auditory presentation may be especially useful in subpopulations where literacy problems are common. Listening imposes its own burdens, however. Auditory presentation (without simultaneous visual display) of long or complicated questions may overtax the respondents' listening ability, reducing their comprehension. Moreover, when the question has numerous response options, it may be difficult for respondents to keep them all in mind. Because of concerns about exceeding the capacity of the respondent's working memory, survey researchers often use *show cards* – written lists of the answer options – with questions that offer a large number of options. The channel of presentation may also affect the order in which respondents consider the response options. When the questions are only read aloud, respondents have little control over the pace at which questions and response options are presented and may begin by considering the options that come at the end of the list (Krosnick & Alwin, 1987; Schwarz, Hippler, & Noelle-Neumann, 1991).

A final difference among the methods involves the mode of responding. With some methods of data collection, respondents indicate their answers orally; with others, they indicate their answers on paper; with still others, they click on a mouse, enter a number using the keyboard of a computer, or press a number on the handset of a touchtone telephone. These different methods impose different cognitive requirements. For instance, because responding by hitting a key requires some familiarity with numbers and keyboards, oral responding is probably easier for many respondents. The different methods of responding may also differ in the apparent level of privacy they afford respondents. Respondents may worry about being overheard when they have to answer aloud.

In summary, then, the methods of data collection presented in Table 10.1 differ in five major characteristics – the method of contacting respondents (telephone, in person, mail, or e-mail), the medium in which the questions are presented (paper or electronic), the method of administering the questions (by an interviewer or by the respondents themselves), the channel used in conveying the questions (auditory or visual), and the mode of responding (oral, written, or electronic). Each of these characteristics of the data collection method may affect the response process and the data that are ultimately collected.

10.2   The Method of Contact and Administration

10.2.1   Method of Contact

It is difficult to isolate the effects of the method of contact from other differences among the modes of data collection. In the first place, the different methods of contact offer access to somewhat different populations. About 6% of the U.S. population cannot be reached by telephone, and this portion differs systematically from the rest of the population (Thornberry & Massey, 1988). Similarly, mail surveys are usually based on lists of the members of limited subpopulations. In addition to this confounding with coverage, the effects of the method of contact are generally difficult to separate from those of the method of administering the questions: Mail surveys almost always employ some form of self-administration, and telephone surveys almost always employ administration by interviewer (although TDE and VRE may change that arrangement).

These problems limit what we can say about how the method of contact alters the process of answering the questions. Moreover, the comparisons done so far have often yielded inconsistent results. A study by Groves and Kahn (1979) found few differences between the answers obtained from telephone and in-person interviews, at least for items that were not sensitive. This picture changed somewhat with sensitive questions; respondents were more willing to answer questions about such topics as income and racial attitudes in PAPI than in conventional telephone interviews. A study by Johnson and his colleagues found even more striking results: students at the University of Kentucky were more willing to admit illicit drug use in a PAPI survey than in a paper-and-pencil telephone survey (Johnson, Hougland, & Clayton, 1989). Two other studies, however, demonstrated just the opposite pattern: A study by Hochstim (1967) found higher levels of reporting medical problems in a face-to-face PAPI survey than in a parallel survey conducted by telephone, and a study by McQueen (1989) that compared CATI and PAPI found higher levels of reported sexual activity in the telephone survey. A final study found mixed results in a comparison of PAPI and conventional telephone interviews for collecting information about alcohol consumption and drug use (Aquilino, 1994). This pattern of contradictory and inconclusive results echoes the findings of an earlier review by T. W. Smith (1984b), who summarized a dozen studies and found no clear indication of any reduction in social desirability effects from telephone data collection

The different methods of contact also differ in whether (and to what degree) they involve an interviewer in the collection of the data. Interviewers can affect the results in two ways – through their personal characteristics (such as their race or sex) or their behaviors in conducting the interviews. Mail surveys eliminate interviewers entirely (although they may make the sponsor of the survey more salient than the other methods of contact do). It also seems likely that contact by telephone would reduce the impact of the interviewers on the responses relative to in-person contact. Not only are the physical characteristics of the interviewers less apparent over the telephone than in a face-to-face interview, there is also some evidence that telephone interviewers depart from the script less often than in-person interviewers do (Presser & Zhao, 1992). There is, however, no clear evidence that telephone interviewers have any less influence on the answers they obtain than in-person interviewers do (see, e.g., the discussion in Chapter 8 of Groves, 1989).

10.2.2   Method of Administration and the Reporting of Sensitive Behaviors

The effects of the method of administration are far easier to summarize; more studies have been done on this issue, and the studies have produced clearer results. Most of this work has been carried out to test the hypothesis that, relative to interviewer administration, self-administration will reduce respondents' unwillingness to report socially undesirable behaviors (such as illicit drug use). As we noted in Chapter 9, the results strongly support this hypothesis.

Table 10.2 illustrates the impact of self-administration, summarizing the results of six similar experiments investigating the impact of the method of administration on the reporting of illicit drug use. (Several of the studies also examined reports about the consumption of alcohol.) The entries in the table are the ratios of the proportion of respondents reporting drug use (or alcohol consumption) when the questions were self-administered to the corresponding proportion when the questions were administered by interviewers. For example, if 6% of the respondents admitted that they had used cocaine in the last year when the questions were self-administered but only 4% admitted this to an interviewer, the table shows a ratio of 1.5. Most of the ratios are greater than 1.0, indicating that higher levels of drug use were reported when the questions were self-administered than when they were administered by interviewers. Of the 63 comparisons in the table, 57 show higher levels of reporting under self-administration. The table also indicates that the effects of self-administration are generally more marked for more sensitive behaviors. The ratios between levels of reporting under self- and interviewer administration of the questions tend to be more extreme for cocaine and marijuana than for alcohol, and for use in the month prior to the interview than for longer time spans. Results like those in Table 10.2 have been reported for several other types of sensitive behaviors as well, leading Bradburn (1983) to conclude that self-administration generally yields higher levels of reporting of sensitive

TABLE 10.2 Self-Administration and Reports of Illicit Drug Use: Ratios of Estimated Prevalence under Self- and Interviewer Administration

Study	Methods of Data Collection	Drug	Time Frame		
			Past Month	Past Year	Lifetime
Aquilino (1994)	SAQ vs. PAPI	Cocaine	1.00	1.50	1.14
		Marijuana	1.20	1.30	1.02
		Alcohol	1.07	1.05	1.01
	SAQ vs. conventional telephone	Cocaine	1.00	1.00	1.32
		Marijuana	1.50	1.62	1.04
		Alcohol	1.07	1.03	0.98
Aquilino and LoSciuto (1990)	SAQ vs. conventional telephone (Whites)	Cocaine	1.20	1.18	0.91
		Marijuana	1.00	1.04	1.00
		Alcohol	1.09	—	—
	SAQ vs. conventional telephone (Blacks)	Cocaine	1.67	1.22	1.21
		Marijuana	2.43	1.38	1.25
		Alcohol	1.15	—	—
Gfroerer and Hughes (1992)	SAQ vs. conventional telephone	Cocaine	—	2.21	1.43
		Marijuana	—	1.54	1.33
Schober, Caces, Pergamit, and Branden (1992)	SAQ vs. PAPI	Cocaine	1.67	1.33	1.12
		Marijuana	1.34	1.20	1.01
Tourangeau and Smith (1996)	CASI vs. CAPI	Cocaine	0.95	1.37	1.01
		Marijuana	1.19	0.99	1.29
	ACASI vs. CAPI	Cocaine	1.74	2.84	1.81
		Marijuana	1.66	1.61	1.48
Turner, Lessler, and Devore (1992)	SAQ vs. PAPI	Cocaine	2.46	1.58	1.05
		Marijuana	1.61	1.30	1.05
		Alcohol	1.06	1.04	0.99

Note: SAQ refers to self-administered questionnaires; PAPI to paper-and-pencil interviews; CASI to computer-assisted self-administered interviews; and ACASI to audio computer-assisted self-administered interviews.

behaviors than questions administered by interviewers, particularly in face-to-face interviews.

Besides increasing reports of undesirable behaviors, self-administration can also decrease overreports of desirable ones, such as attendance at religious services (Presser & Stinson, 1998). In studies of sexual behavior, self-administration sometimes has both effects at the same time, decreasing the number of sex partners reported by men and increasing the number reported by women. Table 10.3 summarizes the

TABLE 10.3 Ratios Comparing Average Number of Sexual Partners, by Method of Data Collection and Sex

Study	Methods of Data Collection	Sex	Past Year	Past 5 Years	Lifetime
Tourangeau, Rasinski, Jobe, Smith, and Pratt (1997)	SAQ vs. PAPI	Females	1.00	1.18	1.50
	CASI vs. CAPI	Females	1.39	1.58	1.00
Tourangeau and Smith (1996)	CASI vs. CAPI	Females	1.48	1.16	1.24
		Males	0.54	0.70	0.90
	ACASI vs. CAPI	Females	1.64	1.88	1.66
		Males	0.75	1.00	1.01

Note: SAQ refers to self-administered questionnaires; PAPI to paper-and-pencil interviews; CASI to computer-assisted self-administered interviews; and ACASI to audio computer-assisted self-administered interviews.

results of two experiments on reports about sexual partners (Tourangeau, Rasinski, Jobe, Smith, & Pratt, 1997; Tourangeau & Smith, 1996). In both, self-administration increased the average number of partners reported by the women; the ratios between the averages reported in self-administered questionnaires to those reported under interviewer administration of the questions range from 1.00 to as high as 1.88. In the experiment that included a representative sample of men, self-administration also tended to decrease the average number of sexual partners reported by the men; for the men, the ratios between self- and interviewer administration range from a high of 1.01 to a low of 0.54. Under certain conditions, self-administration eliminated the disparity between the reports of men and women entirely (Tourangeau & Smith, 1996).

10.2.3 Method of Administration and the Impact of the Interviewers

Self-administration, then, increases the willingness of respondents to report socially disapproved or illegal behaviors. Another potential benefit of self-administration is that it lowers the profile of the interviewers, reducing their impact on the data they collect. Of course, when a self-administered questionnaire is sent by mail or e-mail or linked to a Web site, no interviewer is ever present. Self-administration is, however, sometimes used in surveys conducted in person, with interviewers delivering the questionnaire and recruiting the respondent to take part but not actually administering the questions. In such settings, the characteristics or behaviors of the interviewers can still affect the results.

When they do administer the questions, the interviewers carry out several specific tasks:

- They follow the routing instructions and determine which question to administer;
- they read the question verbatim or generate a paraphrase of it;
- they field any questions from the respondent or assist respondents who exhibit other signs of difficulty;
- they determine whether the respondent's answer meets the demands of the question and, if it does not, probe for further information; and
- they record the respondent's answer, in some cases determining which answer category best fits the answer.

(See Sander et al., 1992, for a more detailed model of interviewer behavior.) Interviewers inevitably vary in how they perform each of these duties, and these variations can affect the answers obtained. Self-administration transfers most of these burdens from the interviewer to the respondent. (Similarly, computer assistance shifts at least some of these burdens to the data collection software.) A study by Tourangeau and his colleagues indicated that even when the questionnaires were delivered to the respondents by interviewers, self-administration completely eliminated variation attributable to the interviewers (Tourangeau, Rasinski, Jobe, Smith, & Pratt; 1997). Apparently, even the personal characteristics of the interviewer had little effect on the respondents when the questions were self-administered.

10.3   Other Characteristics of the Data Collection Method

The remaining characteristics that distinguish the different methods of data collection – the medium in which the questionnaire is embodied, the channel through which the questions are conveyed, and the mode of responding – have effects that are both subtler and less well documented than those of the method of administration.

10.3.1   The Effects of Computer Assistance

Missing Data

Perhaps the most obvious effect of the computerization of survey questionnaires is that it automates the process of determining which question comes next and, as a result, virtually eliminates data missing because a question was inadvertently skipped. Such skip errors are substantial contributors to missing data in surveys. The reduction in the rate of missing data has been demonstrated repeatedly in studies of computer-assisted data collection (e.g., Baker, Bradburn, & Johnson, 1995; Catlin & Ingram, 1988; Kiesler & Sproull, 1986; Martin, O'Muircheartaigh, & Curtice, 1993; Tourangeau, Rasinski, Jobe, Smith, & Pratt, 1997). An additional finding is that interviewers tend to be better at figuring out which item comes next than respondents are; relative to self-administration, interviewer administration tends to reduce skip errors. Table 10.4 shows the impact of both computer assistance and self-administration on the rate of missing data in a survey on sexual behavior conducted by Tourangeau, Rasinski, Jobe, Smith, and Pratt (1997).

Impact on Reporting

Aside from increasing the completeness of the data, computerization of the data collection process appears to have little consistent impact on

TABLE 10.4 Proportion of Questions
Answered by Method of Data Collection

Method of Data Collection	Mean Proportion (n)
PAPI	97.8 (261)
SAQ	94.6 (256)
CAPI	99.2 (244)
CASI	97.9 (244)
Interviewer-administered	98.5 (505)
Self-administered	96.2 (500)
Computer-assisted	98.6 (488)
Paper-and-pencil	96.2 (517)

Note: SAQ refers to self-administered questionnaires; PAPI to paper-and-pencil interviews; CASI to computer-assisted self-administered interviews. Data are from Tourangeau et al. (1997).

the answers to nonsensitive questions. Baker, Bradburn, and Johnson (1995) compared interviews done by CAPI and PAPI and found scattered differences between the two methods of data collection. Another experimental comparison between CAPI and PAPI (Martin et al., 1993), which focused on attitude questions, found some evidence that respondents were more willing to give extreme answers to the CAPI version of the questions than to the PAPI version. But two other studies, which compared CATI and conventional telephone interviews, found no particular pattern to the difference between the two methods (Catlin & Ingram, 1988; Groves & Mathiowetz, 1984). The study by Groves and Mathiowetz used a questionnaire that focused on health topics; the one by Catlin and Ingram used a questionnaire on labor force behavior. Neither study found much difference between the responses obtained in computer-assisted and conventional telephone interviews.

The picture changes somewhat when the questions are sensitive. Baker and his colleagues found that CAPI increased reporting relative to PAPI on a number of sensitive items (involving income, assets, use of condoms, and spells of unemployment) (Baker et al., 1995). By contrast, Tourangeau and his colleagues compared data collected by four modes (CAPI, PAPI, SAQ, and CASI) and found that whether the questions were administered on paper or by computer had little effect on the answers, although there were marked differences between the self- and interviewer-administered methods of data collection (Tourangeau, Rasinski, Jobe, Smith, & Pratt, 1997).

Three experiments comparing ACASI with other methods of self-administration indicate that ACASI increases the reporting of sensitive behaviors compared to the other methods, especially self-administration on a paper questionnaire (O'Reilly, Hubbard, Lessler, Biemer, & Turner, 1994; Tourangeau & Smith, 1996; Turner et al., 1998). The results of Tourangeau and Smith, however, suggest that at least part of ACASI's advantage over other methods of self-administration reflects its use of auditory presentation rather than computer assistance. They compared computer-assisted self-administration with and without sound (i.e., ACASI and CASI) and found an advantage for ACASI with some very sensitive items (e.g., questions about anal sex). These results parallel the findings of Turner and his colleagues, who reported striking differences between ACASI and paper self-administration on the reporting of homosexual behaviors. It remains to be determined how much of the increase in reporting under ACASI can be traced to its use of computerization, auditory presentation, or other features of that mode of data collection.

Other Effects of Computer Assistance

There are some indications that computerization may have still other effects on the response process. Several studies find slightly, although in some cases significantly, higher rates of unit nonresponse with computer-assisted data collection than with conventional paper methods (Baker et al., 1995; Catlin & Ingram, 1988; Groves & Mathiowetz, 1984; Kiesler & Sproull, 1986; Tourangeau, Rasinski, Jobe, Smith, & Pratt, 1997). Although these differences are usually attributed to the inevitable hardware difficulties when a new technology is introduced, it is also possible that they reflect some resistance to the computer on the part of interviewers or respondents. Resistance to computers may be particularly high among respondents with little prior experience with computers (such as older respondents), especially when the method of data collection requires them to interact with the computer directly (as CASI and ACASI do; see Couper & Rowe, 1996).

Another effect of computerization may be to slow down the interview. Increases in the total administration time with computer-assisted methods have been noted by Catlin and Ingram (1988), Groves and Mathiowetz (1984), Martin and her colleagues (1993), and Waterton and Duffy (1984). Many observers believe that, by giving respondents more time to think about their answers, slower-paced interviews will yield more accurate answers (e.g., Cannell et al., 1981).

A final effect of computerization involves the impact of the interviewers on the results. Two studies suggest that computer assistance reduces variability across interviewers (Groves & Mathiowetz, 1984; Tourangeau, Rasinski, Jobe, Smith, & Pratt, 1997). It is quite plausible that computerization reduces variation in interviewers' behavior, thereby reducing their effects on the answers.

Humanizing the Interface

In computer-assisted methods that don't involve an interviewer, questionnaire designers may be tempted to enhance the attractiveness of the interface or to humanize it in various ways to increase respondents' interest in the task of completing the questionnaire. The design resources available in a Web survey allow considerable opportunities in this regard, including images of faces, recordings of voices, and animated drawings. A growing body of evidence suggests that far subtler cues than these (such as *gendered text* or simple inanimate line drawings of a face) can evoke reactions similar to those produced by an interviewer, including social desirability effects.

Nass, Moon, and Green (1997), for example, conclude that the tendency to stereotype by gender can be triggered by such minimal cues as the voice on a computer program. Based on the results of a series of experiments that varied a number of cues in computer tutoring and other tasks, Nass and his colleagues (Fogg & Nass, 1997; Nass, Fogg, & Moon, 1996; Reeves & Nass, 1996) argue that computer interfaces (even the words used in a text-based tutoring task) can trigger reactions from subjects similar to those evoked by interactions with other people. Their central thesis is that people treat computers as social actors rather than as inanimate tools (see also Walker, Sproull, & Subramani, 1994). To the extent that people respond to computers as though they had human characteristics, adding a variety of humanizing visual and aural touches may offset or reduce the benefits of computer-assisted self-administration for items on sensitive topics.

10.3.2   Channel of Presentation and Mode of Responding

Cognitive Burden

To date, there have been few studies on the impact of the channel of presentation and the mode of responding. It seems likely, however, that these features of the method of data collection markedly affect the cognitive requirements placed on the respondents, in particular the demand for literacy (O'Reilly et al., 1994). At what is perhaps the least demanding extreme, the questions are read aloud to the respondents, who answer them orally. The combination of the auditory channel of presentation with the oral mode of response characterizes several methods of data collection, including PAPI, CAPI, CATI, VRE, and paper-and-pencil telephone interviews. This combination requires only that the respondent speak the language in which the questions are written. Still, the auditory channel does require at least minimal listening skills on the part of th respondents. When the question is complicated and respondents can read, visual presentation may produce more accurate understanding of the question than auditory presentation (cf. Chaiken & Eagly, 1976, on the interaction between communication channel and message complexity in determining the effectiveness of a persuasion message).

At the other extreme of cognitive difficulty are methods of data collection in which the questions are presented visually and the respondents must answer them by pressing a key, typically a number on the keyboard of the computer (as in PDE and CASI) or handset of a touchtone telephone (as in TDE). With this combination of presentation and response modes, the respondents must be able to read, recognize numbers, and key their answers accurately. These requirements are not trivial. According to the National Adult Literacy Survey, nearly one-fourth of the U.S. adult population has extremely limited literacy in English (Kirsh, Jungeblut, Jenkins, & Kolstad, 1993). This subgroup is able to read only brief, uncomplicated prose. About a fifth of those in this category have visual difficulties that interfere with their ability to read printed material; almost a quarter are immigrants who may not yet have mastered English. Individuals at this level of literacy are likely to have difficulty completing all but the simplest questionnaires and, in some cases, even that will exceed their ability to process written material.

The level of cognitive difficulty associated with the method of data collection is likely to affect both the proportion of the sample able to participate in the survey and the rate of missing data among those who do take part. It may also affect the reliability of the data that are obtained. Table 10.5 displays the different skills required from the respondents by the different methods of data collection.

Layout and Format

The cognitive requirements imposed by a particular method of data collection aren't necessarily inherent in that method but can vary with the layout and formatting of the questionnaire. Although few substantive differences between computer-assisted and paper-and-pencil interviews have been found (see Nicholls, Baker, & Martin, 1997), those differences that have been found often reflect changes in the design of the instrument (e.g., Baker, Bradburn, & Johnson, 1995; Bergman, Kristiansson, Olofsson, & Säfström, 1994). Most of these changes involve apparently innocuous modifications of the layout; still, such changes may make it harder or easier to complete the questions, and they may convey different expectations about the kinds of information required.

The literature on computerization of standardized psychological tests leads to similar conclusions about the importance of seemingly minor characteristics of the method of presenting the items and eliciting the answers. Honaker (1988) reviewed the results of nine experiments comparing computer administration of the MMPI with the traditional paper-

TABLE 10.5 Cognitive Demands Imposed by Different Methods of Data Collection

Channel of Presentation	Mode of Response	Method of Data Collection	Cognitive Requirements
Auditory	Oral	PAPI, CAPI, VRE, CATI, conventional telephone	Listening skills
	Written	ASAQ	Listening skills
			Limited literacy and numeracy
	Keypad	TDE	Listening skills
			Limited numeracy
		ACASI (also visual presentation)	Listening skills
			Limited numeracy and computer skills
Visual	Oral	—	—
	Written	SAQ	Literacy
			Ability to follow routing instructions
	Keypad	CASI, PDE, Website	Literacy
			Limited numeracy and computer skills

Note: PAPI refers to paper-and-pencil interviews; CAPI to computer-assisted personal interviews; VRE to voice recognition entry; CATI to computer-assisted telephone interviews; ASAQ to audio self-administered questionnaires; TDE to touchtone data entry; ACASI to audio computer-assisted self-administered interviews; SAQ to self-administered questionnairs; CASI to audio computer-assisted self-administered interviews; and PDE to prepared data entry.

and-pencil administration. There were no consistent patterns regarding the presence or direction of differences across the two modes. He argued that one reason for these mixed results was that features of the computer interface differed across the various studies. Some programs allowed respondents to skip items; others did not. Some allowed respondents to change their earlier answers, some allowed respondents only to review their earlier answers but not to change them, and some did not allow respondents to backtrack at all. The more the computer interface allowed the same freedom as the paper version of the MMPI, the more the answers converged.

Channel of Presentation and Response Order Effects

The channel of presentation has another potential effect on the response process. As Krosnick and Alwin (1987) have argued, when the items are presented visually, respondents are likely to begin by process-ing the first response option presented; by contrast, when the items are presented aurally, respondents are likely to begin processing the final option they heard (see Chapter 8). This difference, in turn, can lead to different response order effects, particularly if the respondents have adopted a satisficing criterion for selecting their answers. If respondents select the first acceptable option that they consider, then the order of the options will interact with the channel of presentation to determine the final distribution of responses. This predicted interaction between re-sponse order and presentation channel has been demonstrated empiri-cally by Schwarz, Hippler, and Noelle-Neumann (1991).

10.4   Psychological Effects of the Differences among Data Collection Methods

So far, we have reviewed the different methods of data collection and their consequences for the data that are collected – the rate at which answers are missing, whether the order of the response options affects the answers, the impact of the interviewers, and the level of reporting sensitive information. Here we propose a model of the processes that mediate these effects. The model described here is an extension of one originally proposed by Tourangeau and Smith (1996, 1998).

Figure 10.1 depicts the model, showing the main hypothesized links among the features of the different methods of data collection, the psy-chological variables affected by these features, and the consequences of these psychological variables for the answers ultimately obtained. The model assumes that three key variables are responsible for the effects of data collection mode on data quality – the sense of impersonality the method fosters, the cognitive burdens it imposes, and the legitimacy it seems to confer. These psychological variables are affected by the char-acteristics of the method of data collection and, in turn, affect the prop-erties of the data obtained. Although this model has not yet been syste-matically tested, it provides a useful summary of much of what is known about the effects of the method of data collection. It also suggests a number of specific hypotheses for future research. For example, the model incorporates the hypothesis that self-administration increases the perceived impersonality of the data collection process and that this effect underlies the differences in reporting sensitive behaviors by the method of administration.

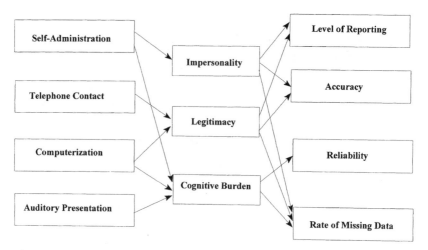

Figure 10.1 Model of the impact of the mode of data collection on the data collected. Features of the method of data collection (on the left) affect three key mediating variables (in the middle), which in turn affect the properties of the data that are collected (on the right).

10.4.1   Impersonality of the Data Collection Process

According to Figure 10.1, self-administration increases respondents' willingness to report sensitive information by reducing the sense that this information is being disclosed to another person. The combination of auditory presentation and oral response may also affect the respondent's sense that others are present, at least in settings where other members of the household can overhear the questions and answers. As we noted in Chapter 9, however, the presence of third parties during an interview seems to have little impact on the answers that respondents give (T. W. Smith, 1997).

What does seem to matter is the respondent's concern over the interviewer's approval or disapproval. Respondents are reluctant to disclose certain types of information directly to an interviewer. In Chapter 9, we suggested that this reluctance is largely a matter of their fear of embarrassment. The interview situation has the all key ingredients found in descriptions of the experience of embarrassment – exposure in the presence of a stranger of some failure or moral lapse on the part of the respondent (cf. Tangney et al., 1996). This view implies that efforts to humanize the interfaces of computer-assisted methods of self-administration may, by creating a virtual human presence, increase the level of misreporting about sensitive topics.

10.4.2   Legitimacy

The second variable that, according to our model, mediates the effects of the different methods of data collection is their impact on the perceived legitimacy and importance of the study.

Legitimacy and importance are also major determinants of whether members of the sample agree to take part in the survey in the first place. Because of their impact on response rates, many surveys put substantial effort into fostering a sense of legitimacy and importance: Interviewers may be given picture identification badges; letters may be sent to the members of the sample ahead of time explaining the purposes and sponsorship of the study; official stationary may be used in correspondence with sample members, and letters may be signed by senior government officials or academic researchers; 800 numbers may be set up for answering questions about the study; incentives may be offered for taking part. Advance letters, government or academic sponsorship of the survey, and incentives are known to be effective means of increasing response rates (Heberlein & Baumgartner, 1978; Yammarino et al., 1991). Several studies have, for example, demonstrated the effect of the study's sponsorship on response rates, sometimes by varying the affiliation of the author of the advance letter (Brunner & Carroll, 1969; Ferber & Sudman, 1976; see also Panel on Privacy and Confidentiality as Factors in Survey Response, 1979).

We suspect that these same variables may sometimes affect the data obtained from those who do consent to take part. Just as the perceived importance of the topic affects the depth of processing of persuasive messages (e.g., Petty & Cacioppo, 1984), it may affect the depth of processing of survey questions. For the most part, however, survey sponsorship doesn't seem to have large effects on the answers given, although there are occasional exceptions (e.g., Presser, Blair, & Triplett, 1992).

The method of data collection is likely to affect the perceived importance and legitimacy of the survey in two ways. First, when the contact with the respondent is solely by telephone, it limits the possibilities for establishing the survey's credentials. Advance letters are difficult to use in a telephone survey; interviewers cannot show their identification badges or point to official letters from the sponsors of the survey. This reduced sense of legitimacy may account for the greater reluctance of respondents to report sensitive information over the telephone (despite the reduced psychological presence of the interviewer). The second postulated effect involves computerization. At least for the time being, a computer is still a relative novelty for many respondents, and the use of a computer to collect the data is likely to impress respondents with the study's importance and objectivity. This heightened sense of legitimacy may increase the respondents' willingness to report socially undesirable behaviors. Although the impact of computer assistance is not always found, at least three studies suggest that computer assistance by itself may increase the proportion of respondents reporting sensitive behaviors (Baker et al., 1995; O'Reilly et al., 1994; Turner et al., 1998).

10.4.3   Cognitive Burden

The final mediating variable in the model is cognitive burden. The different methods of data collection make different demands on such skills as reading, listening, following directions, recognizing numbers, and keying, as summarized in Table 10.5. As computerization and self-administration are adopted more widely in surveys, new design principles are likely to emerge that reduce the demands of the new methods on respondents and interviewers.

In his *Design of Everyday Things*, Norman (1990) argues for seven such design principles. According to Norman, designs should

- take advantage of knowledge that is available externally, as well as knowledge stored in long-term memory;
- simplify the structure of the tasks;
- make both controls and the actions they perform visible to the user;
- rely on natural mappings between actions and their consequences;
- exploit both physical and cultural constraints;
- allow for errors; and
- rely on standardization when other design principles do not apply.

Many computer-assisted data collection programs embody these principles. These programs often have help bars with reminders about which key to press to back up or to advance; these make external knowledge readily available. Many programs also require a numerical answer, using this constraint to simplify the task. They typically display the answers back to the respondent or interviewer, making the action of keying the answer more visible. It is usually possible to back up and change an earlier answer, allowing for errors.

In a similar vein, Couper (1994) argues that a well-designed computer-assisted data collection system should exhibit ten characteristics:

- Functionality (i.e., the system should meet the requirements for carrying out the tasks);
- Consistency (the system's conventions and mappings between actions and consequences should be the same within a questionnaire and, if possible, across questionnaires and other interviewer tools);
- Informative feedback (the system should provide some feedback, such as a confirmation message or movement to the next screen, for every user action);
- Transparency (the system should carry out certain functions – such as checking that the answer entered corresponds to one of the options – without drawing the user's attention to them);
- Explicitness (the system should make it obvious what actions are possible and how they are to be performed);
- Comprehensibility (the system should avoid jargon, abbreviations, and arbitrary conventions);
- Tolerance (the system should allow for errors, incorporating facilities to prevent, detect, and correct errors);
- Efficiency (the system should minimize user effort by, for example, simplifying the actions needed to carry out common operations);
- Supportiveness (the system should recognize the cognitive limits of the users and make it unnecessary for them to memorize large numbers of commands, providing ready access to online help instead);
- Optimal complexity (the system should avoid both over-simplification and extreme complexity).

Couper's principles are derived from the growing literature on human–computer interaction (e.g., Galitz, 1993).

Finally, drawing on findings on visual perception and on patterns of eye movements during reading, Jenkins and Dillman (1997) advocate five principles for the design of self-administered paper questionnaires:

- Consistently using graphical elements (such as contrast and spacing) to define a clear path through the questionnaire;

- Using prominent visual guides to redirect respondents when conventions within a questionnaire must change;
- Placing directions where they are easily seen and close to where they are needed;
- Keeping separate pieces of information physically close when they must be connected to be understood; and
- Asking only one question at a time.

Dillman, Tortora, Conradt, and Bowker (1998) have extended these principles to Web surveys.

There is clearly considerable overlap in these prescriptions. For example, all three sets of principles emphasize consistency with the natural inclinations of the respondents. In the case of self-administered questionnaires, for instance, the eye is drawn to areas of high contrast. Questionnaire designers can use this tendency to help respondents find the next item in the questionnaire (by reserving bold type for question numbers and question text). Similarly, questionnaires should follow the normal reading order of the respondents (in English, from left to right and from top to bottom). All three sets of principles also point out the importance of consistency across questions and an appropriate level of complexity. Unfortunately, the principles are vague enough that applying them is likely to remain more of an art than a science. For the same reason, it may be difficult to test them empirically or to determine the gains that can be achieved with questionnaires that embody them.

10.4.4   Other Mediators

Figure 10.1 omits at least three additional variables that may mediate the effects of the different methods of data collection. The first of these possible mediators is the pace of the interview. Several studies suggest that computer assistance slows down the pace of interviews somewhat; of course, as computers become faster, this difference between electronic and paper questionnaires may disappear. As Bishop and his colleagues have observed, however, self-administration may have similar effects, slowing down or at least giving the respondents control over the pace of administration (Bishop et al., 1988). So far, however, no clear evidence has emerged that variations in pace affect the quality of the data, at least within the range of speeds found in surveys. Although it is reasonable to expect the same speed–accuracy trade-offs with survey questions that are observed with other cognitive tasks, at least for now pace does not seem to play a key role in explaining differences among different methods of data collection.

A second omitted mediator involves the order of processing the questions. When an interviewer or the computer administers the questions, the questions are, with few exceptions, asked and answered in the intended order. Backtracking and jumping ahead appear to be quite rare. As a result, with computer assistance or interviewer administration, the order in which the questions are presented and the order in which they are answered are virtually identical. With self-administered paper questionnaires, however, respondents are free to look ahead and backtrack. (Although in principle respondents may have the same freedom to move about the questionnaire with a computer-assisted instrument, they are probably far less likely to exercise that freedom than with a paper SAQ.)

Bishop and his colleagues presented some evidence that question order effects are reduced or eliminated with paper SAQs, but the evidence for the crucial interaction between question order and data collection method was significant only once in four tests; similarly, a more recent study by Schwarz and Hippler (1995) found only a marginally significant interaction between question order and method of administration. It is plausible that these interactions *should* be weak. After all, even with a paper questionnaire, most respondents probably proceed through the questions in the intended order. Because the order of processing the questions is unlikely to vary dramatically by method and because this variable appears to mediate only the effects of question order – not the effects of other question characteristics, such as wording or the order of the response options (Bishop et al., 1988) – we have not included this variable in the model in Figure 10.1.

Norman (1990) emphasizes the importance of mental models of everyday devices. Mental models are likely to play a key role in surveys as well. Available evidence as is available suggests that survey respondents do not always have clear notions about what is expected of them. For example, Cannell and his colleagues report that respondents in the National Health Interview Survey were unsure about whether they were supposed to report exact information (Cannell, Fowler, & Marquis, 1968). Because of the relative unfamiliarity of the survey interview situation, respondents may draw on their models of other situations in interpreting the survey task. They may see being interviewed as similar to having an everyday conversation, casting a vote, or dealing with an inflexible bureaucracy (cf. Suchman & Jordan, 1990). When the questions are self-administered, respondents may see the survey situation as resembling taking a multiple-choice examination, filing a government form, or playing a computer game. When an SAQ is sent through the mail, the greatest danger is that the respondent will see the survey as just another piece of junk mail. The model that respondents adopt is likely to be affected by the method of data collection and is likely to affect, in turn, the respondents' perceptions of the overall situation and their understanding of the importance of accuracy, completeness, and detail in their answers. Unfortunately, we know very little about respondents' mental models of the survey. They may turn out to be one of the most important mediators of respondent behavior.

10.5 Conclusions

There's considerable evidence that the method of data collection affects the answers that are obtained. As new methods of data collection are introduced, it will become even more important to understand the differences among them. The methods in current use different along many dimensions, but three of the differences stand out psychologically. Methods of survey data collection vary in the actual or virtual presence of an interviewer; methods that lower the salience of the interviewers or dispense with them entirely seem to offer a number of advantages, especially when the questions are about sensitive topics. Data collection methods also differ in the opportunities they provide for establishing the legitimacy and importance of the survey. Telephone surveys may be at a particular disadvantage here. Finally, different methods impose different burdens on the respondent's reading, numeracy, and listening skills. These cognitive demands aren't necessarily fixed but instead vary with the layout and formatting of the questionnaires.

CHAPTER ELEVEN

Impact of Cognitive Models on Survey Measurement

During the past decade, cognitive theories have swept through survey methodology as they had earlier swept through psychology in 1970s and 1980s. Although the adoption of cognitive concepts and methods may seem quite rapid, it's still uncertain how much impact these ideas will ultimately have.

The first effort to foster collaboration between cognitive scientists and survey researchers took place in the late 1970s, when the British Social Science Research Council sponsored a conference on retrospective data in surveys. The conference brought psychologists and survey researchers together, apparently for the first time, to explore measurement problems in surveys; the immediate product of the conference was a volume edited by Moss and Goldstein (1979) focusing on problems of recall. Similar efforts to spark collaborations between cognitive psychologists and survey researchers began in the United States in 1980 and reached an early watershed in 1983, when the Committee on National Statistics, with support from the National Science Foundation (NSF), sponsored a seminar on cognitive aspects of survey methodology (see Jabine, Straf, Tanur, & Tourangeau, 1984).[1] This seminar marked the beginning of

[1] In one such effort, a workshop was convened by the Bureau of Social Science Research on recall issues in the National Crime Survey (NCS). The NCS was undergoing a redesign, and one of the key questions was how to prompt more accurate memory for crime victimizations over the year-long recall period used in the survey. A panel of cognitive psychologists, including Elizabeth Loftus and Endel Tulving, took part in the workshop (see Biderman, 1980). In the same year, the Committee on National Statistics (CNSTAT, a branch of the National Research Council) organized a panel on problems in the measurement of subjective phenomena, such as attitudes. The work of that panel culminated in an widely cited two-volume discussion of the issues involved in measuring such phenomena in surveys (Turner & Martin, 1984). The CNSTAT panel helped widen the

long-term institutional support for the interdisciplinary movement, in the form of NSF grants to researchers outside the government and inter-agency transfers from NSF to the National Center for Health Statistics (NCHS). Much of the research reviewed in this book was carried out under grants from NSF, contracts from NCHS, or both. In addition, the title of the conference – Cognitive Aspects of Survey Methodology (CASM) – has come to stand for the interdisciplinary movement as a whole.[2]

The diffusion of the cognitive approach to measurement problems in surveys seems to have accelerated since the time of CASM. During the late 1980s and early 1990s, several major U.S. statistical agencies (the Bureau of the Census, the Bureau of Labor Statistics, and the NCHS) established cognitive laboratories, primarily for the purpose of pretesting survey questionnaires. (As one observer noted, "cognitoria" seemed to be springing up all around Washington.) And a textbook appeared, summarizing much of the cognitive work on survey measurement error (Sudman, Bradburn, & Schwarz, 1996). More subtle developments also signaled the widespread acceptance of the new approach among survey methodologists. For example, mainstream investigations of survey error have taken on an increasingly cognitive flavor (see, e.g., Chapter 9 in Groves, 1989, or the papers in the volume on survey measurement error edited by Biemer, Groves, Lyberg, Mathiowetz, & Sudman, 1991).

The seemingly rapid adoption of the cognitive approaches to survey errors in part reflected prior developments within survey research that had paved the way for the flurry of activity in the last 15 years. The "new" methods and concepts were in some ways extensions of long-term trends in mainstream approaches to survey error. We have reviewed many of these antecedents in earlier chapters. For example, Cannell, Miller, and Oksensberg (1981) had briefly outlined a model of survey

---

focus of the movement to apply cognitive models from the narrow problem of recall errors in surveys to the broader issues of measurement errors in general.

[2] At the same time, parallel developments were taking place in Germany, where a group of researchers centered at ZUMA, a research center in Mannheim, were also applying cognitive models to account for problems in the survey measurement, especially the measurement of attitudes. A workshop was held in the summer of 1984 that included both German (Hans-Jurgen Hippler, Norbert Schwarz, and Fritz Strack) and American researchers (Reid Hastie, Roger Tourangeau; see the volume by Hippler, Schwarz, & Sudman, 1987). At both the CASM and ZUMA conferences, detailed cognitive models of the survey response process were presented (Strack & Martin, 1987; Tourangeau, 1984, 1987).

responding that anticipated the one we present here. Earlier, classic methodological papers by Neter and Waksberg (1964) and Sudman and Bradburn (1973) had presented sophisticated analyses of the effects of memory errors on survey reports that inspired much of the later work on forgetting and telescoping in surveys. The volume by Schuman and Presser (1981) paved the way for later psychological models of question wording and context effects, providing both a rich set of carefully documented examples and intriguing hypotheses about the sources of the effects. These and other precursors within survey research helped lay the foundation for the collaborative efforts of the 1980s and 1990s.

This chapter offers an assessment of these developments. It examines the impact of the application of cognitive methods and models on conceptions of survey error and on survey practice, especially the practice of developing and testing survey questionnaires. First, though, we summarize what we take to be the main features of the cognitive approach as we have developed it in the preceding chapters. (We won't interrupt this summary for commercial breaks, so see the relevant earlier chapters for citations to the cognitive and survey literature.)

11.1 The Anatomy of a Survey Response

We began this book with a picture of the mental steps people go through in answering a survey question. Although people can short-circuit some of these steps on occasion, it's clear that responding to a question often enough involves understanding the question, retrieving relevant information from memory, making some sort of judgment, and then formulating the judgment in a way that's consistent with the question's demands (see Table 1.1). Our effort in the intermediate chapters has been to improve the resolution of this picture. We view respondents as pragmatists – at times, as opportunists – in their approach to these mental steps. Respondents have relevant experience in dealing with a range of questions in everyday life, and they use the strategies they've developed in the course of this experience to make sense of the questions in surveys and to satisfy the perceived demands of the interview.

For concreteness, let's suppose that an interviewer has just asked Jones, "How many times during the last two months have you consulted a doctor or health care professional about a medical condition?" It's natural to think of Jones's first task as grasping this question. Every survey item conveys, either implicitly or explicitly, uncertainty about which of a set of propositions happens to be true, and it requests the respondent to supply an answer by specifying the true one. In the case of the question about medical consultations, this space is roughly the set of propositions: "Jones consulted a doctor zero times in the last two months," "Jones consulted a doctor one time in the last two months," and so on. If the question comes with response options, then the options correspond to this uncertainty space. But whether or not response options are available, Jones has to understand the question in enough detail to determine which set of propositions the survey researcher has in mind as potential answers. This entails parsing the sentence, identifying the questioned element, and determining the boundaries and potential overlap among the propositions that would constitute an answer. To do this, Jones is likely to use not only information internal to the question itself, but also the relation of the item to others in the questionnaire and the additional cues available from the interviewer and the setting.

To determine which of the candidate propositions is true, Jones must typically consult memory for the type of event in question. Although there is no consensus on how memory for autobiographical events is organized, there is some agreement about how people retrieve information about these events. Jones might start with a set of cues that includes an abstract of the question itself (e.g., "I consulted a doctor x times in the last two months"). This information may call up relevant facts from long-term memory – in the best case, the answer to the question itself. In many situations, however, memory won't deliver the right answer but might provide relevant information (e.g., "Two months ago I visited Smith in Florida"; "I've had lower back pain recently"; and so on) that supplements the initial memory cues. Inferences based on these cues (e.g., "If I had back pain, I probably consulted Dr. Alberts") can also fill out the information Jones is using to probe memory. This cycle can continue until Jones has found the needed facts or has extracted as much from memory as is possible under the conditions of the interview. How successful this process will be depends on the richness of the cue, the match between the cue and the event-as-encoded, and the time that's elapsed since the event took place, among other factors.

For many questions, memory won't suffice to pick out the true proposition that the question seeks. People usually don't encode in memory the calendar dates of personal events; so if the question asks when some event happened, respondents probably have to reconstruct the date, perhaps using the sort of constraint-satisfaction process that we outlined in Chapter 4. This process can take into account landmark events (e.g., Jones's wedding, birth of her child, start of her new job), calendar information (e.g., beginnings and ends of school terms, dates of holidays), personal time periods (e.g., when Jones lived in Lincoln, Nebraska; when Jones was in college), and other facts that have temporal implications. In a similar way, people don't usually encode a running tally of the number of occurrences of each type of event they've experienced; so, when Jones is asked how many times she's consulted a doctor, there is no ready-made answer she can retrieve. Jones could try to recall and count individual incidents or she could estimate the number based on typical rates (e.g., that she usually sees a doctor three times a year). Which of these strategies she uses will depend on the perceived magnitude of the answer, the length of the reference period, the availability of the incident information, and the regularity of the event type.

Answers to attitude questions, like answers to behavioral questions, usually aren't preformed, waiting for the respondent to retrieve them from long-term memory. If Jones has to answer a question about her attitude toward gun control, for example, she is likely to base her answer on a sample of considerations that bear on the question (e.g., constitutional rights, dangers associated with gun accidents, criminal activity), combining them to yield an overall opinion. This sampling process helps explain the instability of attitudes over time, as well as their susceptibility to context effects. Earlier items in the interview can make certain considerations more salient and thus more likely to be included later in the sample for the target item. Of course, not all considerations that come to mind are necessarily incorporated in Jones's answer. Perceived redundancy between items, perceived irrelevance, or warnings about possible biasing effects can cause Jones to discard considerations that might otherwise have affected her judgment about an issue.

Whether the question calls for a judgment about time, frequency, or an attitude issue, Jones is likely to come up with an answer using similar processes. Sometimes she'll be able to report an answer she formed earlier, retrieving an exact date, a tally, or an existing judgment about the issue. Much of the time, though, she'll arrive at an answer via some other route. For example, her report may be based on an impression. With time or frequency questions, this impression may reflect how hard it was for her to recall the target event(s); with an attitude question, it may reflect a vague evaluation. Or Jones may make a new judgment derived from general information she recalls at the time the question is asked. With temporal questions, this general information may take the form of a lifetime period or some other higher-level temporal unit that helps her date the target event; with frequency questions, the general information may be the event's typical rate of occurrence; with attitude questions, it may involve Jones's broader values or ideological predispositions. Finally, Jones's judgments may be based on specific information she retrieves in thinking about her answer. She may remember specific details about the incident from which she can infer its date, specific episodes from which she can compute a total, or specific considerations from which she can arrive at an overall view. Regardless of the exact nature of the judgment she is called on to make, Jones is likely to use one of these broad strategies to make it.

Finally, Jones's response to the question depends on the fit between the internal information she's retrieved or inferred and the external constraints of the interview. For questions that demand a numeric answer, such as the question about doctor consultations, she may have to adjust her answer to the perceived range and distribution of allowable responses, to the perceived meaning of scale labels, and to other constraints. (If no response options are present, she may also have to decide on how exact the response should be and then round her answer accordingly.) She may also give more weight to certain response options, depending on their order (first or last in a list) and channel of presentation (visual or auditory). If the topic is a sensitive one, she may shade her answer up or down or she may refuse to answer entirely. This response censoring is more likely to happen when she perceives clear risks in admitting to some taboo, when an interviewer is present than when the survey is self-administered, and when she thinks there is no danger in being caught in a lie.

This picture of question answering in surveys comes in part from traditional research in cognitive and social psychology. As we hope our earlier chapters make clear, however, research on cognitive aspects of surveys has become a special stream of investigation in its own right. The professed aim of this investigation is to understand and to reduce survey error, and it thus seems fair to ask how far it's come in its own terms. That's the task for the remainder of this chapter (and the remainder of this book).

11.2 Impact on Conceptions of Survey Measurement Error

Perhaps the most obvious change the CASM movement has produced is the way survey researchers view measurement errors. Before the new approach, empirical investigations of survey measurement often had a piecemeal character: Problems were cataloged, but the origins of these problems and the relations between the different types of problems were often unclear. For example, the "quality" profiles for several federal surveys provided a rich and detailed account of the sources of potential errors but made little effort to develop hypotheses about the causes of these problems (see, e.g., Brooks & Bailar, 1978, and Jabine, 1990). We do not intend this as criticism; developing theories about the sources of problems was not the purpose of these documents. They do, however, reflect the state of the art in survey methodology prior to the new approach. Since the advent of the CASM movement, researchers have traced these measurement errors to the psychological processes of the respondent (e.g., Strack & Martin, 1987; Tourangeau, 1984), the interviewer (Sander et al., 1992), and the character of the interaction (Schaeffer, 1991a; Schober, 1999; Suchman & Jordan, 1990). Discussions of measurement problems in surveys now often organize them in terms of the mental components of the response process that give rise to the problem (e.g., Groves, 1989, Chapter 9), and researchers have developed checklists that tie problems in individual survey questions to the underlying cognitive operations (e.g., Lessler & Forsyth, 1995). The cognitive models of the response process have provided a new paradigm for understanding – or at least classifying – the different types of measurement errors in surveys.

11.2.1 Statistical Conceptions of Survey Error

Until recently, the reigning conception of survey errors was statistical rather than psychological in character. The new cognitive models do not so much contradict these earlier statistical models of error as supplement them. The statistical models concern the consequences of different types of survey errors for the estimates derived from the survey; the cognitive models, by contrast, focus almost exclusively on the causes of errors. Survey errors have two main consequences for survey estimates. When the errors are systematic, they bias the estimates; when the errors are random, they increase their variance. Not surprisingly, the statistical models fall into two categories: variance models and bias models.

The Hansen–Hurwitz–Bershad Model

As Lessler and Kalsbeek (1992) have pointed out, the U.S. Census Bureau has been the leader in the development of variance models, and no single model developed at the Bureau has been more influential than the one proposed by Hansen, Hurwitz, and Bershad (1961). The model assumes that, in effect, in any survey, there is an initial random selection of respondents from a population of potential respondents, followed by a random selection by each respondent of an answer from a distribution of his or her potential answers. Both factors – the sample and the specific response – contribute to the overall variance of the survey estimate. The model also allows for the possibility that bias inflates the total error, where bias is conceptualized as the difference between the population mean and the true value for the quantity in question. We give the mathematical details of the model in the appendix to this chapter.

This conception of measurement or response errors applies most naturally in situations in which there *is* a true value. For example, it is easy to see how it applies when the question asks about the number of doctor visits the respondent made over the last six months or the number of hours he or she worked during the past week. We might expect answers to these questions to be biased downward by forgetting (or upward by telescoping), and we might also expect some variation if we were to readminister the question to the same respondent. It is still possible to apply the model even in situations in which there is no "platonic" true score, but the true score is instead defined as the mean across repetitions of the interview. In such cases – for example, when attitudes are being measured – the model is equivalent to the classical psychometric formulation (see Chapter 1 and Biemer & Stokes, 1991).

Bias Models

Although the Hansen–Hurwitz–Bershad model includes a bias term, its focus is clearly on the variance components of the error. There are, however, a number of statistical models that focus on biases as contributors to the overall error in survey statistics. One member of this family of models concerns the impact of nonresponse on survey estimates. In the simplest formulation, each member of the survey sample is seen as belonging to one of two subpopulations, or strata: those who would consistently become nonrespondents if they were part of the sample and those who would consistently become respondents. By definition, data are never obtained for members of the nonrespondent stratum. If the unadjusted sample mean is used as an estimate of the overall population mean, then the nonresponse bias (B_{NR}) will be the product of two factors – the proportion of the population in the nonrespondent stratum (P_{NR}) and the difference between the means for the two strata ($\bar{Y}_R$ *and* $\bar{Y}_{NR}$):

$$B_{NR}(\bar{y}) = P_{NR}(\bar{Y}_R - \bar{Y}_{NR})$$

More sophisticated formulations express the bias in terms of the response propensity for each member of the population; this propensity represents the probability that an individual will provide data if he or she is part of the sample. Under this stochastic model of nonresponse, the bias in the unadjusted sample mean will depend on the shortfall in the sample total due to nonresponse and the covariance of the response propensity and the substantive variable of interest.[3] The shortfall in the total can be eliminated by increasing the sample size (or adjusting the sample weights). It is far more difficult to eliminate the portion of the bias that reflects the relationship between response propensities and the characteristic that the survey is attempting to measure. For example, we saw in Chapter 9 that income is related to the likelihood that sample members will opt out of the income supplement to the CPS (Moore et al., 1999). It's not easy to compensate for the bias introduced by such relationships.

11.2.2 Combining the Statistical and Cognitive Approaches to Error

On the surface, statistical models like the ones summarized here seem at best unconnected with the cognitive models described in the rest of this book. But the great virtue of the statistical error models is their flexibility. They apply in almost any situation because they make very minimal assumptions. For example, it is always possible to see an answer as the sum of the true answer and an error, as in the Hansen et al. model, since the error is *defined* as the difference between the reported and the true answers. The cognitive models, by contrast, make more substantive assumptions. Their great virtue is that they make stronger predictions about the nature and direction of the errors than the statistical models do. This suggests the possibility of combining statistical models' methods of partitioning error with the cognitive models' ideas

---

[3] Formally,

$$B_{NR}(\bar{y}) = - \frac{\sum_{i=1}^{N} (1 - p_j)Y_j}{N}$$
$$= \text{Cov}(p_j, Y_j) - (1 - \bar{p})\bar{Y}$$

where p_j is the response propensity for person j and where $\bar{p}$ is the population mean of the response propensities (so that $1 - \bar{p}$ represents the expected nonresponse rate across samples).

about the sources of these errors (see Groves, 1999, for an extended discussion).[4]

O'Muircheartaigh's (1991) work on simple response variance illustrates the development of statistical models that reflect theoretical considerations. Using data from the CPS reinterview program, O'Muircheartaigh argues that the estimated *simple response variance* – the variability of the responses across hypothetical repetitions of the interview – takes on different values, depending on whether the data come from self-reporters or proxies. (See the appendix for a formal definition of simple response variance.) The usual procedure for estimating the simple response variance involves comparing the data in the CPS interview with those obtained from a reinterview; the procedure assumes that the errors in the answers are uncorrelated across trials. The assumption of independence may not be tenable when the interval between the initial interview and the reinterview is short – say, a week or less – and the same person provides the data both times. The respondent may remember his or her earlier answer, a circumstance that will presumably increase the consistency of the responses and lead to an underestimate of the simple response variance. O'Muircheartaigh attempts to estimate

---

[4] Cognitive models can sometimes play a direct role in *reducing* errors. It is possible, for example, to use results from the memory literature to provide better cues to respondents or to develop such memory aids as life event calendars. We discuss such techniques later in this chapter.

It is also possible that results from cognitive models could be useful in *adjusting* survey estimates to reduce errors. For example, a statistical model can be adjusted for nonresponse by using a substantive model of the causes of the nonresponse. Because data about the nonrespondents are typically sparse, these "theoretical" models tend to be fairly simple. In principle, other substantive models also provide a basis for adjusting survey estimates in order to reduce bias. Neter and Waksberg (1964), for example, argued that reports about the frequency of home repairs were the product of four factors, reflecting the actual frequency of relevant repairs (X_j), the proportion retained in memory (ρ_j), the proportion reported in error due to telescoping (α_j), and the proportion deliberately left out of the respondents' reports (β_j):

$$Y_j = X_j \, \rho_j \, (1 + \alpha_j) \, (1 - \beta_j)$$

As a practical matter, estimating values for the relevant parameters may not be easy. It may require varying the length of the reference period or other features of the design (which is how Neter and Waksberg derived their estimates of the values of ρ and α) or collecting additional information about the events (such as records data) that is not susceptible to distortion by memory errors. Analysts may be reluctant to apply such corrections for fear of introducing new errors into the final estimates. Still, the current practice of ignoring large sources of error clearly has its drawbacks.

and compensate for this correlation; in addition, he provides separate estimates of the simple response variance for proxies and self-respondents.

O'Muircheartaigh's model and the belief-sampling model of attitude responses presented in Chapter 6 both attempt to bring theoretical notions to bear on what appear as random error components in the standard statistical models. In each case, the new models attempt to pull fixed or systematic components out of what had been previously written off as random. Because estimating these fixed components may require relatively complex alterations to the design of a survey (the addition of reinterviews or the imposition of split-ballot designs in which different respondents get the items under different modes of data collection), it seems unlikely that researchers will routinely apply the new, more theoretically based models of survey error. Still, efforts to reconcile the statistical and cognitive approaches to error are likely to continue and likely to yield worthwhile results (e.g., Groves, 1999).

11.3   Impact on Survey Practice

If the CASM movement has had a dramatic impact on how researchers conceive survey errors, it has had an equally dramatic impact on their attempts to reduce measurement error. These attempts encompass changes in questionnaire design and methods to assist survey respondents (Jobe & Mingay, 1989, 1991).

11.3.1   Questionnaire Development and Pretesting

From the outset, the movement to apply cognitive methods to survey problems has focused on tools for developing questionnaires (Jobe & Mingay, 1989; Willis et al., 1991). During the past 15 years, survey researchers have imported a variety of methods for designing questionnaires, including card sorts, vignettes, focus groups, reaction time measures, interaction coding, and cognitive interviewing.

Card Sorts and Vignettes

The different techniques have somewhat different aims. The goal of focus groups, card sorts, and vignettes is to explore respondents' cognitive structures for specific domains. Focus groups have been popular in market research settings for some time, but the federal statistical agencies and their contractors have come to use them only recently. Focus groups are not really a cognitive method, and there is already an extensive literature on their use (see Krueger, 1994, for an introduction), so we will not discuss them here beyond noting that their application in federal surveys seems to reflect increased concerns about the potential mismatch between the concepts that the survey questions presuppose and those that survey respondents actually hold. These same concerns spurred the use of some of the other tools described here. In card sorting, respondents group objects, concepts, or statements into piles based on their apparent similarity. Researchers typically analyze the sort data by means of a statistical clustering procedure (see, e.g., Everitt, 1974) in order to discover the cognitive structures underlying the similarity judgments. Card sorts have occasionally aided in developing or improving questionnaires. For example, Brewer, Dull, and Jobe (1989) used such data to explore people's conceptions of chronic medical conditions; their findings provide an empirical basis for improving the conditions checklist in the HIS. (For a more extended discussion of the card sorting technique, see Brewer & Lui, 1995).

Vignettes are short descriptions of hypothetical scenarios, and researchers employ them to understand how respondents would answer questions about these situations (e.g., Gerber, 1990). One drawback to card sorting is that it is difficult for interviewers to administer in a survey. Vignettes, by contrast, can be part of an ordinary interview, thus providing some evidence about varying conceptions of a topic or domain. Vignettes were extensively used in redesigning the CPS questionnaire (Martin & Polivka, 1995; see also Esposito, Campanelli, Rothgeb, & Polivka, 1991). In the early stages of that effort, vignettes explored respondents' conceptions of work by describing various hard-to-classify activities (such as volunteer work or unpaid work in a family business) and helped reveal whether respondents categorized these situations according to the CPS definition. A later study examined how changes in the CPS questions about work affected respondents' answers to the vignettes. Table 11.1 displays some of the findings from that study (Martin & Polivka, 1995, Table 1). The vignettes revealed that respondents' definitions of work sometimes differ markedly from the CPS definition, with the majority of respondents misclassifying two of the scenarios in which the workers (Amy and Sarah) received no pay. A new version of the work question affected classifications, helping in some cases but hurting in others.

TABLE 11.1 Percentage Classifying a Vignette as Work

| | 1991 | |
| | Old Version | New Version |
Vignette	Would you report him/her as working last week, not counting work around the house?	Would you report him/her as working for pay (or profit) last week?
Bill attended his college classes and got paid to tend bar for a fraternity party one night last week.	78	85
Last week, Amy spent 20 hours at home doing the accounting for her husband's business. She did not receive a paycheck.	46	29
Sam spent 2 hours last week painting a friend's house and was given 20 dollars.	61	71
Last week, Sarah cleaned and painted the back room of her house in preparation for setting up an antique shop there.	47	42
Cathy works as a real estate agent for commissions. Last week she showed houses but didn't sign any contract.	89	61
Fred helped his daughter out by taking care of his grandson 2 days last week while the boy's mother worked	13	2
Last week, Susan put in 20 hours of volunteer service at a local hospital	36	4

Note: Sample size of approximately 300 per version and vignette. The first five vignettes meet the CPS definition for work and the final two do not.
Source: Data from Martin and Polivka (1995). Copyright © 1995. Reprinted with permission of the University of Chicago Press.

Reaction Time and Interaction Coding

Traditionally, cognitive psychologists have used reaction time measures to test hypotheses about the mental processes people use in carrying out some task (e.g., Sternberg, 1969) or about the way their memory for some domain is organized (e.g., Collins & Quillian, 1969). Studies on reaction times to attitude questions have followed this pattern, testing hypotheses about the process of answering attitude questions, about attitude structure, or both (Fazio et al., 1986; Judd et al., 1991; Tourangeau, Rasinski, & D'Andrade, 1991). Recently, however, Bassili

(1996b; Bassili & Scott, 1996) has extended the use of reaction times to identify poorly worded questions; in addition, the speed with which respondents are able to answer attitude questions may predict their susceptibility to context effects.

Coding of interactions between respondents and interviewers also serves as a method for identifying problematic survey items (Fowler, 1992). The proportion of respondents who ask for clarification of the item's meaning or who give unacceptable answers provides an index of the presence and severity of problems. As in the case of response time, survey methodologists' use of this method reflects concerns about potential hitches in the response process, especially about whether respondents interpret the questions as intended.

Cognitive Interviewing

By far the most widely adopted new tool for questionnaire development has been the cognitive interview. As Conrad and Blair (1996, p. 1) point out, "The most tangible result of the dialogue between survey methods research and cognitive psychology is the widespread use of think aloud methods for pretesting questionnaires – so-called cognitive interviews." In its pure form, this method requires respondents to report aloud everything they are thinking as they attempt to answer a survey question; researchers record these reports and analyze them for evidence of misunderstanding and other difficulties. More than ten years earlier, Loftus (1984) had suggested that protocol analysis (i.e., analysis of verbal reports about thought processes) might serve as a useful means for exploring how respondents answer specific survey questions. Shortly thereafter, NCHS set up a cognitive laboratory to carry out cognitive interviewing and conducted a study to evaluate this new method for developing questionnaires. The evaluation pitted a version of a questionnaire on dental health that researchers developed in the traditional way with one they developed using cognitive interviews or other "cognitive" methods, such as experimental comparisons of multiple versions of the items (Lessler et al., 1989).

Although it is clear that *cognitive interviewing* is the direct descendant of the protocol analysis that Herbert Simon and his colleagues invented (Ericsson & Simon, 1980, 1984), the term now has somewhat broader scope, encompassing most of the cognitively inspired procedures we have touched on here. Jobe and Mingay (1989), for example, included nine methods in their list of cognitive interviewing techniques:

- Concurrent think-alouds (in which respondents verbalize their thoughts while they answer a question);
- Retrospective think-alouds (in which respondents describe how they arrived at their answers either just after they provide them or at the end of the interview);
- Focus group discussions (in which the respondents take part in a semistructured discussion of the topic);
- Confidence ratings (in which respondents assess their confidence in their answers);
- Paraphrasing (in which respondents restate the question in their own words);
- Sorting (in which respondents group items based on similarity or rank them on one or more scales);
- Response latency (in which response times are measured);
- Probes (in which respondents answer follow-up questions designed to reveal their response strategies); and
- Memory cues (in which the respondents receive various aids to recall).

At many survey organizations, the practice of cognitive interviewing appears to encompass a narrower set of activities, including concurrent and retrospective protocols, probes designed to identify response strategies, and requests to the respondent to paraphrase items or to define unfamiliar terms (see also Willis & Schechter, 1997). Most of the follow-up probes (including those eliciting paraphrases and definitions) are scripted ahead of time, but some are generated during the interview. However, it is clear that the method is new, and there are no shared standards for carrying out cognitive interviews (Willis, DeMaio, & Harris-Kojetin, 1999).

Coding Schemes for Cognitive Interviews

Another issue on which there is little consensus is how to code the information obtained from a cognitive interview. One method is to produce a kind of "gist" transcript for each interview, summarizing each respondent's protocol (or answers to probes). Researchers may further summarize these transcripts in a report pointing out the problems in each item. An obvious weakness of this and similar procedures is that cognitive interviews become the basis for nonquantitative, essentially impressionist analyses of the results of the interviews – hardly a desirable situation. Conrad and Blair (1996, p. 8) note that the success of cognitive psychology is

attributable [in part] to the use of rigorous experimental methods that rely on objective, quantifiable data. It is ironic, therefore, that the . . . survey methods community has adapted cognitive psychology as a set of largely impressionist methods.

Several researchers, including Conrad and Blair, have attempted to rectify this situation by creating coding schemes that allow more rigorous analysis of the results of cognitive interviews. Conrad and Blair's scheme groups problems by the cognitive process that gives rise to them – understanding the question, performing the implied task, or formatting and reporting the answer. In addition, their coding scheme includes a second component reflecting the aspect of the question responsible for the difficulty. This second component distinguishes five problem types: lexical problems, which derive from the meaning of the words or their use in the current context; inclusion/exclusion problems, which arise in determining the scope of a term or concept; temporal problems, which involve the boundaries of the reference period or the duration of the activity in question; logical problems, which result from the logical form or presuppositions of the question; and computational problems, which derive from the capacity of working memory.

Quite a few alternative coding schemes have appeared in recent proposals, and we summarize them in Table 11.2 (see Blair et al., 1991; Bolton, 1993; Conrad and Blair, 1996; Lessler & Forsyth, 1995; Presser & Blair, 1994; Willis, 1997b). Most of these distinguish trouble spots associated with each of the major components of the response process that we have discussed in this book: comprehension, memory, judgment, and response formulation. Presser and Blair (1994), however, also code for interviewer difficulties, such as problems in reading the question or recording an answer. Blair et al.'s (1991) scheme is specialized for identifying the strategies that respondents use to estimate behavioral frequencies, such as the recall-and-count and rate-based estimation strategies that we reviewed in Chapter 5.

11.3.2   Evaluating the New Methods for Questionnaire Development

It might seem obvious that the new methods for developing and pretesting survey questions would yield improvements in the questions

TABLE 11.2 Systems for Coding Cognitive Interviews

Scheme	Basic Categories	Other Dimensions/ Categories	Additional Features

Blair, Menon, and Bickart (1991)	Strategies for frequency questions
	  Automatic
	  Recall-and-count
	  Rate-based estimation
	  Enumeration-based
	For proxy attitude questions
	  Anchoring-and-adjustment
	  Other
	For recall
	  Search strategies
	  Use of cues
	  Reference period
		—	Focus on identifying response strategy rather than question problems

Bolton (1993)	Fourteen categories of verbalization	—	Automated coding based on presence of key words in verbal protocol

Conrad and Blair (1996)	Three response components
	  Understanding
	  Task performance
	  Response formatting
		Five problem types
		  Lexical
		  Temporal
		  Logical
		  Computational
		  Omission/inclusion
			—

(continued)

TABLE 11.2 (*continued*)

Scheme	Basic Categories	Other Dimensions/ Categories	Additional Features
Lessler and Forsyth (1995)	Four response components Comprehension Retrieval Judgment Response generation	Detailed subcategories for each component	To be used for appraisal of questionnaires without cognitive interview data
Presser and Blair (1994)	Two response components Semantic Respondent task	Analysis problems Interviewer problems	Can also be used to code interactions between interviewers and respondents and expert appraisal of questions
Willis (1997b)	Four response components Comprehension Retrieval Judgment Response generation	Logical problems	—

and reductions in measurement error. So far, however, there is relatively little direct evidence of this impact. As Willis and Schechter (1997) note, "a skeptic might remain unconvinced, and based on the available evidence, argue that there has been little direct empirical demonstration of the effectiveness of these methods." The evidence favoring the new techniques is largely anecdotal, often consisting of apparently improved versions of the questions (see, e.g., Bassili & Scott, 1996, and Fowler, 1992). Although these examples often seem compelling, they do not in themselves demonstrate any reduction in measurement errors. Respondents surely answer questions more accurately when they understand them, but we still cannot quantify the improvement that a more comprehensible question provides, and we cannot rule out the possibility that some other problem with the revised question offsets potential gains from improved comprehension. Moreover, the anecdotal evidence cannot demonstrate that the new methods are more effective or cheaper than existing methods.

Empirical Evaluations

To date, three studies have attempted to evaluate cognitive interviewing as a tool for questionnaire. The first was carried out by Lessler et al. (1989) for NCHS. It compared a version of a questionnaire concerning dental health that reflected the results from cognitive interviews (as well as several laboratory studies) against a version developed using standard methods. The comparison of the two versions involved both field and laboratory experiments, but both produced inconclusive results. Both experiments had relatively small samples (385 and 146 respondents, respectively), especially considering the rarity of some of the dental practices the questions asked about (e.g., fluoride mouth rinses); in addition, outside data (from dental records) were available only for a minority of the laboratory respondents.

Presser and Blair (1994) carried out a more successful investigation of the relative effectiveness of cognitive interviewing. Their study compared four pretesting methods: conventional pretests, behavior coding, cognitive interviewing, and expert panels. The conventional pretests consisted of telephone interviews with two small samples, each with about 40 respondents; the pretest interviewers then reported on their overall experiences and their experiences with each item in the questionnaire. These same pretest interviews were also monitored, and certain respondent behaviors were coded. Both the interviewer debriefings and the behavior codings were summarized in reports detailing the problems with each item. The cognitive interviewing pretest included 10–12 cognitive interviews conducted by each of three interviewers. Finally, two panels of survey research experts reviewed the questions. Each of the cognitive interviewers and the chairs of the two expert panels also wrote summaries describing the problems with each item.

The Presser–Blair study produced some clear results. First, the expert panels reported the most problems with the questions, on average identifying about 160 problems compared to about 90 for the other methods. In addition, the methods differed somewhat in the types of problems they picked out. The interviewer debriefing and behavior coding reported most of the interviewer problems; by contrast, the cognitive interviews and expert reviews reported most of the comprehension and analysis problems. These findings are quite plausible; why shouldn't the methods differ in the number and type of problems they identify? Still, without any evidence that the suspect items actually exhibit the problems they are supposed to have, it is not clear how much weight to give to these two findings. A third finding concerned the reliability of the problems reported for each item. The agreement across replications of each method on whether a particular question contained a specific type of problem was discouragingly low (a median value of Yule's Q of .51 for the three cognitive interviewers). Not surprisingly, an assessment of the relative costs of the four methods found expert reviews and cognitive interviews to be the least expensive methods.

Finally, Willis and Schechter (1997) tested several hypotheses based on the results of cognitive interviews in a series of field experiments. In some sense, the ultimate product of a pretesting technique is a hypothesis about how an item or an alternative will work in a field setting. Based on the results of cognitive interviews, Willis and Schechter derived explicit hypotheses about the performance of five pairs of items. They then tested these hypotheses in three split-ballot experiments. For example, one experiment compared responses to the item "On a typical day, how much time do you spend doing strenuous physical activities, such as lifting, pushing, or pulling?" One group received that item by itself; the other group received the same item after a preliminary, filter question (*On a typical day, do you spend any time doing strenuous physical activities, such as lifting, pushing, or pulling?*). Willis and Schechter hypothesized that the version with the filter item would yield a higher percentage of respondents admitting that they spent little or no time on strenuous activities. This hypothesis was confirmed in all three split ballots. The results of these studies offer some assurance that the processes observed in cognitive laboratories are real and that similar processes affect the answers of actual survey respondents.

Limitations of Cognitive Interviews

There is spotty evidence, then, for the effectiveness of the new procedures. Although the new techniques in general and cognitive interviewing in particular are high in face validity – it just seems sensible that they would produce better questions – there are both practical and theoretical reasons why their effectiveness may be limited.

The practical reasons involve the reliability of the results of cognitive interviews. The conclusions from a cognitive pretest are typically based on a small number of interviews, often 20 or fewer. Even if these sample sizes were adequate for purposes of questionnaire development, the method itself is still new and unstandardized; it is easy to believe that organizations and individual interviewers differ widely in their conduct of cognitive interviews. Moreover, as Conrad and Blair (1996) point out, the conclusions drawn from the interviews are only loosely constrained by the actual data they produce. Even if the interviews were formally coded using one of the available systems, coders would still sometimes disagree about the code to be assigned. With all these sources of unreliability at work, it is hardly surprising that Presser and Blair (1994) found low levels of agreement across cognitive interviewers about the nature of the problems with specific items.

Even if the conduct and coding of cognitive interviews were (or at least could be) reliable, there are other possible problems. Laboratory and field settings are likely to differ in a number of ways, some of them relevant to the processes respondents use in answering the questions. For instance, the interview is likely to have more distractions and to be conducted at a faster pace in a field setting than in the laboratory. The implicit assumption seems to be that if a problem is observed in the laboratory it will probably also be found in the field, where conditions are less conducive to formulating careful, accurate answers. This assumption may often hold, but sometimes it may not; precisely *because* of the distractions and fast pace, respondents in an actual survey may switch to less effortful (but potentially more accurate) response strategies than the ones they would use in the lab setting.

There are, in addition, theoretical limits on the usefulness of cognitive interviews. Certain processes occur too rapidly to leave any trace in working memory, and neither retrospective nor concurrent protocols are likely to shed much light on what took place. Ask respondents their date of birth and they will be unable to say much about how they arrived at their answers; sometimes the answer just pops into mind. An influential paper by Nisbett and Wilson (1977) gives the most widely cited arguments regarding the limits of introspective access. These authors marshaled evidence that we may be unaware of the stimuli that affect our responses, unaware of the responses themselves, and unaware of the connection between the two. More recently, Wilson and his colleagues have conducted several studies showing that simply asking respondents to list the reasons for their attitudes can change those attitudes (see Wilson & Hodges, 1992, and Wilson, LaFleur, & Anderson, 1995, for recent summaries). At least sometimes, probes can alter the process they were intended to shed light on.

In advocating the use of verbal protocols, Ericsson and Simon (1980) were hardly unaware of these limitations. They noted that "only information in focal attention can be verbalized" (p. 235). People may omit from a verbal report information they used in performing a task because the information never came to focal attention, because it left working memory before they could report it, or because they could no longer access it in long-term memory when the retrospective probe came along. In addition, respondents may have to recode information in order to report it (for instance, when the information is visual) or they may have to summarize it to reduce the memory load. These "intermediate processes" may introduce distortions into the verbal reports. Ericsson and Simon acknowledge that both the nature and the timing of the probe can affect the validity of a verbal report. Requests for reports that summarize performance across a number of tasks or for reports of hypothetical states yield data with a less direct relation to the contents of working memory than requests for a concurrent think-aloud. If Ericsson and Simon are right, concurrent and immediate retrospective protocols can provide a relatively direct indication about the information respondents are attending to or just attended to; such protocols may provide valuable clues about the processes respondents use to answer a question. Other verbalization tasks, however, may yield reports with little or no relation to the contents of working memory. It is not clear how closely cognitive interviews conform to these guidelines.

There is one final difficulty. Even if the results of cognitive interviews were both reliable and valid, merely knowing that there is a problem, even knowing the nature of that problem, is not the same as knowing the solution. Cognitive interviewing may provide an accurate diagnosis, but a diagnosis does not always point to a cure.

11.3.3   Response Aids

After pretesting methods, the area in which the collaboration between cognitive psychologists and survey researchers has had the greatest practical impact on surveys is in the use of aids for the respondents. In some cases, these tools were developed in collaborative efforts; in other cases, cognitive psychologists have extended and supported existing survey techniques. For example, Freedman and her colleagues had developed a life events calendar as a useful method for collecting retrospective data over long periods (Freedman, Thornton, Camburn, Alwin, & Young-DeMarco, 1988). Means and Loftus (1991) then investigated the effectiveness of such calendars as an aid to recall. They hypothesized that first gathering data on employment and educational milestones may improve recall and dating for other events, such as those related to health care. Table 11.3 lists six such response aids.

This list is not exhaustive, and additional tactics for reducing the burden on respondents will doubtless be forthcoming. But the results thus far are encouraging; most of the techniques appear to produce the expected improvements in reporting.

11.4   Impact on Psychology

The organizers of the 1983 CASM seminar hoped that the movement would affect not only survey practice, but psychological theory as well (Jabine et al., 1984). In retrospect, this hope seems a little naive. The idea that some survey errors are cognitive in origin implies that conceptual and methodological tools from psychology should be useful in understanding and reducing them. It does not imply, however, that tools or concepts from the survey literature would suddenly apply to psychological topics or appeal to psychologists. Still, one area of potential payoff for psychology is that surveys can reveal cognitive phenomena that were unknown or at least relatively unfamiliar to psychologists.

In three areas, this potential seems to have been realized. The first is memory for time. Telescoping had long been a methodological concern among survey researchers (e.g., Neter & Waksberg, 1964), and as early as 1973, Sudman and Bradburn had applied psychological concepts in attempting to explain the phenomenon. Since the early 1980s, telescoping and memory for the dates of events has become a lively research topic within cognitive psychology. This recent cognitive work draws on the earlier contributions by survey researchers (see, e.g., Friedman's 1993

TABLE 11.3 Aids for Reducing Cognitive Burdens

Response Aid	Description and Rationale	Study	Result
Life event calendar	Calendar for recording job histories or other personal landmarks to improve dating and increase recall	Means and Loftus (1991)	The calendar increased the level of reporting
Landmark events	The generation by the respondent of memorable events that fix the beginning of the reference period and reduce telescoping	Loftus and Marburger (1983)	Landmark events reduced levels of reporting
Added retrieval cues	Providing additional retrieval cues	Means, Swan, Jobe, and Esposito (1991)	Added cues increase accuracy of recall
Branching format for attitude questions	Breaking a rating task into simpler components to improve reliability	Krosnick and Berent (1993)	Branching and labeling all the options increased reliability
Backward search	Respondent told to retrieve most recent events first	Loftus and Fathi (1985) Loftus, Smith, Klinger, and Fiedler (1992) Jobe, White, Kelley, Mingay, Sanchez, & Loftus (1990)	Search order produced inconclusive results
Second guess	Giving respondent a second try to answer the question	Lessler, Tourangeau, and Salter (1989)	Additional events reported in second try

review), and much of it has been done by participants in the 1983 CASM seminar or their collaborators (e.g., Brown et al., 1985; Huttenlocher, Hedges, & Bradburn, 1990; Loftus & Marburger, 1983).

Two other topics – context effects and frequency estimation – that are sources of methodological concern have become the focus of substantive cognitive research. In both cases, existing methodological and psychological streams of work converged as a result of the CASM movement. Social psychologists and psychophysicists had studied the impact of context on judgments at least since the 1950s (e.g., Brown, 1953; Hovland, Harvey, & Sherif, 1957); within survey research, methodologists had described context as a source of error for at least that long a period (e.g., Hyman & Sheatsley, 1950). Interest in context effects intensified in both fields during the early 1980s. Social cognition researchers had carried out and published influential studies on the "priming" of personality constructs (Herr et al., 1983; Higgins et al., 1977); at roughly the same time, Schuman and Presser (1981) published their careful investigations of a large number of well-known survey context effects. Thereafter, investigators consciously drew concepts and examples from both literatures (e.g., Schwarz & Bless, 1992a; Strack & Martin, 1987; Tourangeau & Rasinski, 1988) and published similar papers in psychology and survey journals. Increasingly, it is hard to say where the survey work on this topic leaves off and the psychological work begins.

A similar convergence seems to have taken place with the study of frequency estimation. There was a strong tradition within both the cognitive and the survey literatures concerning reports of behavioral frequencies, as we noted in Chapter 5. In the 1980s, researchers began drawing on work from both traditions (e.g., Burton & Blair, 1991, and Lessler et al., 1989), and soon it became hard to draw the line separating survey from psychological research (e.g., Brown & Siegler, 1993; Conrad et al., 1998; Menon, Raghubir, & Schwarz, 1995).

11.5 Barriers to Further Accomplishments

Overall, the attempt to apply cognitive models to survey measurement has achieved a modest success. It has led to the acceptance of a new psychological conception of survey errors, although it has had little impact on survey estimation. It has affected the pretesting and development of survey questionnaires, although it remains unclear whether the new methods have *improved* the questionnaires. It has led to the wider use of aids to the respondents (such as life event calendars), with some gains in response accuracy. And, in a few areas, it has altered the focus of psychological research. The widespread acceptance of the new approach, however, raises the question of why progress hasn't been more impressive.

In adapting methods and concepts from one discipline to the problems of another, we run several general risks: We may focus on the wrong problems in the new discipline, apply the wrong theories from the old one, propose the wrong strategies for solutions, or fail in implementing potentially successful strategies. At various points, the movement to apply cognitive methods to surveys has, we believe, fallen into each of these traps.

11.5.1   Wrong Problems

From the outset, the CASM movement has focused on one set of problems – measurement errors arising from the respondent's cognitive processes – and has neglected others, such as nonresponse or the character of the interaction between the interviewer and the respondent. Other perspectives might have directed attention to these latter problems (e.g., Groves, Cialdini, & Couper, 1992; Suchman & Jordan, 1990). Any set of tools is useful for some tasks and useless for others, and adopting a particular set of tools inevitably raises the question of the salience of tasks for which it is suited. Even within the range of problems for which cognitive psychology is appropriate, the CASM movement has tended to focus on some issues (e.g., retrieval) at the expense of others (e.g., the initial encoding of events or the fit between the respondent's situation and the concepts embodied in the questionnaire). Some of these choices may have directed research away from the most pressing problems, the largest sources of errors.

11.5.2   Wrong Theories

Even when they address the right problems, interdisciplinary researchers may seize on discredited theories or outmoded methods. Concepts sometimes seem to take on a second life in a new discipline long after the source discipline has discarded them. Psychoanalysis, for example, seems to linger on in literary theory long after psychology has abandoned it. In the case of the CASM movement, the heavy reliance on protocol analysis may provide a case in point. Within cognitive and social psychology, there is a keen appreciation of the limits of verbal protocols; however, the survey community often seems to accept uncritically the results of cognitive interviews, even though these results are based on looser data collection methods and less formal coding procedures than most psychologists would allow. Another case in point might be early attempts to apply the concept of schemas to survey problems; the concept is simply too vague to give much leverage on the concrete problems that survey researchers face.[5]

11.5.3 Wrong Applications

A third obstacle arises in applying theories – even perfectly correct ones – to survey practice. Having decided that retrieval failure is an important source of error in a question, we can adopt any of a number of strategies in an effort to improve the answers. We can provide additional cues, encourage estimation strategies in place of retrieval, suggest a particular search order, give the respondents life event calendars, ask respondents to try a second time, and so on. Some strategies may prove generally useful, but others may not. Cognitive research has more often provided clearer conclusions about the sources of error than about the best methods for reducing them; as we noted earlier, diagnosis is not the same as cure. Because there are few ready-made strategies that apply to the problems found in surveys, we often need "engineering" research to develop and test proposed aids to the respondents. And, in some cases, it may be that no good solutions exist. If parents never knew what vaccinations their children received, then no amount of prompting their memories will enable them to report their children's shots accurately (Willis et al., 1999). Rather than response aids, statistical corrections based on medical records data may be the only way to improve the estimates from national immunization surveys.

11.5.4 Wrong Implementations

Even if a strategy for reducing errors is right in principle, implementing it may pose difficulties. The work of Lessler and her colleagues illustrates

---

[5] It seems possible that further progress in the cognition-and-surveys area will require a cadre of professionals who are equally well acquainted with both areas' methods and theories. As yet, there are few places where graduate students can receive systematic training in both approaches; instead, they are forced to put together their own interdisciplinary program from the bottom up. One hopeful sign for the CASM movement is the Joint Program on Survey Methodology – a consortium of the University of Maryland, the University of Michigan, and Westat – which is devoted to training survey researchers with skills in both statistical and cognitive methods.

some of the pitfalls here (Lessler et al., 1989). Strategies that seem to improve recall in the laboratory are less successful in the field, in part because their success depends on such procedural variables as the pace and length of the interview. Strategies that are sound in general may fail in specific instances because of difficulties in implementation. Defining unfamiliar terms may generally reduce comprehension problems, but the definition provided must be clear and simple, as we noted in Chapter 2; otherwise, the cure can be worse than the illness. Fowler (1992) discusses an example that illustrates this point. The revised wording of a question about HMOs defined that term:

Do you belong to an HMO or health plan that has a list of people or places you go to, in order for the plan to cover your health care costs? Was your last visit to a medical doctor covered by your health care plan?

The new version led to more requests for clarification from respondents than the old one. Different wording of the definition might well have produced better results.

11.5.5   Conclusions

These are difficulties that any interdisciplinary enterprise encounters, and the CASM movement has had to confront each of them. New tools, such as a conversation analysis, continue to be added to the array (Schaeffer, 1991b; Schober, 1999), and older concepts and methods continue to yield results. Within a relatively short period, the cognitive approach to survey errors has helped to change the face of an old art form. It is still too soon to say how profound those changes will turn out to be.

APPENDIX: STATISTICAL MODELS FOR SURVEY ERROR

The Hansen–Hurwitz–Bershad model, and its numerous descendants and variants, decompose an observation (Y_{jt}) obtained from a respondent (say, respondent j) on a specific occasion (survey interview t) into various components – typically, a true score (X_j) and an error (ε_{jt}):

$$Y_{jt} = X_{jt} + \varepsilon_{jt} \tag{11.1}$$

The error (ε_{jt}) is conceived as a random variable whose value is not correlated across respondents or across repetitions of the interview; its mean is not necessarily zero. That is, the expected value of the observation obtained from the same respondent across repetitions of the interview (t) and samples (s) is not necessarily X_j, the respondent's true value:

$$E(Y_{jt}) = E_s \, E_t \, (Y_{jt}) = Y_j$$

Similarly, the population mean for the observed values ($\bar{Y} = \Sigma \, Y_j \, / \, N$) may differ by some amount (B, the average bias) from the population mean for the true values ($\bar{X}$).

Under the assumptions of the model, the mean squared error of the estimated mean derived from a specific sample of respondents on a given occasion ($\bar{y}_t$) reflects both the bias in the estimate and its variance:

$$MSE(\bar{y}_t) = E[(\bar{y}_t - \bar{X})^2] = V\,(\bar{y}_t) + B^2 \qquad (11.2)$$

The bias term is just the squared difference between the population mean of the expected values for the observations (i.e., the Y_j's) and the mean of the true values (the X_j's). The variance term can be analyzed further into components that reflect measurement and sampling error:

$$V(\bar{y}_t) = E([(\bar{y}_t - \bar{y}) + (\bar{y} - \bar{Y})]^2) \quad \text{where} \quad \bar{y} = \Sigma \, Y_i \, / \, n$$
$$= E[(\bar{y}_t - \bar{y})^2 + (\bar{y} - \bar{Y})^2 + (\bar{y}_t - \bar{y})(\bar{y} - \bar{Y})] \qquad (11.3)$$

The first of the three terms in Equation 11.3 reflects variation in the answers across trials, or response variance; the second, variation across samples, or sampling variance; and the third, the covariance between the measurement and sampling errors. The latter term is usually assumed to be zero; that is, variation in the composition of the sample is assumed to have no impact on the errors of measurement.

It is not always plausible to assume that the reporting errors of different members of the sample are completely uncorrelated. In many survey designs, the same informant provides multiple observations (e.g., a single respondent provides information about all members of the household) or a single interviewer collects data from multiple respondents. In these situations, it is probably more realistic to assume that the errors in the observations from a single informant or in those collected by a single interviewer will be correlated with each other. When there is some correlation among the errors, it is possible to break down the response variance term in Equation 11.3. We will use the subscript i to denote observations sharing the same source of error (e.g., the same interviewer). The usual assumption is that the errors arising from the same source will covary but that those from different sources will be independent:

$$\mathrm{Cov}(\varepsilon_{ij}, \varepsilon_{i'j'}) = 0 \quad \text{if} \quad i \neq i'$$
$$= \rho_w \, \sigma_\varepsilon^2 \quad \text{if} \quad i = i', j \neq j'$$

Under this assumption, the response variance has two components – the simple response variance and the correlated response variance. If each of m interviewers collects observations from k respondents (and if each of the m samples is selected via simple random sampling), the response variance term in Equation 11.3 can be reexpressed:

$$E[(\bar{y}_t - \bar{y})^2] = \frac{\sigma_\varepsilon^2}{km} + \frac{(m-1)\rho_w \sigma_\varepsilon^2}{km}$$

The first term is the simple response variance; the second, the correlated response variance.

In a closely related formulation, each observation is seen as consisting of three components – the true score, the random error, and the shared error (representing, for example, the impact of the interviewer):

$$Y_{ij} = X_{ij} + b_i + e_{ij}$$

This formulation breaks the error (ε_{ij}) defined in Equation 11.1 into two additive components, one that is unique to the observation (e_{ij}) and one that is shared with other observations (b_i). The overall variance in the sample mean has three corresponding components – the sampling variance, the simple response variance, and the correlated response variance.

$$V(\bar{y}_t) = \frac{1}{n} (\sigma_X^2 + \sigma_b^2 + \sigma_e^2) [(m-1)\rho_y]$$

where

$$\rho_y = \frac{\sigma_b^2}{\sigma_X^2 + \sigma_b^2 + \sigma_e^2} \tag{11.4}$$

References

Abbott, V., Black, J. B., & Smith, E. E. (1985). The representation of scripts in memory. *Journal of Memory and Language, 24,* 179–199.

Abelson, R. P. (1981). The psychological status of the script concept. *American Psychologist, 36,* 715–729.

Abelson, R. P., Loftus, E. F., & Greenwald, A. G. (1992). Attempts to improve the accuracy of self-reports of voting. In J. Tanur (Ed.), *Questions about questions: Inquiries into the cognitive bases of surveys* (pp. 138–153). New York: Russell Sage Foundation.

Abernathy, J., Greenberg, B., & Horvitz, D. (1970). Estimates of induced abortion in urban North Carolina. *Demography, 7,* 19–29.

Abramson, P. R., & Claggett, W. (1984). Race-related differences in self-reported and validated turnout. *Journal of Politics, 46,* 719–738.

Aguinis, H., Pierce, C., & Quigley, B. (1993). Conditions under which a bogus pipeline procedure enhances the validity of self-reported cigarette smoking: A meta-analytic review. *Journal of Applied Social Psychology, 23,* 352–373.

Allan, L. G. (1979). The perception of time. *Perception & Psychophysics, 26,* 340–354.

Allen, J. (1995). *Natural language understanding* (2nd ed.). Redwood City, CA: Benjamin/Cummings.

Allen, J. F., & Kautz, H. A. (1985). A model of naive temporal reasoning. In J. R. Hobbs & R. C. Moore (Eds.), *Formal theories of the commonsense world* (pp. 251–268). Norwood, NJ: Ablex.

Allport, G. W. (1935). Attitudes. In C. Murchison (Ed.), *A handbook of social psychology* (pp. 798–844). Worcester, MA: Clark University Press.

Alwin, D., & Krosnick, J. (1991). The reliability of survey attitude measurement: The influence of question and respondent attributes. *Sociological Methods and Research, 20,* 139–181.

Anderson, B. A., Silver, B. D., & Abramson, P. R. (1988a). The effects of the race of the interviewer on measures of electoral participation by blacks in SRC National Election Studies. *Public Opinion Quarterly, 52,* 53–88.

Anderson, B. A., Silver, B. D., & Abramson, P. R. (1988b). The effects of the race of the interviewer on race-related attitudes of black respondents in SRC/CPS National Election Studies. *Public Opinion Quarterly, 52,* 289–324.

Anderson, J. R. (1983). *The architecture of cognition.* Cambridge, MA: Harvard University Press.

Anderson, J. R., & Schooler, L. J. (1991). Reflections of the environment in memory. *Psychological Science, 2,* 396–408.

Anderson, N. (1981). *Foundations of information integration theory.* New York: Academic Press.

Anglin, D., Hser, Y., & Chou, C. (1993). Reliability and validity of retrospective behavioral self-report by narcotics addicts. *Evaluation Review, 17,* 91–108.

Aquilino, W. S. (1993). Effects of spouse presence during the interview on survey responses concerning marriage. *Public Opinion Quarterly, 57,* 358–376.

Aquilino, W. S. (1994). Interview mode effects in surveys of drug and alcohol use. *Public Opinion Quarterly, 58,* 210–240.

Aquilino, W. S., & LoScuito, L. A. (1990). Effect of interview mode on self-reported drug use. *Public Opinion Quarterly, 54,* 362–395.

Armstrong, J. S., Denniston, W. B., Jr., & Gordon, M. M. (1975). The use of the decomposition principle in making judgments. *Organizational Behavior and Human Performance, 14,* 257–263.

Armstrong, S. L., Gleitman, L. R., & Gleitman, H. (1983). What some concepts might not be. *Cognition, 13,* 263–308.

Ayidiya, S. A., & McClendon, M. J. (1990) Response effects in mail surveys. *Public Opinion Quarterly, 54,* 229–247.

Bachrach, C. A., Evans, V. J., Ellison, S. A., & Stolley, K. S. (1992, May). *What price do we pay for single sex fertility surveys?* Paper presented to the Population Association of America, Denver.

Baddeley, A. D. (1986). *Working memory.* Oxford: Clarendon.

Baddeley, A. D., Lewis, V., & Nimmo-Smith, I. (1978). When did you last . . . ? In M. M. Gruneberg, P. E. Morris, & R. N. Sykes (Eds.), *Practical aspects of memory* (pp. 77–83). London: Academic Press.

Bahrick, H. P. (1983). The cognitive map of a city: Fifty years of learning and memory. In G. H. Bower (Ed.), *The psychology of learning and motivation* (Vol. 17, pp. 125–163). Orlando, FL: Academic Press.

Bahrick, H. P., Bahrick, P. O., & Wittlinger, R. P. (1975). Fifty years of memory for names and faces: A cross sectional approach. *Journal of Experimental Psychology: General, 104,* 54–75.

Bahrick, H. P., Hall, L. K., & Dunlosky, J. (1993). Reconstructive processing of memory content for high versus low test scores and grades. *Applied Cognitive Psychology, 7,* 1–10.

Baker, R. P., Bradburn, N. M., & Johnson, R. (1995). Computer-assisted personal interviewing: An experimental evaluation of data quality and survey costs. *Journal of Official Statistics, 11,* 415–434.

Bargh, J., Chaiken, S., Govender, R., & Pratto, F. (1992). The generality of the automatic activation effect. *Journal of Personality and Social Psychology, 62,* 893–912.

Bargh, J., Chaiken, S., Raymond, P., & Hymes, C. (1996). The automatic activation effect: Unconditional automatic attitude activation with a pronunciation task. *Journal of Experimental Social Psychology, 32,* 104–128.

Barsalou, L. W. (1988). The content and organization of autobiographical memories. In U. Neisser & E. Winograd (Eds.), *Remembering reconsidered: Ecological and traditional approaches to the study of memory* (pp. 193–243). Cambridge: Cambridge University Press.

Barsalou, L. W., & Sewell, D. R. (1985). Contrasting the representations of scripts and categories. *Journal of Memory and Language, 24,* 646–665.

Bartlett, F. C. (1932). *Remembering.* Cambridge: Cambridge University Press.

Bassili, J. N. (1996a). Meta-judgmental versus operative indexes of psychological attributes: The case of measures of attitude strength. *Journal of Personality & Social Psychology, 71,* 637–653.

Bassili, J. N. (1996b). The how and the why of response latency measurement in telephone surveys. In N. Schwarz & S. Sudman (Eds.), *Answering questions: Methodology for determining cognitive and communicative processes in survey research* (pp. 319–346). San Francisco: Jossey-Bass.

Bassili, J. N., & Fletcher, J. (1991). Response-time measurement in survey research: A method for CATI and a new look at non-attitudes. *Public Opinion Quarterly, 55,* 331–346.

Bassili, J. N., & Scott, B. S. (1996b). Response latency as a signal to question problems in survey research. *Public Opinion Quarterly, 60,* 390–399.

Bauman, K., & Dent, C. (1982). Influence of an objective measure on self-reports of behavior. *Journal of Applied Psychology, 67,* 623–628.

Beatty, P., Herrmann, D., Puskar, C., & Kerwin, J. (1998). "Don't know" responses in surveys: Is what I know what you want to know and do I want you to know it? *Memory, 6,* 407–426.

Begg, I., Maxwell, D., Mitterer, J. O., & Harris, G. (1986). Estimates of frequency: Attribute or attribution. *Journal of Experimental Psychology: Learning, Memory, and Cognition, 12,* 496–508.

Bell, C. (1992). Memory for an early school report. In M. A. Conway, D. C. Rubin, H. Spinnler, & W. A. Wagenaar (Eds.), *Theoretical perspectives on autobiographical memory* (pp. 151–165). Dordrecht: Kluwer.

Belli, R. F. (1989). Influences of misleading postevent information: Misinformation, interference, and acceptance. *Journal of Experimental Psychology: General, 118,* 72–85.

Belli, R. F., Traugott, M. W., Young, M., & McGonagle, K. (1999). Reducing vote overreporting in surveys: A source monitoring approach. *Public Opinion Quarterly, 63,* 90–108.

Belson, W. A. (1981). *The design and understanding of survey questions.* Aldershot, U.K.: Gower.

Bergman, L. R., Kristiansson, K. E., Olofsson, A., & Säfström, M. (1994). Decentralised CATI versus paper and pencil interviewing: Effects on the results of the Swedish labor force surveys. *Journal of Official Statistics, 10,* 181–195.

Bickart, B. A. (1992). Question order effects and brand evaluations: The moderating role of consumer knowledge. In N. Schwarz & S. Sudman (Eds.), *Context effects in social and psychological research* (pp. 63–79). New York: Springer-Verlag.

Bickart, B. A., Blair, J., Menon, G., & Sudman, S. (1990). Cognitive aspects of proxy reporting of behavior. *Advances in Consumer Research, 17,* 198–206.

Biderman, A. (1980). *Report of a workshop on applying cognitive psychology to recall problems of the National Crime Survey.* Washington, DC: Bureau of Social Science Research.

Biemer, P. P., Groves, R. M., Lyberg, L. E., Mathiowetz, N. A., & Sudman, S. (1991). *Measurement errors in surveys.* New York: Wiley.

Biemer, P. P., & Stokes, L. (1991). Approaches to the modeling of measurement error. In P. Biemer, R. Groves, L. Lyberg, N. Mathiowetz, & S. Sudman (Eds.), *Measurement errors in surveys* (pp. 487–516). New York: Wiley.

Binnick, R. I. (1991). *Time and the verb.* Oxford: Oxford University Press.

Bishop, G. (1987). Context effects in self-perceptions of interest in government and public affairs. In H. Hippler, N. Schwarz, & S. Sudman (Eds.), *Social information processing and survey methodology* (pp. 179–199). New York: Springer-Verlag.

Bishop, G., Hippler, H., Schwarz, N., & Strack, F. (1988). A comparison of response effects in self-administered and telephone surveys. In R. Groves, P. Biemer, L. Lyberg, J. Massey, W. Nicholls, & J. Waksberg (Eds.), *Telephone survey methodology* (pp. 321–340). New York: Wiley.

Bishop, G., Oldendick, R., & Tuchfarber, A. (1986). Opinions on fictitious issues: The pressure to answer survey questions. *Public Opinion Quarterly, 50,* 240–250.

Bjork, R. A., & Landauer, T. K. (1978). On keeping track of the present status of people and things. In M. M. Gruneberg, P. E. Morris, & R. N. Sykes (Eds.), *Practical aspects of memory* (pp. 52–60). London: Academic Press.

Blair, E. A., & Burton, S. (1987). Cognitive processes used by survey respondents to answer behavioral frequency questions. *Journal of Consumer Research, 14,* 280–288.

Blair, E. A., & Ganesh, G. K. (1991). Characteristics of interval-based estimates of autobiographical frequencies. *Applied Cognitive Psychology, 5,* 237–250.

Blair, J., Menon, G., & Bickart, B. (1991). Measurement effects in self vs. proxy responses: An information-processing perspective. In P. P. Biemer, R. M. Groves, L. E. Lyberg, N. A. Mathiowetz, & S. Sudman (Eds.), *Measurement errors in surveys* (pp. 145–166). New York: Wiley.

Bless, H., Bohner, G., Hild, T., & Schwarz, N. (1992). Asking difficult questions: Task complexity increases the impact of response alternatives. *European Journal of Social Psychology, 22,* 309–312.

Block, R. A. (1985). Contextual coding in memory: Studies of remembered duration. In J. A. Michon & J. L. Jackson (Eds.), *Time, mind, and behavior* (pp. 169–178). Berlin: Springer-Verlag.

Boekeloo, B., Schiavo, L., Rabin, D., Conlon, R., Jordan, C., & Mundt, D. (1994). Self-reports of HIV risk factors at a sexually transmitted disease clinic: Audio vs. written questionnaires. *American Journal of Public Health, 84,* 754–760.

Bolinger, D. L. (1957). *Interrogative structures of American English (The direct question).* Tuscaloosa: University of Alabama Press.

Bolton, R. N. (1993). Pretesting questionnaires: Content analyses of respondents' concurrent verbal protocols. *Marketing Science, 12,* 280–303.

Boltz, M. (1995). Effects of event structure on retrospective duration judgments. *Perception & Psychophysics, 57,* 1080–1096.

Bower, G. H., Black, J. B., & Turner, T. J. (1979). Scripts in memory for text. *Cognitive Psychology, 11,* 177–220.

Bradburn, N. M. (1982). Question-wording effects in surveys. In R. Hogarth (Ed.), *Question framing and response consistency* (pp. 65–76). San Francisco: Jossey-Bass.

Bradburn, N. M. (1983). Response effects. In P. Rossi, J. Wright, & A. Anderson (Eds.), *Handbook of survey research* (pp. 289–328). New York: Academic Press.

Bradburn, N. M., & Danis, C. (1984). Potential contributions of cognitive research to survey questionnaire design. In J. Tanur, T. Jabine, M. Straf, & R. Tourangeau (Eds.), *Cognitive aspects of survey methodology: Building a bridge between disciplines* (pp. 101–129). Washington, DC: National Academy of Sciences.

Bradburn, N. M., & Miles, C. (1979). Vague quantifiers. *Public Opinion Quarterly, 43,* 92–101.

Bradburn, N. M., Rips, L., & Shevell, S. (1987). Answering autobiographical questions: The impact of memory and inference on surveys. *Science, 236,* 157–161.

Bradburn, N. M., & Sudman, S. (1979). *Improving interview method and questionnaire design.* San Francisco: Jossey-Bass.

Bradburn, N. M., Sudman, S., & Associates. (1979). *Improving interview method and questionnaire design.* San Francisco: Jossey-Bass.

Bransford, J., & Johnson, M. (1972). Contextual prerequisites for understanding: Some investigations of comprehension and recall. *Journal of Verbal Learning and Verbal Behavior, 11,* 717–726.

Breckler, S., & Wiggins, S. (1989). Affect versus evaluation in the structure of attitudes. *Journal of Experimental Social Psychology, 25,* 253–271.

Brewer, M. B., Dull, V. T., & Jobe, J. B. (1989). *Social cognition approach to reporting chronic conditions in health surveys.* Vital and Health Statistics, Series 6, Number 3. Hyattsville, MD: National Center for Health Statistics.

Brewer, M. B., & Lui, L. J. (1995). Use of sorting tasks to assess cognitive structure. In N. Schwarz & S. Sudman (Eds.), *Answering questions: Methodology for determining cognitive and communicative processes in survey research* (pp. 373–387). San Francisco: Jossey-Bass.

Brewer, W. F. (1988). Memory for randomly sampled autobiographical events. In U. Neisser & E. Winograd (Eds.), *Remembering reconsidered: Ecological and traditional approaches to the study of memory* (pp. 21–90). Cambridge: Cambridge University Press.

Brittingham, A., Tourangeau, R., & Kay, W. (1998). Reports of smoking in a national survey: Self and proxy reports in self-and interviewer-administered questionnaires. *Annals of Epidemiology, 8,* 393–401.

Brooks, C., & Bailar, B. (1978). *An error profile: Employment as measured by the Current Population Survey. Statistical Policy Working Paper 3.* Washington, DC: Office of Federal Statistical Policy and Standards.

Brown, D. R. (1953). Stimulus similarity and the anchoring of subjective scale. *American Journal of Psychology, 66,* 199–214.

Brown, N. R., Rips, L. J., & Shevell, S. K. (1985). The subjective dates of natural events in very-long-term memory. *Cognitive Psychology, 17,* 139–177.

Brown, N. R., Shevell, S. K., & Rips, L. J. (1986). Public memories and their personal context. In D. C. Rubin (Ed.), *Autobiographical memory* (pp. 137–158). Cambridge: Cambridge University Press.

Brown, N., & Siegler, R. (1993). Metrics and mappings: A framework for understanding real-world quantitative estimation. *Psychological Review, 100,* 311–325.

Brown, N. R., & Sinclair, R. C. (1997). *Estimating the number of lifetime sexual partners: Men and women do it differently.* Paper presented at the 52nd Conference of the American Association for Public Opinion Research, May 15–18, Norfolk, VA.

Brown, P., & Levinson, S. (1987). *Politeness: Some universals in language usage.* Cambridge: Cambridge University Press.

Bruce, D., Hockley, W. E., & Craik, F. I. M. (1991). Availability and category-frequency estimation. *Memory & Cognition, 19,* 301–312.

Bruner, J. S. (1990). *Acts of meaning.* Cambridge, MA: Harvard University Press.

Brunner, G., & Carroll, S. (1969). The effect of prior notification on refusal rate in fixed address surveys. *Journal of Advertising, 9,* 42–44.

Budescu, D. V., & Wallsten, T. S. (1985). Consistency in interpretation of probabilistic phrases. *Organizational Behavior and Human Decision Processes, 36,* 391–405.

Burt, C. D. B. (1992a). Retrieval characteristics of autobiographical memories. *Applied Cognitive Psychology, 6,* 389–404.

Burt, C. D. B. (1992b). Reconstruction of the duration of autobiographical events. *Memory & Cognition, 20,* 124–132.

Burton, S., & Blair, E. (1991). Task conditions, response formulation processes, and response accuracy for behavioral frequency questions in surveys. *Public Opinion Quarterly, 55,* 50–79.

Cannell, C., Fowler, F. J., & Marquis, K. (1968). The influence of interviewer and respondent psychological and behavioral variables on the reporting in household interviews. *Vital and Health Statistics,* Series 2, No. 26 (PB80–128275). Washington, DC.: U.S. Government Printing Office.

Cannell, C., Marquis, K. H., & Laurent, A. (1977). A summary of studies of interviewing methodology. *Vital and Health Statistics,* Series 2, No. 69 (DHEW Pub. No. HRA 77–1343). Washington, D.C.: U.S. Government Printing Office.

Cannell, C., Miller, P., & Oksenberg, L. (1981). Research on interviewing techniques. In S. Leinhardt (Ed.), *Sociological methodology 1981* (pp. 389–437). San Francisco: Jossey-Bass.

Card, J. J. (1978). The correspondence of data gathered from husband and wife: Implications for family planning studies. *Social Biology, 25,* 196–204.

Catania, J. A., Binson, D., Canchola, J., Pollack, L. M., Hauck, W., & Coates, T. J. (1996). Effects of interviewer gender, interviewer choice, and item wording on responses to questions concerning sexual behavior. *Public Opinion Quarterly, 60*, 345–375.

Catania, J. A., Gibson, D., Coates, D. D., Chitwood, D. D., & Coates, T. J. (1990), Methodological problems in AIDS behavioral research: Influences of measurement error and participation bias in studies of sexual behavior. *Psychological Bulletin, 108*, 339–362.

Catlin, O., & Ingram, S. (1988). The effects of CATI on costs and data quality: A comparison of CATI and paper methods in centralized interviewing. In R. Groves, P. Biemer, L. Lyberg, J. Massey, W. Nicholls, & J. Waksberg (Eds.), *Telephone survey methodology* (pp. 437–450). New York: Wiley.

Chaiken, S. (1980). Heuristic versus systematic information processing and the use of source versus message cues in persuasion. *Journal of Personality and Social Psychology, 39*, 752–766.

Chaiken, S., & Bargh, J. (1993). Occurrence versus moderation of the automatic activation effect: Reply to Fazio. *Journal of Personality and Social Psychology, 64*, 759–765.

Chaiken, S., & Eagly, A. (1976). Communication modality as determinant of message persuasiveness and message comprehensibility. *Journal of Personality and Social Psychology, 34*, 605–614.

Chaiken, S., & Yates, S. (1985). Attitude schematicity and thought-induced attitude polarization. *Journal of Personality and Social Psychology, 49*, 1470–1481.

Chang, P., & Novick, L. (1990). A probabilistic contrast model of causal induction. *Journal of Personality and Social Psychology, 58*, 545–567.

Chu, A., Eisenhower, D., Hay, M., Morganstein, D., Neter, J., & Waksberg, J. (1992). Measuring the recall error in self-reported fishing and hunting activities. *Journal of Official Statistics, 8*, 19–39.

Clark, A. L., & Tifft, L. L. (1966). Polygraph and interviewer self-reported deviant behavior. *American Sociological Review, 31*, 516–523.

Clark, A. L., & Wallin, P. (1964). The accuracy of husbands' and wives' reports of the frequency of marital coitus. *Population Studies, 18*, 165–173.

Clark, H. H. (1985). Language use and language users. In G. Lindzey & E. Aronson (Eds.), *The handbook of social psychology: Volume 2. Special fields and applications* (pp. 179–231). New York: Random House.

Clark, H. H., & Schaefer, E. F. (1989). Contributing to discourse. *Cognitive Science, 13*, 259–294.

Clark, H. H., & Schober, M. F. (1992). Asking questions and influencing answers. In J. M. Tanur (Ed.), *Questions about questions: Inquiries into the cognitive bases of surveys* (pp. 15–48). New York: Russell Sage.

Cochran, W. (1953). *Sampling techniques.* New York: Wiley.

Coder, J., & Scoon-Rogers, L. (1995). *Evaluating the quality of income data collected in the annual supplement to the March Current Population Survey and the Survey of Income and Program Participation.* Paper presented at the Joint Statistical Meetings, August 1995, Orlando, FL.

Collins, A. M., & Michalski, R. (1989). The logic of plausible reasoning: A core theory. *Cognitive Science, 13,* 1–50.

Collins, A. M., & Quillian, M. R. (1969). Retrieval time from semantic memory. *Journal of Verbal Learning and Verbal Behavior, 8,* 240–247.

Conrad, F. G., & Blair, J. (1996). *From impressions to data: Increasing the objectivity of cognitive interviews.* Paper presented at the 1996 Joint Statistical Meetings, Chicago, August 4, 1996.

Conrad, F. G., Brown, N. R., & Cashman, E. R. (1998). Strategies for estimating behavioral frequency in survey interviews. *Memory, 6,* 339–366.

Converse, J. M., & Presser, S. (1986). *Survey questions: Handcrafting the standardized questionnaire.* Beverly Hills, CA: Sage.

Converse, P. (1964). The nature of belief systems in mass publics. In D. Apter (Ed.), *Ideology and discontent* (pp. 206–261). New York: Free Press.

Converse, P. (1970). Attitudes and non-attitudes: Continuation of a dialogue. In E. Tufte (Ed.), *The quantitative analysis of social problems* (pp. 168–189). Reading, MA: Addison-Wesley.

Conway, M. A. (1993). Impairments of autobiographical memory. In F. Boller & J. Grafman (Eds.), *Handbook of neuropsychology* (Vol. 8, pp. 175–191). Dordrecht, the Netherlands: Elsevier.

Conway, M. A. (1996). Autobiographical knowledge and autobiographical memories. In D. C. Rubin (Ed.), *Remembering our past* (pp. 67–93). Cambridge: Cambridge University Press.

Conway, M. A., & Bekerian, D. A. (1987). Organization in autobiographical memory. *Memory & Cognition, 15,* 119–132.

Couper, M. P. (1994). *What can CAI learn from HCI?* Paper presented at the COPAFS Seminar on New Directions in Statistical Methodology, June 1994, Bethesda, MD.

Couper, M. P., & Nicholls W., II. (1998). The history and development of computer assisted survey information collection methods. In M. P. Couper, R. P. Baker, J. Bethlehem, C. Z. Clark, J. Martin, W. L. Nicholls, & J. O'Reilly (Eds.), *Computer assisted survey information collection* (pp. 1–22). New York: Wiley.

Couper, M. P., & Rowe, B. (1996). Computer-assisted self-interviews. *Public Opinion Quarterly, 60,* 89–105.

Couper, M. P., Singer, E., & Kulka, R. A. (1998). Participation in the 1990 decennial census: Politics, privacy, pressures. *American Politics Quarterly, 26,* 59–80.

Crain, S., & Fodor, J. D. (1985). How can grammars help parsers? In D. R. Dowty, L. Karttunen, & A. M. Zwicky (Eds.), *Natural language parsing* (pp. 94–128). Cambridge: Cambridge University Press.

Crowne, D., & Marlowe, D. (1964). *The approval motive.* New York: Wiley.

Daamen, D. D. L., & de Bie, S. E. (1992). Serial context effects in survey items. In N. Schwarz & S. Sudman (Eds.), *Context effects in social and psychological research* (pp. 97–114). New York: Springer-Verlag.

DeMaio, T. J. (1984). Social desirability and survey measurement: A review. In C. F. Turner & E. Martin (Eds.), *Surveying subjective phenomena* (Vol. 2, pp. 257–281). New York: Russell Sage Foundation.

Deming, W. (1950). *Some theory of sampling.* New York: Wiley.

DePaulo, B. M., & Bell, K. L. (1996). Truth and investment: Lies are told to those who care. *Journal of Personality and Social Psychology, 71,* 703–716.

DePaulo, B. M., Kashy, D. A., Kirkendol, S. E., Wyer, M. W., & Epstein, J. A. (1996). Lying in everyday life. *Journal of Personality and Social Psychology, 70,* 979–995.

Devine, P. G. (1989). Stereotypes and prejudice: Their automatic and controlled components. *Journal of Personality and Social Psychology, 56,* 5–18.

Dillman, D. A., Tortora, R. D., Conradt, J., & Bowker, D. (1998). *Influence of plain vs. fancy design on response rates for web surveys.* Paper presented at the 1998 Joint Statistical Meetings, Dallas, TX, August 1998.

Dominitz, J., & Manski, C. F. (1997). Perceptions of economic insecurity: Evidence from the Survey of Economic Expectations. *Public Opinion Quarterly, 61,* 261–287.

Dovidio, J. F., & Fazio, R. H. (1992). New technologies for the direct and indirect assessment of attitudes. In J. Tanur (Ed.), *Questions about questions: Inquiries into the cognitive bases of surveys* (pp. 204–237). New York: Russell Sage Foundation.

Dowty, D. R. (1979). *Word meaning and Montague grammar.* Dordrecht, the Netherlands: Reidel.

Duffy, J. C., & Waterton, J. J. (1984). Under-reporting of alcohol consumption in sample surveys: The effect of computer interviewing in fieldwork. *British Journal of Addiction, 79,* 303–308.

Ellsworth, P., & Gross, S. (1994). Hardening of the attitudes: Americans' views on the death penalty. *Journal of Social Issues, 50,* 19–52.

Ericsson, K. A., & Simon, H. A. (1980). Verbal reports as data. *Psychological Review, 87,* 215–257.

Ericsson, K. A., & Simon, H. A. (1984). *Protocol analysis: Verbal reports as data.* Cambridge, MA: MIT Press.

Esposito, J. L., Campanelli, P. C., Rothgeb, J., & Polivka, A. E. (1991). Determining which questions are best: Methodologies for evaluating survey questions. In *Proceedings of the American Statistical Association, Survey Research Methods Section.* Alexandria, VA: American Statistical Association.

Esposito, J., & Jobe, J. (1991). A general model of the survey interaction process. *Bureau of the Census Seventh Annual Research Conference Proceedings* (pp. 537–560). Washington, DC: U.S. Bureau of the Census.

Everitt, B. (1974). *Cluster analysis.* London: Heinemann.

Fay, R. L., Carter, W., & Dowd, K. (1991). Multiple causes of nonresponse: Analysis of the survey of 1990 census participation. In *Proceedings of the Social Statistics Section.* Alexandria, VA: American Statistical Association.

Fazio, R. (1989). On the power and functionality of attitudes: The role of attitude accessibility. In A. Pratkanis, S. Breckler, & A. Greenwald (Eds.), *Attitude structure and function* (pp. 153–179). Hillsdale, NJ: Erlbaum.

Fazio, R. (1993). Variability in the likelihood of automatic attitude activation: Data analysis and commentary on Bargh, Chaiken, Govender, and Pratto (1992). *Journal of Personality and Social Psychology, 64,* 753–758.

Fazio, R., Chen, D., McDonel, E., & Sherman, S. J. (1982). Attitude accessibility, attitude-behavior consistency, and the strength of the object-evaluation association. *Journal of Experimental Social Psychology, 18,* 339–357.

Fazio, R., Sanbonmatsu, D., Powell, M., & Kardes, F. (1986). On the automatic activation of attitudes. *Journal of Personality and Social Psychology, 37,* 229–238.

Fazio, R., & Williams, C. (1986). Attitude accessibility as a moderator of the attitude–perception and attitude–behavior relations: An investigation of the 1984 Presidential election. *Journal of Personality and Social Psychology, 51,* 505–514.

Fein, D. J., & West, K. K. (1988). Towards a theory of coverage error: An exploratory assessment of data from the 1986 Los Angeles test census. In *Proceedings of the Annual Research Conference* (pp. 540–562). Washington, DC: U.S. Bureau of the Census.

Felcher, E. M., & Calder, B. (1990). Cognitive models for behavioral frequency questions. *Advances in Consumer Research, 17,* 207–211.

Feldman, J. M., & Lynch, J. G. (1988). Self-generated validity and other effects of measurement on belief, attitude, intention, and behavior. *Journal of Applied Psychology, 73,* 421–435.

Fendrich, M., & Vaughn, C. M. (1994). Diminished lifetime substance use over time: An inquiry into differential underreporting. *Public Opinion Quarterly, 58,* 96–123.

Fendrich, M., & Xu, Y. (1994). The validity of drug use reports from juvenile arrestees. *The International Journal of the Addictions, 29,* 971–985.

Ferber, R., & Sudman, S. (1974). A comparison of alternative procedures for collecting consumer expenditure data for frequently purchased products. *Journal of Marketing Research, 11,* 128–135.

Ferber, R., & Sudman, S. (1976). The effects of compensation in consumer expenditure studies. *Annals of Economic and Social Measurement, 3,* 319–331.

Ferguson, R. P., & Martin, P. (1983). Long-term temporal estimation in humans. *Perception & Psychophysics, 33,* 585–592.

Fillmore, C. J. (1999). A linguistic look at survey research. In M. Sirken, D. J. Herrmann, S. Schechter, N. Schwarz, J. Tanur, & R. Tourangeau (Eds.), *Cognition and survey research* (pp. 183–198). New York: Wiley.

Fischhoff, B. (1991). Value elicitation: Is there anything in there? *American Psychologist, 46,* 835–847.

Fodor, J. A. (1981). The present status of the innateness controversy. In *Representations.* Cambridge, MA: MIT Press.

Fodor, J. A. (1994). Concepts: A pot boiler. *Cognition, 50,* 93–113.

Fogg, B. J., & Nass, C. (1997). Silicon sycophants: The effects of computers that flatter. *International Journal of Human-Computer Studies, 46,* 551–561.

Forsyth, B. H., Lessler, J. L., & Hubbard, M. L. (1992). Cognitive evaluation of the questionnaire. In C. Turner, J. Lessler, & J. Gfroerer (Eds.), *Survey measurement of drug use: Methodological studies* (pp. 13–52). Rockville, MD: National Institute on Drug Abuse.

Fowler, F. J. (1992). How unclear terms affect survey data. *Public Opinion Quarterly, 56,* 218–231.

Fowler, F. J., & Mangione, T. W. (1990). *Standardized survey interviewing: Minimizing interviewer error*. Newbury Park, CA: Sage.

Freedman, D., Thornton, A., Camburn, D., Alwin, D., & Young-DeMarco, L. (1988). The life history calendar: A technique for collecting retrospective data. In C. Clogg (Ed.), *Sociological methodology 1988* (pp. 37–68). Washington, DC: American Sociological Association.

Friedman, W. J. (1987). A follow-up to "Scale effects in memory for the time of events." *Memory & Cognition, 15*, 518–520.

Friedman, W. J. (1993). Memory for the time of past events. *Psychological Bulletin, 113*, 44–66.

Friedman, W. J., & Wilkins, A. J. (1985). Scale effects in memory for the time of events. *Memory & Cognition, 13*, 168–175.

Fuhrman, R. W., & Wyer, R. S., Jr. (1988). Event memory: Temporal order judgments of personal life experiences. *Journal of Personality and Social Psychology, 54*, 365–384.

Fujii, E. T, Hennessy, M., & Mak, J. (1985). An evaluation of the validity and reliability of survey response data on household electricity conservation. *Evaluation Review, 9*, 93–104.

Galambos, J. A., & Rips, L. J. (1982). Memory for routines. *Journal of Verbal Learning and Verbal Behavior, 21*, 260–281.

Galinat, W. H., & Borg, I. (1987). On symbolic temporal information: Beliefs about the experience of duration. *Memory & Cognition, 15*, 308–317.

Galitz, W. (1993). *User-interface screen design*. Boston: QED.

Gaskell, G. D., O'Muircheartaigh, C. A., & Wright, D. B. (1994). Survey questions about the frequency of vaguely defined events: The effect of response alternatives. *Public Opinion Quarterly, 58*, 241–254.

Gentner, D., & Collins, A. (1981). Studies of inference from lack of knowledge. *Memory & Cognition, 9*, 434–443.

Gerber, E. R. (1990). Calculating residence: *A cognitive approach to household membership judgments among low income blacks*. Unpublished report submitted to the U.S. Bureau of the Census.

Gfroerer, J., & Hughes, A. (1992). Collecting data on illicit drug use by phone. In C. Turner, J. Lessler, & J. Gfroerer (Eds.), *Survey measurement of drug use: Methodological studies* (pp. 277–295). DHHS Pub. No. ADM 92-1929. Rockville, MD: National Institute on Drug Abuse.

Gigerenzer, G. (1991). How to make cognitive illusions disappear: "Beyond heuristics and biases." In W. Stroche & M. Hewstone (Eds.), *European review of social psychology* (Vol. 2, pp. 83–115). New York: Wiley.

Gigerenzer, G., & Goldstein, D. G. (1996). Reasoning the fast and frugal way: Models of bounded rationality. *Psychological Review, 103*, 650–669.

Gillund, G., & Shiffrin, R. M. (1984). A retrieval model for both recognition and recall. *Psychological Review, 91*, 1–67.

Gilpin, E. A., Pierce, J. P., Cavin, S. W., Berry, C. C., Evans, N. J., Johnson, M., & Bal, D. G. (1994). Estimates of population smoking prevalence: Self- vs proxy reports of smoking status. *American Journal of Public Health, 84*, 1576–1579.

Graesser, A. C., Bommareddy, S., Swamer, S., & Golding, J. M. (1996). Integrating questionnaire design with a cognitive computational model of human question answering. In N. Schwarz & S. Sudman (Eds.), *Answering questions* (pp. 143–174). San Francisco: Jossey-Bass.

Graesser, A. C., Huber, J. D., & Person, N. K. (1992). *Question-asking in tutoring sessions.* Paper presented at the 32nd Annual Meeting of the Psychonomic Society, San Francisco.

Graesser, A. C., McMahen, C. L., & Johnson, B. K. (1994). Question asking and answering. In M. A. Gernsbacher (Ed.), *Handbook of psycholinguistics* (pp. 517–538). San Diego, CA: Academic Press.

Graesser, A. C., Roberts, R. M., & Hackett-Renner, C. (1990). Question-answering in the context of telephone surveys, business interactions, and interviews. *Discourse Processing, 13,* 327–348.

Graesser, A. C., Singer, M., & Trabasso, T. (1994). Constructing inferences during narrative comprehension. *Psychological Review, 101,* 371–395.

Grice, H. (1975). Logic and conversation. In P. Cole & T. Morgan (Eds.), *Syntax and semantics: Vol. 3, Speech acts* (pp. 41–58). New York: Seminar Press.

Grice, H. P. (1989). *Studies in the way of words.* Cambridge, MA: Harvard University Press.

Groenendijk, J., & Stokhof, M. (1997). Questions. In J. van Benthem & A. ter Meulen (Eds.), *Handbook of logic and language* (pp. 1055–1124). Amsterdam: Elsevier.

Groves, R. (1989). *Survey costs and survey errors.* New York: Wiley.

Groves, R. M. (1999). Survey error models and cognitive theories of response behavior. In M. G. Sirken, D. J. Herrmann, S. Schechter, N. Schwarz, J. M. Tanur, & R. Tourangeau (Eds.), *Cognition and survey research* (pp. 235–250). New York: Wiley.

Groves, R. M., Cialdini, R., & Couper, M. (1992). Understanding the decision to participate in a survey. *Public Opinion Quarterly, 56,* 475–495.

Groves, R. M., & Couper, M. P. (1998). *Nonresponse in household surveys.* New York: Wiley.

Groves, R. M., & Kahn, R. (1979). *Surveys by telephone: A national comparison with personal interviews.* New York: Academic Press.

Groves, R. M., & Mathiowetz, N. (1984). Computer assisted telephone interviewing: Effects on interviewers and respondents. *Public Opinion Quarterly, 48,* 356–369.

Hadaway, K., Marler, P., & Chaves, M. (1993). What the polls don't show: A closer look at U.S. church attendance. *American Sociological Review, 58,* 741–752.

Hainer, P., Hines, C., Martin, E., & Shapiro, G. (1988). Research on improving coverage in household surveys. In *Proceedings of the Annual Research Conference* (pp. 513–539). Washington, DC: U.S. Bureau of the Census.

Hansen, M. H., Hurwitz, W. N., & Bershad, M. A. (1961). Measurement errors in censuses and in surveys. *Bulletin of the International Statistical Institute, 38,* 359–374.

Hansen, M. H., Hurwitz, W., & Madow, W. (1953). *Sample survey methods and theory.* New York: John Wiley.

Hanson, C., & Hirst, W. (1989). On the representation of events: A study of orientation, recall, and recognition. *Journal of Experimental Psychology: General, 118*, 136–147.

Harrell, L., & Clayton, R. (1991). *Voice recognition technology in survey data collection: Results of the first field tests.* Paper presented at the National Field Technologies Conference, May 1991, San Diego, CA.

Harrell, L., Rosen, R., & Manning, C. (1998), *Web-based data collection in the Current Employment Statistics program.* Paper presented at the Joint Statistical Meetings, August, 1998, Dallas, TX.

Harrison, L. D. (1995). The validity of self-reported data on drug use. *The Journal of Drug Issues, 25*, 91–111.

Hasher, L., & Zacks, R. (1984). Automatic processing of fundamental information: The case of frequency of occurrence. *American Psychologist, 39*, 1372–1388.

Hastie, R. (1981). Schematic principles in human memory. In E. T. Higgins, C. P. Herman, & M. P. Zanna (Eds.), *Social cognition: The Ontario Symposium* (Vol. 1, pp. 39–88). Hillsdale, NJ: Erlbaum.

Hastie, R., & Park, B. (1986). The relationship between memory and judgement depends on whether the judgement is memory-based or on-line. *Psychological Review, 93*, 258–268.

Hatchett, S., & Schuman, H. (1975–1976). White respondents and race-of-interviewer effects. *Public Opinion Quarterly, 39*, 523–528.

Haviland, S., & Clark, H. (1974). What's new? Acquiring new information as a process in comprehension. *Journal of Verbal Learning and Verbal Behavior, 13*, 512–521.

Heberlein, T. A., & Baumgartner, R. (1978). Factors affecting response rates to mailed questionnaires: A quantitative analysis of the published literature. *American Sociological Review, 43*, 447–462.

Henrion, M., Fischer, G. W., & Mullin, T. (1993). Divide and conquer? Effects of decomposition on the accuracy and calibration of subjective probability distributions. *Organizational Behavior and Human Decision Processes, 55*, 207–227.

Herold, E., & Way, L. (1988). Sexual self-disclosure among university women, *Journal of Sex Research, 24*, 1–14.

Herr, P., Sherman, S. J., & Fazio, R. (1983). On the consequences of priming: Assimilation and contrast effects. *Journal of Experimental Social Psychology, 19*, 323–340.

Herrmann, D. J. (1992). *The contributions of the CASM Collaborative Research Program II. Contributions to cognitive and survey theory: Question answering strategies.* Hyattsville, MD: National Center for Health Statistics.

Herrmann, D. J. (1994). The validity of retrospective reports as a function of the directness of the retrieval process. In N. Schwarz & S. Sudman (Eds.), *Autobiographical memory and the validity of retrospective reports* (pp. 21–37). Berlin: Springer-Verlag.

Higginbotham, J. (1996). The semantics of questions. In S. Lappin (Ed.), *The handbook of contemporary semantic theory* (pp. 361–384). Oxford: Blackwell.

Higgins, E. T., Rholes, W. S., & Jones, C. R. (1977). Category accessibility and impression formation. *Journal of Experimental Social Psychology, 13*, 141–154.

Hill, D. H. (1987). Response errors around the seam: Analysis of change in a panel with overlapping reference periods. *Proceedings of the Section on Survey Research Methods, American Statistical Association* (pp. 210–215).

Hilton, D. (1990). Conversational processes and causal reasoning. *Psychological Bulletin, 107*, 65–81.

Hintzman, D. L. (1984). Episodic versus semantic memory: A distinction whose time has come – and gone? *Behavioral and Brain Sciences, 7*, 240–241.

Hintzman, D. L. (1988). Judgments of frequency and recognition memory in a multiple-trace memory model. *Psychological Review, 95*, 528–551.

Hintzman, D. L., & Curran, T. (1994). Retrieval dynamics of recognition and frequency judgments: Evidence for separate processes of familiarity and recall. *Journal of Memory and Language, 33*, 1–18.

Hochstim, J. (1967). A critical comparison of three strategies of collecting data from households. *Journal of the American Statistical Association, 62*, 976–989.

Holmes, D. S. (1970). Differential change in affective intensity and the forgetting of unpleasant personal experiences. *Journal of Personality and Social Psychology, 15*, 234–239.

Holyoak, K., & Mah, W. (1982). Cognitive reference points in judgments of symbolic magnitude. *Cognitive Psychology, 14*, 328–352.

Honaker, L. M. (1988). The equivalency of computerized and conventional MMPI administration: A critical review. *Clinical Psychology Review, 8*, 561–577.

Hornik, J. (1981). Time cue and time perception effect on response to mail surveys. *Journal of Marketing Research, 18*, 243–248.

Hovland, C. I., Harvey, O. J., & Sherif, M. (1957). Assimilation and contrast effects in reaction to communication and attitude change. *Journal of Abnormal and Social Psychology, 55*, 244–252.

Howell, W. C. (1973). Representation of frequency in memory. *Psychological Bulletin, 80*, 44–53.

Huttenlocher, J., Hedges, L. V., & Bradburn, N. M. (1990). Reports of elapsed time: Bounding and rounding processes in estimation. *Journal of Experimental Psychology: Learning, Memory, and Cognition, 16*, 196–213.

Huttenlocher, J., Hedges, L., & Prohaska, V. (1988). Hierarchical organization in ordered domains: Estimating the dates of events. *Psychological Review, 95*, 471–484.

Hyman, H. H., Cobb, W., Feldman, J., Hart, C., & Stember, C. (1954). *Interviewing in social research*. Chicago: University of Chicago Press.

Hyman, H. H., & Sheatsley, P. B. (1950) The current status of American public opinion. In J. C. Payne (Ed.), *The teaching of contemporary affairs: Twenty-first yearbook of the National Council for the Social Studies* (pp. 11–34). New York: National Education Association.

Jabine, T. (1990). *Survey of Income and Program Participation (SIPP): Quality profile*. Washington, DC: U.S. Department of Commerce, Bureau of the Census.

Jabine, T. B., King, K. E., & Petroni, R. J. (1990). *Quality profile, Survey of Income and Program Participation*. Washington, DC: Bureau of the Census.

Jabine, T., Straf, M., Tanur, J., & Tourangeau, R. (1984). *Cognitive aspects of survey methodology: Building a bridge between disciplines*. Washington, DC: National Academy of Sciences.

Jackendoff, R. (1991). Parts and boundaries. *Cognition, 41,* 9–45.

Jacoby, L. L., & Whitehouse, K. (1989) An illusion of memory: False recognition influenced by unconscious perception. *Journal of Experimental Psychology: General, 118,* 126–135.

Jenkins, C., & Dillman, D. (1997). Towards a theory of self-administered questionnaire design. In L. Lyberg, P. Biemer, M. Collins, E. DeLeeuw, C. Dippo, N. Schwarz, & D. Trewin (Eds.), *Survey measurement and process quality* (pp. 165–196). New York: Wiley.

Jobe, J. B., & Herrmann, D. (1996). Implications of models of survey cognition for memory theory. In D. Herrmann, M. Johnson, C. McEvoy, C. Herzog, & P. Hertel (Eds.), *Basic and applied memory research: Volume 2: Practical applications* (pp. 193–205) Hillsdale, NJ: Erlbaum.

Jobe, J. B., & Mingay, D. J. (1989). Cognitive research improves questionnaires. *American Journal of Public Health, 79,* 1053–1055.

Jobe, J. B., & Mingay, D. J. (1991). Cognition and survey measurement: History and overview. *Applied Cognitive Psychology, 5,* 175–192.

Jobe, J. B., Pratt, W. F., Tourangeau, R., Baldwin, A., & Rasinski, K. (1997). Effects of interview mode on sensitive questions in a fertility survey. In L. Lyberg, P. Biemer, M. Collins, E. de Leeuw, C. Dippo, N. Schwarz, & D. Trewin (Eds.), *Survey measurement and process quality* (pp. 311–329). New York: Wiley.

Jobe, J. B., Tourangeau, R., & Smith, A. F. (1993). Contributions of survey research to the understanding of memory. *Applied Cognitive Psychology, 7,* 567–584.

Jobe, J. B., White, A. A., Kelley, C. L., Mingay, D. J., Sanchez, M. J., & Loftus, E. F. (1990). Recall strategies and memory for health-care visits. *Milbank Memorial Fund Quarterly, 68,* 171–189.

Johnson, E., & Tversky, A. (1983). Affect, generalization, and the perception of risk. *Journal of Personality and Social Psychology, 45,* 20–31.

Johnson, L. D., & O'Malley, P. M. (1997). The recanting of earlier reported drug use by young adults. In L. Harrison & A. Hughes (Eds.), *The validity of self-reported drug use: Improving the accuracy of survey estimates* (pp. 59–80). Rockville, MD: National Institute on Drug Abuse.

Johnson, M. K. (1983). A multiple-entry, modular memory system. In G. H. Bower (Ed.), *The psychology of learning and motivation* (Vol. 17, pp. 81–123). Orlando, FL: Academic Press.

Johnson, M. K., Hashtroudi, S., & Lindsay, D. S. (1993). Source monitoring. *Psychological Bulletin, 144,* 3–28.

Johnson, T., Hougland, J., & Clayton, R. (1989). Obtaining reports of sensitive behaviors: A comparison of substance use reports from telephone and face-to-face interviews. *Social Science Quarterly, 70,* 174–183.

Jones, E. E., & Sigall, H. (1971). The bogus pipeline: A new paradigm for measuring affect and attitude. *Psychological Bulletin, 76*, 349–364.

Jones, E. F., & Forrest, J. D. (1992). Underreporting of abortion in surveys of U.S. women: 1976 to 1988. *Demography, 29*, 113–126.

Jonides, J., & Naveh-Benjamin, M. (1987). Estimating frequency of occurrence. *Journal of Experimental Psychology: Learning, Memory, & Cognition, 13*, 230–240.

Judd, C., Drake, R., Downing, J., & Krosnick, J. (1991). Some dynamic properties of attitude structures: Context-induced response facilitation and polarization. *Journal of Personality and Social Psychology, 60*, 193–202.

Judd, C., & Krosnick, J. (1982). Attitude centrality, organization, and measurement. *Journal of Personality and Social Psychology, 42*, 436–447.

Judd, C., & Milburn, J. (1980). The structure of attitude systems in the general public: Comparison of a structural equation model. *American Sociological Review, 46*, 660–669.

Just, M. A., & Carpenter, P. A. (1992). A capacity theory of comprehension. *Psychological Review, 99*, 122–149.

Juster, T. (1966). Consumer buying intentions and purchase probability. An experiment in survey design. *Journal of the American Statistical Association, 61*, 658–696.

Kahn, J. R., Lasbeek, W. D., & Hofferth, S. L. (1988). National estimates of teenage sexual activity: Evaluating the comparability of three national surveys. *Demography, 25*, 189–204.

Kalton, G., Collins, M., & Brook, L. (1978). Experiments in wording opinion questions. *Journal of the Royal Statistical Society (Series C), 27*, 149–161.

Kalton, G., & Miller, M. E. (1991). The seam effect with social security income in the Survey of Income and Program Participation. *Journal of Official Statistics, 7*, 235–245.

Kane, E. W., & Macaulay, L. J. (1993). Interviewer gender and gender attitudes. *Public Opinion Quarterly, 53*, 1–28.

Kaplan, K. (1972). On the ambivalence-indifference problem in attitude theory and measurement: A suggested modification of the semantic differential technique. *Psychological Review, 77*, 361–372.

Katz, D. (1942). Do interviewers bias poll results? *Public Opinion Quarterly, 6*, 248–268.

Keenan, J. M., & Baillet, S. D. (1980). Memory for personally and socially significant events. In R. S. Nickerson (Ed.), *Attention and performance, VIII* (pp. 651–670). Hillsdale, NJ: Erlbaum.

Kennickell, A. B. (1996). *Using range techniques with CAPI in the 1995 Survey of Consumer Finances.* Paper presented at the Joint Statistical Meetings, August 1995, Chicago.

Kenny, D. (1991). A general model of consensus and accuracy in interpersonal perception. *Psychological Review, 98*, 155–163.

Kiesler, S., & Sproull, L. (1986). Response effects in the electronic survey. *Public Opinion Quarterly, 50*, 402–413.

Kinder, D., & Sanders, L. (1990). Mimicking political debate with survey questions. *Social Cognition, 8*, 73–103.

Kirsh, I. S., Jungeblut, A., Jenkins, L., & Kolstad, A. (1993). *Adult literacy in America: A first look at the results of the National Adult Literacy Survey*. Washington, DC: National Center for Education Statistics.

Klassen, A., Williams, C., & Levitt, E. (1989). *Sex and morality in the U.S.: An empirical enquiry under the auspices of the Kinsey Institute*. Middletown, CT: Wesleyan University Press.

Knäuper, B. (1998a). *The impact of age and education on response order effects in attitude measurement*. Unpublished manuscript.

Knäuper, B. (1998b). Age differences in question and response order effects. In N. Schwarz, D. C. Park, B. Knäuper, & S. Sudman (Eds.), *Cognition, aging, and self-reports* (pp. 341–363). Philadelphia: Psychology Press.

Knowles, E. S. (1988). Item context effects on personality scales: Measuring changes the measure. *Journal of Personality and Social Psychology, 55*, 312–320.

Kolodner, J. (1985). Memory for experience. In G. H. Bower (Ed.), *The psychology of learning and motivation* (Vol. 19, pp. 1–57). Orlando, FL: Academic Press.

Krosnick, J. A. (1988). The role of attitude importance in social evaluation: A study of policy preferences, presidential candidate evaluations, and voting behavior. *Journal of Personality and Social Psychology, 55*, 196–210.

Krosnick, J. A. (1989). Attitude importance and attitude accessibility. *Personality and Social Psychology Bulletin, 15*, 295–306.

Krosnick, J. A. (1991). Response strategies for coping with the cognitive demands of attitude measures in surveys. *Applied Cognitive Psychology, 5*, 213–236.

Krosnick, J. A., & Abelson, R. P. (1992). The case for measuring attitude strength in surveys. In J. Tanur (Ed.), *Questions about questions: Inquiries into the cognitive bases of surveys* (pp. 177–203). New York: Russell Sage Foundation.

Krosnick, J. A., & Alwin, D. (1987). An evaluation of a cognitive theory of response-order effects in survey measurement. *Public Opinion Quarterly, 51*, 201–219.

Krosnick, J. A., & Berent, M. (1993). Comparisons of party identification and policy preferences: The impact of survey question format. *American Journal of Political Science, 37*, 941–964.

Krosnick, J. A., & Fabrigar, L. R. (1997). Designing rating scales for effective measurement in surveys. In L. Lyberg, P. Biemer, M. Collins, E. deLeeuw, C. Dippo, N. Schwarz, & D. Trewin (Eds.), *Survey measurement and process quality* (pp. 141–164). New York: Wiley.

Krosnick, J. A., & Schuman, H. (1988). Attitude intensity, importance, certainty, and susceptibility to response effects. *Journal of Personality and Social Psychology, 54*, 940–952.

Krueger, R. A. (1994). *Focus groups*. Newbury Park, CA: Sage.

Kubovy, M., & Psotka, J. (1976). The predominance of seven and the apparent spontaneity of numerical choices. *Journal of Experimental Psychology: Human Perception and Performance, 2*, 291–294.

Kurbat, M. A., Shevell, S. K., & Rips, L. J. (1998). A year's memories: Effects of the calendar on recalled autobiographical events. *Memory & Cognition, 26,* 532–552.

Lakoff, G. (1972). Hedges: A study in meaning criteria and the logic of fuzzy concepts. In *Papers from the Eighth Regional Meeting, Chicago Linguistic Society* (pp. 183–228). Chicago: Chicago Linguistic Society.

Landy, F. J., & Farr, J. L. (1980). Performance rating. *Psychological Bulletin, 87,* 72–107.

Lanier, A., Burrelli, J., & Fecso, R. (1998). *Web-based data collection in NSF surveys.* Paper presented at the Joint Statistical Meetings, August 1998, Dallas, TX.

Larsen, S. F. (1988). Remembering without experiencing: Memory for reported events. In U. Neisser & E. Winograd (Eds.), *Remembering reconsidered: Ecological and traditional approaches to the study of memory* (pp. 326–355). Cambridge: Cambridge University Press.

Larson, R., & Segal, G. (1995). *Knowledge of meaning.* Cambridge, MA: MIT Press.

Lau, R. R., Sears, D. O, & Centers, R. (1979). The "positivity bias" in evaluations of public figures: Evidence against instrument artifacts. *Public Opinion Quarterly, 43,* 347–358.

Laumann, E., Gagnon, J., Michael, R., & Michaels, S. (1994). *The social organization of sexuality: Sexual practices in the United States.* Chicago: University of Chicago Press.

Lavine, H., Huff, J. W., Wagner, S. H., & Sweeney, D. (1998). The moderating influence of attitude strength on the susceptibility to context effects in attitude surveys. *Journal of Personality and Social Psychology, 75,* 359–373.

Lehnert, W. (1978). *The process of question answering: A computer simulation of cognition.* Hillsdale, NJ: Erlbaum.

Lemmens, P., Tan, E. S., & Knibbe, R. A. (1992). Measuring quantity and frequency of drinking in a general population survey: A comparison of five indices. *Journal of Studies on Alcohol, 53,* 476–486.

Lessler, J. T., & Forsyth, B. H. (1995). A coding system for appraising questionnaires. In N. Schwarz & S. Sudman (Eds.), *Answering questions: Methodology for determining cognitive and communicative processes in survey research* (pp. 259–291). San Francisco: Jossey-Bass.

Lessler, J. T., & Kalsbeek, W. (1992). *Nonsampling error in surveys.* New York: Wiley.

Lessler, J. T., & O'Reilly, J. M. (1997). Mode of interview and reporting of sensitive issues: Design and implementation of audio computer-assisted self-interviewing. In L. Harrison & A. Hughes (Eds.), *The validity of self-reported drug use: Improving the accuracy of survey estimates* (pp. 366–382). Rockville, MD: National Institute on Drug Abuse.

Lessler, J. T., Tourangeau, P., & Salter, W. (1989). *Questionnaire design in the cognitive research laboratory: Results of an experimental prototype.* Vital and Health Statistics, Series 6, No. 1 (DHHS Pub. No. PHS 89–1076). Washington, DC: U.S. Government Printing Office.

Lewis, D. K. (1975). Adverbs of quantification. In E. L. Keenan (Ed.), *Formal semantics of natural language* (pp. 3–15). Cambridge: Cambridge University Press.

Lewis, D. K. (1979). Scorekeeping in a language game. *Journal of Philosophical Logic, 8,* 339–359.

Lichtenstein, S., Fischhoff, B., & Phillips, L. D. (1982). Calibration of probabilities: The state of the art to 1980. In D. Kahneman, P. Slovic, & A. Tversky (Eds.), *Judgment under uncertainty: Heuristics and biases* (pp. 306–334). Cambridge: Cambridge University Press.

Lichtenstein, S., Slovic, P., Fischhoff, B., Layman, M., & Combs, B. (1978). Judged frequency of lethal events. *Journal of Experimental Psychology: Human Learning and Memory, 4,* 551–578.

Linde, C. (1993). *Life stories: The creation of coherence.* Oxford: Oxford University Press.

Linton, M. (1975). Memory for real-world events. In D. A. Norman & D. E. Rumelhart (Eds.), *Explorations in cognition* (pp. 376–404). San Francisco: Freeman.

Linton, M. (1982). Transformations of memory in everyday life. In U. Neisser (Ed.), *Memory observed* (pp. 77–91). San Francisco: Freeman.

Linville, P. (1982). The complexity-extremity effect and age-based stereotyping. *Journal of Personality and Social Psychology, 42,* 193–210.

Linville, P., & Jones, E. (1980). Polarized appraisal of out-group members. *Journal of Personality and Social Psychology, 38,* 689–703.

Locander, W. B., Sudman, S., & Bradburn, N. M. (1976). An investigation of interview method, threat, and response distortion. *Journal of the American Statistical Association, 71,* 269–275.

Lodge, M., McGraw, K., & Stroh, P. (1989). An impression-driven model of candidate evaluation. *American Political Science Review, 83,* 399–419.

Loftus, E. F. (1979). *Eyewitness testimony.* Cambridge, MA: Harvard University Press.

Loftus, E. F. (1984). Protocol analysis of responses to survey recall questions. In T. Jabine, M. Straf, J. Tanur, & R. Tourangeau (Eds.), *Cognitive aspects of survey design: Building a bridge between disciplines* (pp. 61–64). Washington, DC: National Academy Press.

Loftus, E. F., & Fathi, D. C. (1985). Retrieving multiple autobiographical memories. *Social Cognition, 3,* 280–295.

Loftus, E. F., & Marburger, W. (1983). Since the eruption of Mt. St. Helens, has anyone beaten you up? Improving the accuracy of retrospective reports with landmark events. *Memory & Cognition, 11,* 114–120.

Loftus, E. F., Schooler, J. W., Boone, S. M., & Kline, D. (1987). Time went by so slowly: Overestimation of event duration by males and females. *Applied Cognitive Psychology, 1,* 3–13.

Loftus, E. F., Smith, K. D., Klinger, M. R., & Fiedler, J. (1992). Memory and mismemory for health events. In J. M. Tanur (Ed.), *Questions about questions: Inquiries into the cognitive basis of surveys* (pp. 102–137). New York: Russell Sage Foundation.

London, K., & Williams, L. (1990). *A comparison of abortion underreporting in an in-person interview and self-administered questionnaire*. Paper presented at the Annual Meeting of the Population Association of America, Toronto, May 3–5, 1990.

Lopes, L. (1982). *Toward a procedural theory of judgment*. Unpublished manuscript, University of Wisconsin-Madison.

Luker, K. (1984). *Abortion and the politics of motherhood*. Berkeley: University of California Press.

MacGregor, D. G., & Lichtenstein, S. (1991). Problem structuring aids for quantitative estimation. *Journal of Behavioral Decision Making, 4*, 101–116.

MacGregor, D. G., Lichtenstein, S., & Slovic, P. (1988). Structuring knowledge retrieval: An analysis of decomposed quantitative judgments. *Organizational Behavior and Human Decision Processes, 42*, 303–323.

Madigan, S. A. (1971). Modality and recall order interactions in short term memory for serial order. *Journal of Experimental Psychology, 87*, 294–296.

Magura, S., & Kang, S.-Y. (1997). The validity of self-reported cocaine use in two high risk populations. In L. Harrison & A. Hughes (Eds.), *The validity of self-reported drug use: Improving the accuracy of survey estimates* (pp. 227–246). Rockville, MD: National Institute on Drug Abuse.

Malt, B. C., & Johnson, E. C. (1992). Do artifact concepts have cores? *Journal of Memory & Language, 31*, 195–217.

Mandler, J., & Johnson, N. (1977). Remembrance of things parsed: Story structure and recall. *Cognitive Psychology, 9*, 111–151.

Manis, M., Biernat, M., & Nelson, T. F. (1991). Comparison and expectancy processes in human judgment. *Journal of Personality and Social Psychology, 61*, 203–211.

Marquis, K. H., & Moore, J. C. (1989). Response errors in SIPP: Preliminary results. *Proceedings, 1989 Annual Research Conference, U.S. Bureau of the Census* (Arlington, VA, March 19–22, 1989) (pp. 515–535). Washington, DC: U.S. Bureau of the Census.

Martin, E., & Polivka, A. E. (1995). Diagnostics for redesigning survey questionnaires: Measuring work in the Current Population Survey. *Public Opinion Quarterly, 59*, 547–567.

Martin, J., O'Muircheartaigh, C., & Curtice, J. (1993). The use of CAPI for attitude surveys: An experimental comparison with traditional methods. *Journal of Official Statistics, 9*, 641–661.

Martin, L. (1986). Set/reset: Use and disuse of concepts in impression formation. *Journal of Personality and Social Psychology, 51*, 493–504.

Martin, L., Seta, J., & Crelia, R. (1990). Assimilation and contrast as a function of people's willingness and ability to expend effort in forming an impression. *Journal of Personality and Social Psychology, 59*, 27–37.

Martini, A. (1989). Seam effect, recall bias, and the estimation of labor force transition rates from SIPP. *Proceedings of the Section on Survey Research Methods, American Statistical Association* (pp. 387–392). Alexandria, Va: American Statistical Association.

Mason, R., Carlson, J., & Tourangeau, R. (1995). Contrast effects and subtraction in part-whole questions. *Public Opinion Quarterly, 58*, 569–578.

Mathiowetz, N. A., & Duncan, G. J. (1988). Out of work, out of mind: Response errors in retrospective reports of unemployment. *Journal of Business and Economic Statistics, 6,* 221–229.

May, R., Anderson, R., & Blower, S. (1989). The epidemiology and transmission dynamics of HIV-AIDS. *Daedalus, 118,* 163–201.

McCauley, R. N. (1984). Inference and temporal coding in episodic memory. *Behavioral and Brain Sciences, 7,* 246–247.

McClelland, J. L., McNaughton, B. L., & O'Reilly, R. C. (1995). Why there are complementary learning systems in the hippocampus and neocortex: Insights from the successes and failures of connectionist models of learning and memory. *Psychological Review, 102,* 419–457.

McClendon, M., & O'Brien, D. (1988). Question-order effects on subjective well-being. *Public Opinion Quarterly, 52,* 351–364.

McCloskey, M., Wible, C., & Cohen, N. (1988). Is there a special flashbulb memory mechanism? *Journal of Experimental Psychology: General, 117,* 171–181.

McGill, A. (1989). Context effects in judgments of causation. *Journal of Personality and Social Psychology, 57,* 189–200.

McGuire, W. J. (1960). A syllogistic analysis of cognitive relationships. In M. Rosenberg, C. Hovland, W. McGuire, R. Abelson, & J. Brehm (Eds.), *Attitude organization and change* (pp. 65–111). New Haven, CT: Yale University Press.

McMullen, M. (1997). Affective contrast and assimilation in counterfactual thinking. *Journal of Experimental Social Psychology, 33,* 77–100.

McQueen, D. V. (1989). Comparison of results of personal interview and telephone surveys of behavior related to risk of AIDS: Advantages of telephone techniques. In *Conference Proceedings: Health Survey Research Methods* (pp. 247–252) (DHHS Pub. No. (PHS) 89–3447). Washington, D.C.: U.S. Department of Health and Human Services.

Means, B., & Loftus, E. (1991). When personal history repeats itself: Decomposing memories for recurring events. *Applied Cognitive Psychology, 5,* 297–318.

Means, B., Nigam, A., Zarrow, M., Loftus, E., & Donaldson, M. (1989). Autobiographical memory for health-related events. *Vital and Health Statistics,* Series 6, No. 2 (DHHS Pub. No. (PHS) 89–1077). Washington, DC: U.S. Government Printing Office.

Means, B., Swan, G. E., Jobe, J. B., & Esposito, J. L. (1991). An alternative approach to obtaining personal history data. In P. Biemer, R. Groves, L. Lyberg, N. Mathiowetz, & S. Sudman (Eds.), *Measurement errors in surveys* (pp. 167–184). New York: Wiley.

Means, B., Swan, G. E., Jobe, J. B., & Esposito, J. L. (1994). The effects of estimation strategies on the accuracy of respondents' reports of cigarette smoking. In N. Schwarz & S. Sudman (Eds.), *Autobiographical memory and the validity of retrospective reports* (pp. 107–119). Berlin: Springer-Verlag.

Menon, G. (1993). The effects of accessibility of information on judgments of behavioral frequencies. *Journal of Consumer Research, 20,* 431–460.

Menon, G. (1996). *Are the parts better than the whole? The effects of decompositional questions on judgments of frequent behaviors.* Paper presented at the Conference on the Science of Self-Report, Bethesda, MD, November 7, 1996.

Menon, G., Raghubir, P., & Schwarz, N. (1995). Behavioral frequency judgments: An accessibility-diagnosticity framework. *Journal of Consumer Research, 22,* 212–228.

Mieczkowski, T., Barzelay, D., Gropper, B., & Wish, E. (1991). Concordance of three measures of cocaine use in an arrestee population: Hair, urine, and self-report. *Journal of Psychoactive Drugs, 23,* 241–249.

Mieczkowski, T., & Newel, R. (1997). Patterns of concordance between hair assays and urinalysis for cocaine: Longitudinal analysis of probationers in Pinellas County, Florida. In L. Harrison & A. Hughes (Eds.), *The validity of self-reported drug use: Improving the accuracy of survey estimates* (pp. 161–199). Rockville, MD: National Institute on Drug Abuse.

Millar, M. G., & Tesser, A. (1986). Thought-induced attitude change: The effects of schema structure and commitment. *Journal of Personality and Social Psychology, 51,* 259–269.

Miller, P. B., & Groves, R. M. (1985) Matching survey responses to official records: An exploration of validity in victimization reporting. *Public Opinion Quarterly, 49,* 366–380.

Mingay, D. J., Shevell, S. K., Bradburn, N. M., & Ramirez, C. (1994). Self and proxy reports of everyday events. In N. Schwarz & S. Sudman (Eds.), *Autobiographical memory and validity of retrospective reports* (pp. 225–250). New York: Springer-Verlag.

Moore, J. C. (1988). Self-proxy response status and survey response quality. *Journal of Official Statistics, 4,* 155–172.

Moore, J. C., & Kasprzyk, D. (1984). Month-to-month recipiency turnover in the ISDP. *Proceedings of the Section on Survey Research Methods, American Statistical Association* (pp. 210–215). Alexandria, VA: American Statistical Association.

Moore, J. C., Stinson, L. L., & Welniak, E. J. (1999). Income reporting in surveys: Cognitive issues and measurement error. In M. G. Sirken, D. J. Herrmann, S. Schechter, N. Schwarz, J. M. Tanur, & R. Tourangeau (Eds.), *Cognition and Survey Research.* New York: Wiley.

Morris, M. (1993). Telling tails explain the discrepancy in sexual partner reports. *Nature, 365,* 437–440.

Morris, M. W., & Murphy, G. L. (1990). Converging operations on a basic level in event taxonomies. *Memory & Cognition, 18,* 407–418.

Mosher, W. D., & Duffer, A. P., Jr. (1994). *Experiments in survey data collection: The National Survey of Family Growth pretest.* Paper presented at the meeting of the Population Association of America, May, 1994, Miami, FL.

Moss, L., & Goldstein, H. (1979). *The recall method in social surveys.* London: University of London Institute of Education.

Mott, F. (1985). *Evaluation of fertility data and preliminary analytic results from the 1983 survey of the National Longitudinal Surveys of Work Experience of Youth.* A report to the National Institute of Child Health and Human Development by the Center for Human Resources Research, January 1985.

Moxey, L. M., & Sanford, A. J. (1993). *Communicating quantities.* Hillsdale, NJ: Erlbaum.

Mueller, J. (1973). *War, presidents, and public opinion.* New York: Wiley.

Murray, D., O'Connell, C., Schmid, L., & Perry, C. (1987). The validity of smoking self-reports by adolescents: A reexamination of the bogus pipeline procedure. *Addictive Behaviors, 12,* 7–15.

Myers, S. L. (1980). Why are crimes underreported? What is the crime rate? Does it really matter? *Social Science Quarterly, 61,* 23–42.

Narayan, S., & Krosnick, J. (1996). Education moderates some response effects in attitude measurement. *Public Opinion Quarterly, 60,* 58–88.

Nass, C., Fogg, B. J., & Moon, Y. (1996). Can computers be teammates? *International Journal of Human-Computer Studies, 45,* 669–678.

Nass, C., Moon, Y., & Green, N. (1997). Are machines gender neutral? Gender-stereotypic responses to computers with voices. *Journal of Applied Social Psychology, 27,* 864–876.

Nathan, G., Sirken, M., Willis, G., & Esposito, J. (1990). *Laboratory experiments on the cognitive aspects of sensitive questions.* Paper presented at the International Conference on Measurement Error in Surveys, Tucson, AZ, November, 1990.

Neisser, U., & Harsch, N. (1992). Phantom flashbulbs: False recollections of hearing the news about Challenger. In E. Winograd & U. Neisser (Eds.), *Affect and accuracy in recall* (pp. 9–31). Cambridge: Cambridge University Press.

Neter, J., & Waksberg, J. (1964). A study of response errors in expenditures data from household interviews. *Journal of the American Statistical Association, 59,* 17–55.

Newell, A. (1973). You can't play 20 questions with nature and win. In W. G. Chase (Ed.), *Visual information processing* (pp. 283–308). New York: Academic Press.

Newstead, S. E. (1988). Quantifiers as fuzzy concepts. In T. Zétényi (Ed.), *Fuzzy sets in psychology* (pp. 51–72). Amsterdam: Elsevier.

Newtson, D. (1973). Attribution and the unit of perception of ongoing behavior. *Journal of Personality and Social Psychology, 28,* 28–38.

Nicholls, W. L., II, Baker, R. P., & Martin, J. (1997). The effect of new data collection technologies on survey data quality. In L. Lyberg, P. Biemer, M. Collins, E. deLeeuw, C. Dippo, N. Schwarz, & D. Trewin (Eds.), *Survey measurement and process quality* (pp. 221–248). New York: Wiley.

Nisbett, R. E., & Wilson, T. D. (1977). Telling more than we can know: Verbal reports on mental processes. *Psychological Review, 84,* 231–259.

Norman, D. A. (1990). *The design of everyday things.* New York: Doubleday.

Nottenburg, G., & Shoben, E. J. (1980). Scripts as linear orders. *Journal of Experimental Social Psychology, 16,* 329–347.

O'Muircheartaigh, C. (1991). Simple response variance: Estimation and determinants. In P. Biemer, R. Groves, L. Lyberg, N. Mathiowetz, & S. Sudman (Eds.), *Measurement errors in surveys* (pp. 551–574). New York: Wiley.

O'Reilly, J., Hubbard, M., Lessler, J., Biemer, P., & Turner, C. (1994). Audio and video computer assisted self-interviewing: Preliminary tests of new technology for data collection. *Journal of Official Statistics, 10,* 197–214.

Ornstein, R. E. (1969). *On the experience of time.* New York: Penguin.

Osherson, D. N., Smith, E. E., & Shafir, E. B. (1986). Some origins of belief. *Cognition, 24,* 197–224.

Ostrom, T. M., & Upshaw, H. L. (1968). Psychological perspective and attitude change. In A. C. Greenwald, T. C. Brock, & T. M. Ostrom (Eds.), *Psychological foundations of attitudes* (pp. 65–111). New York: Academic Press.

Ottati, V., Riggle, E., Wyer, R., Schwarz, N., & Kuklinski, J. (1989). Cognitive and affective bases of opinion survey responses. *Journal of Personality and Social Psychology, 57,* 404–415.

Padian, N. S. (1990). Sexual histories of heterosexual couples with one HIV infected partner. *American Journal of Public Health, 80,* 990–991.

Panel on Privacy and Confidentiality as Factors in Survey Response. (1979). *Privacy and confidentiality as factors in survey response.* Washington, DC: National Academy of Sciences.

Parducci, A. (1965). Category judgment: A range-frequency model. *Psychological Review, 72,* 407–418.

Parducci, A. (1974). Contextual effects: A range-frequency analysis. In E. Carterette & M. Friedman (Eds.), *Handbook of perception: Psychophysical judgment and measurement.* (Vol. II, pp. 127–141). New York: Academic Press.

Patrick, D. L., Cheadle, A., Thompson, D. C., Diehr, P., Koepsell, T., & Kinne, S. (1994). The validity of self-reported smoking: A review and meta-analysis. *American Journal of Public Health, 84,* 1086–1093.

Payne, J. W., Bettman, J. R., & Johnson, E. J. (1993). *The adaptive decision maker.* Cambridge: Cambridge University Press.

Pelham, B. W., Sumarta, T. T., & Myaskovsky, L. (1994). The easy path from many to much: The numerosity heuristic. *Cognitive Psychology, 26,* 103–133.

Pepper, S. (1981). Problems in the quantification of frequency expressions. In D. W. Fiske (Ed.), *New directions for methodology of social and behavioral sciences* (Vol. 9, pp. 25–41). San Francisco: Jossey-Bass.

Petty, R. E., & Cacioppo, J. T. (1981). *Attitudes and persuasion: Classical and contemporary approaches.* Dubuque, IA: Brown.

Petty, R. E., & Cacioppo, J. T. (1984). The effects of involvement on responses to argument quality and quantity: Central and peripheral routes to persuasion. *Journal of Personality and Social Psychology, 46,* 69–81.

Petty, R. E., & Cacioppo, J. (1986). *Communication and persuasion: Central and peripheral routes to attitude change.* New York: Springer-Verlag.

Petty, R. E., & Wegener, D. T. (1993) Flexible correction processes in social judgment: Correcting for context-induced contrast. *Journal of Experimental Social Psychology, 29,* 136–165.

Phipps, P., & Tupek, A. (1990). *Assessing measurement errors in a touchtone recognition survey.* Paper presented at the International Conference on Measurement Errors in Surveys, November 1990, Tucson, AZ.

Pillemer, D. B., Goldsmith, L. R., Panter, A. T., & White, S. H. (1988). Very long-term memories of the first year in college. *Journal of Experimental Psychology: Learning, Memory, and Cognition, 14,* 709–715.

Pillemer, D. B., Krensky, L., Kleinman, S. N., Goldsmith, L. R., & White, S. H. (1991). Chapters in narratives: Evidence from oral histories of the first year in college. *Journal of Narrative and Life History, 1,* 3–14.

Pillemer, D. B., Rhinehart, E. D., & White, S. H. (1986). Memory of life transitions: The first year in college. *Human Learning, 5,* 109–123.

Poulton, E. C. (1989) *Bias in quantifying judgments*. Hillsdale, NJ: Erlbaum.

Poynter, W. D. (1983). Duration judgment and the segmentation of experience. *Memory & Cognition, 11*, 77–82.

Pratt, J. W., Raiffa, H., & Schlaifer, R. (1964). The foundations of decision under uncertainty: An elementary exposition. *Journal of the American Statistical Association, 59*, 353–375.

Presser, S. (1990). Can changes in context reduce vote overreporting in surveys? *Public Opinion Quarterly, 54*, 586–593.

Presser, S., & Blair, J. (1994). Survey pretesting: Do different methods produce different results? In P. V. Marsden (Ed.), *Sociological methodology* (Vol. 24, pp. 73–104). Beverly Hills, CA: Sage.

Presser, S., Blair, J., & Triplett, T. (1992). Survey sponsorship, response rates, and response effects. *Social Science Quarterly, 73*, 699–702.

Presser, S., & Stinson, L. (1998). Data collection mode and social desirability bias in self-reported religious attendance. *American Sociological Review, 63*, 137–145.

Presser, S., & Zhao, S. (1992). Attributes of questions and interviewers as determinants of interviewing performance. *Public Opinion Quarterly, 56*, 236–240.

Priester, J., & Petty, R. (1996). The gradual threshold model of ambivalence: Relating the positive and negative bases of attitudes to subjective ambivalence. *Journal of Personality and Social Psychology, 71*, 431–449.

Quadrel, M., Fischhoff, B., & Davis, W. (1993). Adolescent (in)vulnerability. *American Psychologist, 48*, 102–116.

Raden, D. (1985). Strength-related attitude dimensions. *Social Psychology Quarterly, 48*, 312–330.

Radford, A. (1997). *Syntactic theory and the structure of English: A minimalist approach*. Cambridge; England: Cambridge University Press.

Ramsey, F. (1931). Truth and probability. In R. B. Braithwaite (Ed.), *The foundations of mathematics and other logical essays* (pp. 156–198). London: Routledge and Kegan Paul.

Rasinski, K. A. (1989). The effect of question wording on support for government spending. *Public Opinion Quarterly, 53*, 388–394.

Rasinski, K. A., Baldwin, A. K., Willis, G. B., & Jobe, J. B. (1994). *Risk and loss perceptions associated with survey reporting of sensitive behaviors*. Paper presented at the annual meeting of the American Statistical Association, August 1994, Toronto, Canada.

Rasinski, K. A., Mingay, D., & Bradburn, N. M. (1994). Do respondents really "mark all that apply" on self-administered questions? *Public Opinion Quarterly, 58*, 400–408.

Rasinski, K. A., & Tourangeau, R. (1991). Psychological aspects of judgments about the economy. *Political Psychology, 12*, 27–40.

Reder, L. (1987). Strategy selection in question answering. *Cognitive Psychology, 19*, 90–138.

Reeves, B., & Nass, C. (1996). *The media equation: How people treat computers, television, and new media like real people and places*. Cambridge: CSLI and Cambridge University Press.

Reichenbach, H. (1947). *Elements of symbolic logic.* New York: Free Press.

Reiser, B. J., Black, J. B., & Abelson, R. P. (1985). Knowledge structures in the organization and retrieval of autobiographical memories. *Cognitive Psychology, 17,* 89–137.

Rifkin, A. (1985). Evidence for a basic level in event taxonomies. *Memory & Cognition, 13,* 538–556.

Rips, L. J. (1995). The current status of research on concept combination. *Mind & Language, 10,* 72–104.

Rips, L. J., Shoben, E. J., & Smith, E. E. (1973). Semantic distance and the verification of semantic relations. *Journal of Verbal Learning and Verbal Behavior, 12,* 1–20.

Robinson, J. A. (1986). Temporal reference systems and autobiographical memory. In D. C. Rubin (Ed.), *Autobiographical memory* (pp. 159–188). Cambridge: Cambridge University Press.

Robinson, J. A. (1992). First experience memories: Contexts and functions in personal histories. In M. A. Conway, D. C. Rubin, H. Spinnler, & W. A. Wagenaar (Eds.), *Theoretical perspectives on autobiographical memory* (pp. 223–240). Dordrecht, the Netherlands: Kluwer.

Roese, N. (1997). Counterfactual thinking. *Psychological Bulletin, 121,* 133–148.

Rokeach, M., & Ball-Rokeach, S. (1989). Stability and change in American value priorities, 1968–1981. *American Psychologist, 44,* 775–784.

Rosch, E. H. (1973). On the internal structure of perceptual and semantic categories. In T. E. Moore (Ed.), *Cognitive development and the acquisition of language* (pp. 111–144). New York: Academic Press.

Rosch, E. (1975). Cognitive reference points. *Cognitive Psychology, 7,* 532–547.

Rosch, E. H. (1978). Principles of categorization. In E. Rosch & B. B. Lloyd (Eds.), *Principles of categorization* (pp. 27–48). Hillsdale, NJ: Erlbaum.

Ross, M. (1988). The relation of implicit theories to the construction of personal histories. *Psychological Review, 96,* 341–357.

Ross, M., & Sicoly, F. (1979). Egocentric biases in availability and attribution. *Journal of Personality and Social Psychology, 37,* 322–336.

Rubin, D. C. (1982). On the retention function for autobiographical memory. *Journal of Verbal Learning and Verbal Behavior, 19,* 21–38.

Rubin, D. C., & Baddeley, A. D. (1989). Telescoping is not time compression: A model of the dating of autobiographical events. *Memory & Cognition, 17,* 653–661.

Rubin, D. C., & Wetzel, A. E. (1996). One hundred years of forgetting: A quantitative description of retention. *Psychological Review, 103,* 734–760.

Rubin, D. C., Wetzler, S. E., & Nebes, R. D. (1986). Autobiographical memory across the lifespan. In D. C. Rubin (Ed.), *Autobiographical memory* (pp. 202–221). Cambridge, England: Cambridge University Press.

Sadock, J. M. (1977). Truth and approximations. In K. Whistler, R. D., Van Valin, Jr., C. Chiarello, J. J. Jaeger, M. Petruck, H. Thompson, R. Javkin, & A. Woodbury (Eds.), *Proceedings of the third annual meeting of the Berkeley Linguistics Society* (pp. 430–439). Department of Linguistics, University of California, Berkeley.

Sadock, J. M. (1981). Almost. In P. Cole (Ed.), *Radical pragmatics* (pp. 257–272). New York: Academic Press.

Sanbonmatsu, D., & Fazio, R. (1990). The role of attitudes in memory-based decision-making. *Journal of Personality and Social Psychology, 59,* 614–622.

Sander, J., Conrad, F., Mullen, P., & Herrmann, D. (1992). Cognitive modeling of the survey interview. *1992 Proceedings of the Section on Survey Research Methods* (pp. 818–823). Alexandria, VA: American Statistical Association.

Saris, W., & Pijper, M. (1986). Computer assisted interviewing using home computers. *European Research, 14,* 144–150.

Schab, F. R., & Crowder, R. G. (1989). Accuracy of temporal coding: Auditory-visual comparisons. *Memory & Cognition, 17,* 384–397.

Schacter, D. L. (1987). Implicit memory: History and current status. *Journal of Experimental Psychology: Learning, Memory, and Cognition, 13,* 501–518.

Schaeffer, N. C. (1980). Evaluating race-of-interviewer effects in a national survey. *Sociological Methods and Research, 8,* 400–419.

Schaeffer, N. C. (1991a). Hardly ever or constantly? Group comparisons using vague quantifiers. *Public Opinion Quarterly, 55,* 395–423.

Schaeffer, N. C. (1991b). Conversation with a purpose – or conversation? Interaction in the standardized interview. In P. P. Biemer, R. M. Groves, L. E. Lyberg, N. A. Mathiowetz, & S. Sudman (Eds.), *Measurement error in surveys* (pp. 367–391). New York: Wiley.

Schaeffer, N. C. (1994). Errors of experience: Response errors in reports about child support and their implications for questionnaire design. In N. Schwarz & S. Sudman (Eds.), *Autobiographical memory and the validity of retrospective reports* (pp. 141–160). Berlin: Springer-Verlag.

Schaeffer, N. C. (in press). Asking questions about threatening topics: A selective overview. In A. Stone, J. Turkkan, C. Bachrach, V. Cain, J. Jobe, & H. Kurtzman (Eds.), *The science of self-report: Implications for research and practice*. Mahwah, NJ: Erlbaum.

Schaeffer, N. C., & Barker, K. (1995). *Issues in using bipolar response categories: Numeric labels and the middle category*. Paper presented at the annual meeting of the American Association for Public Opinion Research, Ft. Lauderdale, FL, May 23, 1995.

Schaeffer, N. C., & Bradburn, N. M. (1989). Respondent behavior in magnitude estimation. *Journal of the American Statistical Association, 84,* 402–413.

Schafer, R. (1992). *Retelling a life: Narration and dialogue in psychoanalysis*. New York: Basic Books.

Schank, R. C. (1975). *Conceptual information processing*. Amsterdam: North-Holland.

Schank, R. C. (1982). *Dynamic memory*. Cambridge: Cambridge University Press.

Schank, R. C., & Abelson, R. P. (1977). *Scripts, plans, goals, and understanding*. Hillsdale, NJ: Erlbaum.

Schober, M. (1999). Making sense of questions: An interactional approach. In M. G. Sirken, D. J. Herrmann, S. Schechter, N. Schwarz, J. M. Tanur, & R.

Tourangeau (Eds.), *Cognition and survey research* (pp. 77–93). New York: Wiley.

Schober, M. F., & Clark, H. H. (1989). Understanding by addressees and over-hearers. *Cognitive Psychology, 21,* 211–232.

Schober, M. F., & Conrad, F. G. (1997). Does conversational interviewing reduce survey measurement error? *Public Opinion Quarterly, 60,* 576–602.

Schober, S., Caces, M. F., Pergamit, M., & Branden, L. (1992). Effects of mode of administration on reporting of drug use in the National Longitudinal Survey. In C. Turner, J. Lessler, & J. Gfroerer (Eds.), *Survey measurement of drug use: Methodological studies* (pp. 267–276). Rockville, MD: National Institute on Drug Abuse.

Schooler, J. W., & Herrmann, D. J. (1992). There is more to episodic memory than just episodes. In M. A. Conway, D. C. Rubin, H. Spinnler, & W. A. Wagenaar (Eds.), *Theoretical perspectives on autobiographical memory* (pp. 241–262). Dordrecht, the Netherlands: Kluwer.

Schuman, H. (1972). Attitudes vs. actions versus attitudes vs. attitudes. *Public Opinion Quarterly, 36,* 347–354.

Schuman, H. (1992). Context effects: State of the art/state of the past. In N. Schwarz & S. Sudman (Eds.), *Context effects in social and psychological research* (pp. 35–47). New York: Springer-Verlag.

Schuman, H., & Converse, J. (1971). The effects of black and white interviewers on white respondents in 1968. *Public Opinion Quarterly, 35,* 44–68.

Schuman, H., & Ludwig, J. (1983). The norm of evenhandedness in surveys as in life. *American Sociological Review, 48,* 112–120.

Schuman, H., & Presser, S. (1981). *Questions and answers in attitude surveys: Experiments in question form, wording, and context.* New York: Academic Press.

Schwarz, N. (1990). Assessing frequency reports of mundane behaviors: Contributions of cognitive psychology to questionnaire construction. In C. Hendrick & M. Clark (Eds.), *Review of personality and social psychology* (Vol. 11, pp. 98–119). Beverly Hills, CA: Sage.

Schwarz, N. (1996). *Cognition and communication: Judgmental biases, research methods, and the logic of conversation.* Mahwah, NJ: Erlbaum.

Schwarz, N., & Bienas, J. (1990). What mediates the impact of response alternatives on frequency reports of mundane behaviors? *Applied Cognitive Psychology, 4,* 61–72.

Schwarz, N., & Bless, H. (1992a). Constructing reality and its alternatives: Assimilation and contrasts effects in social judgment. In L. L. Martin & A. Tesser (Eds.), *The construction of social judgment* (pp. 217–245). Hillsdale, NJ: Erlbaum.

Schwarz, N., & Bless, H. (1992b). Scandals and public trust in politicians: Assimilation and contrast effects. *Personality and Social Psychology Bulletin, 18,* 574–579.

Schwarz, N., Bless, H., & Bohner, G. (1991). Mood and persuasion: Affective states influence the procession of persuasive communications. *Advances in Experimental Social Psychology, 24,* 161–199.

Schwarz, N., Bless, H., Strack, F., Klumpp, G., Rittenauer-Schatka, H., & Simons, A. (1991). Ease of retrieval as information: Another look at the availability heuristic. *Journal of Personality and Social Psychology, 61,* 195–202.

Schwarz, N., & Clore, G. L. (1983). Mood, misattribution, and judgments of well-being: Informative and directive functions of affective states. *Journal of Personality and Social Psychology, 45,* 513–523.

Schwarz, N., & Hippler, H.-J. (1987). What response scales may tell your respondents: Information functions of response alternatives. In H.-J. Hippler, N. Schwarz, & S. Sudman (Eds), *Social information processing and survey methodology* (pp. 163–178). New York: Springer-Verlag.

Schwarz, N., & Hippler, H.-J. (1995). Subsequent questions may influence answers to preceding questions in mail surveys. *Public Opinion Quarterly, 59,* 93–97.

Schwarz, N., Hippler, H.-J., Deutsch, B., & Strack, F. (1985). Response categories: Effects on behavioral reports and comparative judgments. *Public Opinion Quarterly, 49,* 388–395.

Schwarz, N., Hippler, H., & Noelle-Neumann, E. (1991). A cognitive model of response-order effects in survey measurement. In N. Schwarz & S. Sudman (Eds.), *Context effects in social and psychological research* (pp. 187–201). New York: Springer-Verlag.

Schwarz, N., Knauper, B., Hippler, H.-J., Noelle-Neumann, E., & Clark, F. (1991). Rating scales: Numeric values may change the meaning of scale labels. *Public Opinion Quarterly, 55,* 618–630.

Schwarz, N., Strack, F., & Mai, H. (1991). Assimilation and contrast effects in part-whole question sequences: A conversational logic analysis. *Public Opinion Quarterly, 55,* 3–23.

Schwarz, N., & Sudman, S. (1992). *Context effects in social and psychological research.* New York: Springer-Verlag.

Searle, J. (1969). *Speech acts.* Cambridge: Cambridge University Press.

Sears, D. O. (1983). The person-positivity bias. *Journal of Personality and Social Psychology, 44,* 233–250.

Sheatsley, P. (1983). Questionnaire construction and item writing. In P. Rossi, J. Wright, & A. Anderson (Eds.), *Handbook of survey research* (pp. 195–230). New York: Academic Press.

Sheingold, K., & Tenney, Y. J. (1982). Memory for a salient childhood event. In U. Neisser (Ed.), *Memory observed* (pp. 201–212). New York: Freeman.

Shimizu, I., & Bonham, G. (1978). Randomized response technique in a national survey. *Journal of the American Statistical Association, 73,* 35–39.

Shum, M. (1997). Unpublished dissertation research, Northwestern University.

Shum, M. (1998). The role of temporal landmarks in autobiographical memory processes. *Psychological Bulletin, 124,* 423–442.

Shyrock, H. S., Siegel, J. S., & Stockwell, E. G. (1976). *The methods and materials of demography* (condensed ed.). San Diego, CA: Academic Press.

Siegel, A. W., Goldsmith, L. T., & Madson, C. R. (1982). Skill in estimation problems of extent and numerosity. *Journal for Research in Mathematics Education, 13,* 211–232.

Sikkel, D. (1985). Models for memory effects. *Journal of the American Statistical Association, 80,* 835–841.

Silver, B. D., Abramson, P. R., & Anderson, B. A. (1986). The presence of others and overreporting of voting in American national elections. *Public Opinion Quarterly, 50*, 228–239.

Simon, H. (1957). *Models of man.* New York: Wiley.

Simon, H. A., & Feigenbaum, E. A. (1964). Effects of similarity, familiarization, and meaningfulness in verbal learning. *Journal of Verbal Learning and Verbal Behavior, 3*, 385–396.

Singer, E., Hippler, H., & Schwarz, N. (1992). Confidentiality assurances in surveys: Reassurance or threat. *International Journal of Public Opinion Research, 4*, 256–268.

Singer, E., Mathiowetz, N., & Couper, M. (1993). The impact of privacy and confidentiality concerns on survey participation: The case of the 1990 U.S. census. *Public Opinion Quarterly, 57*, 465–482.

Singer, E., von Thurn, D., & Miller, E. (1995). Confidentiality assurances and response: A quantitative review of the experimental literature. *Public Opinion Quarterly, 59*, 66–77.

Singer, M. (1985). Mental processes of question answering. In A. C. Graesser & J. B. Black (Eds.), *The psychology of questions* (pp. 121–156). Hillsdale, NJ: Erlbaum.

Skowronski, J. J., Betz, A. L., Thompson, C. P., & Shannon, L. (1991). Social memory in everyday life: The recall of self-events and other-events. *Journal of Personality and Social Psychology, 60*, 831–843.

Skowronski, J. J., Betz, A. L., Thompson, C. P., & Walker, W. R. (1994). The impact of differing memory domains on event-dating processes in self and proxy reports. In N. Schwarz & S. Sudman (Eds.), *Autobiographical memory and the validity of retrospective reports* (pp. 217–234). New York: Springer-Verlag.

Smith, A. F. (1991). Cognitive processes in long-term dietary recall. *Vital and Health Statistics*, Series 6, No. 4 (DHHS Pub. No. PHS 92–1079). Washington, DC: U.S. Government Printing Office.

Smith, A. F., & Jobe, J. B. (1994). Validity of reports of long-term dietary memories: Data and a model. In N. Schwarz & S. Sudman (Eds.), *Autobiographical memory and the validity of retrospective reports* (pp. 121–140). Berlin: Springer-Verlag.

Smith, A. F., Jobe, J. B., & Mingay, D. (1991). Retrieval from memory of dietary information. *Applied Cognitive Psychology, 5*, 269–296.

Smith, E. R. (1999). New connectionist models of mental representation: Implications for survey research. In M. G. Sirken, D. J. Herrmann, S. Schechter, N. Schwarz, J. M. Tanur, & R. Tourangeau (Eds.), *Cognition and survey research* (pp. 251–266). New York: Wiley.

Smith, T. W. (1983). An experimental comparison between clustered and scattered scale items. *Social Psychology Quarterly, 46*, 163–168.

Smith, T. W. (1984a). Non-attitudes: A review and evaluation. In C. F. Turner & E. Martin (Eds.), *Surveying subjective phenomena* (Vol. 2, pp. 215–255). New York: Russell Sage Foundation.

Smith, T. W. (1984b), *A comparison of telephone and personal interviewing.*

GSS Methodological Report No. 28. Chicago: National Opinion Research Center.

Smith, T. W. (1986). *Conditional order effects.* GSS Methodological Report No. 20. Chicago: National Opinion Research Center.

Smith, T. W. (1987). That which we call welfare by any other name would smell sweeter: An analysis of the impact of question wording on response patterns. *Public Opinion Quarterly, 51,* 75–83.

Smith, T. W. (1988). *Ballot position: An analysis of context effects related to rotation design.* GSS Methodological Report No. 55. Chicago: National Opinion Research Center.

Smith, T. W. (1992a). Thoughts on the nature of context effects. In N. Schwarz & S. Sudman (Eds.), *Context effects in social and psychological research* (pp. 163–184). New York: Springer-Verlag.

Smith, T. W. (1992b). Discrepancies between men and women in reporting number of sexual partners: A summary from four countries. *Social Biology, 39,* 203–211.

Smith, T. W. (1996). American sexual behavior: Trends, socio-demographic differences, and risk behavior. In J. Garrison, M. D. Smith, & D. Bersharov (Eds.), *The demography of sexual behavior* (pp. 1–77). Menlo Park, CA: Kaiser Family Foundation.

Smith. T. W. (1997). The impact of the presence of others on a respondent's answers to questions. *International Journal of Public Opinion Research, 9,* 33–47.

Sonenstein, F. L., Pleck, J. H., & Ku, L. C. (1989). Sexual activity, condom use, and AIDS awareness among adolescent males. *Family Planning Perspectives, 21,* 152–158.

Sperber, D., & Wilson, D. (1986). *Relevance: Communication and cognition.* Cambridge, MA: Harvard University Press.

Srull, T. K., & Wyer, R. S. (1979). The role of category accessibility in the interpretation of information about persons: Some determinants and implications. *Journal of Personality and Social Psychology, 37,* 1660–1672.

Stalnaker, R. C. (1974). Pragmatic presuppositions. In M. K. Munitz & P. K. Unger (Eds.), *Semantics and philosophy* (pp. 197–214). New York: New York University Press.

Stapel, D. A., Martin, L. L., & Schwarz, N. (1998). The smell of bias: What instigates correction processes in social judgments? *Personality and Social Psychology Bulletin, 24,* 797–806.

Stefanowska, M. (1977). The feeling of "cultural inadequacy" and the validity of respondent's answers to questions about reading books. *Studia Socjologiczne, 2,* 133–143.

Sternberg, S. (1969). Memory-scanning: Mental processes revealed by reaction time experiments. *Acta Psychologica, 60,* 276–315.

Stevens, S. S. (1975). *Psychophysics: Introduction to its perceptual, neural, and social prospects.* New York:Wiley.

Stinson, L. L. (1997). *Final report: The subjective assessment of income and expenses: Cognitive test results.* Washington, DC: Bureau of Labor Statistics.

Strack, F. (1992). Order effects in survey research: Activation and informative functions of preceding questions. In N. Schwarz & S. Sudman (Eds.), *Context effects in social and psychological research* (pp. 23–34). New York: Springer-Verlag.

Strack, F., & Martin, L. (1987). Thinking, judging, and communicating: A process account of context effects in attitude surveys. In H. Hippler, N. Schwarz, & S. Sudman (Eds.), *Social information processing and survey methodology* (pp. 123–148). New York: Springer-Verlag.

Strack, F., Martin, L., & Schwarz, N. (1988). Priming and communication: The social determinants of information use in judgments of life satisfaction. *European Journal of Social Psychology, 18*, 429–442.

Strack, F., Schwarz, N., & Gschneidinger, E. (1985). Happiness and reminiscing: The role of time perspective, affect, and mode of thinking. *Journal of Personality and Social Psychology, 47*, 1460–1469.

Strack, F., Schwarz, N., & Wänke, M. (1991). Semantic and pragmatic aspects of context effects in social and psychological research. *Social Cognition, 9*, 111–125.

Stulginskas, J. V., Verreault, R., & Pless, I. B. (1985). A comparison of observed and reported restraint use by children and adults. *Accident Analysis & Prevention, 17*, 381–386.

Suchman, L., & Jordan, B. (1990). Interactional troubles in face-to-face survey interviews. *Journal of the American Statistical Association, 85*, 232–241.

Suchman, L., & Jordan, B. (1992). Validity and the collaborative construction of meaning in face-to-face surveys. In J. M. Tanur (Ed.), *Questions about questions: Inquiries into the cognitive bases of surveys* (pp. 241–267). New York: Russell Sage Foundation.

Sudman, S., Bickart, B., Blair, J., & Menon, G. (1994). The effects of level of participation on reports of behavior and attitudes by proxy reporters. In N. Schwartz & S. Sudman (Eds.), *Autobiographical memory and validity of retrospective reports* (pp. 251–265). New York: Springer-Verlag.

Sudman, S., & Bradburn, N. (1973). Effects of time and memory factors on response in surveys. *Journal of the American Statistical Association, 68*, 805–815.

Sudman, S., & Bradburn, N. (1974). *Response effects in surveys: A review and synthesis.* Chicago: Aldine.

Sudman, S., & Bradburn, N. (1982). *Asking questions: A practical guide to questionnaire design.* San Francisco: Jossey-Bass.

Sudman, S., Bradburn, N., & Schwarz, N. (1996). *Thinking about answers: The application of cognitive processes to survey methodology.* San Francisco: Jossey-Bass.

Sudman, S., Finn, A., & Lannom, L. (1984). The use of bounded recall procedures in single interviews. *Public Opinion Quarterly, 48*, 520–524.

Tanfer, K., & Cubbins, L. A. (1992). Coital frequency among single women: Normative constraints and situational opportunities. *Journal of Sex Research, 29*, 221–250.

Tangney, J. P., & Fischer, K. (1995). *Self-conscious emotions: Shame, guilt, embarrassment, and pride.* New York: Guilford Press.

Tangney, J. P., Miller, R. W., Flicker, L., & Barlow, D. H. (1996). Are shame, guilt, and embarrassment distinct emotions? *Journal of Personality and Social Psychology, 70*, 1256–1269.

Tannenhaus, M. K., Boland, J. E., Mauner, G. A., & Carlson, G. N. (1993). More on combinatory lexical information: Thematic structure in parsing and interpretation. In G. Altmann & R. Shillcock (Eds.), *Cognitive models of speech processing* (pp. 297–319). Hillsdale, NJ: Erlbaum.

Tesser, A. (1978). Self-generated attitude change. In L. Berkowitz (Ed.), *Advances in experimental social psychology* (Vol. 11, pp. 289–338). New York: Academic Press.

Tesser, A., & Leone, C. (1977). Cognitive schemas and thoughts as determinants of attitude change. *Journal of Experimental Social Psychology, 13*, 340–356.

Tesser, A., & Rosen, S. (1975). The reluctance to transmit bad news. In L. Berkowitz (Ed.), *Advances in experimental social psychology* (Vol. 8, pp. 193–232). New York: Academic Press.

Thomas, E. A. C., & Brown, I., Jr. (1974). Time perception and the filled-duration illusion. *Perception & Psychophysics, 16*, 449–458.

Thompson, C. P. (1982). Memory for unique personal events: The roommate study. *Memory and Cognition, 10*, 324–332.

Thompson, C. P., Skowronski, J. J., Larsen, S. F., & Betz, A. L. (1996). *Autobiographical memory.* Mahwah, NJ: Erlbaum.

Thornberry, O., & Massey, J. (1988). Trends in United States telephone coverage across time and subgroups. In R. Groves, P. Biemer, L. Lyberg, J. Massey, W. Nicholls, & J. Waksberg (Eds.), *Telephone survey methodology* (pp. 25–49). New York: John Wiley.

Thurstone, L. (1927). A law of comparative judgment. *Psychological Review, 34*, 273–286.

Tourangeau, R. (1984). Cognitive science and survey methods. In T. Jabine, M. Straf, J. Tanur, & R. Tourangeau (Eds.), *Cognitive aspects of survey design: Building a bridge between disciplines* (pp. 73–100). Washington, DC: National Academy Press.

Tourangeau, R. (1987). Attitude measurement: A cognitive perspective. In H. Hippler, N. Schwarz, & S. Sudman (Eds.), *Social information processing and survey methodology* (pp. 149–162). New York: Springer-Verlag.

Tourangeau, R. (1990). Comment. *Journal of the American Statistical Association, 85*, 250–251.

Tourangeau, R. (1992). Context effects on attitude responses: The role of retrieval and memory structures. In N. Schwarz & S. Sudman (Eds.), *Context effects in social and psychological research* (pp. 35–47). New York: Springer-Verlag.

Tourangeau, R., & Rasinski, K. (1986). *Context effects in attitude surveys.* Unpublished manuscript.

Tourangeau, R., & Rasinski, K. (1988). Cognitive processes underlying context effects in attitude measurement. *Psychological Bulletin, 103*, 299–314.

Tourangeau, R., Rasinski, K., & Bradburn, N. (1991). Measuring happiness in surveys: A test of the subtraction hypothesis. *Public Opinion Quarterly, 55*, 255–266.

Tourangeau, R., Rasinski, K., Bradburn, N., & D'Andrade, R. (1989a). Carry-over effects in attitude surveys. *Public Opinion Quarterly, 53*, 495–524.

Tourangeau, R., Rasinski, K., Bradburn, N., & D'Andrade, R. (1989b). Belief accessibility and context effects in attitude measurement. *Journal of Experimental Social Psychology, 25*, 401–421.

Tourangeau, R., Rasinski, K., & D'Andrade, R. (1991). Attitude structure and belief accessibility. *Journal of Experimental Social Psychology, 27*, 48–75.

Tourangeau, R., Rasinski, K., Jobe, J. B., Smith, T. W., & Pratt, W. (1997). Sources of error in a survey of sexual behavior. *Journal of Official Statistics, 13*, 341–365.

Tourangeau, R., Shapiro, G., Kearney, A., & Ernst, L. (1997). Who lives here? Survey undercoverage and household roster questions. *Journal of Official Statistics, 13*, 1–18.

Tourangeau, R., & Smith, T. W. (1996). Asking sensitive questions: The impact of data collection mode, question format, and question context. *Public Opinion Quarterly, 60*, 275–304.

Tourangeau, R., & Smith, T. W. (1998). Collecting sensitive information with different modes of data collection. In M. P. Couper, R. P. Baker, J. Bethlehem, C. Z. Clark, J. Martin, W. L. Nicholls, & J. O'Reilly (Eds.), *Computer assisted survey information collection* (pp. 431–454). New York: Wiley.

Tourangeau, R., Smith, T. W., & Rasinski, K. A. (1997). Motivation to report sensitive behaviors on surveys: Evidence from a bogus pipeline experiment. *Journal of Applied Social Psychology, 27*, 209–222.

Traugott, M. W., & Katosh, J. P. (1979). Response validity in surveys of voting behavior. *Public Opinion Quarterly, 43*, 359–377.

Trope, Y. (1986). Identification and inferential processes in dispositional attribution. *Psychological Review, 93*, 239–257.

Tulving, E. (1983). *Elements of episodic memory*. Oxford: Oxford University Press.

Tulving, E. (1984). Relations among components and processes of memory. *Behavioral and Brain Sciences, 7*, 257–263.

Tulving, E. (1985). Memory and consciousness. *Canadian Psychology, 26*, 1–12.

Tulving, E., & Thomson, D. M. (1973). Encoding specificity and retrieval processes in episodic memory. *Psychological Review, 80*, 352–373.

Turner, C. F., Ku, L., Rogers, S. M., Lindberg, L. D., Pleck, J. H., & Sonenstein, F. L. (1998). Adolescent sexual behavior, drug use, and violence: Increased reporting with computer survey technology. *Science, 280*, 867–873.

Turner, C. F., Lessler, J. T., & Devore, J. (1992). Effects of mode of administration and wording on reporting of drug use. In C. Turner, J. Lessler, & J. Gfroerer (Eds.), *Survey measurement of drug use: Methodological studies* (pp. 177–220). Rockville, MD: National Institute on Drug Abuse.

Turner, C. F., Lessler, J. T., & Gfroerer, J. (1992). *Survey measurement of drug use: Methodological studies*. Rockville, MD: National Institute on Drug Abuse.

Turner, C. F., & Martin, E. (1984). *Surveying subjective phenomena*. New York: Russell Sage Foundation.

Tversky, A., & Kahneman, D. (1973). Availability: A heuristic for judging frequency and probability. *Cognitive Psychology, 5*, 207–232.

Tversky, A., & Kahneman, D. (1974). Judgment under uncertainty: Heuristics and biases. *Science, 185*, 1124–1131.

Tversky, A., & Kahneman, D. (1979). Prospect theory: An analysis of decision under risk. *Econometrica, 47*, 263–291.

Tversky, A., & Kahneman, D. (1982). Judgments of and by representativeness. In D. Kahneman, P. Slovic, & A. Tversky (Eds), *Judgment under uncertainty: Heuristics and biases* (pp. 84–98). Cambridge: Cambridge University Press.

Tversky, A., & Koehler, D. J. (1994). Support theory: A nonextensional representation of subjective probability. *Psychological Review, 101*, 547–567.

Tversky, B., & Tuchin, M. (1989). A conciliation of the evidence in eyewitness testimony: Comments on McCloskey and Zaragoza. *Journal of Experimental Psychology: General, 118*, 86–91.

Udry, J. R. (1980). Changes in the frequency of marital intercourse from panel data. *Archives of Sexual Behavior, 9*, 319–325.

Underwood, B. J., Zimmerman, J., & Freund, J. S. (1971). Retention of frequency information with observations on recognition and recall. *Journal of Experimental Psychology, 87*, 149–162.

Underwood, G. (1975). Attention and the perception of duration during encoding and retrieval. *Perception, 4*, 291–296.

Upchurch, D. M., Weisman, C. S., Shepherd, M., Brookmeyer, R., Fox, R., Celentano, D. D., Colletta, L., & Hook, E. W., III. (1991). Interpartner reliability of reporting of recent sexual behaviors. *American Journal of Epidemiology, 134*, 1159–1166.

Usher, J. A., & Neisser, U. (1993). Childhood amnesia and the beginnings of memory for four early life events. *Journal of Experimental Psychology: General, 122*, 155–165.

Von Neumann, J., & Morgenstern, O. (1947). *Theory of games and economic behavior* (2nd ed.). Princeton, NJ: Princeton University Press.

Wadsworth, J., Johnson, A. M., Wellings, K., & Field, J. (1996). What's in a mean? An examination of the inconsistency between men and women in reporting sexual partnerships. *Journal of the Royal Statistical Society, 159*, 111–123.

Wagenaar, W. A. (1986). My memory: A study of autobiographical memory over six years. *Cognitive Psychology, 18*, 225–252.

Walker, J. H., Sproull, L., & Subramani, M. (1994). Using a human face in an interface. *Proceedings of the Conference on Human Factors in Computers '94*, (pp. 85–91). Boston: ACM.

Wallsten, T. S., Budescu, D. V., & Zwick, R. (1992). Comparing the calibration and coherence of numerical and verbal probability judgments. *Management Science, 39*, 176–190.

Warner, S. (1965). Randomized response: A survey technique for eliminating evasive answer bias. *Journal of the American Statistical Association, 60*, 63–69.

Warriner, G. K., McDougall, G. H. G., & Claxton, J. D. (1984). Any data or none at all? Living with inaccuracies in self-reports of residential energy consumption. *Environment and Behavior, 16,* 502–526.

Waterton, J., & Duffy, J. (1984). A comparison of computer interviewing techniques and traditional methods for the collection of self-report alcohol consumption data in a field survey. *International Statistical Review, 52,* 173–182.

Waterworth, J. A. (1985). Memory mechanisms and the psychophysical scaling of duration. *Perception, 14,* 81–92.

Watkins, M. J., & Kerkar, S. P. (1985). Recall of a twice-presented item without recall of either presentation. *Journal of Memory and Language, 24,* 666–678.

Watkins, M. J., & LeCompte, D. C. (1991). Inadequacy of recall as a basis for frequency knowledge. *Journal of Experimental Psychology: Learning, Memory, & Cognition, 17,* 1161–1176.

Wedell, D. H., Parducci, A., & Geiselman, R. E. (1987). A formal analysis of ratings of physical attractiveness: Successive contrast and simultaneous assimilation. *Journal of Experimental Social Psychology, 23,* 230–249.

Weeks, M. (1992). Computer-assisted survey information collection: A review of CASIC methods and their implications for survey operations. *Journal of Official Statistics, 9,* 445–465.

Wegener, D. T., & Petty, R. E. (1995). Flexible correction processes in social judgment: The role of naive theories in corrections for perceived bias. *Journal of Personality and Social Psychology, 68,* 36–51.

Wells, G., & Gavanski, I. (1989). Mental simulation of causality. *Journal of Personality and Social Psychology, 56,* 161–169.

Whisman, M. A., & Allan, L. E. (1996). Attachment and social cognition theories of romantic relationships: Convergent or complementary perspectives. *Journal of Social and Personal Relationships, 13,* 263–278.

White, R. T. (1982). Memory for personal events. *Human Learning, 1,* 171–183.

Whitten, W. B., & Leonard, J. M. (1981). Directed search through autobiographical memory. *Memory & Cognition, 9,* 566–579.

Whittlesea, B W. A. (1993). Illusions of familiarity. *Journal of Experimental Psychology: Learning, Memory, and Cognition, 19,* 1235–1253.

Wickelgren, W. A. (1973). The long and short of memory. *Psychological Bulletin, 80,* 425–438.

Wickelgren, W. A. (1974). Single-trace fragility theory of memory dynamics. *Memory & Cognition, 2,* 775–780.

Williams, M. D., & Hollan, J. D. (1981). The process of retrieval from very long-term memory. *Cognitive Science, 5,* 87–119.

Willis, G. (1997a). The use of the psychological laboratory to study sensitive topics. In L. Harrison & A. Hughes (Eds.), *The validity of self-reported drug use: Improving the accuracy of survey estimates* (pp. 416–438). NIDA Monograph 167. Rockville, MD: National Institute on Drug Abuse.

Willis, G. (1997b). *NCHS Cognitive Interviewing Project: General coding scheme for questionnaire problems.* Hyattsville, MD: National Center for Health Statistics.

Willis, G., Brittingham, A., Lee, L., Tourangeau, R., & Ching, P. (1999). *Response errors in surveys of children's immunizations.*Vital and Health Statistics, Series 6, Number 8. Hyattsville, MD: National Center for Health Statistics.

Willis, G., DeMaio, T., & Harris-Kojetin, B. (1999). Is the bandwagon headed to the methodological promised land? Evaluating the validity of cognitive interviewing techniques. In M. Sirken, D. J. Herrmann, S. Schechter, N. Schwarz, J. Tanur, & R. Tourangeau (Eds.), *Cognition and survey research* (pp. 133–154). New York: Wiley.

Willis, G., Rasinski, K., & Baldwin, A. (1998). *Cognitive research on responses to sensitive survey questions* (Working Paper Series, No. 24). Hyattsville, MD: National Center for Health Statistics, Cognitive Methods Staff.

Willis, G., Royston, P., & Bercini, D. (1991). The use of verbal report methods in the development and testing of survey questionnaires. *Applied Cognitive Psychology, 5,* 251–267.

Willis, G. B., & Schechter, S. (1997). Evaluation of cognitive interviewing techniques: Do the results generalize to the field? *Bulletin de Methodologie Sociologique, 55,* 40–66.

Willis, G., Sirken, M., & Nathan, G. (1994). *The cognitive aspects of responses to sensitive survey questions* (Working Paper Series, No. 9). Hyattsville, MD: National Center for Health Statistics, Cognitive Methods Staff.

Wilson, T. D., & Brekke (1994). Mental contamination and mental correction: Unwanted influences on judgments and evaluation. *Psychological Bulletin, 116,* 117–142.

Wilson, T. D., & Dunn, D. (1986). Effects of introspection on attitude–behavior consistency: Analyzing reasons versus focusing on feelings. *Journal of Experimental Social Psychology, 22,* 249–263.

Wilson, T. D., & Hodges, S. (1992). Attitudes as temporary constructions. In L. Martin & A. Tesser (Eds.), *The construction of social judgments* (pp. 37–66). New York: Springer-Verlag.

Wilson, T. D., Hodges, S., & LaFleur, S. (1995). Effects of introspecting about reasons: Inferring attitudes from accessible thoughts. *Journal of Personality and Social Psychology, 69,* 16–28.

Wilson, T. D., Houston, C. E., Etling, K. M., & Brekke, N. (1996). A new look at anchoring effects: Basic anchoring and its antecedents. *Journal of Experimental Psychology: General, 125,* 387–402.

Wilson, T. D., Kraft, D., & Dunn, D. (1989). The disruptive effects of explaining attitudes: The moderating effect of knowledge about the attitude object. *Journal of Experimental Social Psychology, 25,* 379–400.

Wilson, T. D., LaFleur, S. J., & Anderson, D. A. (1995). The validity and consequences of verbal reports about attitudes. In N. Schwarz & S. Sudman (Eds.), *Answering questions: Methodology for determining cognitive and communicative processes in survey research* (pp. 91–114). San Francisco: Jossey-Bass.

Woodberry, R. (1997). *The missing fifty percent: Accounting for the gap between survey estimates and head counts of church attendance.* Master's thesis, Sociology Department, University of Notre Dame, South Bend, IN.

Woodrow, H. (1951). Time perception. In S. S. Stevens (Ed.), *Handbook of experimental psychology* (pp. 1224–1236). New York: Wiley.

Wyer, R., & Hartwick, J. (1984). The recall and use of belief statements as bases for judgments: Some determinants and implications. *Journal of Experimental Social Psychology, 20,* 65–85.

Wyer, R., & Rosen, N. (1972). Some further evidence for the Socratic effect using a subjective probability model of cognitive organization. *Journal of Personality and Social Psychology, 24,* 420–424.

Wyner, G. A. (1980). Response errors in self-reported number of arrests. *Sociological Methods and Research, 9,* 161–177.

Yammarino, F. J., Skinner, S. J., & Childers, T. L. (1991). Understanding mail survey response behavior. *Public Opinion Quarterly, 55,* 613–639.

Young, N. (1989). Wave-seam effects in the SIPP. *Proceedings of the Section on Survey Research Methods, American Statistical Association* (pp. 393–398). Alexandria, VA: American Statistical Association.

Yzerbyt, V. Y., Schadron, G., Leyens, J.-P., & Rocher, S. (1994). Social judgeability: The impact of meta-informational cues on the use of stereotypes. *Journal of Personality and Social Psychology, 66,* 48–55.

Zajonc, R. B. (1968). Cognitive theories in social psychology. In G. Lindzey & E. Aronson (Eds.), *Handbook of social psychology* (2nd ed., Vol. 1, pp. 320–411). Reading, MA: Addison-Wesley.

Zakay, D. (1990). The evasive art of subjective time measurement: Some methodological dilemmas. In R. A. Block (Ed.), *Cognitive models of psychological time* (pp. 59–84). Hillsdale, NJ: Erlbaum.

Zakay, D., Tsal, Y., Moses, M., & Shahar, I. (1994). The role of segmentation in prospective and retrospective time estimation processes. *Memory & Cognition, 22,* 344–351.

Zaller, J. R. (1992). *The nature and origins of mass opinion.* Cambridge: Cambridge University Press.

Zaller, J., R., & Feldman, S. (1992). A simple theory of the survey response: Answering questions versus revealing preferences. *American Journal of Political Science, 36,* 579–616.

Zaragoza, M. S., & McCloskey, M. (1989). Misleading postevent information and the memory impairment hypothesis: Comment on Belli and reply to Tversky and Tuchin. *Journal of Experimental Psychology: General, 118,* 92–99.

Author Index

Abbott, V., 69
Abelson, R., 69, 78, 79, 81, 172,
    202, 273, 274
Abernathy, J., 272
Abramson, P., 273, 274, 280, 287
Aguinis, H., 271
Allan, L., 117, 276
Allen, J., 3, 36, 110
Allport, G., 167
Alwin, D., 17, 249, 250, 251, 252,
    293, 304, 335
Anderson, B., 273, 274, 280, 287
Anderson, D., 179, 208
Anderson, J., 14, 32, 77, 87, 91, 207
Anderson, N., 11, 13, 181, 210
Anderson, R., 276
Anglin, D., 270, 334
Aquilino, W., 270, 281, 294, 296
Armstrong, J., 95, 162, 163
Armstrong, S., 46
Ayidiya, S., 200

Bachrach, C., 276
Baddeley, A., 77, 84, 115, 132, 133
Bahrick, H., 83, 84
Bahrick, P., 83, 84
Bailar, B., 319
Baillet, S., 66
Baker, R., 299, 300, 301, 303, 308
Bal, D., 269
Baldwin, A., 233, 235, 265, 271,
    281, 282, 283, 284, 291
Ball-Rokeach, S., 174

Bargh, J., 169
Barker, K., 243
Barlow, D., 285, 306
Barsalou, L., 69, 70, 78, 79, 96,
    115
Bartlett, F., 22
Barzelay, D., 270
Bassili, J., 14, 217, 325–326, 331
Bauman, K., 271
Baumgartner, R., 261, 307
Beatty, P., 66
Begg, I., 139
Bekerian, D., 80
Bell, C., 83, 84
Bell, K., 285, 286, 287
Belli, R., 42, 274
Belson, W., 24, 25
Bercini, D., 19, 323
Berent, M., 249
Bergman, L., 303
Berry, C., 269
Bershad, M., 319, 320, 321, 340
Bettman, J., 8
Betz, A., 11, 67, 91, 92, 112, 114,
    115, 116, 121, 133, 244
Bickart, B., 22, 65, 66, 117, 147,
    151, 328, 329
Biederman, A., 313
Biemer, P., 300, 302, 308, 314, 320
Bienas, J., 248
Biernat, M., 212, 221, 222, 228
Binnick, R., 101
Binson, D., 276

Bishop, G., 170, 200, 207, 216, 246, 310, 311
Bjork, R., 63
Black, J., 69, 78, 79, 81, 326
Blair, E., 12, 21, 86, 94, 139, 146, 148, 149, 151, 152, 154, 155, 156, 159, 160, 163, 337
Blair, J., 22, 65, 66, 147, 151, 307, 328, 329, 330, 331, 332, 333
Bless, H., 150, 156, 160, 201, 207, 208, 209, 211, 212, 216, 221, 224, 225, 226, 337
Block, R., 118
Blower, S., 276
Bohner, G., 150
Boland, J., 37
Bolinger, D., 26, 30
Bolton, R., 328, 329
Boltz, M., 118
Bommareddy, S., 32
Bonham, G., 272
Boone, S., 118
Borg, I., 119
Bower, G., 69
Bowker, D., 210
Bradburn, N., 2, 22, 42, 47, 49, 60, 66, 81, 83, 86, 87, 88, 92, 94, 120, 121, 129–130, 132, 133, 137, 145, 146, 147, 174, 179, 180, 182, 197, 199, 201, 203, 204, 205, 206, 207, 209, 224, 225, 228, 234, 235, 236, 237, 238, 251, 257, 259, 260, 268, 269, 280, 295, 299, 300, 301, 303, 308, 314, 315, 335, 337
Branden, L., 270, 280, 296
Bransford, J., 202
Breckler, S., 185
Brekke, N., 144, 207
Brewer, M., 324
Brewer, W., 68, 84, 85, 96
Brittingham, A., 66, 146, 149, 152, 269, 271, 339
Brook, L., 203
Brookmeyer, R., 276
Brooks, C., 319
Brown, D., 216, 337

Brown, I., Jr., 118
Brown, N., 10, 79, 88, 137, 146, 147, 149, 150, 151, 152, 154, 155, 156, 157, 278, 337
Brown, P., 287
Bruce, D., 142, 145
Bruner, J., 71
Brunner, G., 307
Budescu, D., 47, 162
Burrelli, J., 291
Burt, C., 112–113, 114, 115, 119, 120, 133
Burton, S., 12, 21, 86, 94, 139, 146, 149, 151, 152, 154, 155, 156, 157, 160, 163, 337

Caces, M., 270, 280, 296
Cacioppo, J., 7, 167, 252, 307
Calder, B., 141
Camburn, D., 335
Campanelli, P., 351
Canchola, J., 276
Cannell, C., 5, 6, 7, 16, 17, 85, 92, 94, 301, 311, 314
Card, J., 269
Carlson, G., 37
Carlson, J., 176, 180, 203, 209
Carpenter, P., 25, 36, 40
Carroll, S., 307
Carter, W., 262
Cashman, E., 137, 146, 147, 150, 151, 152, 154, 155, 156, 157, 337
Catania, J., 261, 276
Catlin, O., 299, 300, 301
Cavin, S., 269
Celentano, D., 276
Centers, R., 240, 241
Chaiken, S., 7, 169, 171, 184, 302
Chang, P., 212
Chaves, M., 274
Cheadle, A., 269, 271
Chen, D., 168
Childers, T., 261, 307
Ching, P., 146, 149, 152, 339
Chitwood, D., 261
Chou, C., 270
Chu, A., 86, 97, 155

Cialdini, R., 338
Claggett, W., 274
Clark, A., 269, 277
Clark, F., 241–243
Clark, H., 9, 53, 54, 55, 56, 57, 202
Claxton, J., 269
Clayton, R., 290, 294
Clore, G., 177, 200, 207, 208
Coates, D., 261
Coates, T., 261, 267
Cobb, W., 286
Cochran, W., 2
Coder, J., 272
Cohen, N., 81
Colletta, L., 276
Collins, A., 10, 43, 77, 110, 157, 159, 203, 325
Combs, B., 161, 162
Conrad, F., 19, 55, 56, 137, 146, 147, 150, 151, 152, 154, 155, 156, 157, 298, 319, 326, 327, 328, 329, 333, 337
Conradt, J., 310
Converse, J., 39, 40, 43, 60, 286
Converse, P., 13, 22, 169
Conway, M., 70, 75–76, 79, 80, 110, 115
Couper, M., 259, 261, 262, 263, 279, 289, 290, 291, 301, 309, 338
Craik, F., 142, 145
Crain, S., 37
Crelia, R., 180, 220, 222
Crowder, R., 118
Crowne, D., 258
Cubbins, L., 256
Curran, T., 138, 139, 142, 157
Curtice, J., 299, 300, 301

Daamen, D., 240
D'Andrade, R., 14, 176, 177, 179, 182, 199, 206, 207, 325
Danis, C., 174
Davis, W., 161
deBie, S., 240
DeMaio, T., 23, 258, 327
Deming, W., 2
Denniston, W., Jr., 95, 162, 163

Dent, C., 271
DePaulo, B., 285, 286, 287
Deutsch, B., 150, 247, 248
Devine, P., 269
Devore, J., 270, 280, 296
Diehr, P., 269, 271
Dillman, D., 26, 309, 310
Dominitz, J., 160, 161, 162, 163
Donaldson, M., 12, 21, 78, 85, 95, 96, 134
Dovidio, J., 269
Dowd, K., 262
Downing, J., 167, 176, 177, 206, 325
Dowty, D., 101
Drake, R., 167, 176, 177, 206, 325
Duffer, A., Jr., 271, 281
Duffy, J., 269, 301
Dull, V., 324
Duncan, G., 82, 85, 86
Dunn, D., 171, 179, 185

Eagly, A., 302
Eisenhower, D., 86, 97, 155
Ellison, S., 276
Ellsworth, P., 178
Epstein, J., 285, 287
Ericsson, K., 326, 334
Ernst, L., 14, 281
Esposito, J., 19, 94, 95, 281, 324, 336, 337
Etling, K., 144
Evans, N., 269
Evans, V., 276
Everitt, B., 324

Fabrigar, L., 249
Farr, J., 240, 241
Fathi, D., 93, 336, 337
Fay, R., 262
Fazio, R., 12, 167, 168, 169, 172, 173, 177, 178, 179, 203, 221, 222, 247, 269, 325, 337
Fecso, R., 291
Feigenbaum, E., 73
Fein, D., 281
Felcher, E., 141

Feldman, J., 159, 175, 185, 186, 187, 188, 189, 190, 286
Fendrich, M., 269, 270
Ferber, R., 307
Ferguson, R., 120, 121
Fiedler, J., 82, 85, 93, 336, 337
Field, J., 276
Fillmore, C., 23, 25, 49
Finn, A., 89
Fischer, G., 163
Fischer, K., 285
Fischhoff, B., 12, 18, 161, 162, 175
Fletcher, J., 14
Flicker, L., 285, 306
Fodor, J., 32, 37
Fogg, B., 302
Forrest, J., 265, 268, 269
Forsyth, B., 19, 319, 328, 330
Fowler, F., 38, 40, 55, 311, 325, 331, 340
Fox, R., 276
Freedman, D., 335
Freund, J., 138, 139
Friedman, W., 11, 112, 114, 335
Fuhrman, R., 80
Fujii, E., 273

Gagnon, J., 256, 280
Galambos, J., 69
Galinat, W., 119
Galitz, W., 309
Ganesh, G., 148
Gaskell, G., 150, 156
Gavanski, I., 212
Geiselman, R., 212, 220, 223
Gentner, D., 10, 43, 157
Gerber, E., 324
Gfroerer, J., 256, 296
Gibson, D., 261
Gigerenzer, G., 145, 160
Gillund, G., 82
Gilpin, E., 269
Gleitman, H., 46
Gleitman, L., 46
Golding, J., 31
Goldsmith, L., 67, 70, 95, 114
Goldstein, D., 145

Goldstein, H., 313
Gordon, M., 95, 162, 163
Govender, R., 169
Graesser, A., 3, 9, 29, 32, 33, 41, 55
Green, N., 302
Greenberg, B., 272
Greenwald, A., 273, 274
Grice, P., 9, 50–53, 54, 202, 203, 204, 205, 209
Groenendijk, J., 27
Gropper, B., 270
Gross, S., 178
Groves, R., 4, 261, 268, 294, 295, 300, 301, 314, 319, 322, 323, 338
Gschneidinger, E., 176, 207, 211, 212, 223, 226

Hackett-Renner, C., 41
Hadaway, K., 274
Hainer, P., 256, 281
Hansen, M., 2, 4, 319, 320, 321, 340
Hanson, C., 68
Harrell, L., 290, 291
Harris, G., 139
Harris-Kojetin, B., 23, 327
Harrison, L., 270
Harsch, N., 81
Hart, C., 286
Hartwick, J., 179
Harvey, O., 337
Hasher, L., 139, 140, 141
Hashtroudi, S., 78
Hastie, R., 7, 13, 173, 179, 314
Hatchett, S., 286
Hauck, W., 276
Hay, M., 86, 87, 155
Heberlein, T., 261, 307
Hedges, L., 22, 116, 120, 121, 132, 235 , 238 , 337
Hennessy, M., 273
Henrion, M., 163
Herold, E., 276
Herr, P., 203, 221, 222, 337
Herrmann, D., 19, 21, 66, 71, 82, 298, 319
Higginbotham, J., 27, 29, 31

Higgins, E., 207, 337
Hild, T., 150, 156, 160
Hill, D., 122
Hilton, D., 212
Hines, C., 256, 281
Hintzman, D., 72, 138, 139, 141, 142, 144, 157
Hippler, H., 150, 200, 232, 241–243, 247, 248, 252, 253, 262, 288, 293, 310, 311, 314
Hirst, W., 68
Hochstim, J., 294
Hockley, W., 142, 145
Hodges, S., 167, 177 , 194, 197, 208, 334
Hofferth, S., 276
Hollan, J., 94
Holmes, D., 92
Holyoak, K., 246
Honaker, L., 303
Hook, E., 276
Hornik, J., 121
Horvitz, D., 272
Hougland, J., 294
Houston, C., 144
Hovland, C., 337
Howell, W., 140
Hser, Y., 270
Hubbard, M., 19, 300, 302, 308
Huber, J., 29, 55
Huff, J., 217
Hughes, A., 296
Hurwitz, W., 2, 319, 320, 321, 340
Huttenlocher, J., 22, 116, 120, 121, 132, 234, 235, 238, 337
Hyman, H., 210, 286, 337
Hymes, C., 169

Ingram, S., 299, 300, 301

Jabine, T., 122, 313, 319, 335
Jackendoff, R., 32
Jacoby, L., 143
Jenkins, C., 26, 309
Jenkins, L., 303
Jobe, J., 9, 19, 70, 85, 86, 93, 94, 95, 97, 126, 148, 233, 234, 235,

263, 265, 271, 281, 282, 283, 284, 291, 297, 298, 299, 300, 301, 305, 323, 324, 326, 336, 337
Johnson, A., 276
Johnson, B., 3, 9
Johnson, E., 8, 211
Johnson, E. C., 46
Johnson, L., 269, 270
Johnson, M., 78, 82, 202, 269
Johnson, N., 202
Johnson, R., 299, 300, 301, 303, 308
Johnson, T., 294
Jones, C., 207, 337
Jones, E. E., 171, 269
Jones, E. F., 265, 268, 269
Jonides, J., 139, 141, 142
Jordan, B., 55, 57, 311, 319, 338
Judd, C., 167, 169, 176, 177, 206, 217, 325
Jungeblut, A., 303
Just, M., 36, 40
Juster, T., 160

Kahn, J., 276
Kahn, R., 294
Kahneman, D., 10, 125, 137, 139, 143, 144, 145, 151, 161, 162
Kalsbeek, W., 319
Kalton, G., 124, 125, 126, 203
Kane, E., 286, 287
Kang, S., 270
Kaplan, K., 188
Kardes, F., 167, 168, 179, 325
Kashy, D., 285, 287
Kasprzyk, D., 123
Katosh, J., 274
Katz, D., 286
Kautz, H., 110
Kay, W., 66, 269, 271
Kearney, A., 14, 281
Keenan, J., 66
Kelley, C., 93, 336, 337
Kennickell, A., 234, 264
Kenny, D., 183
Kerkar, S., 151
Kerwin, J., 66
Kiesler, S., 290, 299, 301

Kinder, D., 175
King, K., 122
Kinne, S., 269, 271
Kirkenol, S., 285, 287
Kirsh, I., 303
Klassen, A., 276
Kleinman, S., 70
Kline, D., 118
Klinger, M., 82, 85, 93, 336, 337
Klumpp, G., 208
Knauper, B., 241–243, 252
Knibbe, R., 269
Knowles, E., 228, 229
Koehler, D., 119, 160, 162, 163
Koepsell, T., 269, 271
Kolodner, J., 70, 73–75, 91
Kolstad, A., 303
Kraft, D., 171, 179, 185
Krensky, L., 70
Kristiansson, K., 303
Krosnick, J., 17, 167, 169, 171, 172,
    176, 177, 206, 217, 249, 250,
    251, 252, 253, 293, 304, 325
Krueger, R., 324
Ku, L., 256, 276, 290, 300, 308
Kubovy, M., 245
Kuklinski, J., 179, 201, 222
Kulka, R., 259, 262, 263
Kurbat, M., 89, 90, 91, 114, 116,
    244

LaFleur, S., 177, 179, 208, 334
Lakoff, G., 234
Landauer, T., 63
Landy, F., 240, 241
Lanier, A., 291
Lannom, L., 89
Larsen, S., 11, 22, 65, 91, 92, 112,
    114, 115, 116, 133, 244
Larson, R., 31
Lasbeek, W., 276
Lau, R., 240, 241
Laumann, E., 256, 280
Laurent, A., 5
Lavine, H., 217
Layman, M., 161, 162
LeCompte, D., 142, 145, 151

Lee, L., 146, 149, 152, 339
Lehnert, W., 3, 9
Lemmens, P., 269
Leonard, J., 83, 84, 93
Leone, C., 171, 184
Lessler, J., 12, 19, 43, 147, 148, 149,
    151, 256, 270, 271, 280, 281,
    296, 300, 302, 308, 319, 326,
    328, 330, 331, 336, 337, 340
Levinson, S., 287
Levitt, E., 276
Lewis, D., 9, 42, 108
Lewis, V., 84, 115, 133
Leyens, J., 13
Lichtenstein, S., 95, 161, 162, 163
Lindberg, L., 276, 290, 300, 308
Linde, C., 71
Lindsay, D., 78
Linton, M., 78, 33
Linville, P., 171
Locander, W., 268, 269
Lodge, M., 173, 174
Loftus, E., 12, 21, 42, 78, 82, 85,
    89, 91, 93, 95, 96, 118, 134, 146,
    148, 154, 155, 160, 163, 273,
    274, 326, 335, 336, 337
London, K., 271
Lopes, L., 180
LoScuito, L., 270, 296
Ludwig, J., 210, 211
Lui, L., 324
Luker, K., 174
Lyberg, L., 314
Lynch, J., 159

Macaulay, L., 286, 287
MacGregor, D., 95, 163
Madigan, S., 93
Madow, W., 2
Madson, C., 95
Magura, S., 270
Mah, W., 246
Mai, H., 180, 203, 204, 205, 209,
    223
Mak, J., 273
Malt, B., 46
Mandler, J., 202

Mangione, T., 55
Manis, M., 212, 221, 222, 228
Manning, C., 291
Manski, C., 160, 161, 162, 163
Marburger, W., 89, 336, 337
Marler, P., 274
Marlowe, D., 258
Marquis, K., 5, 125, 126, 311
Martin, E., 203, 256, 281, 313, 324, 325
Martin, J., 299, 300, 301, 303
Martin, L., 7, 17, 18, 20, 172, 178, 180, 201, 203, 207, 209, 213, 220, 221, 222, 314, 319, 337
Martin, P., 120, 121
Martini, A., 123
Mason, R., 176, 180, 203, 209
Massey, J., 293
Mathiowetz, N., 82, 85, 86, 259, 262, 263, 279, 300, 301, 314
Mauner, G., 37
Maxwell, D., 139
May, R., 276
McCauley, R., 72
McClelland, J., 76
McClendon, M., 176, 200, 204
McCloskey, M., 42, 81
McDonel, E., 168
McDougall, G., 269
McGill, A., 212
McGonagle, K., 274
McGraw, K., 173, 174
McGuire, W., 213, 287
McMahen, C., 3, 9
McMullen, M., 211, 221, 222
McNaughton, B., 76
McQueen, D., 294
Means, B., 12, 21, 78, 85, 91, 94, 95, 96, 134, 146, 148, 154, 155, 160, 163, 335, 336
Menon, G., 22, 65, 66, 146, 147, 148, 150, 151, 155, 156, 159, 160, 163, 328, 329, 337
Michael, R., 256, 280
Michaels, S., 256, 280
Michalski, R., 110, 159
Mieczkowski, T., 270

Milburn, J., 169
Miles, C., 47, 101
Millar, M., 185
Miller, E., 262, 288
Miller, M., 124, 125, 126
Miller, P., 5, 6, 16, 85, 92, 94, 268, 301, 314
Miller, R., 285, 306
Mingay, D., 66, 70, 93, 148, 228, 251, 322, 326, 336, 337
Mitterer, J., 139
Moon, Y., 302
Moore, J., 67, 123, 125, 126, 264, 268, 269, 272, 321
Morganstein, D., 86, 87, 155
Morgenstern, O., 281
Morris, M., 69, 278
Moses, M., 118
Mosher, W., 271, 281
Moss, L., 313
Mott, F., 271
Moxey, L., 47, 49
Mueller, J., 174
Mullen, P., 298, 319
Mullin, T., 19, 163
Murphy, G., 69
Murray, D., 265, 268, 269, 271
Myaskovsky, L., 119
Myers, S., 270

Narayan, S., 252, 253
Nass, C., 302
Nathan, G., 281, 282
Nebes, R., 87
Neisser, U., 67, 71, 81
Nelson, T., 212, 221, 222, 228
Neter, J., 11, 86, 88, 89, 92, 97, 126, 127, 128, 129, 130, 133, 146, 155, 228, 315, 322, 335
Neveh-Benjamin, M., 139, 141, 142
Newel, R., 270
Newell, A., 3
Newstead, S., 47
Newtson, D., 68
Nicholls, W., II, 289, 290, 303
Nigam, A., 12, 21, 78, 85, 95, 96, 134

Nimmo-Smith, I., 84, 115, 133
Nisbett, R., 112, 334
Noelle-Neumann, E., 241–243, 252,
    253, 293, 305
Norman, D., 308, 311
Nottenburg, G., 69
Novick, L., 212

O'Brien, D., 176, 204
O'Connell, C., 265, 268, 269, 271
Oksenberg, L., 5, 6, 16, 85, 92, 94,
    301, 314
Oldendick, R., 170, 246
Olofsson, A., 303
O'Malley, P., 269, 270
O'Muircheartaigh, C., 150, 156, 266,
    299, 300, 301, 322, 323
O'Reilly, J., 271, 281, 300, 302, 308
O'Reilly, R., 76
Ornstein, R., 118
Osherson, D., 226
Ostrom, T., 214
Ottati, V., 179, 201, 222

Padian, N., 276
Panter, A., 67, 114
Parducci, A., 212, 214, 220, 223,
    239
Park, B., 7, 173, 179
Patrick, D., 269, 271
Payne, J., 8
Pelham, B., 119
Pepper, S., 47
Pergamit, M., 270, 280, 296
Perry, C., 265, 268, 269, 271
Person, N., 29, 55
Petroni, R., 122
Petty, R., 7, 167, 187, 213, 221,
    252, 307
Phillips, L., 161
Phipps, P., 290
Pierce, C., 271
Pierce, J., 269
Pijper, M., 290
Pillemer, D., 67, 70, 89, 114
Pleck, J., 256, 276, 290, 300, 308
Pless, I., 273
Polivka, A., 324, 325

Pollack, L., 276
Poulton, E., 117, 244, 245
Powell, M., 167, 168, 179, 325
Poynter, W., 118
Pratt, J., 281
Pratt, W., 233, 234, 235, 263, 264,
    265, 271, 281, 291, 297, 298,
    299, 300, 301
Pratto, F., 169
Presser, S., 1, 22, 39, 40, 43, 60,
    170, 174, 175, 197, 200, 201,
    202, 203, 210, 215, 216, 273,
    274, 275, 295, 296, 307, 315,
    328, 330, 331, 332, 333, 337
Priester, J., 187
Prohaska, V., 116, 121, 132
Psotka, J., 245
Puskar, C., 66

Quadrel, M., 161
Quigley, B., 271
Quillian, M., 77, 325

Raden, D., 172
Radford, A., 26, 35
Raghubir, P., 150, 155, 156, 159,
    337
Raiffa, H., 281
Ramirez, C., 66
Ramsey, F., 4
Rasinski, K., 7, 14, 20, 22, 172, 175,
    176, 177, 179, 180, 181, 182,
    186, 187, 188, 189, 190, 191,
    199, 201, 202, 203, 205, 206,
    207, 209, 228, 233, 234, 235,
    251, 263, 264, 265, 271, 273,
    276, 281, 282, 283, 284, 291,
    297, 298, 299, 300, 301, 325,
    337
Raymond, P., 169
Reder, L., 11, 157
Reeves, B., 302
Reichenbach, H., 64
Reiser, B., 78, 79, 81
Rhinehart, E., 67, 89, 114
Rholes, W., 207, 337
Rifkin, A., 69
Riggle, E., 79, 201, 222

Rips, L., 10, 31, 46, 69, 79, 81, 83, 88, 89, 90, 91, 114, 116, 137, 147, 244, 337
Rittenauer-Schatka, H., 208
Roberts, R., 41
Robinson, J., 70, 76, 89, 90, 91
Rocher, S., 13
Roese, N., 212
Rogers, S., 276, 290, 300, 308
Rokeach, M., 174
Rosch, E., 46, 68, 245
Rosen, N., 213, 216
Rosen, R., 290
Rosen, S., 287
Ross, M., 13, 125
Rothgeb, J., 324
Rowe, B., 291, 301
Royston, P., 19, 323
Rubin, D., 86, 87, 132, 133

Sadock, J., 106, 108, 234
Säfström, M., 303
Salter, W., 12, 43, 147, 148, 149, 151, 326, 331, 336, 337, 340
Sanbonmatsu, D., 167, 168, 172, 173, 177, 178, 179, 247, 325
Sanchez, M., 93, 336, 337
Sander, J., 19, 298, 319
Sanders, L., 175
Sanford, A., 47, 42
Saris, W., 290
Schab, F., 118
Schacter, D., 77
Schadron, G., 13
Schaefer, E., 55
Schaeffer, N., 47, 79, 86, 235, 236, 237, 258, 284, 286, 319, 340
Schafer, R., 71
Schank, R., 32, 69, 73
Schechter, S., 327, 331, 332
Schlaifer, R., 281
Schmid, L., 265, 268, 269, 271
Schober, M., 9, 53, 55, 56, 57, 319, 340
Schober, S., 55, 270, 280, 296
Schooler, J., 71, 87, 118
Schuman, H., 1, 22, 43, 174, 175, 178, 197, 200, 201, 202, 203, 210, 211, 215, 216, 217, 286, 315, 337
Schwarz, N., 18, 22, 53, 54, 150, 155, 156, 159, 160, 170, 176, 177, 180, 200, 201, 202, 203, 204, 205, 207, 208, 209, 211, 212, 213, 216, 221, 222, 223, 224, 225, 226, 232, 241–243, 247, 248, 252, 253, 262, 288, 291, 305, 310, 311, 314, 337
Scoon-Rogers, L., 272
Scott, B., 326, 331
Searle, J., 29, 246
Sears, D., 240, 241
Segal, G., 31
Seta, J., 180, 220, 222
Sewell, D., 69
Shafir, E., 226
Shahar, I., 118
Shapiro, G., 14, 256, 281
Sheatsley, P., 2, 210, 337
Sheingold, K., 67
Shepherd, M., 276
Sherif, M., 337
Sherman, S., 168, 203, 221, 222, 337
Shevell, S., 10, 66, 79, 81, 83, 88, 89, 90, 91, 114, 116, 137, 147, 244, 337
Shiffrin, R., 82
Shimizu, I., 272
Shoben, E., 46, 69
Shum, M., 114, 134
Shyrock, H., 233
Sicoly, F., 13
Siegel, A., 95
Siegel, J., 233
Siegler, R., 337
Sigall, H., 269
Sikkel, D., 86
Silver, B., 273, 274, 280, 287
Simon, H., 73, 250, 326, 334
Simons, A., 208
Sinclair, R., 146, 149, 150, 152, 156, 278
Singer, E., 259, 262, 263, 279, 288
Singer, M., 33, 41
Sirkin, M., 281, 282
Skinner, S., 261, 307

Skowronski, J., 11, 66, 91, 92, 112, 114, 115, 116, 121, 133, 244
Slovic, P., 95, 161, 162, 163
Smith, A., 9, 12, 21, 70, 85, 86, 97, 126, 148, 149
Smith, E., 46, 69, 70, 148, 226
Smith, K., 82, 85, 93, 336, 337
Smith, T., 150, 154, 169, 175, 199, 203, 213, 215, 216, 228, 233, 234, 247, 263, 264, 268, 269, 273, 276, 277, 280, 287, 290, 294, 296, 297, 298, 299, 300, 301, 305, 306
Sonenstein, F., 256, 276, 290, 300, 308
Sperber, D., 9, 54
Sproull, L., 290, 299, 301, 302
Srull, T., 207
Stalnaker, R., 42
Stapel, D., 180, 213, 221
Stefanowska, M., 273
Stember, C., 286
Sternberg, S., 325
Stevens, S., 235
Stinson, L., 24, 264, 268, 269, 272, 273, 275, 296, 321
Stockwell, E., 233
Stokes, L., 320
Stokhof, M., 27
Stolley, K., 276
Strack, F., 7, 17, 18, 20, 53, 150, 172, 176, 178, 180, 200, 201, 202, 203, 204, 205, 207, 208, 209, 211, 212, 220, 223, 226, 247, 248, 310, 311, 314, 319, 337
Straf, M., 313, 335
Stroh, P., 173, 174
Stulginskas, J., 273
Subramani, M., 302
Suchman, L., 54, 57, 311, 319, 338
Sudman, S., 2, 22, 42, 47, 60, 65, 86, 87, 88, 89, 92, 94, 129–130, 132, 133, 145, 146, 147, 151, 224, 225, 257, 259, 260, 268, 269, 280, 307, 314, 315, 335
Sumarta, T., 119

Swamer, S., 32
Swan, G., 94, 95, 335, 336
Sweeney, D., 217

Tan, E., 269
Tanfer, K., 256
Tangney, J., 285, 306
Tannenhaus, M., 37
Tanur, J., 313, 335
Tenney, Y., 67
Tesser, A., 171, 184, 185, 287
Thomas, E., 118
Thomson, D., 80
Thompson, C., 18, 67, 91, 92, 112, 114, 115, 116, 121, 133, 244
Thompson, D., 269, 271
Thornberry, O., 293
Thornton, A., 335
Thurstone, L., 4
Tifft, L., 276
Tortora, R., 310
Tourangeau, R., 7, 9, 12, 14, 17, 20, 22, 43, 57, 66, 97, 146, 147, 148, 149, 150, 151, 152, 154, 172, 176, 177, 179, 180, 181, 182, 186, 187, 188, 189, 190, 191, 199, 201, 202, 203, 205, 206, 207, 217, 233, 234, 235, 247, 250, 263, 264, 265, 269, 271, 273, 276, 277, 281, 290, 291, 296, 297, 298, 299, 300, 301, 305, 313, 314, 319, 325, 326, 331, 335, 336, 337, 338, 340
Trabasso, T., 33
Traugott, M., 274
Triplett, T., 307
Trope, Y., 203
Tsal, Y., 118
Tuchfarber, A., 170, 246
Tuchin, M., 42
Tulving, E., 71–73, 75, 78, 80
Tupek, A., 290
Turner, C., 203, 256, 270, 276, 280, 290, 296, 300, 302, 308, 313
Turner, T., 69
Tversky, A., 10, 42, 119, 125, 137,

139, 143, 144, 145, 151, 160, 161, 162, 163, 211

Udry, J., 276
Underwood, B., 138, 139
Underwood, G., 118
Upchurch, D., 276
Upshaw, H., 214
Usher, J., 67, 71

Vaughn, C., 269, 270
Verreault, R., 273
Von Neumann, J., 281
von Thurn, D., 262, 288

Wadsworth, J., 276
Wagenaar, W., 11, 75, 84, 87, 92, 96
Wagner, S., 217
Waksberg, J., 11, 86, 88, 89, 92, 97, 126, 127, 128, 129–130, 133, 146, 155, 228, 315, 322, 335
Walker, J., 302
Walker, W., 121
Wallin, P., 269
Wallsten, T., 47, 162
Wänke, M., 53, 202, 203
Warner, S., 272
Warriner, G., 269
Waterton, J., 269, 301
Waterworth, J., 117
Watkins, M., 142, 145, 151
Way, L., 276
Wedell, D., 212, 220, 223
Weeks, M., 290
Wegener, D., 213, 221
Weisman, C., 276
Wellings, K., 276
Wells, G., 212
Welniak, E., 264, 268, 269, 272, 321
West, K., 281
Wetzel, A., 87
Wetzler, S., 86, 87
Whisman, M., 276
White, A., 93, 336, 337
White, R., 114

White, S., 67, 70, 89, 114, 116
Whitehouse, K., 143
Whitten, W., 83, 84, 93
Whittlesea, B., 143
Wible, C., 81
Wickelgren, W., 86
Wiggins, S., 185
Wilkins, A., 112
Williams, C., 167, 168, 171, 276
Williams, L., 271
Williams, M., 94
Willis, G., 19, 23, 146, 149, 152, 258, 281, 282, 283, 284, 323, 327, 328, 330, 331, 332, 339
Wilson, D., 9, 54
Wilson, T., 112, 144, 167, 171, 177, 179, 185, 194, 197, 207, 208, 334
Wish, E., 270
Wittlinger, R., 83, 84
Woodberry, R., 275
Woodrow, H., 118
Wright, D., 150, 156
Wyer, M., 285, 287
Wyer, R., 80, 179, 201, 207, 213, 216, 222
Wyner, G., 270

Xu, Y., 270

Yammarino, F., 261, 307
Yates, S., 171, 184
Young, M., 274
Young, N., 123, 125, 126
Young-DeMarco, L., 335
Yzerbyt, V., 13

Zacks, R., 139, 140, 141
Zajonc, R., 241
Zakay, D., 117, 118
Zaller, J., 170, 172, 174, 175, 179, 185, 186, 187, 188, 189, 190
Zaragoza, M., 42
Zarrow, M., 12, 21, 78, 85, 95, 96, 134
Zhao, S., 295
Zimmerman, J., 138, 139
Zwick, R., 162

Subject Index

abortion reporting, 265, 268, 271–272

ACASI (audio computer-assisted self-administered interviewing), 256, 276, 290, 300, 304

accessibility
of attitudes, 167–169, 179–180
of attitudinal considerations, 206–209
of episodic information, 152, 155, 159
of nonepisodic information, 155–156, 159

accuracy of survey responses (*see also* measurement error), 2
aggregate comparisons, 266–268
attitude questions, 2, 165–166
factual questions, 94, 95
frequency questions, 141, 149, 160
individual comparisons, 266–268
measures of accuracy, 2, 266–269
self vs. proxy responses, 62
sensitive questions, 264–265, 269–279

acquiescence, 5
additive decomposition, 146, 147
adjunct questions, 37–38
adverbial quantifiers, 24
age heaping, 233–234
ambiguity
semantic, 24
syntactic, 23–24, 35, 40

anchoring-and-adjustment, 124, 125–126, 144, 151, 247

anchors, 214, 232, 239, 245–246

argument questions, 37–38

Anderson's information integration theory, 11, 13, 181, 210

artificial intelligence (AI), 36, 110

aspectualizers/aspect markers, 101

assimilation effects, 207, 247–248

attitudes
crystallization, 13, 215
importance, 217
instability, 169–170
intensity, 217
strength, 217

attitude judgments–context effects, 197–229

attitude questions, answers to (*see also* belief-sampling model), 165–198
automatic processes, 168–169
basis for answers, 172–173
considerations, 184–185
construal model, 167–168
determinants of response strategy, 177–178
effects of thought, 170–171
file drawer model, 167, 172
traditional view, 166–167

attitude–behavior correlations, 171

autobiographical events, 62–63

autobiographical memory, 65, 67–99
contents, 68–71

Conway's model, 75–77, 79
  extended events, 70–71
  generic events, 69–70
  Kolodner's model (CYRUS), 73–75, 83
  lifetime periods, 70–71
  retrieval from, 81–99
  structure, 71–76
  Tulving's model, 71–73
audio computer-assisted self-administered interview (ACASI), 256, 276, 290, 300, 304
audio self-administered questionnaires (ASAQ), 291, 304
availability heuristic, 137, 143–144, 151
averaging model, *see* Anderson's information integration theory

backtracking, 15, 19
backward telescoping, *see* telescoping
balanced questions, 39
basic object categories, 68
behavior coding, 331–332
belief-sampling model, 178–194, 197–198, 225–226, 323
  judgment, 180–181
  retrieval, 179–180
  tests of the model, 185–194
bias models, 320–321
  nonresponse, 320
  response propensity, 321
biased rounding rules, 238–239
bogus pipeline, 265, 268, 271, 277–278
bounded interviews, 89–91, 126–128
bounding, 89–91, 115–117

calendar prototypes, 234
Cannell, Miller, and Oksenberg model, 5–7, 16–17, 314–315
card sorting, 323–324
CASM movement (Cognitive Aspects of Survey Methodology), 20–23, 313–317, 338–339
  barriers to progress, 337–340

and conceptions of survey measurement error, 314–315, 318–319
  impact on psychology, 335–337
  other effects on survey practice, 335
  questionnaire development and testing, 323–334
categorical response options (*see also* satisficing), 249–250
censoring, 256, 273, 276, 279
census participation, 262–263, 279
channel of presentation (aural vs. visual), 252, 292–293, 298, 300–305
childhood amnesia, 71
closed-ended questions, 38, 230–231
coding schemes for cognitive interviews, 327–328
cognitive burden, 302–303, 305
cognitive interviewing, 326–328
  coding schemes, 327–328
  concurrent think-alouds, 327
  evaluation of, 331–333
  paraphrasing, 327
  probes, 327
  protocol analysis, 334
  reliability of results, 333
  retrospective think-alouds, 327
cognitive reference points, 245, 248
cognitive sophistication, 252
cognitive toolbox, 8, 15
components of the response process, 5, 7–16, 315–318
comprehension, 7–9, 23–61
  ambiguity, 23–24
  complex syntax, 34
  flexible interviewing, 57–59
  immediate understanding, 30–34
  interpretation, 30, 33–34
  logical form, 31–32
  pragmatics, 25
  role of inference, 33–34
  semantics, 25, 40–50
  standardization, 56–57
  syntax, 25, 34–40
  unfamiliar terms, 24, 43

comprehension (*cont.*)
vague concepts, 24, 45–47
vague quantifiers, 47–50
computer assistance, 289–293, 299–302
cognitive burden, 302–303, 305, 308–310
design principles, 302–312: Couper's, 309; Jenkins and Dillman's, 309–310; Norman's, 308–309
humanizing the interface, 301–302
impact on reporting, 299–301
impersonality, 306–307
legitimacy, 307–308
mental models, 311–312
mode of responding, 298, 302–305
virtual human presence, 301–302
computer-assisted personal interviewing (CAPI), 276, 289–290, 300, 304
computer-assisted self-interviewing (CASI), 276, 289, 300, 304
computer-assisted telephone interviewing (CATI), 290, 300, 304
confidentiality, 259, 261–263, 279
considerations, *see* attitude questions, answers to
consistency, *see* editing
consistency effects, *see* assimilation effects
constant wave response, 125–126
construal model of attitudes, 167–168
Consumer Expenditure Survey (CE), 1, 35, 85, 101, 106, 137
context effects (*see also* assimilation effects *and* contrast effects), 17, 20, 171, 198–229
and causal judgments, 212–213
belief-sampling model, 225–226
conditional, 199
correlational, 198
directional, 198
frequency of, 215–217
inclusion/exclusion model (Schwarz and Bless), 221–225

unconditional, 199
contrast effects, 201, 202–205, 212–215
conversational cues, 246–248
conversational implicature, 51
conversational maxims, *see* Grice's conversational maxims
Conway's model of autobiographical memory, 75–77, 79
cooperative principle, *see* Grice's conversational maxims
correlation between form, meaning, and use, 29–30
cued recall, 84–86
Current Employment Survey, 290
Current Population Survey (CPS), 56, 64, 65, 101, 108, 255, 258, 263, 268, 272, 289, 321, 322, 324
CYRUS (Kolodner's autobiographical memory model), 73–75, 78–79

decennial census, 262, 279
declarative sentence, 29, 35
decomposition, 95–96, 162
deliberate misreporting, *see* censoring
depth of processing, 220, 307
design principles, *see* computer assistance
Detroit Area Study (DAS), 215
diary studies, 66–67, 70, 148
disclosure to third parties, 259, 279–281
to other government agencies, 259, 279–281
within the respondent's household, 258, 279–282
discrimination net, 73
disregarding accessible information, 208–209
mood, 211–212
distinctiveness of events, 91
Drug Use Forcasting (DUF), 270
duration questions, 102–103, 105–107

editing (*see also* censoring *and* misreporting), 1, 13–14, 255–288

consistency, 287
interviewer approval, 257, 275, 279, 286
misreporting, 264–265, 269–279
and nonresponse, 261–264
overreporting, 273–275
politeness to interviewers, 286–287
processes responsible for, 279–285
and reports about sexual behavior, 275–278
underreporting, 269–273
effects of thought on answers to attitude questions, 170–171
elapsed time questions, 102–103, 105–107
embarrassment, 279, 282, 284–286, 306
E-MOPs (event memory organization packets), 73–75, 78, 83
encoding, 139, 235, 317
episodic enumeration, *see* recall-and-count
episodic memory (Tulving's model), 71–73
estimation for frequency questions (*see also* recall-and-count), 21, 88, 143–145, 147, 148–150, 337
additive decomposition, 146, 147
based on general impression, 141, 146, 147, 149–150
based on generic information, 146, 147, 148–149
direct estimation, 149–150
exact tally, 146, 149
recall-and-extrapolate, 146, 147–148, 152
rough approximation, 146, 149–150
strategy selection, 152–159
event series, 101–102
event time, 63–64
event-specific knowledge, 71
exact tally, 141
expert panels, 331–332
extended events, 70–71
external calibration of probability judgments, 161

extrapolation, 141
extreme exemplars, 214

factual questions, 1–2, 9–12, 62–63
false alarm rate, 267
fan effect, 91
faulty presuppositions, 25, 42–44
file drawer model (Wilson and Hodges), 167, 172, 194
filled-duration illusion, 118–120
filter questions, 43
first-hand events, 65–67
Fischhoff's partial perspectives approach, 18, 175
flashbulb memories, 81
flexible vs. standardized interviewing, 55–57
focus groups, 23, 327
focus, sentence, 25
forgetting, 82–91
length of reference period, 86–88
passage of time, 82–86
proximity to temporal boundaries, 88–91
forgetting curves, 86–88
forward telescoping, *see* telescoping
frequency estimates, *see* estimation for frequency questions
frequency of context effects, 215–217
frequency questions, *see* factual questions; estimation for frequency questions

Gallup Poll, 174, 275
Galton method, 87
general happiness-marital happiness, 203–205
general political values, 174
General Social Survey (GSS), 2, 13, 23, 25, 62, 101, 215, 232, 251
general-specific questions, 203–205
generic information, 69–70, 71, 148–149
generic memories, 21, 69–70, 78–79
Gigerenzer and Goldstein's take-the-best heuristic, 145
grammar, *see* syntax

Grice's conversational maxims, 51–53, 202–203, 204–205, 209
  cooperative principle, 51
  maxim of manner, 51
  maxim of quality, 51
  maxim of quantity, 51, 204, 209
  maxim of relation, 51, 202
gross discrepancy rate, 266
grounding, 55

Hansen–Hurwitz–Bershad model, 319–320
high road–low road theories/two track theories, 16–19
Hintzman and Curran theory of recognition judgments, 142–143

ideological predispositions, 174
illicit drug use, 270, 294–296
immediate understanding, question comprehension, 30–31
imperative sentence, 27–28
implicatures in surveys, see also conversational cues), 53–55, 246–248
implicit memory, 77–78
impression-based judgments, 142–143, 149–150, 173–174, 247
  for attitude questions, 173–174
  for frequency questions, 142–143, 149–150, 247
inclusion/exclusion model for context effects (Schwarz and Bless), 221–225
income reporting, 263–264, 268, 272
inductive inference, 226–228
inference, see comprehension; reconstruction
instability of attitudes, 169–170
interaction coding/behavior coding, 326
interactive voice response (IVR), 290, 304
interference effect, 83
Internet surveys, 290
interpretation, see comprehension
interrogative sentence, 27–29, 34–38

interview time, 63–64, 301
interviewer, 1, 5, 276, 286, 292, 294–295, 297–298
interviewer approval, 257, 275, 279, 286
interviewer debriefing, 331–332
intrusive questions, 255–256, 258, 261
item nonresponse, 260–261, 263–264, 273, 299

judgments in surveys (see also estimation for frequency questions and attitude judgments), 7–8, 10–13
judgmental contrast effects, 212–215
judgmental heuristics, 137, 143–145, 151
  anchoring-and-adjustment, 124, 125–126, 144, 151, 247
  availability heuristic, 137, 143–144, 151
  representativeness heuristic, 143, 151
judgments of causality, 212–213

Kolodner's model (CYRUS), 73–75, 83
Krosnick and Alwin's model for response order effects, 17, 250–254
  strong satisficing, 253
  weak satisficing, 253

lack-of-knowledge inference, 43, 157
landmark events, 67, 70–71, 79–80, 89–91, 113–115
leading questions, 42
length of reference period, 86–88
leniency bias, 240–241, 248
level of item generality, 200–209, 226–227
  assimilation effects, 201–203
  contrast effects, 201, 202–205, 212–215
life event calendar, 91, 335–336
life satisfaction, judgments of, 211–212

lifetime periods, 70–71, 75–76, 79–80
logical form, 31–32
long-term memory, 77
lying, 265, 279, 284–286

mapping of response, 13–14, 232–235, 239–249
mean absolute difference, 266
mean squared error, 266
measurement error (*see also* response effects), 4, 121–122, 265–267, 276, 340–342
    random error, 266
    systematic error, 266
medium of questionnaire (paper vs. electronic), 292–293, 298–302
memory-based judgments, 7, 21
memory failure, *see* forgetting
memory for elapsed time, 120–121
memory indices, *see* E-MOPs
Memory Organization Packets (MOPs), 69, 73–75
method of administration (self vs. interviewer; *see also* self-administration), 294–298, 300
method of contact, 293–295
misreporting, 264–265, 269–285
    avoiding embarrassment, 265, 284–285
    confidentiality, 279–281
    lying, 265, 279, 284–286
    privacy, 265, 279–280
    question threat, 264
missing data, *see* item nonresponse
miss rate, 267
mixed views, attitude questions, 186–188
mode of data collection, 20, 276–278, 289–312
    audio computer-assisted self-administered interviewing (ACASI), 256, 276, 290, 300, 304
    audio self-administered questionnaire (ASAQ), 291, 304
    computer-assisted personal interviewing (CAPI), 276, 289–290, 300, 304
    computer-assisted self-administered interviewing (CASI), 276, 289, 300, 304
    computer-assisted telephone interviewing (CATI), 290, 300, 304
    disk by mail (DBM), 290, 304
    interactive voice response (IVR), 290, 304
    Internet surveys, 290
    paper-and-pencil personal interviewing (PAPI), 290–291, 294, 300, 304
    prepared data entry (PDE), 290, 304
    self-administered questionnaire (SAQ), 250, 265, 270–271, 275, 279, 291, 295, 297–298, 300, 304
    touchtone data entry (TDE), 290, 304
    voice recognition entry (VRE), 290, 304
mode of responding, 298, 302–305
Monetary Control Bill, 175, 202–203
mood effects, 211–212

National Crime Survey (NCS), 1, 11, 100, 101, 104, 313
National Education Longitudinal Study of 1988, 2nd Follow-up, 261–263
National Election Studies (NES), 186, 237, 273, 280
National Health Interview Survey (HIS), 12, 38, 62, 63, 101, 103, 136, 165, 231, 311, 313, 324
National Household Survey Of Drug Abuse (NHSDA), 256, 261
National Longitudinal Survey of Youth (NLS-Y), 289
National Medical Expenditure Survey (NMES), 289
National Opinion Research Center (NORC), 174

National Survey of Family Growth (NSFG), 265, 289
need for social approval, 258
net discrepancy rate, 266–267
nonattitudes, 169
norm of evenhandedness, 211
norm of politeness, 286–287
numeric labels, 230, 241–244
numerical reference points, 245
numerosity heuristic, 119

on-line judgments, 7
open-ended questions, 175–176, 186–187, 231–232
optimizing, 251
overlapping considerations, 188–190
overreporting of desirable behaviors, 273–275
   voting, 273–274, 278
   church attendance, 274–275

pace of administration, 310–311, 333–334
Panel Study of Income Dynamics (PSID), 122
paper-and-pencil personal interviewing (PAPI), 290–291, 294, 300, 304
partial prespectives, 173–175
passage of time, 82–86
personal narratives, 71
Petty and Cacioppo's theory of persuasion, 252–253
phonological structure of questions, 26
politeness to interviewers, 286–287
   interviewer class, 286–287
   interviewer race, 286–287
   interviewer sex, 286–287
positional cues, 247–248
positivity bias (see also leniency), 240–245, 248
pragmatics, 25, 51–56
   of interviews, 54–56
prepared data entry (PDE), 290, 304
presupposition, 25, 41–44

pretesting methods, 323–328
   card sorting, 323–324
   cognitive interviews, 23, 326–328
   confidence ratings, 327
   expert panels, 327
   focus group discussions, 23, 327
   response latency, 327
   vignettes, 324–325
primacy effects, see response order effects
priming effects, 176–177
privacy, 258, 259, 263, 275–276, 279
probability judgments, 160–165, 240
   external calibration, 161
   internal consistency, 161–162: conjunction effect, 161; disjunctive events, 162; unpacking, 162
protocol analysis (see also cognitive interviewing), 334
prototypes, 46, 228
   calendar, 234
   numerical, 245
prototypical question, 30
proximity to temporal boundaries, 88–91
proxy reports, 22, 65–67
psychological continuum, 4, 5
psychometric theories of the response process, 3–7

quality profiles, 319
question comprehension, 30–31
   immediate understanding, 30–31
   interpretation, 30–31
question context effects, see context effects
question order effects, see context effects
question wording, 23–44
   adverbial quantifiers, 24, 47–50
   focus, sentence, 25, 32, 35–38
   semantic ambiguity, 23–24
   syntactic ambiguity, 23–24, 34–38, 40
   unfamiliar terms, 24, 42–43

vagueness, 24, 45–50
question wording effects, 174–175
   Korean war items, 174–175

randomized response technique, 272–278
range-frequency model, 214–215, 239–241, 244, 248
   frequency principle, 240–249
   range principle, 214–215, 239
rating scales, 241–246, 249
rational deliberation and misreporting, 279
reaction time, 167–169, 325–326
   attitude questions, 167–169, 325
recall, 81–99, 109
recall order, 93–94
recall-and-count (episodic enumeration), 146, 151, 153–156, 158–160, 175
recall-and-extrapolate (rate estimation), 147–148, 152
recency effects, *see* response order effects
reconstruction, 12, 81–82
reference date, 64–65
reference period, 11, 64–65, 86
reference points, 245, 248
relative temporal order, 112–113
reliability of answers to attitude questions, *see* response stability
representation-about the sentence, 31–34
representation-of the sentence, 31–34
representativeness heuristic, 143, 151
response aids, 335–338
response contraction, 117–118, 244–245, 248
response effects, 2–3, 8, 19
response formats, 230–232
response order effects, 250–254, 304–305
   and channel of presentation, 304–305, 251–252
   cognitive sophistication, 252

individual differences, 252
Krosnick and Alwin's satisficing model, 251–252
primacy effects, 251–252
recency effects, 251–252
response process, models of, 2–7, 16–19, 41, 315–319
   Cannell, Miller, and Oksenberg model, 5–7
   high road–low road/two-track models, 16–19
   Krosnick and Alwin's satisficing model, 17, 251–252
   psychometric models, 3–7
   Strack and Martin's model for attitude questions, 17–19
response stability for attitude questions, 181–184
retrieval, 7–8, 9–10, 77–81
   relation between retrieval and judgment for factual questions, 9–12
retrieval cues, 78–81, 96–97
   relative effectiveness of different cues, 78–79
retrieval-based assimilation effects, 206–207
retrospective bias, 125–126
retrospective probes, 327
rounding, 22, 162–163, 232–239
   encoding, 235
   feeling thermometer, 237–238
   indeterminate quantities, 235–238
   magnitude of quantity being estimated, 234–235
   rounding rules, 238–239

sampling errors, 2
satisficing, 17, 250–251, 305
scale anchors, 245–246
scale labels, 241–245, 248
scale range effects, 249
scale values, 212–213
Schwarz and Bless's inclusion/exclusion model, 221–225
scripts, 69–70

seam effect, 122–126
  constant wave response, 125–126
  forgetting, 124–126
  retrospective bias, 125–126
second-hand events, 65–67
segmentation of events, 118–119
self-administration, 265, 270–271,
  275–276, 279, 282, 295, 297–
  298, 300, 310
self-presentation, 278–291
semantic memory, 72–73
semantic problems, 23–25
sensitive questions (threatening questions), 255–288, 291
sentence parsing, 36, 37
serial position effects, 228–229
sexual partners, 232–234, 268–269,
  275–278, 296–297
show cards, 250–293
simple response variance, 322–323
sincerity conditions, 246
social desirability, 5, 257, 294, 296,
  301
Socratic effect, 213
space of uncertainty, 27–30, 32, 34,
  40–50, 246
spread of activitation, 77
standard of comparison, 210, 212
standardized interviewing, 55–57
statistical models of error, 319–321
Strack and Martin's two-track theory, 17–19
subjective expected utility theory
  (SEU), 281–284
  risks and losses, 281–282
subtraction-based contrast effects,
  205
Sudman–Bradburn theory of time
  compression, 129–132
summarized events, 78
Survey of Consumer Finances, 234–
  235, 289
Survey of Income and Program Participation (SIPP), 122
Survey on Census Participation
  (SCP), 263
syntax, 23–24, 25, 34–38

syntactic ambiguity, 24–25, 34–38,
  40
syntactic problems in question
  wording, 34–50

telescoping, 11, 88–89, 120–121, 126–
  132, 335–337
  backward, 88–89, 120–121
  forward, 11, 88–89, 120–121
  internal, 127–128
  Neter and Waksberg's study, 126–
  129
  temporal compression, 128–132
  variance theories, 132–133
temporal boundaries, 89–91
temporal compression, see telescoping
temporal frequency questions, 102–
  103, 107–108
temporal landmarks, 89–91, 113–115
  calendar based events, 89–91, 114
  landmark events, 89–91, 114
temporal periods/sequences, 115–117
temporal questions
  constraint-satisfaction procedure,
  110–112
  impressions based on retrieval attempt, 109
  and recall of exact temporal information, 109
  and recall of relative order information, 109, 113–117: extended
  event, 109, 115–117; temporal
  landmark, 109, 113–115; temporal period, 115–117
  types of temporal questions, 101–
  108: questions about duration,
  105–107, 117–120; questions
  about elapsed time, 105–107,
  120–121; questions about temporal rates, 107–108; time-of-
  occurrence questions, 104–105,
  112–117
temporal rates, 107–108
third parties, see confidentiality
time on task, 94–95
time-of-occurrence questions, 102–
  103, 104–105

topic saliency, 261
Touchtone Data Entry (TDE), 290, 304
trace position, 36
trace location process, 36–37
traditional view of attitude questions, 165–167
Tulving's model of episodic memory, 71–73
Tversky and Kahneman's judgmental heuristics, *see* judgmental heuristics
typicality effects, 49

unbounded interviews, 126–128
undercoverage, 256, 281
underreporting of undesirable behaviors, 266–278
    abortion, 264, 269, 271–272
    consumption of alcohol, 269
    illicit drug use, 269–270, 295–296
    racist attitudes, 269
    smoking, 269, 271, 278
unfamiliar terms, 24, 43

unit nonresponse, 261, 264, 273, 301
unpacking effect, 119
U.S.-Communist reporters, 210–211

vague concepts, 45–47
vague quantifiers, 47–50
vagueness, 24, 44–50
valuation process, 182
variability of understanding, 45
variance theories of telescoping, 132–133
verbal labels for response options, 230
verification questions, 103–104, 107–108
Vierordt's law, 118–119
vignettes, 282–284
Voice Recognition Entry (VRE), 290, 304

wh-questions, 35–38
working memory, 36–38, 40, 77

ZUMA, 314